Street by Street

GLASGOW

Ist edition May 2001

© Automobile Association Developments Limited 2001

This product includes map data licensed from Ordnance Survey® with the permission of the Controller of Her Majesty's Stationery Office. © Crown copyright 2000. All rights reserved.

Licence No: 399221.

Published by AA Publishing (a trading name of Automobile Association Developments Limited, whose registered office is Norfolk House, Priestley Road, Basingstoke, Hampshire, RG24 9NY. Registered number 1878835).

Mapping produced by the Cartographic Department of The Automobile Association.

A CIP Catalogue record for this book is available from the British Library.

Printed by GRAFIASA S.A., Porto, Portugal

The contents of this atlas are believed to be correct at the time of the latest revision. However, the publishers cannot be held responsible for loss occasioned to any person acting or refraining from action as a result of any material in this atlas, nor for any errors, omissions or changes in such material. The publishers would welcome information to correct any errors or omissions and to keep this atlas up to date. Please write to Publishing, The Automobile Association, Fanum House, Basing View, Basingstoke, Hampshire, RG21 4EA.

Ref: MN069

Key to map pages — ii-iii

Key to map symbols — iv-1

Enlarged scale pages — 2-61

Street by Street — 62-133

Index – towns & villages — 134

Index – streets — 137-183

Index – featured places — 183-192

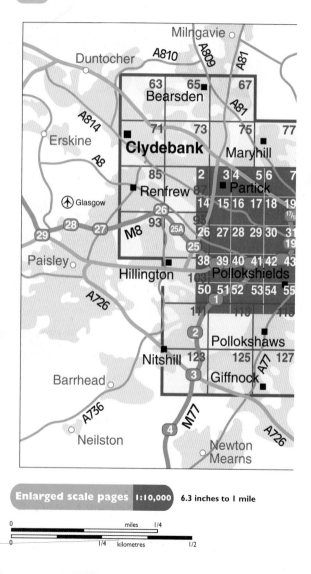

ii

Milngavie

Duntocher

A810

A809

A81

63 65 67

Bearsden

A81

A814

71 73 75 77

Erskine

Clydebank

A8

Maryhill

85 2 3 4 5 6 7

Renfrew 87 Partick

Glasgow

14 15 16 17 18 19

26 17h

95

M8 93 25A 26 27 28 29 30 31

25 19

Paisley

38 39 40 41 42 43

Hillington Pollokshields

103 50 51 52 53 54 55

1

113 115

2

Pollokshaws

Nitshill 123 125 127

A7

Barrhead

3 Giffnock

A736

4 M77

Neilston

Newton
Mearns

A726

Enlarged scale pages 1:10,000 6.3 inches to 1 mile

0   miles   1/4

0   1/4   kilometres   1/2

3.6 inches to 1 mile Scale of main map pages 1:17,500

iv

Junction 9 Motorway & junction	**P+** Park & Ride
Services Motorway service area	Bus/coach station
Primary road single/dual carriageway	Railway & main railway station
Services Primary road service area	Railway & minor railway station
A road single/dual carriageway	Underground station
B road single/dual carriageway	Light railway & station
Other road single/dual carriageway	Preserved private railway
Restricted road	*LC* Level crossing
Private road	Tramway
One way street	Ferry route
Pedestrian street	Airport runway
Track/ footpath	Boundaries- borough/ district
Road under construction	Mounds
Road tunnel	**93** Page continuation 1:17,500
P Parking	**7** Page continuation to enlarged scale 1:10,000

	River/canal lake, pier
	Aqueduct, lock, weir
465 ▲ Winter Hill	Peak (with height in metres)
	Beach
	Coniferous woodland
	Broadleaved woodland
	Mixed woodland
	Park
	Cemetery
	Built-up area
	Featured building
⌐⌐⌐⌐⌐	City wall
A&E	Accident & Emergency hospital
	Toilet

	Toilet with disabled facilities
	Petrol station
PH	Public house
PO	Post Office
	Public library
i	Tourist Information Centre
	Castle
	Historic house/ building
Wakehurst Place NT	National Trust property
M	Museum/ art gallery
†	Church/chapel
	Country park
	Theatre/ performing arts
	Cinema

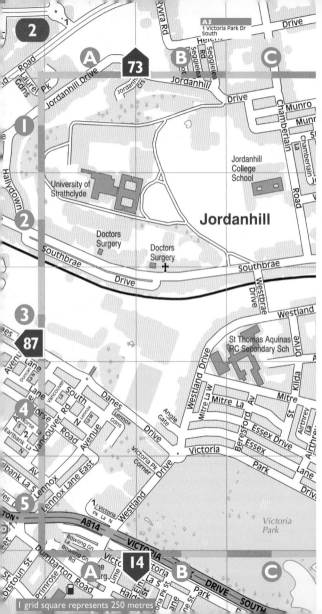

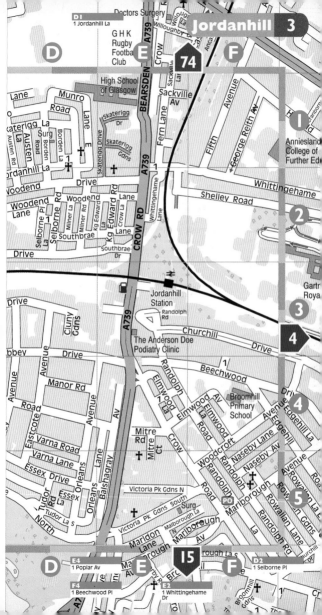

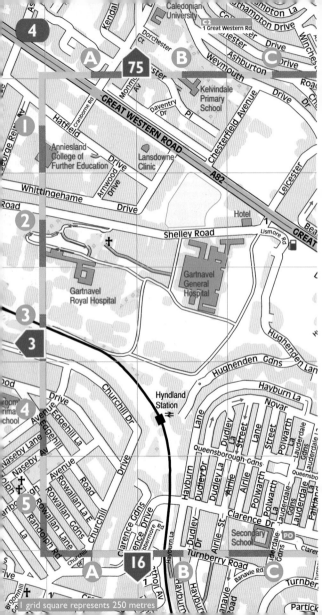

I grid square represents 250 metres

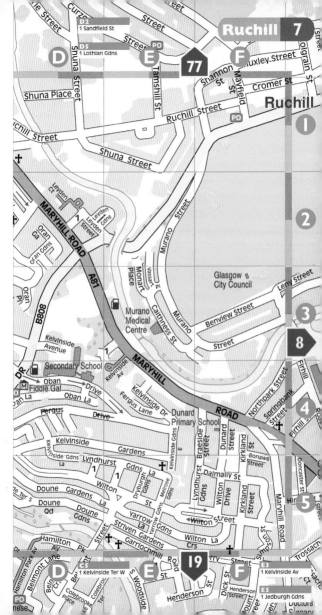

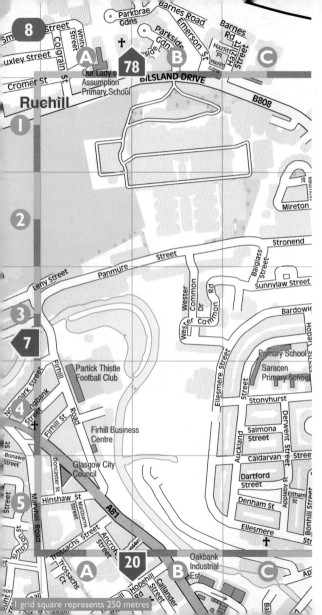

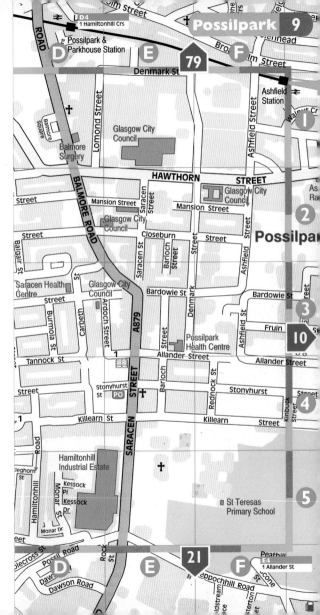

ROAD

D4
1 Hamiltonhill Crs

Possilpark &
Parkhouse Station

D   **E**   Denmark St   **79**   **F**

Broe   Im Street

Ashfield
Station

Walnut Cr

I

Balmore
Square

Lomond Street

Glasgow City
Council

Balmore
Surgery

BALMORE ROAD

Ashfield Street

HAWTHORN   STREET

As
Ra

Glasgow City
Council

Mansion Street

Saracen St

Mansion Street

2

Street

Street

Glasgow City
Council

Closeburn

Street

Possilpa

Balgair

Street

Saracen St

Barloch
Street

Denmark

Street

Ashfield Street

Saracen Health
Centre

Glasgow City
Council

Street

Bardowie St

Bardowie St

reet

3

Burmola
St

Carbeth

Argoch Street

A879

Bardowie St

Street

Ashfield St

Fruin

S

10

Possilpark
Health Centre

Tannock St

SARACEN STREET

Allander Street

Allander Street

Stonyhurst
St

Barloch
Street

Rednock St

Stonyhurst

Kinbuck St

Street

4

Street

1

PO

Killearn St

Killearn   Street

Hamiltonhill
Cleghorn
St

Road

Hamiltonhill
Industrial Estate

Kessock
Pl

Kessock
Dr

Monar Dr

Rock

St Teresas
Primary School

5

lecross St

Possil Road

D   **E**   **21**   **F**   Peathill

E1
1 Allander St

Dawson Road   eppochhill Road

Dawson

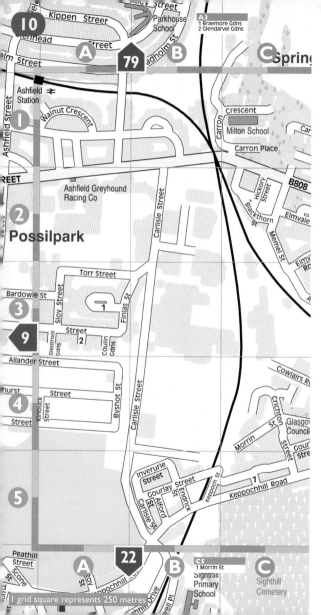

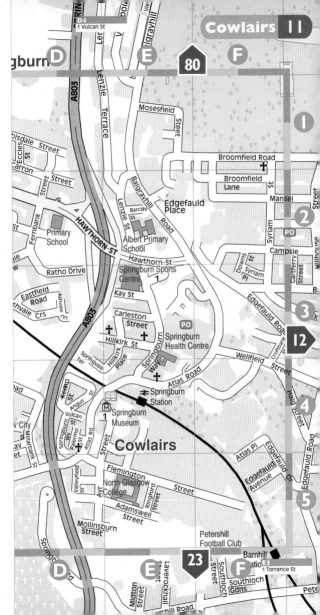

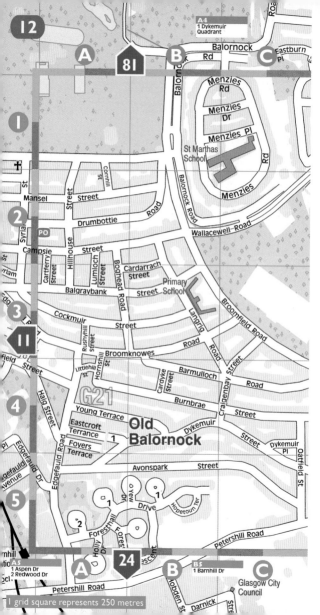

A4
1 Dykemuir
Quadrant

81

Balornock

A   B   C   Eastburn
                      Pl

Balornock
Rd

Menzies
Rd

Menzies
Dr

Menzies Pl

St Marthas
School

Menzies Rd

I

Menzies

Mansel   Cornhill   Street

St

Balornock Road

Drumbottie   Road

Syria   PO

Campsie   Street

Hillhouse   Street

Gartferry   Street   Lumloch   Street   Bothead   Road

Cardarrach
Street

Primary
School

Balgraybank   Street

Cockmuir   Street

Broomfield Road

Langrig Road

Rushyhill
Street

Littlehill   Hornshill   St

St

Broomknowes   Road

field   Street

Cardyke   Street

Barmulloch   Road

Craigenbay   Street

G21

Haghill Street

Young Terrace

Eastcroft
Terrace

Foyers
Terrace

Old
Balornock

Burnbrae   Street

Dykemuir   Street

Dykemuir
Pl

Oatfield St

Edgefauld Road

Edgefauld
Avenue

Avonspark   Street

Yew   Dr

Drive

Hopetoun Ter

Holly Dr   Forehill   Forehill   Crescent

Petershill Road

24

A5
1 Aspen Dr
2 Redwood Dr

A   B   B5
              1 Barnhill Dr   C

Glasgow City
Council

Petershill Road

Jobben St

Darnick

1 grid square represents 250 metres

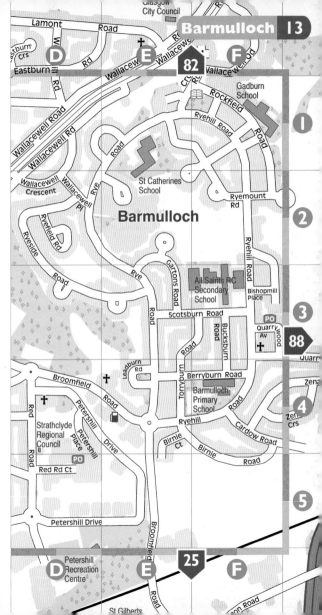

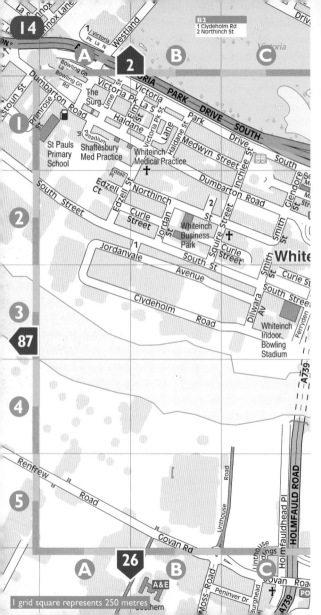

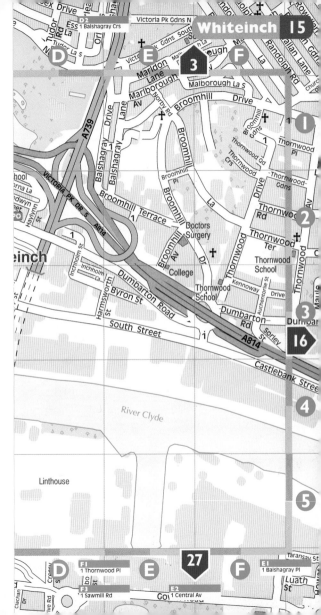

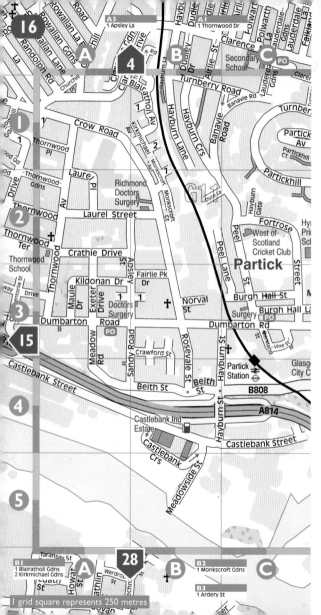

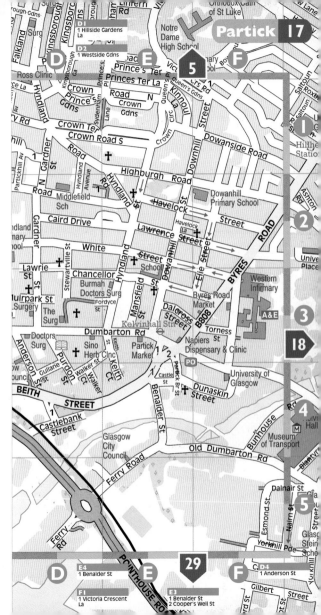

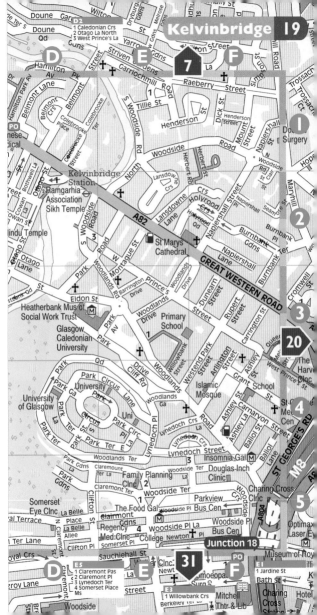

Doune Gdns
Wilton
Doune Ter S
Doune Qd
D2
1 Caledonian Crs
2 Otago La North
3 West Prince's La
Guns
Dryburgh
Melrose
Gdns

Hamilton Av
Belmont Lane
D
Hamilton Park Av
Belmont Pk
Belmont
Belmont Crs
Colebrooke Place
Colebrooke Ter
Chinese
Medical
PO

Yarrow
Striven Gdns
E
Garriochmill Road
Tillie St

7
Newton Street
La
Raeberry Street
St
Dick St
Henderson Street
Henderson Street
Mount Street
Napiershall St
F
Trossachs St
Trossachs Ct
I
Do
Surgery
Hope St

Otago St
Bothwell La
Cowan St
Cowan La
Hindu Temple
Otago
Lane

Kelvinbridge
Station
Ramgarhia
Association
Sikh Temple
North Woodside Road
Woodside Road
A82

Woodside
Lansdowne Crs
Lansdowne Lane
Herbert St
Herbert Rd
Lansdowne Crs
Holyrood Crs
Holyrood Qd
St Marys
Cathedral
Napiershall Pl
Napiershall Lane
Napiershall Street
Burnbank Gdns
Burnbank Pl
Burnbank
GREAT WESTERN ROAD
Cromwell St
Maryhill Road
Seamo
N Woodside Rd
St Clair St
2
Cromwell
3

Eldon St
Heatherbank Mus of
Social Work Trust
Glasgow
Caledonian
University
Park Av
Woodlands Rd
Montague St
Barrington Drive
Prince's St
Woodlands Drive
Woodlands Drive
Woodlands Gdns
Primary
School
Dunearn Street
Rupert Street
Carrington Street
Queens
West Prince's St
20
The
Harv
Clnc

University
of Glasgow
Park Ca
Park Ter
Park Ter E
Park Gdns
Park Circus
University
Park Circus Lane
Park Circus
Uni
Park Circ La
Park Circ
Cliff Rd
Woodlands
Drive
Willowbank St
Woodlands
Road
Westend Park Street
Arlington Street
Ashley St
Grant St
Islamic
Mosque
Ashley St
Carnarvon Street
Ashley La
Baliol St
Insomnia Gal
Ballol
Lane
School
St
Med
Cen
ST GEORGE'S RD
4

Woodlands Ter
Claremont Ter La
Claremont Ter
Claremont Pl
Lynedoch Crs
Lynedoch Cr La
Lynedoch Street
Woodside Ter
Woodside Ter La
Family Planning
Clnc
Douglas-Inch
Clinic
Woodside Pl
Woodside Pl La
Woodside Pl
Bus Cen
Charing
Cross
Clnc
Charing
Cross
M8
5
Optimax
Laser Ey

Somerset
Eye Clnc
La Belle
La Belle
Place
La Belle
Allee
Clifton Pl
Clifton St
Somerset Place Ms
Clairmont
Gdns
Regency
Med Clinc
The Food Gal
Claremont Pl
Newton Street
31
College
Somerset Pl
Parkview Crs
Junction 18
Museum of Roy
illi

D
Royal Crs
Sauchiehall St
Clnc
Newt
E
Homeopa
Sura P
F
PO
Mitchell
Thtr & Lib
Charing
Cross
Hotel
Bath St
1 Jardine St
E1

E5
1 Claremont Pas
2 Claremont Pl
3 Lynedoch Ter
4 Somerset Place
Ms
Claremont
Place
Fitzroy Lane
Woodside
Street
E3
1 Willowbank Crs
Berkeley St

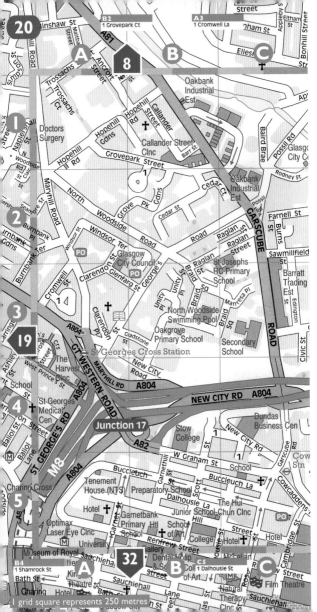

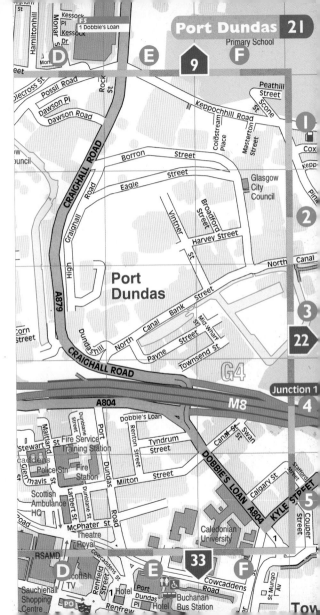

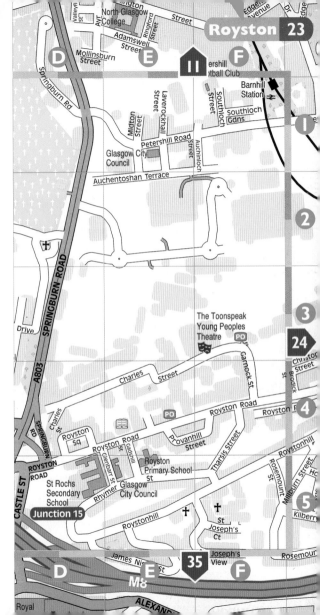

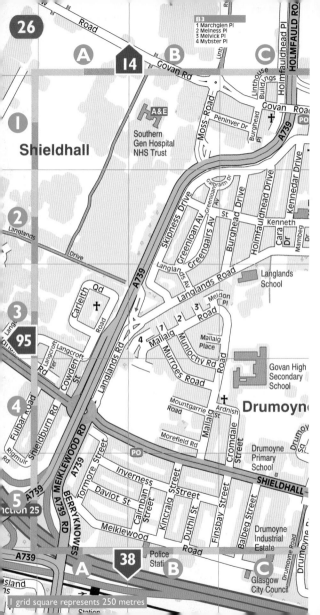

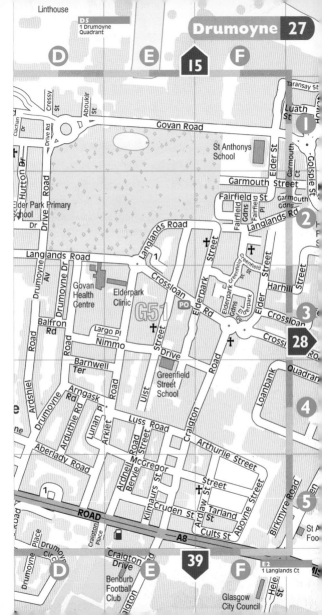

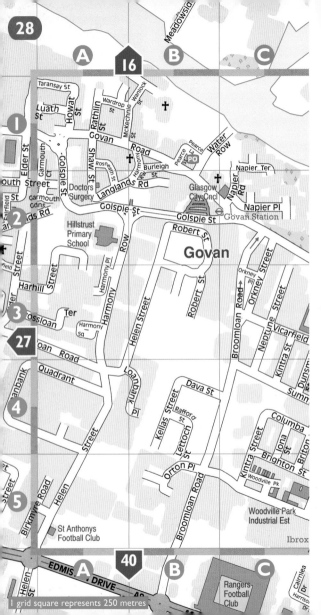

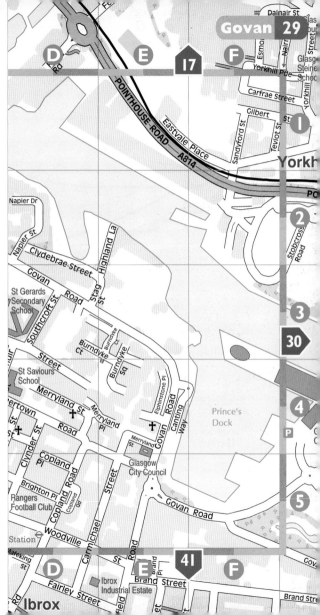

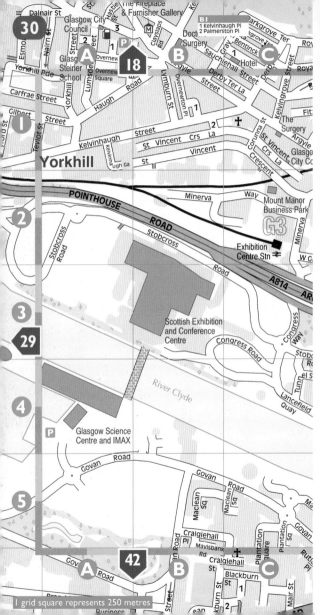

I grid square represents 250 metres

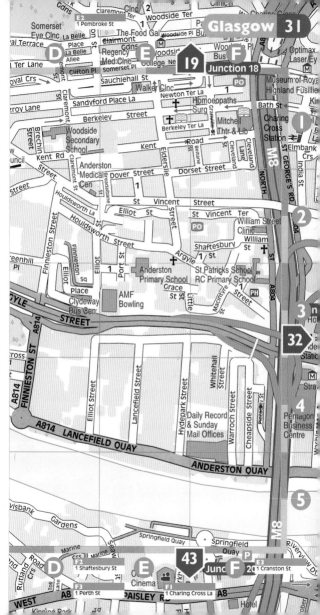

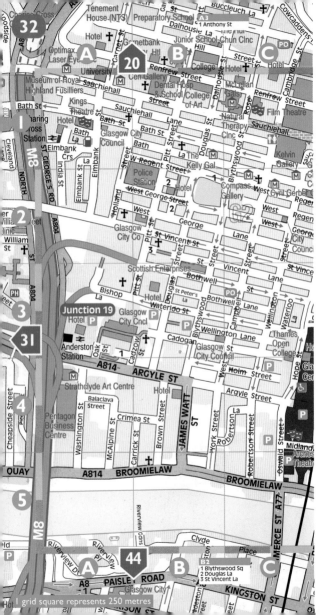

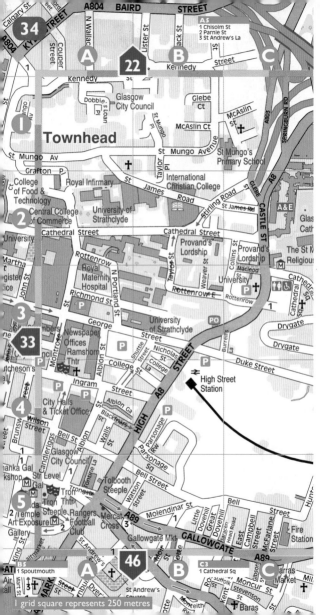

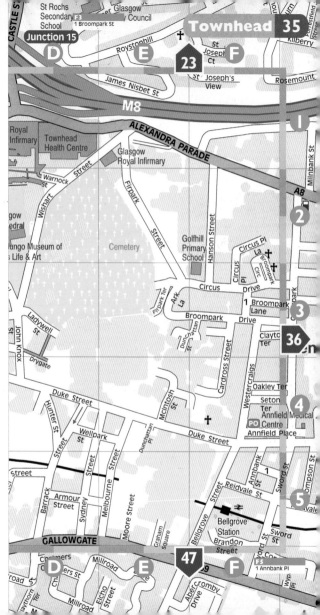

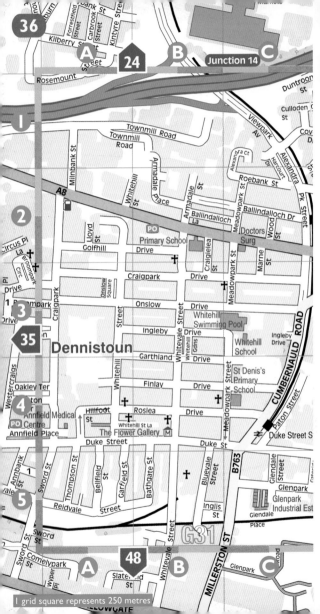

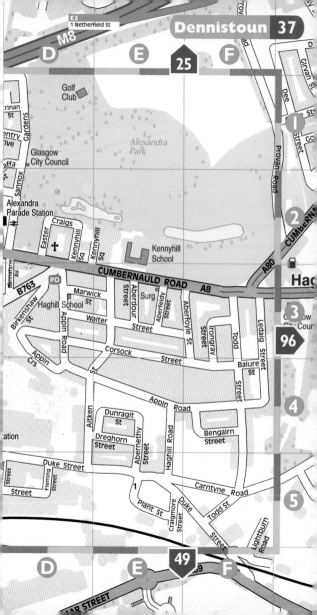

Cemetery

SHIELDHALL

A739 RD

Daviot St

Coyne
Industrial
Estate

Glasgow
City Council

Road

Police
Station

Cardonald
Station

BERRYKNOWES ROAD

A739

Moss Hts Av

Berryknowes Av

Montrave St

Lourdes
Primary
School

Doctors Surgery

PAISLEY ROAD WEST

Police Stn

Lourdes
Avenue

Crosslee St

Maryland Gdns

Maryland Dr

Barlogan

Barfillan

Barfillan Dr

Cemetery Rd

Mosspark Blvd

Corkerhill Road

Corkerhill
Gardens

Kirkdale

Arisaig Dr

Glasgow
City Council

Tarfside Gdns

Tarfside Oval

Tarfside Ov

Cemetery

Kirriemuir Avenue

Avenue

Avenue

Alness Crs

Ardw.

1 grid square represents 250 metres

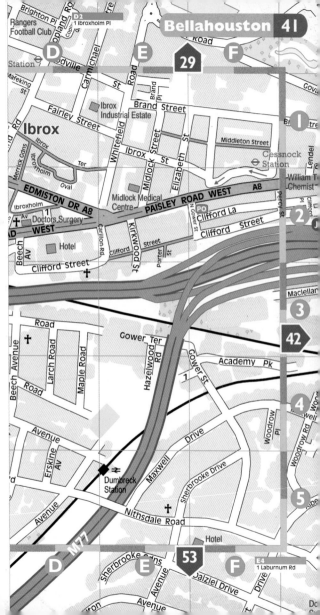

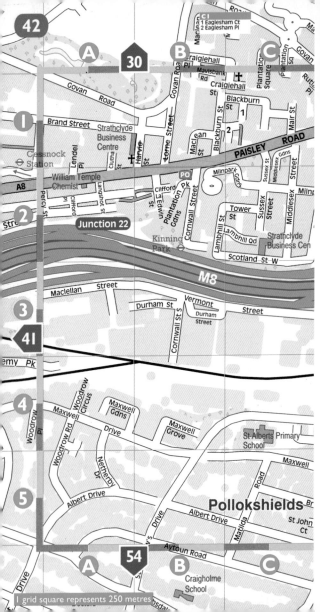

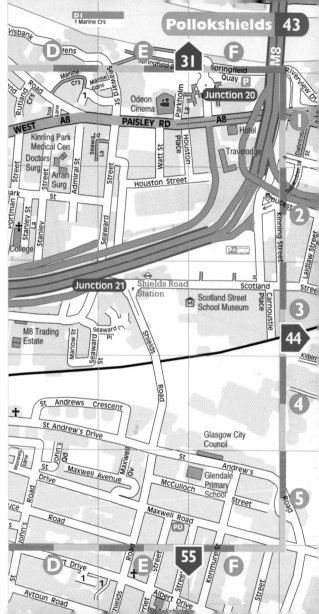

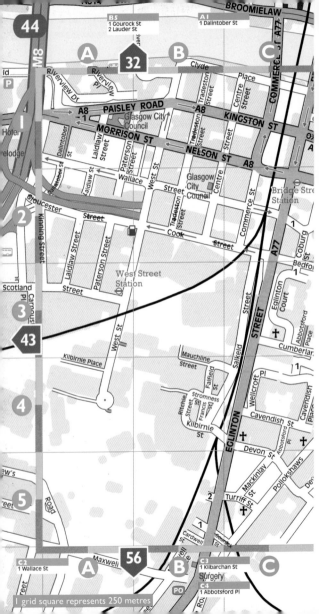

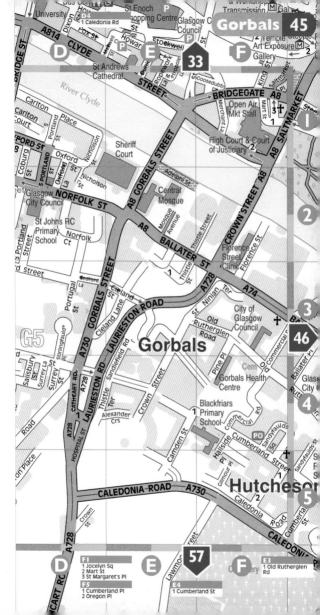

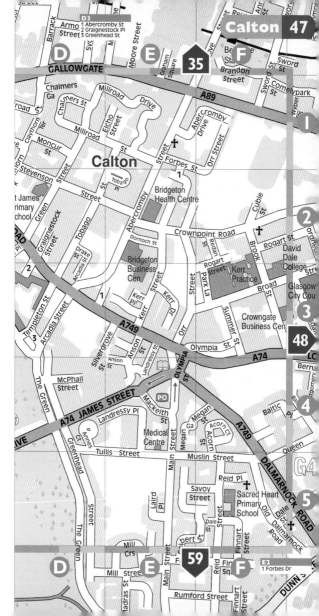

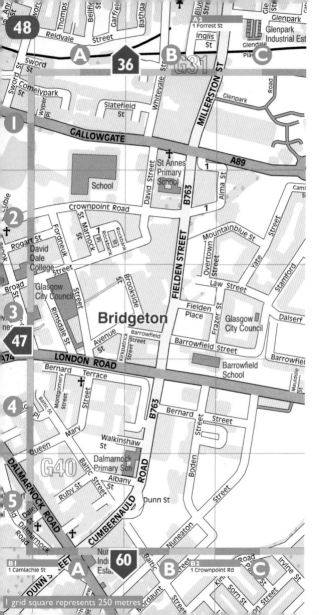

48

A   36   B   G31   C

1 Forrest St
Glenpark
Inglis St
Glenpark
Industrial Est
Glendale
A2
Glendale
Plac

Reidvale   Street
Sword St
Thomps
Bellfi
Garfiel
Bathga

Sword St
Comelypark   Street
Wyper   Pl
Slatefield
St
Whitevale
Glenpark
MILLERSTON ST
Road

1   GALLOWGATE   A89

School
St Annes
Primary
School
David   Street
Alma   Street
Cami
St

2   Crownpoint Road   B763
St Marnock   St
Rockbank
Rockbank St
1

Rogart St
Fordneuk   Street
Fielden
Place
Mountainblue St
Overtown   Street
Yate   Street
Stamford   Street

David
Dale
College
FIELDEN STREET
Law   Street

Broad
Glasgow
City Council
Rimsdale   Street
Brookside   Street
Frazer   St
Glasgow
City Council
Dalserf

3
ne
Bridgeton
Fielden
Place
47

Avenue
St
Kirkpatrick   Street
Barrowfield
Street
Barrowfield   Street
Barrowfiel

A74   LONDON ROAD   Maulside

Bernard   Terrace
Montgomery   Street
Street
B763
Bernard   Street   Street
Barrowfield
School

4
Baltic St
Pl
G
Queen
Mary   St
Baltic   Street
Walkinshaw
St
Boden   Street

G40
Dalmarnock
Primary Sch
DALMARNOCK ROAD
Ruby St
Street
Albany   St
Dunn St

5
1a
Dale   St
Dalmarnock
Road
CUMBERNAULD
Nuneaton   Street

B1
1 Camlachie St
A   60   B   C
DUNN   STREET
Indu
Esta
Baltic   St
B2
1 Crownpoint Rd
Road
Irvine   St
Kin
Sorn St
Jordaunt
Street

1 grid square represents 250 metres

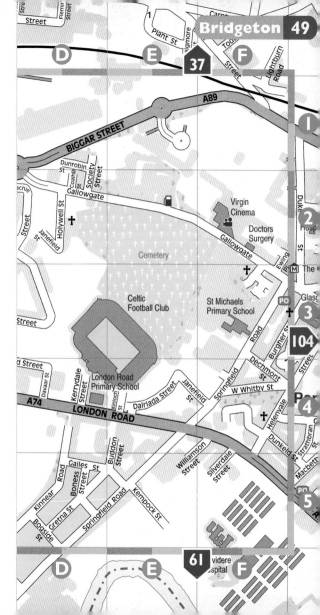

Street
Flemir
Street
Plant St
Carn
Tod
gimore
Lightburn Road
Street

D E F

37

A89

I

BIGGAR STREET

Dunrobin
St
Coalhill
St
Society
Street
Gallowgate

Duke
St
Hosp

2

Virgin
Cinema

Doctors
Surgery

Gallowgate

Ewing

M

The

Holwell St
Janefield
st
Street
achie
Street

Cemetery

Glas

3

Celtic
Football Club

St Michaels
Primary School

Road
Burgher S

104

d Street

London Road
Primary School

Kerrydale
St
Davaar St
Kinloch
Dalriada Street
Janefield
st
Springfield
W Whitby St

Dechmont
St

Street

Helenvale

Po

A74 LONDON ROAD

Dunkeld St

Strathbran

Macbeth

4

Buddon
Street

Williamson
Street

Silverdale
Street

Gailes
Street
Boness
Street
Road
Kinnear
Gretna St
Bosside
St
Springfield Road
Kempock St

PO

5

A

D E F

61

videre
spital

Glasg

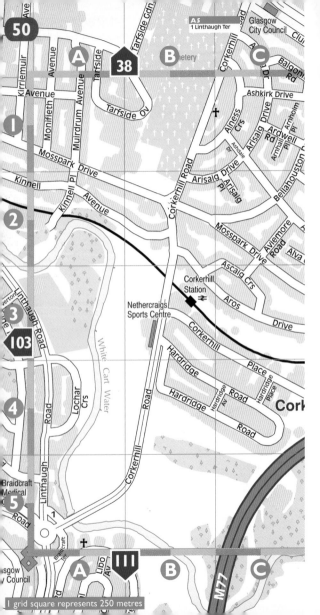

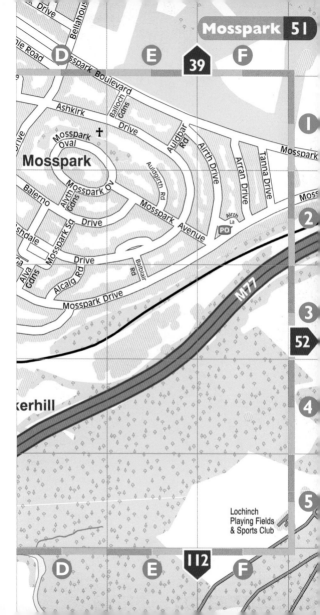

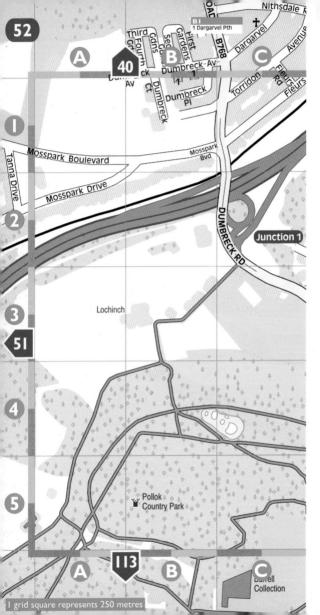

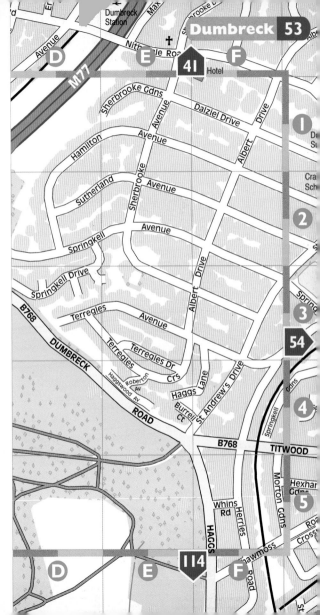

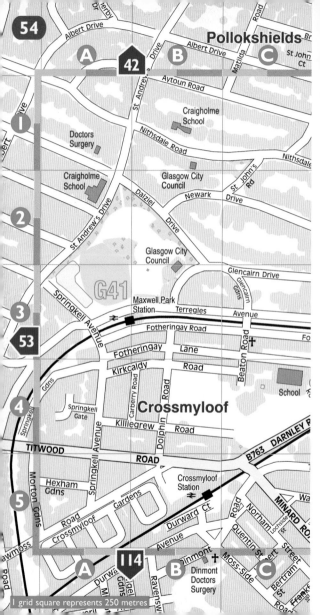

Pollokshields

Albert Drive

42

Ⓐ Ⓑ Ⓒ St John Ct

Albert Drive

Aytoun Road

Matilda

Ⓘ

Craigholme School

Nithsdale Road

Doctors Surgery

Nithsdale

Craigholme School

Glasgow City Council

St John's Rd

Ⓩ

St Andrew's Drive

Dalziel Drive

Newark

Drive

Glasgow City Council

Glencairn Drive

Glencairn Gdns

G41

Maxwell Park Station

Terregles

Avenue

Ⓩ

Springkell Avenue

Fotheringay Road

53

Fotheringay

Lane

Beaton Road

Kirkcaldy

Road

Fo

Ⓩ

Springkell Gate

Carberry Road

Dolphin Road

School

Crossmyloof

Killiegrew

Road

Ⓩ

TITWOOD

Hexham Gdns

Springkell Avenue

Gardens

ROAD

B763 DARNLEY R

Ⓩ

Morton Gdns

Road

Crossmyloof

Gardens

Crossmyloof Station

Durward Ct

MINARD RO

Norham

Lochside

St

Quentin St

Bertram

St

awmoss

Durwa

Mi

glen

Gdns

Ravensw

Avenue

Dinmont

114

Ⓐ Ⓑ Dinmont Doctors Surgery

Moss-Side

Ⓒ

Bertram

St

Frank

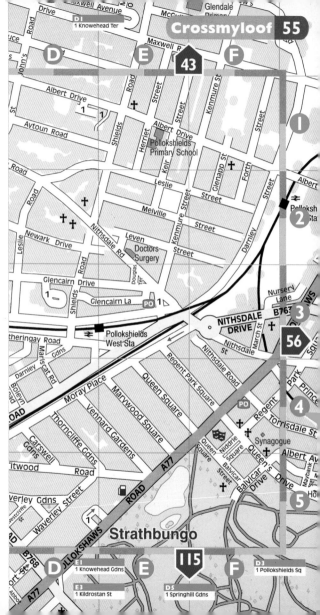

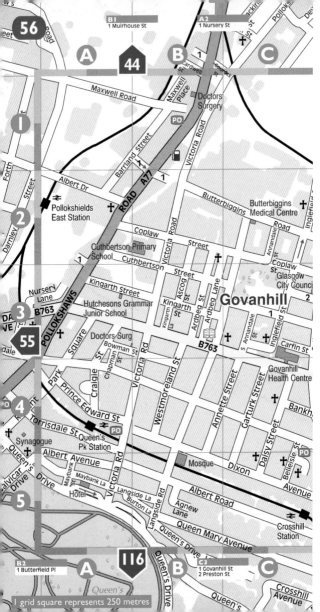

Maxwell Road

Maxwell Place

Doctors Surgery

PO

Victoria Road

Barrland Street

Albert Dr

Forth Street

Darnley Street

ROAD A77

Pollokshields East Station

Butterbiggins Road

Butterbiggins Medical Centre

Coplaw Street

Cuthbertson Primary School

Cuthbertson Street

Victoria Road

Coplaw St

Glasgow City Council

Govanhill

Ascog St

Ardbeg St

Ardbeg Lane

Kingarth Street

55
B763

Nursery Lane

POLLOKSHAWS

Hutchesons Grammar Junior School

Kingarth St

Kingarth St

S Annandale St

Inglefield St

B763

Carfin St

Doctors Surg

Square

Craigie

Chapman St

Bowman St

Victoria Rd

Westmoreland St

Annette Street

Garturk Street

Govanhill Health Centre

Bankh

Park

Prince Edward St

Torrisdale St

Queen's Pk Station

PO

Synagogue

Queen's Drive

Albert Avenue

Maybank St

Maybank La

Victoria Rd

Langside La

Mosque

Dixon

Daisy Street

Belleisle St

Avenue

PO

Hotel

Langside Rd

Burton La

Agnew Lane

Albert Road

Queen Mary Avenue

Crosshill Station

Queen's Drive

Queen's

Crosshill Avenue

1 grid square represents 250 metres

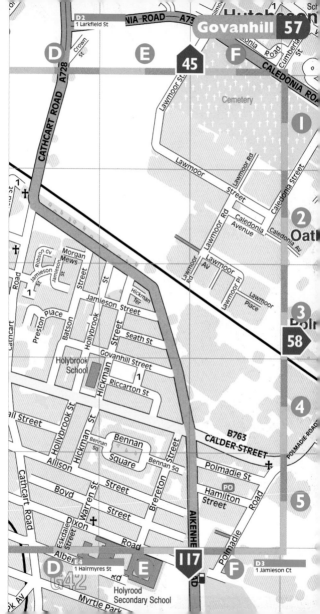

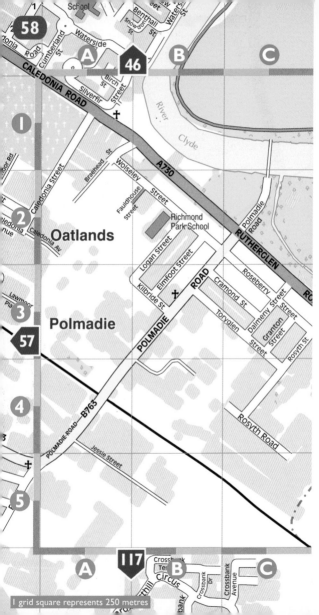

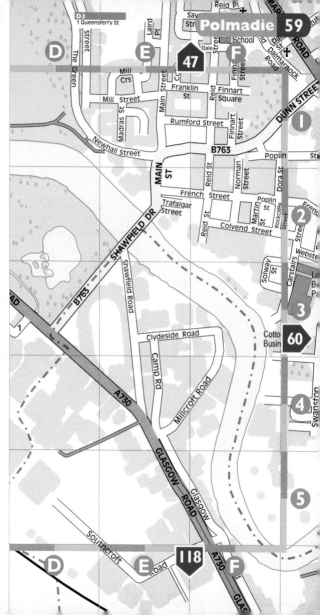

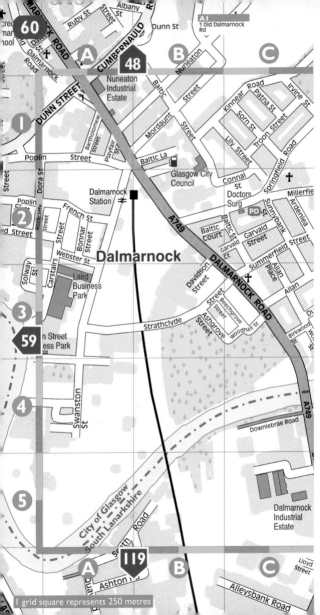

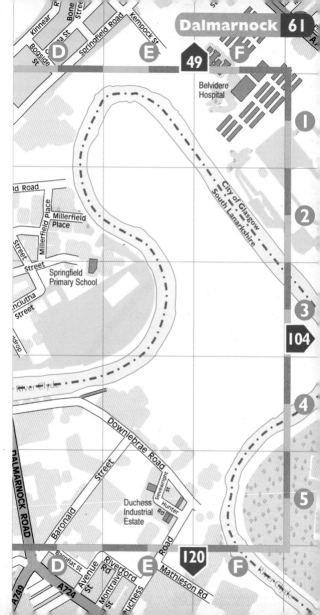

Bone Street

Kinnear

Bogside St

D

Springfield Road

Kempock St

E

49

F

Belvidere Hospital

I

ld Road

Millerfield Place
Millerfield Place

Millerfield Street

Street

enclutna Street

adrop

Springfield Primary School

City of Glasgow
South Lanarkshire

2

3

104

River Clyde

4

Downiebrae Road

Baronald Street

DALMARNOCK ROAD

A749

Duchess Industrial Estate

Sleevewright St

Hunter Rd

Road

5

D

Baroflat St

Avenue St

Riverford Rd

Montraive St

Duchess

A724

E

Mathieson Rd

120

F

River Clyde

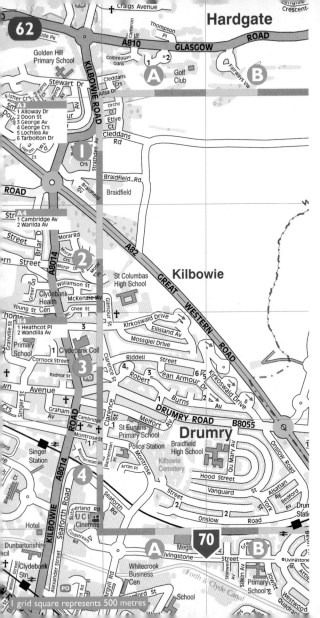

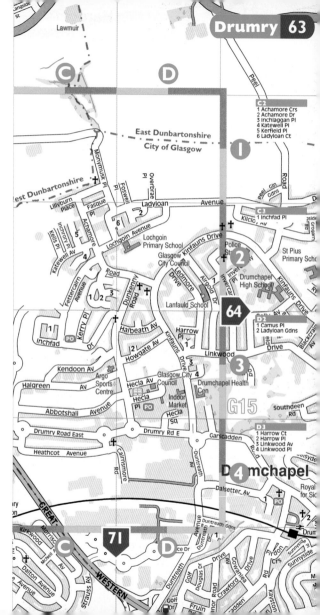

C2
1 Achamore Crs
2 Achamore Dr
3 Inchlaggan Pl
4 Katewell Pl
5 Kerfield Pl
6 Ladyloan Ct

C3
1 Inchfad Pl

D2
1 Camus Pl
2 Ladyloan Gdns

D3
1 Harrow Ct
2 Harrow Pl
3 Linkwood Av
4 Linkwood Pl

Lawmuir

Peel

East Dunbartonshire
City of Glasgow

East Dunbartonshire

Monymusk Pl

Lilliyburn
Place

Fasque

Foswell

Pl

Overdrae
Pl

Ladyloan

Avenue

Peel Gln
Gdns

Road

Kilco

Av

Kells Pl

Incrhory Pl

Achamore

Katewell Av

6

2

5

4

Lochgoin Avenue

Lochgoin
Primary School

Glasgow
City Council

Kinfauns Drive

Ledmore

Drive

Police
St

Inver Ct

Argold Dr

Inver Ct

St Pius
Primary Scho

Drumchapel
High School

Kinfauns

DRIVE

Fettercaim

Avenue

Road

Dunkenny
Road

3

2

1

Lanfauld School

Harrow

Av

2

Linkwood

Kerry Pl

Inchfad

Dr

PO

1

Halbeath Av

Howgate Av

Kinfauns

Drive

Kendoon Av

Argo
Sports
Centre

Hecla Av

Glasgow City
Council

Hecla

Pl

PO

Indoor
Market

Hecla
Av

Drumchapel Health
Cen

G15

Southdeen
Rd

Halgreen

Av

Abbotshall

Avenue

Drumry Road East

Heathcot Avenue

Cairnsmore

Rd

Drumry Rd E

Garscadden

D 4 **mchapel**

Dalsetter Av

1

PO

Royal
for Sic

Drum

GREAT

WESTERN

Kirtwood

Morrisc

Av

McNeil Av

Dalton Avenue

Avenue

71

nce Dr

Duntreath

Avenue

Duntreath Gdns

Golf

Douglas Dr

Crawford Drive

Govan

anor Road

Fruin

Golf

Firdon

Crs

Sunnyside

Kayston

dden

Surnyside

Sunnyside

64

2

3

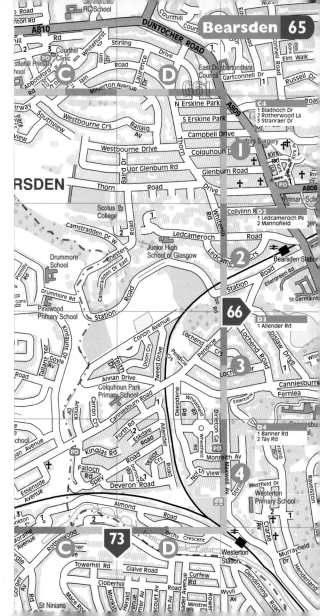

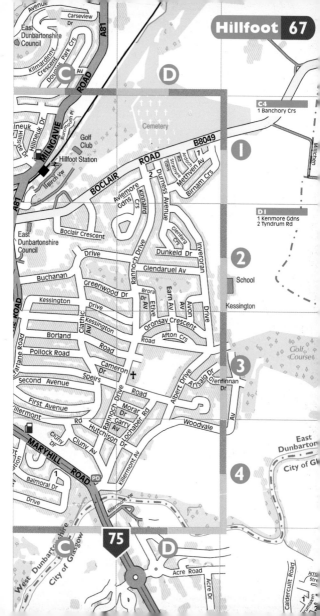

East Dunbartonshire Council

Carseview Dr

Kilmardinny Crescent

Dougrie Park Crs

A81

ROAD

MILNGAVIE

Hillfoot Station

Birch Vw

BOCLAIR

A81

East Dunbartonshire Council

Boclair Crescent

Aviemore Gdns

Kinnaird Crs

Durness Avenue

Drive

Buchanan

Kessington

Drive

Greenwood Dr

Borland

Clathic Av

Kessington

Road

Pollock Road

Cameron Dr

Speirs

Road

Second Avenue

First Avenue

Killermont

Rd

Cluny Dr

Cluny Av

MARYHILL ROAD

Balmoral Dr

Drive

Rannoch Drive

Morar Dr

Garry Av

Lochaber Rd

Hutchison Dr

Killermont Av

PO

Killermont Vw

West Dunbartonshire

City of Glasgow

75

C

D

Cemetery

Golf Club

ROAD

B8049

Stranraer Gdns

Ardoch Gdns

7

Methven Av

Birnam Crs

Glendev Crs

Inveroran

Dunkeld Dr

Glendaruel Av

Brora Dr

Etive Av

Earn Av

Avon Dr

Oronsay Crescent

Afton Crs

Road

+

Albert Drive

Arisaig Dr

Glenfinnan Dr

Woodvale

Av

School

Kessington

Golf Course

East Dunbarton

City of Gl

I

2

3

4

Millichen

Acre Road

Acre Dr

Caldercuilt Road

Arro
Stra

A
B

B2
1 Allander Gdns
2 Calder Ga

1

Balmuildy Road

B4
1 The Rowans

Wilderness
Plantation

2

East Dunbartonshire
Council

Forth & Clyde Canal

Jellyhill

Hilton Pk
1 2

Balmuildy Road

Hilton

Darnley Crs

Terrace

Me

The Surgery

Hilt

3

Westfields

Norfolk Crs

Stirling
Gdns

Stirling

Faskally Av

Muirton

Primary
School

Design
Gdns

Drive

Atholl Gdns

Drive

Lomo

Stirling

Drive

Southesk

Torthill Av

Broadway Avenue

Balmuildy

Gdns

Marchmont

Morga

Carrour G

Dunba

4

Turnbull
High
School

St Andrew's Av

St
Mary's

Bishop Gardens

Torthill
Gdns

Clenburn Gardens

Keir Dr

Lomo

1

Brackenbrae

Avenue

Novar

Gardens

Duncrub Dr

Pollok

A

80

Ins

Brackenbrae

B

Dunbartonshire
cil

Kenmure Dr

Beaufort

Drive

Gardens

(The Fort
Theatre)

Avenue

Laigh
Kenmure

Kenmure

Gardens

Kenmure

Road

Kenmure

PO

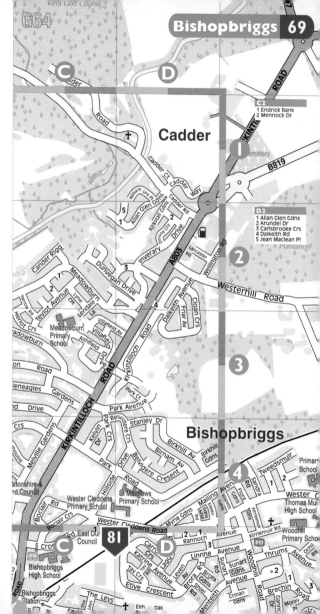

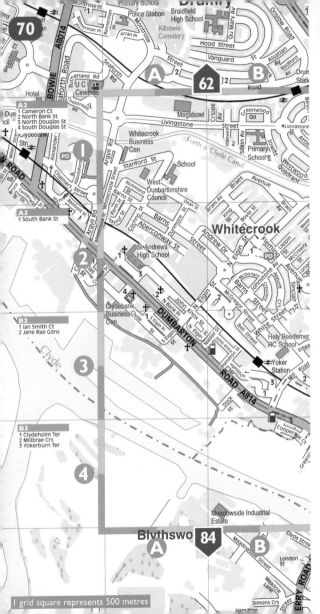

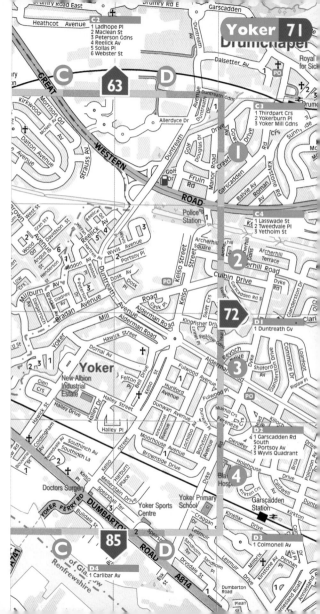

Drumchapel

Royal
for Sick

C2
1 Ladhope Pl
2 Maclean St
3 Peterson Gdns
4 Reellick Av
5 Sollas St
6 Webster St

C3
1 Thirdpart Crs
2 Yokerburn Pl
3 Yoker Mill Gdns

C4
1 Lasswade St
2 Tweedvale Pl
3 Yetholm St

D1
1 Duntreath Gv

D2
1 Garscadden Rd South
2 Portsoy Av
3 Wyvis Quadrant

D3
1 Colmonell Av

D4
1 Carlibar Av

Yoker

New Albion Industrial Estate

Police Station

Yoker Primary School

Yoker Sports Centre

Doctors Surgery

Garscadden Station

63 C D

72

85 C D

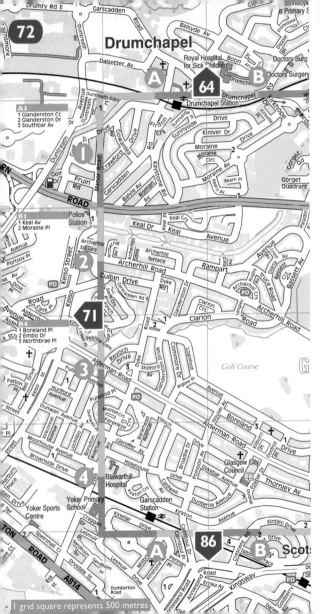

Drumchapel

72

A3
1 Glanderston Ct
2 Glanderston Dr
3 Southbar Av

B1
1 Keal Av
2 Moraine Pl

B4
1 Boreland Pl
2 Embo Dr
3 Northbrae Pl

64

A

B

1

2

71

3

4

86

A

B

Scots

I grid square represents 500 metres

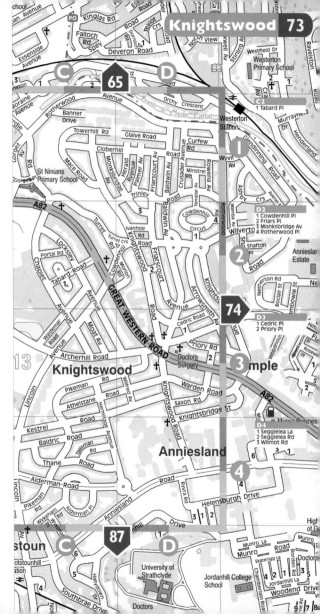

School
Avenue
Kinglas Rd
PO
Falloch
Rd
Spey
Deveron Road
Demon La

Essenside
Avenue

C
D
65

North View

Westfield Dr
Westerton
Primary School

Stirling Av
Crawell Av
Cra Av
C2
1 Tabard Pi

Ravelston

Road

Moraine
Avenue

Rotherwood
Avenue
Banner
Drive

Orchy Crescent

Forth & Clyde Canal

Westerton
Station

Murrayfield
Dr
Henderland

Cardle
Gorget

Towerhill Rd

Glaive Road

Curfew
Road

Glendinning Road

Gorget Av

St Ninians
Primary School

Cloberhill
Road
Mace Road
Monksbridge
Avenue

Herald
Avenue
Palmer Av
Trinley

Flarscourt Av
Baldwin Av
Crusader Avenue
Rowena Av
Minstrel
Rd

Wyvil
Av

Ashby
Crs

Avenue

D2
1 Cowdenhill Pl
2 Friars Pl
3 Monksbridge Av
4 Rotherwood Pl

A82

Turret
Road
Turret Crs
Ivanhoe
Rd

Cowdenhill
Circus

Baldwin Road

4

Wilverton
Rd

Shafton
Road

2

Wamba Av
Rotherwood Avenue

Annieslar
Estate

Chaplet
Portal Rd

Locksley
Avenue

Cowdenhill Road

Morton

Knightswood Road

Friarscourt
Avenue

Arrowsmith Av

Netherton Rd
Boclair St
 Combwee St

Ne

Tabard Road

Waldemar
Road
Moat Av

Cedric Road
1

D3
1 Cedric Pl
2 Priory Pl

74

Priory Rd
2

Hill

Woodhou

Risewa
St

Archerhill Road

Doctors
Surgery

mple

A82

13

Knightswood

Pikeman
Rd
Wilfred Av

Warden Road

Knightswood Road

Lincoln
Avenue

Athelstane
Road

Hermitage Avenue

Saxon Rd

Knightsbridge St

Seggiela La
Seggielea Rd
Wilmot Rd

D4
1 Seggielea La
2 Seggielea Rd
3 Wilmot Rd

Munro Busine

Kestrel
Road

Baldric
Road
Talisman
Rd

Anniesland

Thane
Road

Alderman Road
Pikeman
Rd
Wkenam
W Kenam

Alderman Pl

Anniesland

Road

Rywa Rd

Helensburgh Drive
3 1 2

Hig
of G

stoun

C
87
D

4

Munro La
Munro Road

Borden Rd

Munro

High

otstounhill
ation

Hayburn

Southbrae Drive

University of
Strathclyde

Jordanhill College
School

Skateriga
4
5
Jordanhill La

Chamberlain Rd
3
Doctor

Woodend Drive

Doctors

4

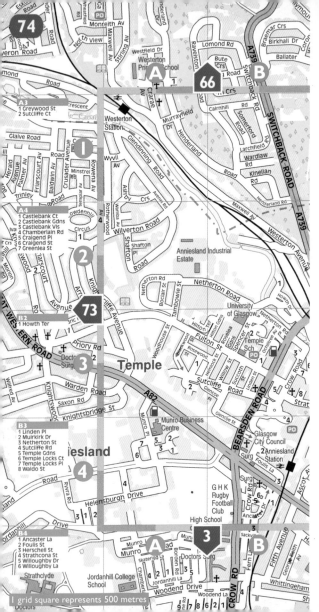

67

C2
1 Ilay Av

I

C4
1 Kendal Av
2 Westerlands

2

76

D4
1 Baronald Ga
2 Cleveden La
3 Daleview Av
4 Ferngrove Av
5 Hertford Av
6 Highfield Pl
7 Lindsay Dr
8 Nottingham Av
9 Nottingham La

3

4

Maryhill

Kelvindale

4

Kelvinside

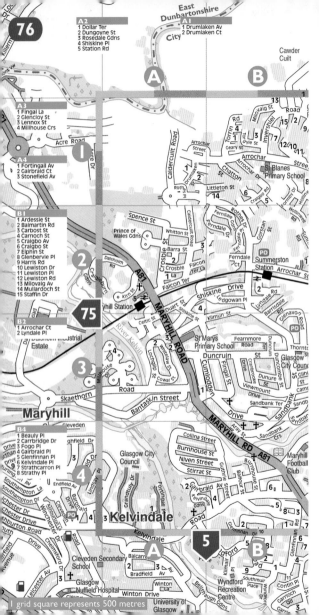

76

A2
1 Dollar Ter
2 Dungoyne St
3 Rosedale Gdns
4 Shiskine Pl
5 Station Rd

B1
1 Drumlaken Av
2 Drumlaken Ct

East
Dunbartonshire
City

Cawder
Cuilt

A3
1 Fingal La
2 Glencloy St
3 Lennox St
4 Millhouse Crs

A4
1 Fortingall Av
2 Gairbraid Ct
3 Stonefield Av

B1
1 Ardessie St
2 Balmartin Rd
3 Carbost St
4 Carnoch St
5 Craigbo Av
6 Craigbo St
7 Elphin St
8 Glenbervie Pl
9 Harris Rd
10 Lewiston Dr
11 Lewiston Pl
12 Lewiston Rd
13 Milovaig Av
14 Mullardoch St
15 Staffin Dr

B2
1 Arrochar Ct
2 Lyndale Pl

B4
1 Beauly Pl
2 Carrbridge Dr
3 Fogo Pl
4 Gairbraid Pl
5 Glenfinnan Pl
6 Kelvindale Pl
7 Strathcarron Pl
8 Strathy Pl

Acre Road

Caldercuilt Road

Arrochar
Street

Chatton

Littleton St

St Blanes
Primary School

Road

Invershiel

Millvaig St

Torrin
Rd

Geary St

Arrochar Dr

Pomeroy

Hollin

Spence St

Whitton St

Prince of
Wales Gdns

Crosbie
Barra St

Crosbie
St

Falcon
St

Ferndale

Ferndale
Ct

Summerston
Station

PO

Arrochar

Dalshoim
Rd

Falcon Ter

Shiskine Drive

Ledgowan Pl

Kilmun St

Lyndale
Rd

Barnsdale

Glenavon
Road

PO

Maryhill Station

75

Celtic St

Duart
St

Shiskine St

River Kelvin

MARYHILL ROAD

St Marys
Primary School

Fearnmore
Road

Duncruin   St

Thornto

Glasgow
City Counc

Dalcholm Industrial
Estate

Millhouse
Dr

Lochgilp
St

Whitelaw St

Lochgip
St Cowal

Cumlodden

Fingal St

Dunure
St

Viewmount
Drive

Cranbrooke
St

Camp

Skaethorn
Road

Bantaskin Street

MARYHILL RD

Aray St

Sandbank Ter

Sandba

Sandbank
Drive

Sandbank
Crs

Maryhill

Clevenden

Collina Street

Burnhouse St

Niven Street

Stirrat St

Glasgow City
Council

Glenfinnan Pl

Gairbraid
Av

Kelvindale
Gdns

Burnhouse
Road

Balfour
Street

Maryhill
Football
Club

Endfield Av

Lindsay Pl

Craigton Dr

Fortinhall Ave

Kelvindale
Road

Glenfinnan Dr

PO

Kelvindale

Kelvindale

Cleveden Secondary
School

Balcarre

Bradfield
Av

Winton Dr

Winton
Drive

Glasgow
Nuffield Hospital

University of
Glasgow

5

Wyndford
Recreation
Centre

Southmuir
Place

Contin

| 1 grid square represents 500 metres |

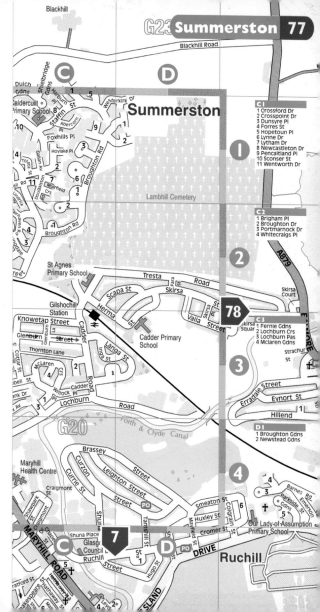

Blackhill

Blackhill Road

C **D**

Summerston

Shielbridge Gdns
Dulch Gdns
Caldercuilt Primary School
Harburn St
Shaftin St
Aberconn Pl
Gallan Av
Foxhills Pl
Hoylake Pl
Muirfield Crs
Douglaston
Westerkirk Dr
Broughton Rd
Broughton Rd
Broughton Rd

Lambhill Cemetery

St Agnes Primary School

Tresta Road
Fara St
Skirsa
Scapa St
Herma St
Vaila Street
Skirsa Square
Skirsa Court

Gilshochill Station
Knowetap Street
Glenburn Street
Cadder
Thornton Lane
Langa St
Inga St
McLaren Crs
Willock Pl
Cadder Pl
Lochburn Road
Cadder Road
Campbell St
Frank Dr
Buckie AV
Lochburn Road

Cadder Primary School

Strachur St
Erradale Street
Eynort St
Hillend

Forth & Clyde Canal

G20

Brassey Street
Curzon Street
Leighton Street
Currie St
Craigmont Street
Maryhill Health Centre

Smeaton St
Huxley St
Cromer St
Coigran St
Mayfield St
Barnes Rd
Emerson
Parkside Rd
Our Lady-of-Assumption Primary School

PO

Shuna Place
Glasgow Council
Ruchill Street
Shuna St
Tamshill St
Hugo St
ISLAND DRIVE
Ruchill

MARYHILL ROAD
Shawpark St
Craigmont St
Stratford St
Shakespeare St
Hathaway La

C **D**

7

I

2

A879

78

3

4

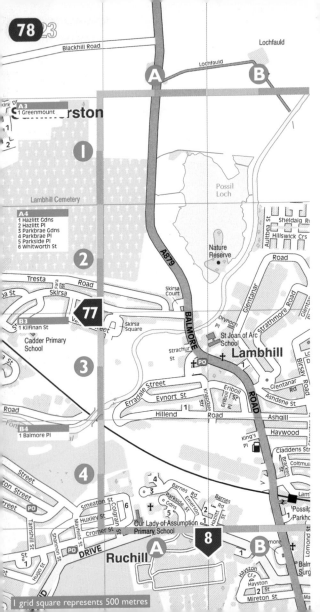

Blackhill Road

Lochfauld

Lochfauld

A

B

...rston

I

Possil
Loch

Lambhill Cemetery

A4
1 Hazlitt Gdns
2 Hazlitt Pl
3 Parkbrae Gdns
4 Parkbrae Pl
5 Parkside Pl
6 Whitworth St

Nature
Reserve

Aultbea St

Sheldaig St

Hillswick Crs

2

Road

Tresta

Skirsa

Road

Skirsa
Court

Glentanar

Strathmore Road

77

B3
1 Kilfinan St

Skirsa
Square

Drynoch
Pl

St Joan of Arc
School

BALMORE

Birsay Road

Cadder Primary
School

3

Strachur
St

PO

Lambhill

Glentanar
Rd

Eriboll
Pl

Knapdale
St

Erradale Street

Eynort St

Eriboll
St

Ashdene St

Road

B4
1 Balmore Pl

Hillend

Road

Ashgill

Haywood

ROAD

King's
Pl

Claddens St

Coltmuil

4

Barnes Rd

4

3

Parkside
Gdns

Emerson

Barnes
Rd

5

2

Hazlitt
St

Possil
Parkho

Smeaton St

Colgrain

Huxley St

6

Mayfield St

Cromer St

Our Lady of Assumption
Primary School

8

Lam

...more

Tamshill St

PO

DRIVE

Ruchill

A

B

Hayston
Crs
Hayston

Surg

Hugo St

1

Shannon St

1

Mireton St

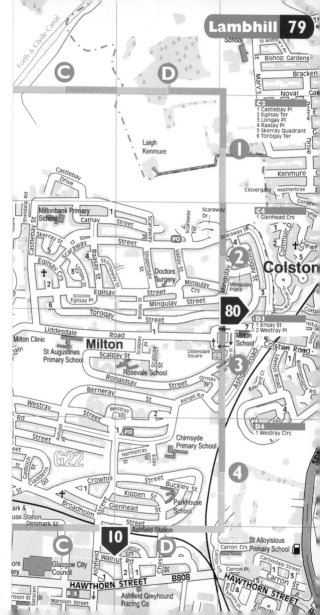

Forth & Clyde Canal

School

St Andrew's N

Bishop Gardens

Bracken

Novar

Gai

St Mary's

C

D

C2
1 Castlebay Pl
2 Egilsay Ter
3 Longay Ter
4 Raasay Pl
5 Skerray Quadrant
6 Torogay Ter

Laigh Kenmure

I

Kenmure

Clovergate   Heatherbrae

Gorsew

Castlebay Drive

Scaraway Dr

Scaraway

Street

C4
1 Glenhead Crs

Miltonbank Primary School

Sheildaig Rd

Cathay

Scaraway

Street

Scaraway St

Coltmuir

Viewf

Castlebay St

Skerray St

Scaraway

Raasay St

Stonehaven St

Shapinsay

Valay St

Scaraway Ter

PO

2

Colston

Egilsay Crs

Longay St

Doctors Surgery

Mingulay Crs

Minguay Place

Colp

Egilsay

Egilsay Pl

Islay Rd

Mingulay

Street

3

D3
1 Ensay St
2 Westray Pl

Torogay

Street

Liddesdale

Road

Scalpay Pl

80

Milton School

Colston Road

Milton Clinic

Milton

Ashfill St

Leehill Road

Bishopbriggs

St Augustines Primary School

Scalpay St

Liddesdale Square

Ronaldsay

Street

Ornsay St

Everard Ct

Colston Road

Rosevale School

Berneray

St

Ashgill Rd

3

Westray

Street

Westray Sq

2

G22

Ashgill St

1

PO

Chirnside Primary School

D4
1 Westray Circ

Gadloch

Claddens

Harmetray St

Eday St

4

Crowhill

Street

Kippen St

Buckley St

Parkhouse School

Broadholm

Glenhead

Street

Ashfield Station

Denmark St

10

Glasgow City Council

Ashfield

Walnut Rd

Walnut Crs

Chester

D

B808

St Alloysious Primary School

Carron Crs Primary School

Carbisdale Street

Carron Pl

Carron

HAWTHORN STREET

Mansion Street

Ashfield Greyhound Racing Co

HAWTHORN STREET

Saracen St

Elmva

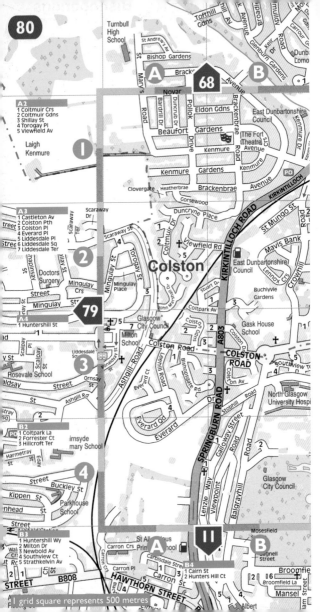

Turnbull High School

St Andrew's St

Bishop Gardens

St Mary's St

A   Brack   **68**   Avenue   **B**

Novar

A2
1 Coitmuir Crs
2 Coitmuir Gdns
3 Shillay St
4 Torogay St
5 Viewfield Av

Laigh Kenmure

I

Eldon Gdns

East Dunbartonshire Council

Pollok Drive

Bardrill Dr

Duncrub Dr

Beaufort

Kenmure

Kenmure   Gardens

Brackenbrae Road

The Fort Theatre Avenue

Kenmure   Avenue

Kenmure

Gardens

Brackenbrae

PO

Clovergate   Heatherbrae

Gorsewood

KIRKINTILLOCH

Scaraway Dr

Duncryne Place

KIRKINTILLOCH ROAD

St Mungo St

A3
1 Castleton Av
2 Colston Pth
3 Coiston Pl
4 Everard Pl
5 Liddesdale Pl
6 Liddesdale Sq
6 Liddesdale Ter

Scaraway St

Scaraway St

Coitmuir Dr

Viewfield Rd

St Mungo St

Mavis Bank

2

Torogay St

Colston

East Dunbartonshire Council

Lennox Cres

Crownhill

Doctors Surgery

Mingulay

Mingulay Crs

Mingulay Place

Stuart Dr

John St

Buchlyvie Gardens

Street

Mingulay

79

Coitpark Av

Coist Gdns

A4
1 Huntershill St

Glasgow City Council

Milton School

Colpark

3

Gask House School

Scalpay Pl

Liddesdale Sq

Ronaldsay St

Colston Road

South View

Rosevale School

Ornsay St

Leemhill Road

Bishopsgate Rd

COLSTON ROAD

North Glasgow University Hospi

Ashgill Rd

Ashgill Road

Everard Ct

Everard Dr

Coiston Av

Springburn Road

B2
PO 1 Coitpark La
2 Forrester Ct
3 Hillcroft Ter

irnside mary School

Everard Gd

Everard

Stronhill Road

Galloway Street

Balgrayhill Road

Glasgow City Council

Harmetray St

Eday

4

Lenzie Way

Viewpoint

Street

Buckley St

Kippen St

nhead St

Parkhouse School

Street

A4
1 Huntershill Wy
2 Milton Dr
3 Newbold Av
4 Southview Ct
5 Strathkelvin Av

St All
School

Carron Crs Prim

A

II

Mosesfield

B

ignell Street

Broomfie

Wa l

St

Carron Pl

Carbisdale Stre

B4
1 Cairn St
2 Hunters Hill Ct

6

Broomfield La

STREET   **B808**   HAWTHORN STREET   Carron   Albert   Mansel

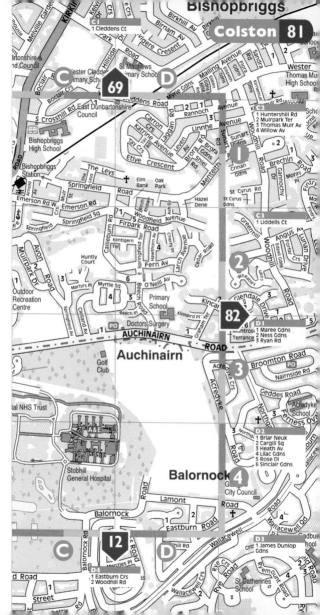

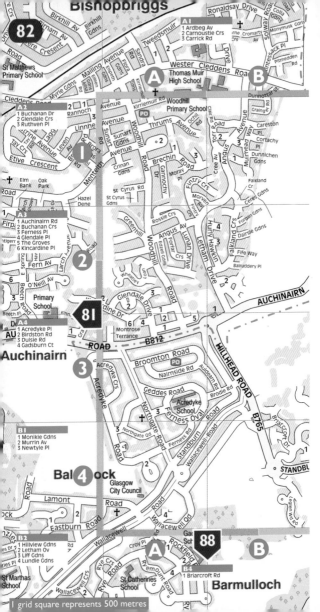

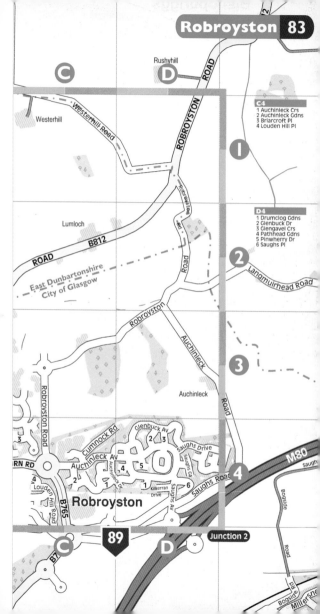

Rushyhill
D

C

ROBROYSTON ROAD

Westerhill Road

Westerhill

C4
1 Auchinleck Crs
2 Auchinleck Gdns
3 Briarcroft Pl
4 Louden Hill Pl

I

Lumloch

Robroyston Road

ROAD **B812**

D4
1 Drumclog Gdns
2 Glenbuck Dr
3 Glengavel Crs
4 Pathhead Gdns
5 Pinwherry Dr
6 Saughs Pl

2

Langmuirhead Road

East Dunbartonshire
City of Glasgow

Robroyston

3

Auchinleck

Robroyston Road

Auchinleck Road

4

M80

Saugh

Cumnock Rd

Glenbuck Av

Auchinleck Av

Auchinleck Dr

Saughs Drive

Saughs Ga

Saughs Rd

3

RN RD

Louden Hill Road

2

4

1

Kilkerran Drive

Saughs Av

5

6

Bogside

Bogside Road

B765

Robroyston

C

B7

89

D

Junction 2

Millers

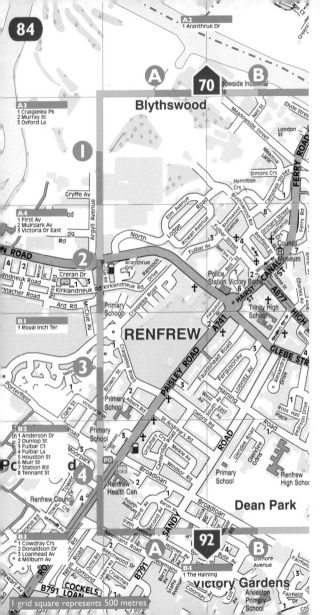

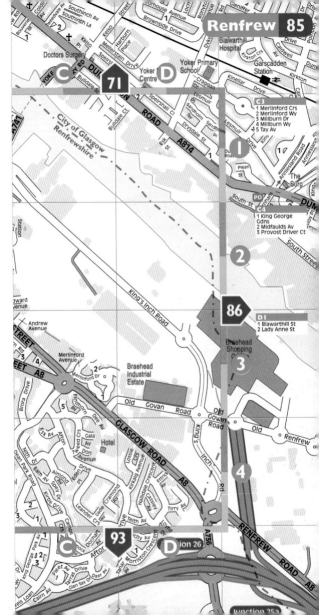

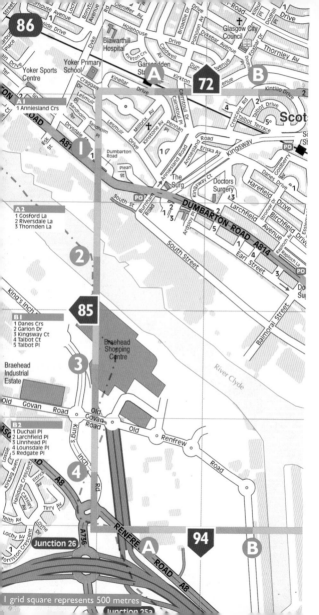

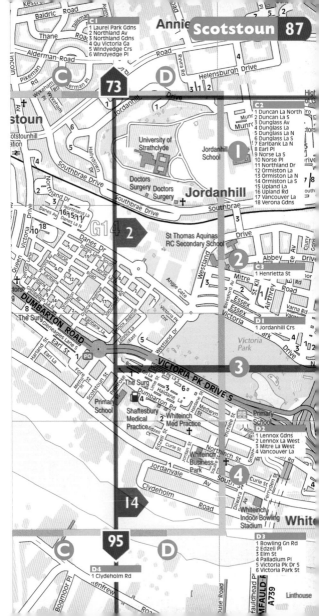

Annie

Baldric Road
Talisman
Thane
Road
Alderman Road
Pikeman Rd
Lincoln

Alderman Pl
Wickham Rd
W Wickham Rd
Wickham Rd

C **73** **D**

Helensburgh Drive
Ryra Rd

Jordanhill Drive

High

Munro

University of Strathclyde

Jordanhill School

Jordanhill

I

Doctors Surgery Doctors Surgery

Southbrae Drive
Hallydown
Northland Dr

Southbrae Drive

G14 **2**

St Thomas Aquinas RC Secondary School

Westland Dr

Abbey Drive

Cluny Av

2

Danes Dr
Danes Av
Danes La N
Danes La S

Victoria Cres

Angle Gate

Mitre Road
St Kilda
Airthrey Av
Essex Drive
Essex
Victoria

Varna Rd

Queen

DUMBARTON ROAD
The Surg
Gleneagles Lane
Earl La
Hartland
Fore
Mitre La
Scotstoun St
PO

Victoria Pk Crt
Earl

Westland Dr

Victoria Park

3 VICTORIA PK DRIVE S

The Surg
Dumbarton Rd
Haldane
Lime
Haldane St
Medwyn

Primary School
Shaftesbury Medical Practice
Whiteinch Med Practice
Edzell St
Curle St

Primary School

Northinch St
Whiteinch Business Park
Jordanvale
Curle St

Jordanhill
South

Fernden St
Dilwara

Whiteinch Indoor Bowling Stadium

4

Clydeholm Road

14

C **95** **D**

Renfrew

Boghorn Pl

Faulds
MFAULD
A739

Linthouse

White

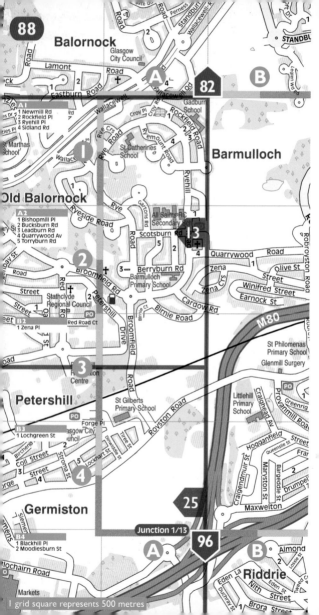

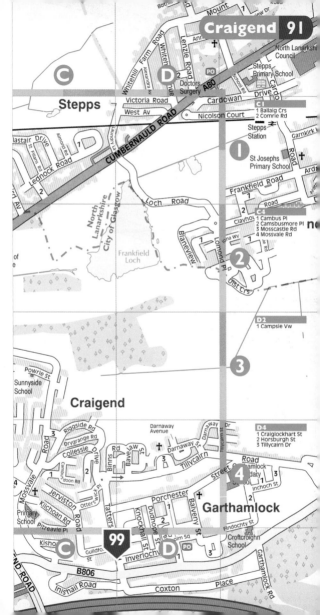

North Lanarkshire
Council

C

Stepps
Primary School

D
Doctors
Surgery **A80**

Whitehill Farm Road
Lenzie Road
Alexandra Av
Whitten
Anr

Cardo
Drive

Stepps

Victoria Road
West Av
Nicolson Court

Cardowan

C1
1 Ballaig Crs
2 Comrie Rd

CUMBERNAULD ROAD

Stepps
Station

Garnkirk

I

St Josephs
Primary School

Alastair
Drive
St Fillans
Almond Av
Lednock Road
7
2

Frankfield Road
Road
Ard

C4
1 Cambus Pl
2 Cambusmore Pl
3 Mosscastle Rd
4 Mossvale Rd

North Lanarkshire
City of Glasgow

Loch Road

Clayhol

ne

Frankfield
Loch

Blaneview
Lomond Pl
Iona Wy
Lona Wy
Ie Rd

2

Uist Crs

D2
1 Campsie Vw

of

3

Powrie St
Sunnyside
School

Craigend

Darnaway Avenue

Riggside Rd
Drygrange Rd
Collessie
Drive
Cambu...doon Rd

Darnaway
Darnaway
Dr

Tillycairn

D4
1 Craiglockhart St
2 Horsburgh St
3 Tillycairn St

Road

Mossvale
Road
Jerviston Road
Kilchoan Rd
Pitreavle Pl
Otter's ...ick Pl

Blins
Rd
Bavelaw
3
3
Porchester
Duchnoe St
Knockhall St
Baveny St

4
Garthamlock
Street
Inchoch St
Findochty St

C
Kisho
Guildfo...
St
Inverlochy

99

D
PO
Dalm Sq
3

Croftcroighn
School

Primary
School

B806
Inishail Road
...ND ROAD

Coxton

Place

Garthamlock Rd

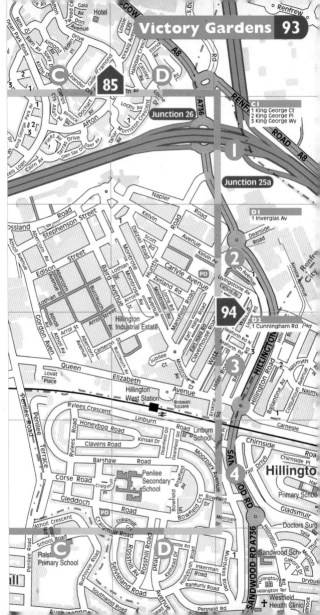

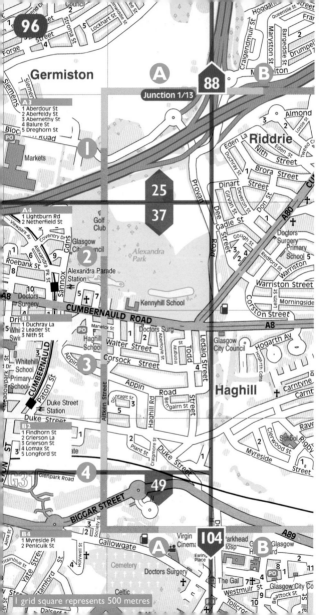

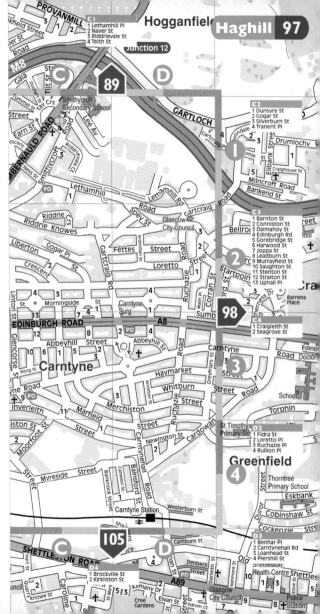

Hogganfield

PROVANMILL

C1
1 Lethamhill Pl
2 Naver St
3 Riddrievale St
4 Teith St

Junction 12

M8

Gala

C

89

D

Tilt Cr

GARTLOCH

Smithycroft
Secondary School

Lee Av

Earn St

CUMBERNAULD ROAD

Ness St

Riddrievale Ct

Smithycroft

PO

C2
1 Dunsyre St
2 Gogar St
3 Silverburn St
4 Tranent Pl

Drumlochy

Avondale

Ellbank Street

Craighouse St

Milncroft Road

Bankend St

LETHAMHILL

Riddrie Crs

Riddrie Knowes

Lethamhill Rd

Road

Gartcraig

Spey St

Glasgow
City Council

Gartcraig Road

C3
1 Barnton St
2 Conniston St
3 Dalmahoy St
4 Edinburgh Rd
5 Gorebridge St
6 Harwood St
7 Joppa St
8 Leadburn St
9 Murrayfield St
10 Saughton St
11 Stenton St
12 Straiton St
13 Uphall Pl

Bellrock

Liberton

Gogar Pl

Fettes

Street

Crescent

Loretto

Street

Gartcraig Rd

Ardmillan St

Ruchazie Road

Startpoint

98

Linton St

Morningside

St

Carntyne
Surg

Malin Pl

Cortan St

Sumb

Chesters Dr

Barness
Place

C4
1 Craigleith St
2 Seagrove St

Glencorse

EDINBURGH ROAD

13

St

A8

PO

2

4

Abbeyhill

Street

Abbeyhill

Carntyne

Road

Edinb

Doctor

Carntyne

Pirrig St

Haymarket

Greyfriars St

Arniston St

Whitburn

Street

3

7

School

Torphin

Inverleith

PO

Marfield

Ruchazie

Street

Cardowan

Street

D2
1 Fidra St
2 Loretto Pl
3 Ruchazie Pl
4 Rullion Pl

St Timothys
Primary Sch

Moorfoot

Street

Carntynehall Road

Newington St

Bainsford St

Camelon St

Greenfield

4

Myreside Street

Bankhock Street

Thorntree
Primary School

Eskbank

Duror

Cobinshaw

Street

Westerburn St

Carntyne Station

Shettleston

Cockenzie

Stre

D3
1 Benhar Pl
2 Carntynehall Rd
3 Loanhead St
4 Piershill St

SHETTLESTON ROAD

C

105

D

Camburn St

Hart St

D4
1 Brockville St
2 Kirkliston St

Caroline

knowe St

A89

Denbeck

St

Kenmore St

PO

Street

Darleith St

Cumany St

Cree Gardens

Elvan St

Edrom St

A89

Glasgow
City Council

Ettrick St

Shettleston
Health Centre

Shettles

Police
Station

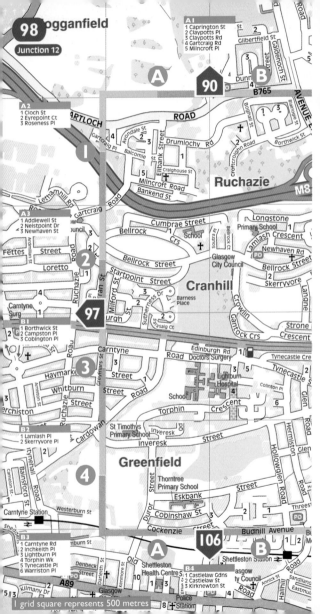

Hogganfield

90

97

106

A1
1 Caprington St
2 Claypotts Pl
3 Claypotts Rd
4 Gartcraig Rd
5 Milncroft Pl

A2
1 Cloch St
2 Eyrepoint Ct
3 Roseness Pl

A3
1 Addiewell St
2 Neistpoint Dr
3 Newhaven St

B1
1 Borthwick St
2 Campston Pl
3 Cobington Pl

B2
1 Lamlash Pl
2 Skerryvore Pl

B3
1 Carntyne Rd
2 Inchkeith Pl
3 Lightburn Pl
4 Torphin Wk
5 Tynecastle Pl
6 Warriston Pl

B4
1 Castielaw Gdns
2 Castielaw St
3 Kirknewton St

HARTLOCH

ROAD

Drumlochy Rd

Gilbertfield St

B765

AVENUE

Borthwick Street

Croftcroighn Road

Ruchazie

M8

Avondale St

Balcomie

Milncroft Road

Bankend St

Craighouse St

Ellbank Street

Cumbrae Street

Bellrock Crs

Bellrock Street

Bellrock Street

School

Startpoint Street

Milford St

Sutherness Dr

Barness Place

Cranhill

Longstone Primary School

Lamlash Crescent

Newhaven Rd

Bellrock Street

Skerryvore

Crowlin

Langne

Camtock Crs

Strone

Crescent

Letham hill Rd

Gartcraig Road

Fettes

Street

Loretto

Carntyne Surg

Ruchazie Road

Bran St

Vasalg Ct

Edinburgh Rd

Doctors Surgery

Tynecastle Cre

Tynecastle

Lightburn Hospital

Colinton Pl

Carntyne

Road

Street

Haymarket

Whitburn Street

Torphin

School

Crescent

Glen

Hermiston

St Timothys Primary School

Inveresk

Inveresk Street

Greenfield

Thorntree Primary School

Eskbank

Cardowan Road

Bainsford Road

Carntyne Road

Rynehall Road

Camlon Rd

Durol Street

Cobinshaw St

Cockenzie Street

Budhill Avenue

Westerburn St

Carntyne Station

Shettleston Health Centre

Shettleston Station

Hollowglen Road

Threest

PO

A89

Glasgow

Police

Denbeck Street

Darleith St

Kilmany Dr

Kenmore St

Amnick St

Eastmui

Sandiland

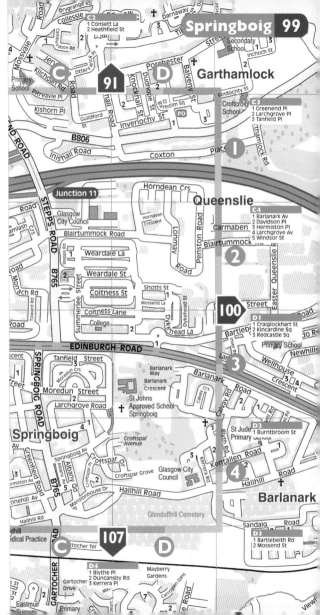

Garthamlock

C2
1 Consett La
2 Heathfield St

Porchester

Secondary School
inchoch St

C3
1 Greenend Pl
2 Larchgrove Pl
3 Tanfield Pl

Croftcroigh School

Findochty St

Coxton Place

1

Horndean Crs

Queenslie

Junction 11

Horndean Crescent

Carmaben

C4
1 Barlanark Av
2 Davidson Pl
3 Hermiston St
4 Larchgrove Av
5 Windsor St

Glasgow City Council

Blairtummock Road

Lonmay Road

Penston Road

Blairtummock

2

Weardale La

Weardale St

Coltness St

Shotts St

Mossend La

Easter Queenslie

Street

100

Coltness Lane

Dykehead La

Bartle

D1
1 Craiglockhart St
2 Kincardine Sq
3 Redcastle St

College

Newhills

Wellhouse Crescent

EDINBURGH ROAD

Tanfield Street

Moredun Crs

3

Barlanark Way

Barlanark Crescent

Barlanark Road

Moredun Street

Calvay Crs

St Johns Approved School Springboig

Larchgrove Road

Springboig

Greenfield Av

Springboig Av

Croftspar Avenue

Croftspar Av

St Jude Primary School

D2
1 Burntbroom St

Kentallen Road

4

Hallhill

Croftspar Grove

Glasgow City Council

Blythe Rd

Hallhill Road

Barlanark

Mansionhouse Dr

Sandaig Road

D3
1 Bartlebeith Rd
2 Mossend St

Glendufthill Cemetery

Medical Practice

Gartocher Ter

Gartocher Drive

Mayberry Gardens

D4
1 Blythe Pl
2 Duncansby Rd
3 Kerrera Pl

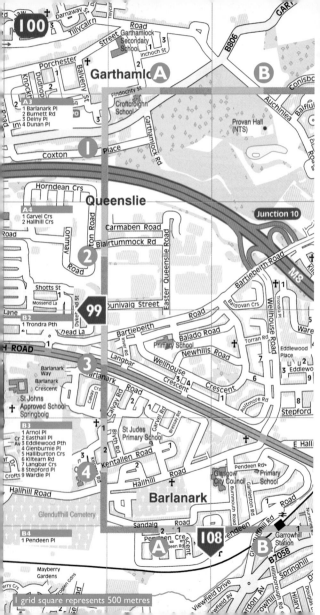

100

Darnaway St

Tillycairn

Tilcarn

Road

Street Garthamlock
Secondary
School

Inchoch St

Porchester

B806

CARL

Conisbo

Auchinlea

Balfu

Knockburn

Dunbob

Balerny St

Garthamlock **A**

B

A3
1 Barlanark Pl
2 Burnett Rd
3 Delny Pl
4 Dunan Pl

Croftcroighn
School

Findochty St

Garthamlock Rd

Provan Hall
(NTS)

Coxton **I** Place

Horndean Crs

Queenslie

A4
1 Garvel Crs
2 Hallhill Crs

Lonmay

Road

ton Road

2

Carmaben Road

Blairtummock Rd

Easter Queenslie Road

Road

Junction 10

M8

Bartiebeith Road

Wellhouse Road

Baldovan Crs

Tronda Pl

Ware

Shotts St

Mossend La

99

Dyke P Rd St

nead La

Dunivaig Street

Bartiebeith

Road

Primary School

Inver Rd

Balado Road

Torran Rd

Newhills Road

Eddlewood
Place

2

Eddle

H ROAD

B2
1 Trondra Pth

3

Barlanark
Way

Barlanark
Crescent

Langbar

Calay St

Barlanark

Road

Road

Wellhouse

Crescent

3 **4**

Wellhouse

Crescent

Aultmore Rd

Stepford

8

St Johns
Approved School
Springboig

Cr

B3
1 Arnol Pl
2 Easthall Pl
3 Eddlewood Pth
4 Glenburnie Pl
5 Haliburton Crs
6 Kiltearn Pl
7 Langbar Crs
8 Stepford Pl
9 Wardie Pl

Av

4

Calvay Rd

Keir St

Garvel Rd

Bressay Rd

Blynn Rd

Kentallen Road

St Judes
Primary School

Glasgow
City Council

Pendeen Rd

Garleston Rd

Primary
School

Crofts

Hallhill Road

Hallhill

Road

Burmmonth Road

Carnbroe Rd

E Hall

Road

Barlanark

Glenduffhill Cemetery

B4
1 Pendeen Pl

Sandaig

Road

Pendeen Cre

cent

2 **1**

A **I08** **B**

Green Rd

Garrowhill
Station

Croduffhill Rd

Garrowhill

B7058

Mayberry
Gardens

Viewfield Drive

Springhill

Hillsborough Rd

Springh

rry Crs

Grovlen cons

don AV

viewfield Av

Hilary

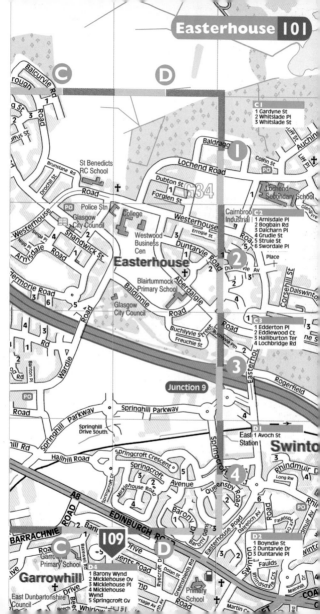

C1
1 Gardyne St
2 Whitslade Pl
3 Whitslade St

C2
1 Arnisdale Pl
2 Bogbain Rd
3 Dalcharn Pl
4 Grudie St
5 Struie St
6 Swordale Pl

C3
1 Edderton Pl
2 Eddiewood Ct
3 Halliburton Ter
4 Lochbridge Rd

D1
East 1 Avoch St
Station

D2
1 Boyndie St
2 Duntarvie Dr
3 Duntarvie Pl

D4
1 Barony Wynd
2 Micklehouse Ov
3 Micklehouse Pl
4 Micklehouse Wynd
5 Springcroft Gv

Baldragg

Lochend Road

Dubton St
Forglen St

Westerhouse
ErroGie St

Duntarvie Road

Duntarvie Av

Lochend Secondary School

Cairnbrook
Industrial

Easterhouse

Abertalgie

Blairtummock Primary School

Glasgow City Council

Road

Buchlyvie Street
Freuchie St

Baldinnie

Road

Rogerfield

Junction 9

Springhill Parkway

Springhill Parkway

Springhill Drive South

Halhill Road

Springcroft Crescent

Springcroft

Avenue

Barony Dr

Swinto

Rhindmuir

Long Rw

AB
EDINBURGH ROAD

109

BARRACHNIE

Garrowhill Primary School

East Dunbartonshire Council

Garrowhill

St Benedicts RC School

Road

College

PO Police Stn
Glasgow City Council

Shandwick St

Westwood Business Cen

Westerhouse Road

Arnisdale Road

hermorie Road

Wardle

Balcurvie Road

brough

St

ifus St

Brunstane

Drochil St

Nigg

Road

Road

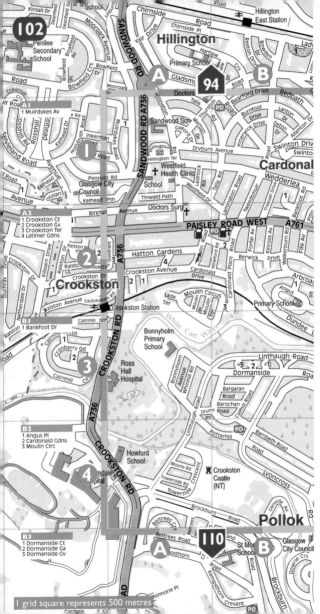

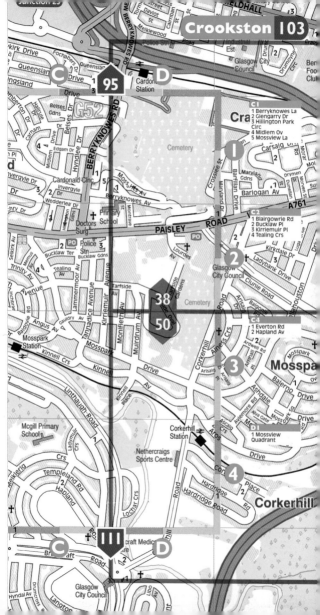

G3

Fr Glenpark
dustrial Estate

Glenpark Road

BIGGAR STREET

A89

Gallowgate

A1
1 Burgher St

Cemetery

Virgin
Cinema

Parkhead
Hosp

Greater Glasgow
Hlth Board

Glasgow City Council

Doctors Surgery

Ewing
Place

PO

I

Glasgow
City Council

Celtic
Football Club

St Michaels
Primary School

The Gal

Westmuir St

Glasgow
City Council

Tollcross Rd

Battock St

10

Westmuir
Medical Centre

Barrowfield St

49

Parkhead

The Surgery

Primary
School

A2
1 Buddon St
2 Janefield St
3 Kinloch St
4 West Whitby St

ndon Road
Primary School

Darleith St

Dechmont

Dunkeld St

Glamis Road

2

Williamson St

silverdale St

Macbeth St

Canmore
Street

Macduff Street

Cutnelton

PO

B1
1 Back Cswy
2 E Wellington St
3 Helenvale St
4 Nisbet St
5 Pharonhill St
6 Powfoot St
7 Ravel Rw
8 Salamanca St
9 Sorby St
10 Southbank St
11 Winning Rw

Kempock St

Belvidere
Hospital

City of Glasgow
South Lanarkshire

A74

LONDON

Surgery

PO

3

Millerfield Pl

Garvald st

Summerfield St

Springfield
Primary School

B2
1 Canmore Pl
2 Dunning St
3 Helenvale St
4 Macbeth Pl
5 Macduff Pl
6 Ogilvie Pl
7 Strathbran St

nclutha
eet

61

4

Downiebrae
Road

Downiebrae

B3
1 Birnam Rd
2 Glenisla St
3 Maukinfauld Ct

Dalmarnock
Trading Estate

Baronald Street

Duchess
Industrial Estate

OAD

Barnfield

River Clyde

Lloyd

1 grid square represents 500 metres

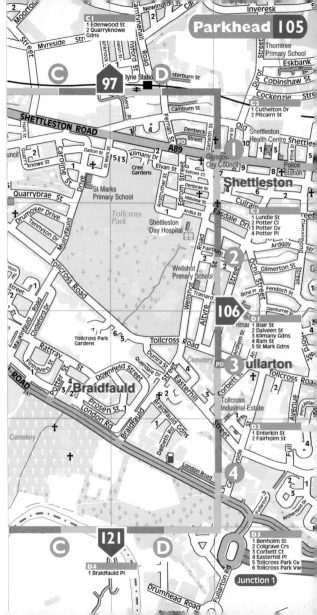

C1
1 Edenwood St
2 Quarryknowe Gdns

97

C **D** sterburn St

Newington St

inveresk

Thorntree Primary School

Eskbank

Cobinshaw St

Cockenzie St

C2
1 Cuthelton Dr
2 Pitcairn St

SHETTLESTON ROAD A89

Shettleston Health Centre Shettles

Glasgow City Council

I

1 3 10

Shettleston

9

8 Police Station

St Marks Primary School

Tollcross Park

Shettleston Day Hospital

Quarrybrae St

Drumover Drive

Tennyson Dr

Culrain

Easdale Dr

D1
1 Lundie St
2 Potter Cl
3 Potter Gv
4 Potter Pl

Ardgay

2

Wellshot Primary School

Gilmerton St

Fendoch St

Ochil St

Glenturret St

106

D1
1 Blair St
2 Dalveen St
3 Kilmany Gdns
4 Ram St
5 St Mark Gdns

Tollcross Park Gardens

6 5

Tollcross Road

Cemetery

3 **ullarton**

Tollcross Road

Rattray

Downfield Street

Prosen St

Braidfauld

Tollcross Industrial Estate

D2
1 Enterkin St
2 Fairholm St

London Rd

Cemetery

4

D3
1 Benholm St
2 Colgrave Crs
3 Corbett Ct
4 Easterhill Pl
5 Tollcross Park Gv
6 Tollcross Park Vw

C **121** **D**

D4
1 Braidfauld Pl

Drumhead Road

Fullarton Rd

Junction 1

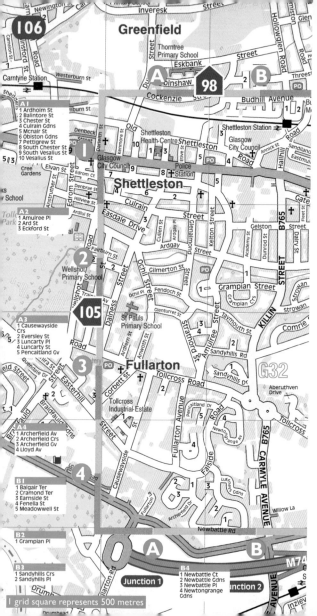

Greenfield

Thorntree Primary School
Eskbank
Carntyne Station Westerburn St Cockenzie
Budhill Avenue
Shettleston Station
Glasgow City Council

A1
1 Ardholm St
2 Balintore St
3 Chester St
4 Culrain Gdns
5 Mcnair St
6 Obiston Gdns
7 Pettigrew St
8 South Chester St
9 South Vesalius St
10 Vesalius St

Denbeck St
Glasgow City Council
Shettleston Health Centre
Shettleston Road
Police Station
Cree Gardens
Elvan St
Edrom Ct

A2
1 Amulree Pl
2 Ard St
3 Eckford St

Shettleston
Culrain Street
Easdale Drive
Cullen St
Ardgay Street
Glenamond Street
Kelton Street
Gelston St
Academy St
Durrod St
Dalry St

Wellshot Primary School
Fairburn St
Gilmerton St
Grampian Street
Grampian Crs
Ochil Pl
Fendoch St
Glenturret St

A3
1 Causewayside Crs
2 Eversley St
3 Luncarty Pl
4 Luncarty St
5 Pencaitland Gv

St Pauls Primary School
Dalness St
Ardheny St
Anworth St
Strathord St
Tavmouth Street
Amulree Street
Comrie St

Fullarton
Tollcross Road
Corbett St
Sandyhills Rd
Sandyhills Dr
Aberuthven Drive
G32

Tollcross Industrial Estate
Fullarton Avenue
Pencaitland Dr
Newtongrange Av
Falside Rd
Tollcross

A4
1 Archerfield Av
2 Archerfield Crs
3 Archerfield Gv
4 Lloyd Av

Braidfauld Gdns
Causewayside
Fullarton Rd
Archerfield Dr
Lukes Gdns

B1
1 Balgair Ter
2 Cramond Ter
3 Earnside St
4 Fenella St
5 Meadowell St

B2
1 Grampian Pl

Newbattle Rd

B3
1 Sandyhills Crs
2 Sandyhills Pl

Junction 1
Junction 2
M74

B4
1 Newbattle Ct
2 Newbattle Gdns
3 Newbattle Pl
4 Newtongrange Gdns

Carmyle Avenue
Willow La

I grid square represents 500 metres

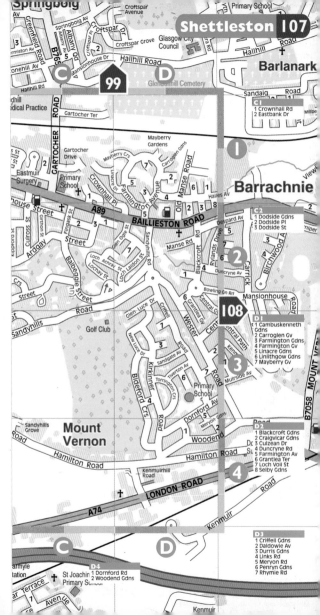

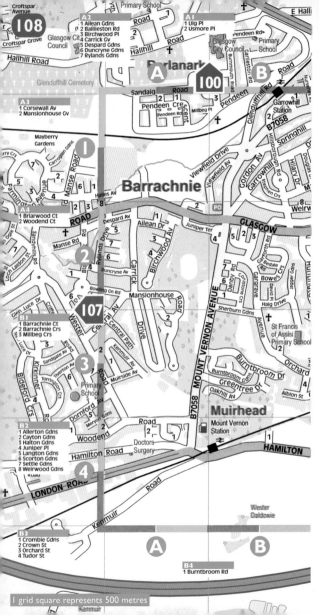

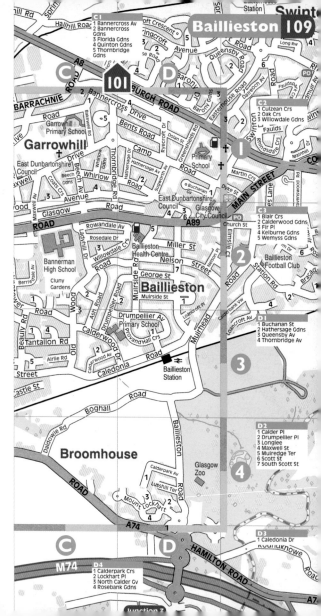

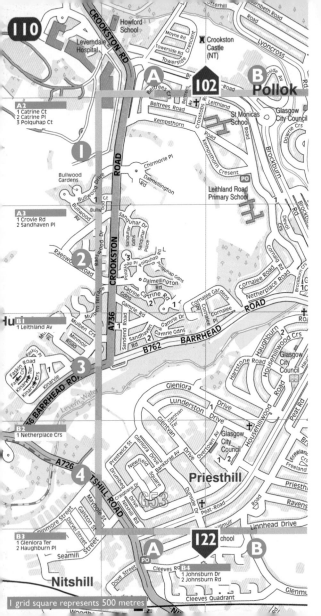

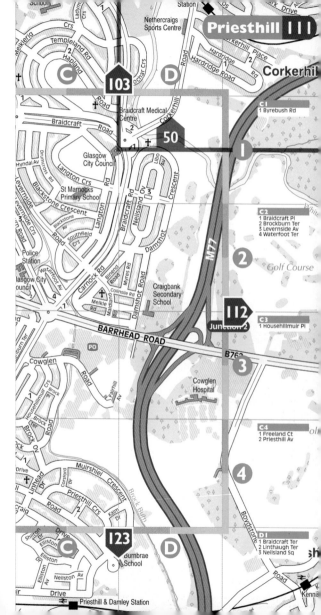

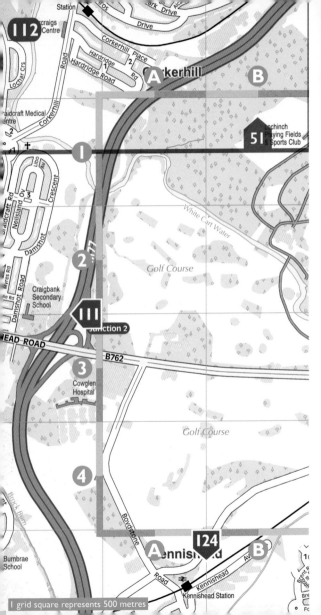

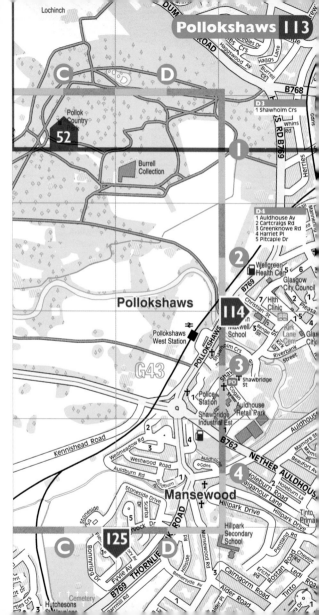

Lochinch

DUM ROAD

ROAD

Eagles Dr

Haggswood Av

Haggs

Burrell Ct

Lane

B768

C

D

D3
1 Shawholm Crs

Pollok
Country

52

S RD B769

Whins Rd

Harriet

Burrell
Collection

1

D4
1 Auldhouse Av
2 Cartcraigs Rd
3 Greenknowe Rd
4 Harriet Pl
5 Pitcaple Dr

2

Wellgreen
Health Cen

6

Glasgow
City Council

B769

7

Hlth
Clinic

Christian St

1

Pleasa

Pollokshaws

114

Maxwell
School

Kirk
Lane

5
4

Bengal St

St

Cem

Gla

Pollokshaws
West Station

Shawholm Crs

Riverbank
Street

G43

3

Sha

Shawbridge
St

PO

Cogan

Police
Station

1

Auldhouse
Retail Park

Auldhous

Shawbridge
Industrial Est

B762

NETHER AUDHOUS

Kennishead Road

2

3

4

Auldhous
Cdns

Mamore S

Mamore

Beaufort

Wellmeadow Rd

Westwood Road

Auldburn Rd

4

Holeburn Rd

Holeburn La

Salganour Lane

Tinto

Stoneside Drive

SCARPA Dr

Mansewood

Hillpark Drive

Hillpark Drive

Tinto

Stoneside
Sq

5

vock
Dr

ROAD

Hillpark
Secondary
School

Pentland Rd

Cheviot

C

D

125

Fyvie Av

THORNLIE

Rd

Mansewood Rd

Cairngorm Rd

Rostan Rd

Rd

Erichst Rd

Bonnyrigg Dr

B769

Bemersyde Av

Alder Road

Cemetery

Hutchesons

3

1

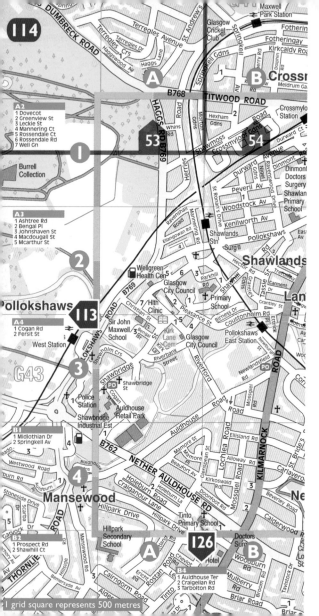

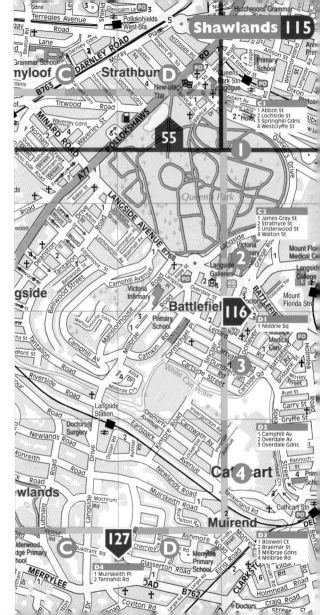

Terregles Avenue

Darnley Road

B763

Titwood Road

MINAR ROAD

A77

Waverley Gdns

Norham

Moss Side Road

Bertram

Framton

Baker St

LANGSIDE AVENUE B768

Deanston

Tantallon

Bellwood Street

Camphill Av

Bedford St

Tantallon

Riverside Road

Langside Station

Doctors Surgery

Newlands Road

Monreith

Road

wlands

Lubhaig

MERRYLEE

Strathbun D

New Stage Thtr

POLLOKSHAWS

55

Queen's Park

Langside Galleries

Victoria Infirmary

Battlefiel 116

Camphill Avenue

Manhouse Gdns

Mansionhouse

Millbrae

Cartkin

Primary School

Carmichael Pl

Alisa

Millbrae Crs

White Cart Water

Cartside Street

Dundenald

Cromarty Avenue

Earlspark

Kintore Road

Carnwadric Avenue

Invergordon Av

Carnwadon Av

Newlands Road

Mochrum Rd

Airlour Rd

Langside Rd

Quadrant Rd

127 D

Cherrybank

Glasserton Road

Muirskeith Road

Ashmore Road

Merrylee Primary School

B762

Coylton Road

Queens Park Stn Synagogue

Albert Av

Maxpark Lane

PO

Primary School

Westmorland

DIXON

C1
1 Abbot St
2 Lochside St
3 Springhill Gdns
4 Westclyffe St

I

Queen's Drive

Victoria Road

Grange Ro

Mount Florida Medical C

Langsi College

Mount Florida Stn

2

C2
1 James Gray St
2 Strathyre St
3 Underwood St
4 Walton St

BATTLEFIE

3

D1
1 Niddrie Sq

Maddick Medical Cen

Battlefield Av

Brisbane St

Morley Street

Garry St

Gryffe St

Ruel St

Sea

D2
1 Camphill Av
2 Overdale Av
3 Overdale Gdns

Cat 4 art

Rannoch

Holmhead

Muirend

DEL

Cathcart Stn

PO

D3
1 Boswell Ct
2 Braemar St
3 Millbrae Gdns
4 Millbrae Rd

CLARKST

Craig Road

Doctors

D4
1 Muirskeith Pl
2 Tannahill Rd

C

D

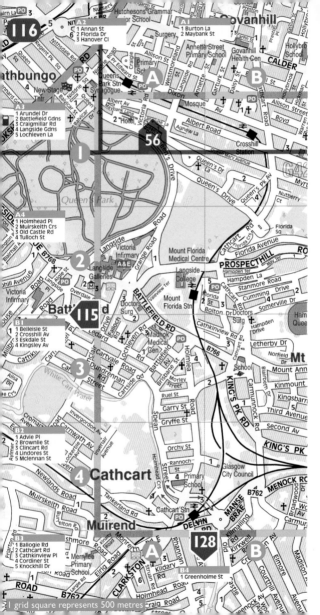

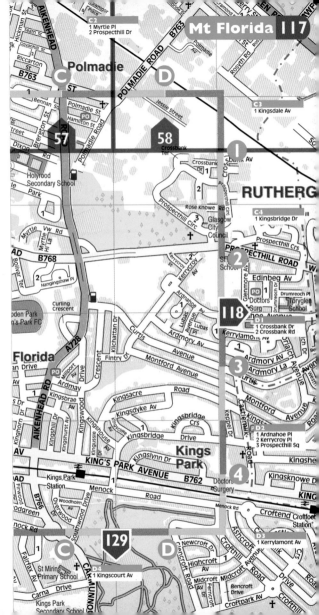

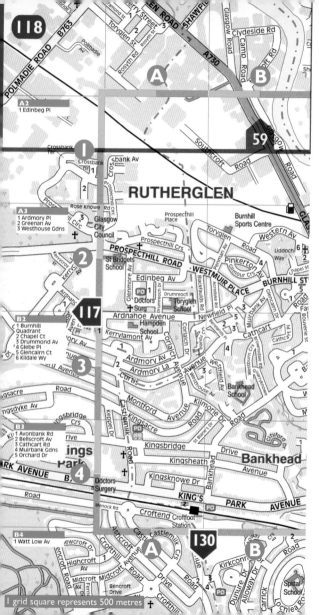

RUTHERGLEN

POLMADIE ROAD
B765

Polmadie Av

A730

SHAWFIELD

Clydeside Rd

Glasgow Road

Camp Rd

ft Rd

A2
1 Edinbeg Pl

Crossbank Ter

Crossbank Dr

sbank Av

Southcroft Road

GLASG

A3
1 Ardmory Pl
2 Greenan Av
3 Westhouse Gdns

Rose Knowe Rd

Glasgow City Council

Prospecthill Circ

Prospecthill Place

Burnhill Sports Centre

Western Av

Liddoch Way

PROSPECTHILL ROAD

Prospecthill Crs

St Bridgets School

Torglen Road

Pinkerton Av

Glenmore Av

Edinbeg Av

WESTMUIR PLACE

BURNHILL ST

PO

Doctors Surg

Drumreoch

Blackfaulds Rd

Acrehoe Rd

B2
1 Burnhill Quadrant
2 Chapel Ct
3 Drummond Av
4 Glebe Pl
5 Glencairn Ct
6 Kildale Wy

Torglen School

Newfield Pl

Cathcart

Ardnahoe Avenue

Hampden School

Kerrylamont Av

Corlaich Dr

Westburn Dr

Cathcart Pl

Ardmory Av

Ardmory La

Avenue

Westhouse Av

Bankhead School

Curtis

Montford

Kilmore Rd

B3
1 Avonbank Rd
2 Bellscroft Av
3 Cathcart Rd
4 Muirbank Gdns
5 Orchard Dr

Kingsacre Road

Kingsbridge Crs

Keppel Dr

Kingsacre

Kingsbridge

St Blane Dr

Clifford Dr

Drive

BANKHEAD

ings Park

Doctors Surgery

Kingsheath Avenue

Kingsknowe Dr

Bankhead Avenue

PARK AVENUE

KING'S PARK AVENUE

Menock Rd

Croftend

Croftfoot Station

PO

B4
1 Watt Low Av

Newcroft Dr

Highcroft Av

Midcroft Av

Bencroft Dr

Crofthill Road

Castlemilk Crs

Croftfoot Road

Kirkconnel

Dunure Dr

Alloway Dr

Carrick

Spittal School

Lochlea Rd

I grid square represents 500 metres

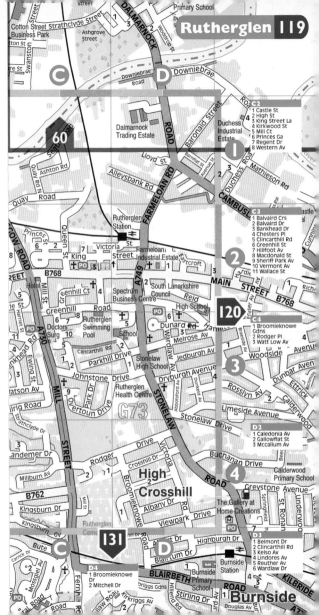

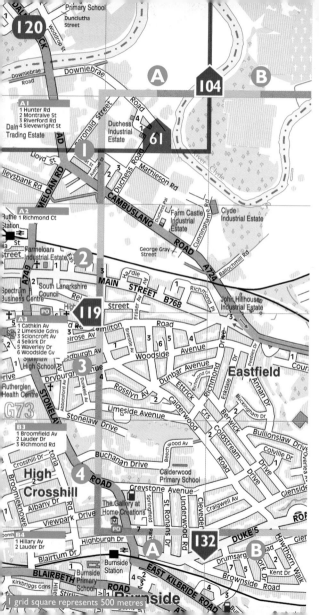

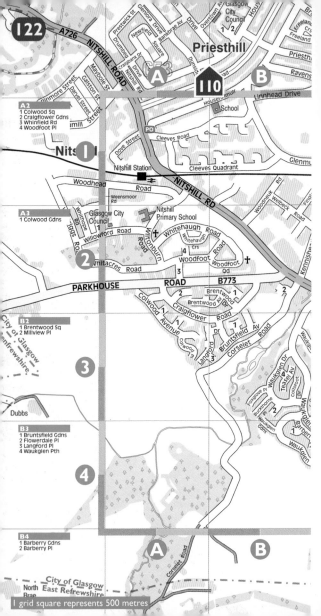

122 A726

NITSHILL ROAD

Prestwick St

Glenora Drive

Newfield Square

Drumbeg Drive

Banbrae Av

Overtown Rd

Drive

Priesthill

Glasgow City Council

1 2

Legglesland

Freeland

Priesth

Raven

A

Mayhole Dr

Nitshill Dr

Dunsiff

Housbmuir

110

Linnhead Drive

B

Kinmore Street

Daniel Street

Galston St

Ravelston Street

Mavisole St

School

A2
1 Colwood Sq
2 Craigflower Gdns
3 Whinfield Rd
4 Woodfoot Pl

PO

Dove Street

Cleeves Road

Nits **I**

Nitshill Station

NITSHILL RD

Woodhead Road

Weensmoor Rd

Cleeves Quadrant

Glenm

Nitshill Primary School

Whinbrae

Hogg Rd

A3
1 Colwood Gdns

Glasgow City Council

Willowford Road

Whinburn

Whitehaugh Road

Road

Woodneuk

Welbeck Road

Fing

2

Whitacres Road

Woodfoot
Crs

4

Woodfoot Qd

Woodfoot

3

Kennishead

PARKHOUSE ROAD B773

Brentwood

1

Brentwood

2

Colwood Avenue

Craigflower Road

Brentwood

Colwood Sq

B2
1 Brentwood Sq
2 Millview Pl

Langford

Dr

3

Bruntsfield Av

Corselet

7

Road

City of Glasgow

Renfrewshire

3

Foxglove Pl

Waukglen Dr

Teasel Av

Buckthorne

Colthorn

Waukglen Gdns

4

Barperrin

Waukglen

Dubbs

B3
1 Bruntsfield Gdns
2 Flowerdale Pl
3 Langford Pl
4 Waukglen Pth

Waukglen

4

B4
1 Barberry Gdns
2 Barberry Pl

A

Corselet Road

B

City of Glasgow

North East Renfrewshire

Brae

I grid square represents 500 metres

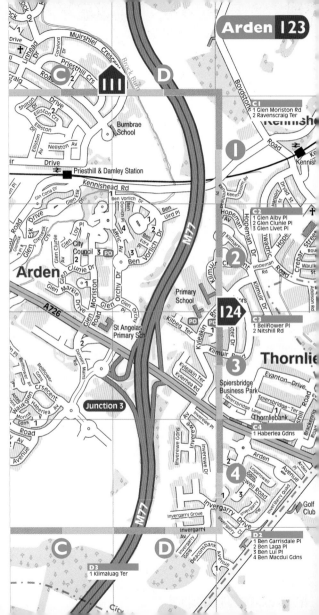

C1
1 Glen Moriston Rd
2 Ravenscraig Ter

C2
1 Glen Alby Pl
2 Glen Clunie Pl
3 Glen Livet Pl

C3
1 Bellflower Rd
2 Nitshill Rd

C4
1 Haberlea Gdns

D2
1 Ben Garrisdale Pl
2 Ben Laga Pl
3 Ben Lui Pl
4 Ben Macdui Gdns

D3
1 Kilmaluag Ter

Muirshiel Crescent
Priesthill Crs
Corsford Dr
Linnhead Drive
Crossstobs Road
Priesthill Road
Shilton Dr
Elliston Cres
Elliston Drive
Elliston Av
Neilston Av
Drive

Burnbrae School

Kennishead Rd

Priesthill & Damley Station

Boydstone Road

Kennishead

Kennishead Road

Kennist

Hopeman Av
Hopeman Dr
Hopeman Rd
Waddic
Kennishead Rd
Kilmaur
Crebar Street
Waulk
Addison Rd

Glen Cona Dr
Glen Esk Dr
Ben Vorlich Pl
Ben Damh Pl
Ben Ulrd Pl
Ben Affric Dr
Ben Edra Pl
Ben Vorlich Dr
Glen Clunie
Glen Clencalk
Glen Esk Drive
Glen Road
Glen Clunie Dr

City Council 3 PO

Arden

A726

Glen Markie Drive
Glen Orchy Drive
Glen Moriston
Glen Orchy Dr
St Angelas Primary Sch

Damley Mains

Primary School
PO PC

Kilbeg Ter
Kyleakin
Kilmuir Dr
Kilmuir Dr
Kyleakin Ter
Kylerhea Rd

Thornlie

Spiersbridge Business Park
Spiersbridge Lane
Evanton Drive
Spiersbridge Road
Thornliebank
Nitshill Road
Electra

Junction 3

Bellflower Court
Crescent
Haberlea
Morista Gdns
Aster Av
Waulkmill Av
Avenue

Inverewe Gdns
Inverewe Av
Inverewe Dr

Arden Avenue
Logansw ell Gdns
Logansw ell Road
Inverdam Quad

Golf Club

Invergarry Gdns
Invergarry Grove
Invergarry Av
Invergarry Drive
Invergarry Vw
Invergarry
Deaconsbank Avenue

M77

124

2

I

3

4

C

D

City

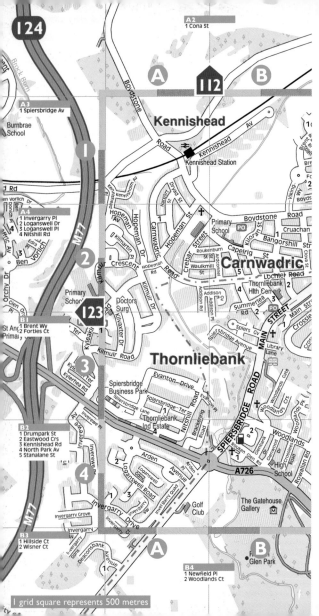

124

A2
1 Cona St

A3
1 Spiersbridge Av

Burnbrae
School

A **112** **B**

Kennishead

Kennishead Road

Kennishead AV

Kennishead Station

1

Ben vorlich

1 Invergarry Pl
2 Loganswell Dr
3 Loganswell Pl
4 Nitshill Rd

Ben Vorlich

Orchy Dr

Glen AV

Ben

2

Kilmuir Dr

Primary
School

123

Kyleakin

B1
1 Brent Wy
2 Forties Ct

St And
Primar

Hopeman
AV

Kimartin Dr

Crescent

Hopeman
Rd

Carnwadric
Road

Hopeman Dr

Crebar
Street

Dryad St

Hopeman St

Harport
St

Roukenburn
St

Waulkmill
St

Primary
School

Carnwadric

Boydstone
Road

Cruachan
St

Bangorshill

Capelrig

Lochiel Road

Thornliebank
Hlth Cen

Addison
Rd

Addison Pl

Summerlea
Rd

Doctors
Surg

Kilwaxter Dr

Kilmuir Road

3

Kylerhea Rd

B2
1 Drumpark St
2 Eastwood Crs
3 Kennishead Rd
4 North Park Av
5 Stanalane St

Inverewe AV

Spiersbridge
Business Park

Spiersbridge
Lane

Evanton Drive

Spiersbridge-Ter

Thornliebank
Ind Estate

Thornliebank

Nitshill Road

Evanton Dr

Braxfield

MAIN

Spiers GV

Spiersbridge Avenue

Library
Lane

Crosslee

STREET

PO

Woodlands Gate

Woodlands Crs

Woodlands PK

SPIERSBRIDGE

ROAD

Rouken Glen Rd

Glenbank

4

Inverewe AV

Loganswell Gdns

Arden
Avenue

Loganswell Road

Invergarry Vw

Arden Av

A726

Golf
Club

Woodlands

Garwood

Crosslees Dr

Rowallan Rd

High
School

The Gatehouse
Gallery

B3
1 Hillside Ct
2 Wisner Ct

Invergarry Grove

Invergarry Drive

Invergarry
Gdns

Deaconsbank
Avenue

A

B4
1 Newfield Pl
2 Woodlands Ct

B
Glen Park

M77

I grid square represents 500 metres

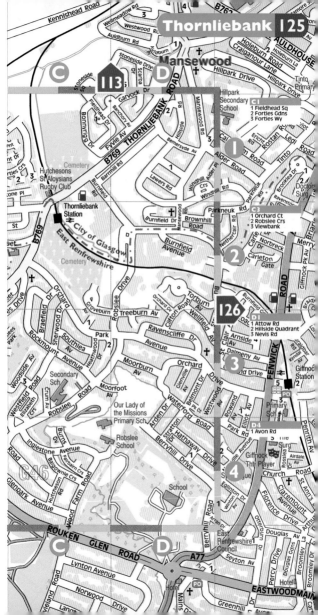

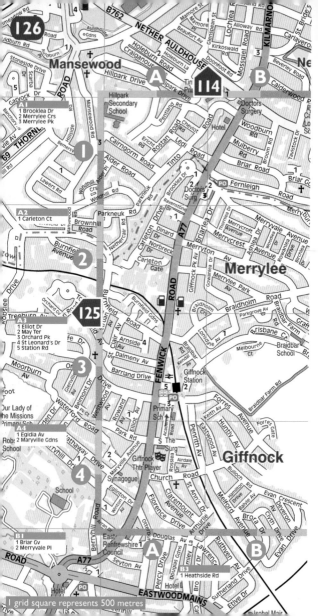

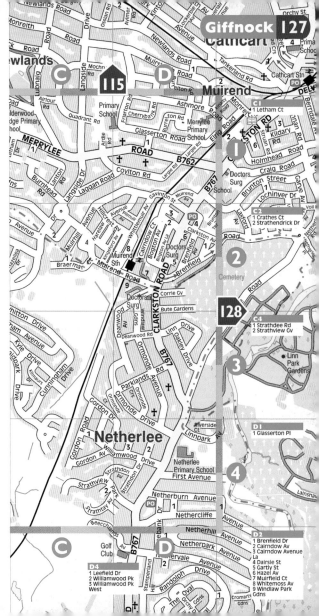

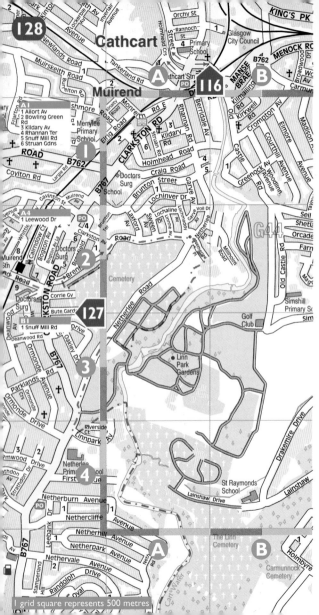

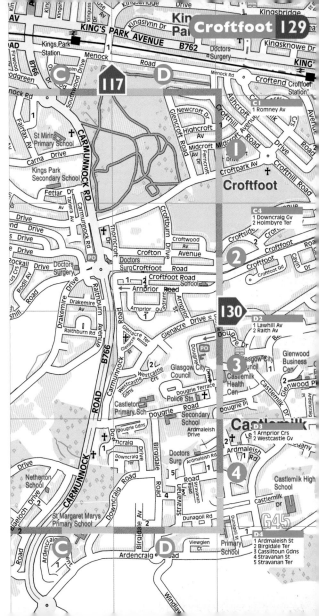

117

Kingsbridge Drive
King's Park
King

Kingslynn Dr
Kingsbridge

Kingsknowe Av

KING'S PARK AVENUE
B762

Doctors
Surgery

Kings Park
Station

Menock

KING

Road

Menock Rd

Croftend Croftfoot
Station

C

D

C1
1 Romney Av

Newcroft
Dr

Highcroft
Av

Midcroft
Av

Ashcroft Av

Crofthill Avenue

Cherry

Drive

St Mirins
Primary School

Carna Drive

Fetlar Dr

CARMUNNOCK RD

Thorncroft Dr

Glencroft Road

Ferncroft Dr

Croftburn Drive

Croftpark Av

Crofthill Road

Midcroft Drive

I

Croftfoot

Kings Park
Secondary School

Fetlar Dr

Tantera Dr

Carmunnock Rd

Drive

Drive

Drive

Rockall Drive

Rodil Av

Roddil Crs

Drakemire

Drakemire Av

Raithburn Rd

Raithburn Avenue

B766

CARMUNNOCK ROAD

Doctors
Surgery

PO

Croftburn Drive

Croftwood
Av

Crofton
Avenue

Croftside Av

Croftfoot

Croftfoot

Croftfoot Qd

Croftfoot Rd

Cavin Dr

C4
1 Downcraig Gv
2 Holmbyre Ter

2

Doctors
Surg

Croftfoot Road

Croftfoot Road
School

Arnprior Road

Arnprior Gdns

Arnprior Rd

Arnprior Gv

Glenacre Dr

Glenacre Ter

Glenacre St

Dougrie Dr

PO

Dougrie Rd

D2
1 Lawhill Av
2 Raith Av

130

3

Glasgow City
Council

Westcastle
Crs

Glasgow City
Council

Castlemilk
Health
Cen

Glenwood
Business
Cen

Glenwood Rd

Glenmilk Dr

Castleton
Primary Sch

Dougrie Terrace

Police Stn

Dougrie
Road

Dougrie
Secondary
School

Castlemilk Pl

Castlemilk

D3
1 Arnprior Crs
2 Westcastle Gv

Dougrie Gdns

Downcraig
Drive

Thorncraig

Birgidale Road

Ardmaleish
Drive

Ardmaleish Rd

Doctors
Surg

Road

Stravanan Road

Ardmaleish Rd

Castlemilk Dr

Ardmaleish

4

Castlemilk High
School

G45

Netherton
School

Glenloch Drive

CARMUNNOCK ROAD

St Margaret Marys
Primary School

Downcraig Road

Birgidale Av

Stravanan

Dunagoil Rd

Primary
School

Viewglen
Ct

D4
1 Ardmaleish St
2 Birgidale Ter
3 Cassiltoun Gdns
4 Stravanan St
5 Stravanan Ter

C

D

Ardencraig

Ardencraig Road

Windlaw

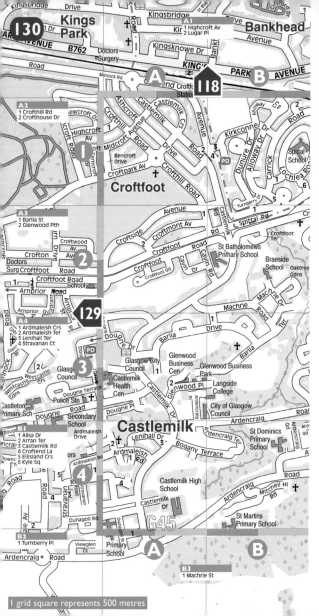

I grid square represents 500 metres

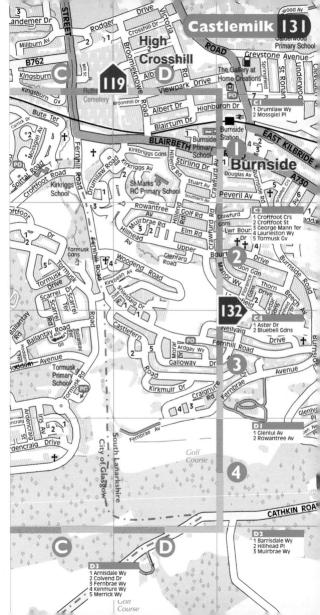

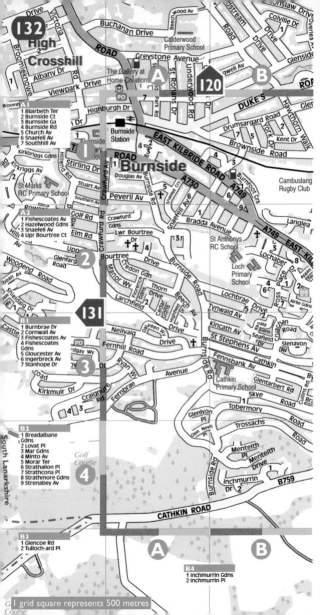

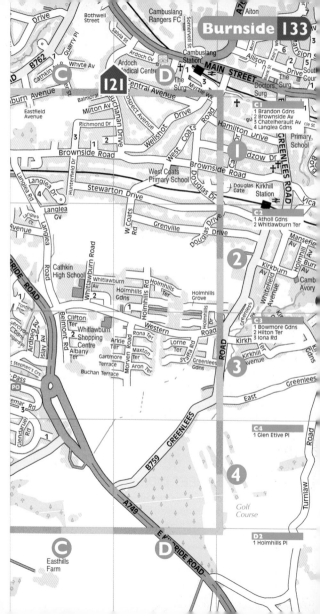

Anniesland	73 D4	Kelvindale	76 A4
Arden	123 C2	Kelvinside	5 D3
Auchinairn	81 D3	Kennishead	124 A1
Baillieston	109 D2	Kilbowie	62 A2
Balornock	81 D4	Kings Park	117 D4
Bankhead	118 B4	Knightswood	73 C3
Barlanark	100 A4	Lambhill	78 B3
Barmulloch	13 E2	Langside	114 B2
Barrachnie	108 A1	Mansewood	113 D4
Battlefield	115 D2	Maryhill	75 D3
Bearsden	64 B1	Merrylee	126 B2
Bellahouston	40 B3	Millerston	90 A2
Bishopbriggs	69 D4	Milton	79 C3
Blythswood	84 A1	Mosspark	51 D1
Braidfauld	105 C3	Mount Florida	116 B3
Bridgeton	48 A3	Mount Vernon	107 C4
Broomhouse	109 C4	Muirend	115 D4
Burnside	132 A1	Muirhead	108 B3
Cadder	69 D1	Netherlee	127 C4
Calton	47 D1	Newlands	114 B4
Cardonald	102 B1	Oatlands	58 A2
Carntyne	97 C3	Old Balornock	12 B4
Carnwadric	124 B2	Parkhead	104 B2
Castlemilk	130 A4	Partick	16 C3
Cathcart	115 D4	Pollok	102 B4
Colston	80 A2	Pollokshaws	113 D2
Corkerhill	50 C4	Pollokshields	54 C1
Cowlairs	11 E4	Polmadie	58 A3
Craigend	91 C3	Port Dundas	21 E3
Craigton	39 D2	Possil Park	9 F2
Cranhill	98 A2	Priesthill	110 A4
Croftfoot	130 A1	Provanmill	89 C3
Crossmyloof	54 B4	Queenslie	99 D2
Dalmarnock	60 A2	Renfrew	84 A3
Dean Park	84 B4	Riddrie	96 B1
Dennistoun	35 F3	Robroyston	83 C4
Drumchapel	64 A4	Royston	22 C4
Drumry	62 A4	Ruchazie	98 B1
Dumbreck	40 C4	Ruchill	7 F1
Easterhouse	101 C2	Rutherglen	56 A4
Eastfield	120 B3	Rutherglen	118 A1
Fullarton	106 A3	Scotstoun	86 B1
Garrowhill	109 C1	Shawlands	114 B2
Garthamlock	91 C4	Shettleston	106 A1
Germiston	24 C3	Sighthill	22 C4
Giffnock	126 B4	Springboig	99 C4
Glasgow	33 F3	Stepps	91 C1
Gorbals	45 E3	Strathbungo	55 E5
Govan	28 B2	Summerston	77 D1
Govanhill	56 B3	Temple	74 A3
Greenfield	98 A4	Thornliebank	124 A3
Haghill	96 B3	Townhead	34 A1
High Crosshill	119 D4	Victory Gardens	92 A1
Hillington	94 A4	West Drumoyne	26 C4
Hogganfield	89 D4	Whitecrook	70 B2
Hutchesontown	45 F5	Whiteinch	14 C2
Ibrox	41 D1	Yoker	71 C3
Jordanhill	2 B2	Yorkhill	29 F1

USING THE STREET INDEX

Street names are listed alphabetically. Each street name is followed by its postal town or area locality, the Postcode District, the page number, and the reference to the square in which the name is found.

Example: **Abbotsford Pl** *GBLS* G5...................... **44** C4 ◨

Some entries are followed by a number in a blue box. This number indicates the location of the street within the referenced grid square. The full street name is listed at the side of the map page.

GENERAL ABBREVIATIONS

ACC	ACCESS
ALY	ALLEY
AP	APPROACH
AR	ARCADE
ASS	ASSOCIATION
AV	AVENUE
BCH	BEACH
BLDS	BUILDINGS
BND	BEND
BNK	BANK
BR	BRIDGE
BRK	BROOK
BTM	BOTTOM
BUS	BUSINESS
BVD	BOULEVARD
BY	BYPASS
CATH	CATHEDRAL
CEM	CEMETERY
CEN	CENTRE
CFT	CROFT
CH	CHURCH
CHA	CHASE
CHYD	CHURCHYARD
CIR	CIRCLE
CIRC	CIRCUS
CL	CLOSE
CLFS	CLIFFS
CMP	CAMP
CNR	CORNER
CO	COUNTY
COLL	COLLEGE
COM	COMMON
COMM	COMMISSION
CON	CONVENT
COT	COTTAGE
COTS	COTTAGES
CP	CAPE
CPS	COPSE
CR	CREEK
CREM	CREMATORIUM
CRS	CRESCENT
CSWY	CAUSEWAY
CT	COURT
CTRL	CENTRAL
CTS	COURTS
CTYD	COURTYARD
CUTT	CUTTINGS
CV	COVE
CYN	CANYON
DEPT	DEPARTMENT
DL	DALE
DM	DAM
DR	DRIVE
DRO	DROVE
DRY	DRIVEWAY
DWGS	DWELLINGS
E	EAST
EMB	EMBANKMENT
EMBY	EMBASSY
ESP	ESPLANADE
EST	ESTATE
EX	EXCHANGE
EXPY	EXPRESSWAY
EXT	EXTENSION
F/O	FLYOVER
FC	FOOTBALL CLUB
FK	FORK
FLD	FIELD
FLDS	FIELDS
FLS	FALLS
FLS	FLATS

FM	FARM
FT	FORT
FWY	FREEWAY
FY	FERRY
GA	GATE
GAL	GALLERY
GDN	GARDEN
GDNS	GARDENS
GLD	GLADE
GLN	GLEN
GN	GREEN
GND	GROUND
GRA	GRANGE
GRG	GARAGE
GT	GREAT
GTWY	GATEWAY
GV	GROVE
HGR	HIGHER
HL	HILL
HLS	HILLS
HO	HOUSE
HOL	HOLLOW
HOSP	HOSPITAL
HRB	HARBOUR
HTH	HEATH
HTS	HEIGHTS
HVN	HAVEN
HWY	HIGHWAY
IMP	IMPERIAL
IN	INLET
IND EST	INDUSTRIAL ESTATE
INF	INFIRMARY
INFO	INFORMATION
INT	INTERCHANGE
IS	ISLAND
JCT	JUNCTION
JTY	JETTY
KG	KING
KNL	KNOLL
L	LAKE
LA	LANE
LDG	LODGE
LGT	LIGHT
LK	LOCK
LKS	LAKES
LNDG	LANDING
LTL	LITTLE
LWR	LOWER
MAG	MAGISTRATE
MAN	MANSIONS
MD	MEAD
MDW	MEADOWS
MEM	MEMORIAL
MKT	MARKET
MKTS	MARKETS
ML	MALL
ML	MILL
MNR	MANOR
MS	MEWS
MSN	MISSION
MT	MOUNT
MTN	MOUNTAIN
MTS	MOUNTAINS
MUS	MUSEUM
MWY	MOTORWAY
N	NORTH
NE	NORTH EAST
NW	NORTH WEST
O/P	OVERPASS
OFF	OFFICE
ORCH	ORCHARD

OV	OVAL
PAL	PALACE
PAS	PASSAGE
PAV	PAVILION
PDE	PARADE
PH	PUBLIC HOUSE
PK	PARK
PKWY	PARKWAY
PL	PLACE
PLN	PLAIN
PLNS	PLAINS
PLZ	PLAZA
POL	POLICE STATION
PR	PRINCE
PREC	PRECINCT
PREP	PREPARATORY
PRIM	PRIMARY
PROM	PROMENADE
PRS	PRINCESS
PRT	PORT
PT	POINT
PTH	PATH
PZ	PIAZZA
QD	QUADRANT
QU	QUEEN
QY	QUAY
R	RIVER
RBT	ROUNDABOUT
RD	ROAD
RDG	RIDGE
REP	REPUBLIC
RES	RESERVOIR
RFC	RUGBY FOOTBALL CLUB
RI	RISE
RP	RAMP
RW	ROW
S	SOUTH
SCH	SCHOOL
SE	SOUTH EAST
SER	SERVICE AREA
SH	SHORE
SHOP	SHOPPING

SKWY	SKYWAY
SMT	SUMMIT
SOC	SOCIETY
SP	SPUR
SPR	SPRING
SQ	SQUARE
ST	STREET
STN	STATION
STR	STREAM
STRD	STRAND
SW	SOUTH WEST
TDG	TRADING
TER	TERRACE
THWY	THROUGHWAY
TNL	TUNNEL
TOLL	TOLLWAY
TPK	TURNPIKE
TR	TRACK
TRL	TRAIL
TWR	TOWER
U/P	UNDERPASS
UNI	UNIVERSITY
UPR	UPPER
V	VALE
VA	VALLEY
VIAD	VIADUCT
VIL	VILLA
VIS	VISTA
VLG	VILLAGE
VLS	VILLAS
VW	VIEW
W	WEST
WD	WOOD
WHF	WHARF
WK	WALK
WKS	WALKS
WLS	WELLS
WY	WAY
YD	YARD
YHA	YOUTH HOSTEL

POSTCODE TOWNS AND AREA ABBREVIATIONS

BAIL/MDB/MHD	Baillieston/Moodiesburn/Muirhead
BLTYR/CAMB	Blantyre/Cambuslang
BSDN	Bearsden
BSHPBGS	Bishopbriggs
CAR/SHTL	Carmyle/Shettleston
CARD/HILL/MSPK	Cardonald/Hillington/Mosspark
CGLE	Central Glasgow east
CGLW	Central Glasgow west
CLYDBK	Clydebank
COWCAD	Cowcaddens
CRMNK/CLK/EAG	Carmunnock/Clarkston/Eaglesham
CSMK	Castlemilk
DEN/PKHD	Dennistoun/Parkhead
DMNK/BRGTN	Dalmarnock/Bridgeton
DRUM	Drumchapel
ESTRH	Easterhouse
GBLS	Gorbals
GIF/THBK	Giffnock/Thornliebank
GOV/IBX	Govan/Ibrox
GVH/MTFL	Govanhill/Mount Florida

KKNTL	Kirkintilloch
KNTSWD	Knightswood
KVD/HLHD	Kelvindale/Hillhead
KVGV	Kelvingrove
LNPK/KPK	Linn Park/King's Park
MRYH/FIRH	Maryhill/Firhill
PLK/PH/NH	Pollock/Priesthill/Nitshill
PLKSD/SHW	Pollockshields/Shawlands
PLKSW/MSWD	Pollockshaws/Mansewood
PPK/MIL	Possil Park/Milton
PSLY	Paisley
PSLYN/LNWD	Paisley north/Linwood
PTCK	Partick
RNFRW	Renfrew
RUTH	Rutherglen
SCOT	Scotstoun
SMSTN	Summerston
SPRGB/BLRNK	Springburn/Balornock
STPS/GTHM/RID	Stepps/Garthamlock/Riddrie
UD/BTH/TAN	Uddingston/Bothwell/Tannochside

A

Abbey Dr *SCOT* G14 .... 2 C3
Abbeyhill St *CAR/SHTL* G32 .... 97 C3
Abbotsford Av *RUTH* G73 .... 119 D3
Abbotsford Pl *GBLS* G5 .... 44 C4
Abbotshall Av *DRUM* G15 .... 63 C3
Abbot St *PLKSD/SHW* G41 .... 115 C1
Abbott Crs *CLYDBK* G81 .... 70 B2
Aberconway St *CLYDBK* G81 .... 70 A2
Abercorn Av *CARD/HILL/MSPK* G52 .... 93 C2
Abercorn Pl *SMSTN* G23 .... 77 C1
Abercromby Dr *DMNK/BRGTN* G40 ..... 47 E1
Abercromby St
  DMNK/BRGTN G40 .... 47 D3
Aberdalgie Rd *ESTRH* G34 .... 101 D2
Aberdour St *DEN/PKHD* G31 .... 37 E3
Aberfeldy St *DEN/PKHD* G31 .... 37 E3
Aberfoyle St *DEN/PKHD* G31 .... 37 E3
Aberlady Rd *GOV/IBX* G51 .... 27 D4
Abernethy Dr *DEN/PKHD* G31 .... 37 E3
Aberuthven Dr *CAR/SHTL* G32 .... 106 B3
Aboukir St *GOV/IBX* G51 .... 27 D1
Aboyne St *GOV/IBX* G51 .... 27 F5
Academy Pk *PLKSD/SHW* G41 .... 41 F4
Academy Rd *GIF/THBK* G46 .... 126 A4
Academy St *CAR/SHTL* G32 .... 106 B2
Achamore Crs *DRUM* G15 .... 63 C2
Achamore Dr *DRUM* G15 .... 63 C2
Achamore Rd *DRUM* G15 .... 63 C2
Acherhill Gdns *KNTSWD* G13 .... 72 A2
Acorn Ct *DMNK/BRGTN* G40 .... 47 F4
Acorn St *DMNK/BRGTN* G40 .... 47 F4
Acre Dr *MRYH/FIRH* G20 .... 75 D3
Acredyke Crs *SPRGB/BLRNK* G21 ...... 81 D3
Acredyke Pl *SPRGB/BLRNK* G21 .... 82 A4
Acredyke Rd *RUTH* G73 .... 118 B2
  SPRGB/BLRNK G21 .... 81 D3
Acre Rd *MRYH/FIRH* G20 .... 75 D1
Adams Court La *CGLE* G1 .... 33 D5
Adamswell St *SPRGB/BLRNK* G21 ...... 11 E5
Addiewell St *CAR/SHTL* G32 .... 98 A3
Addison Gv *GIF/THBK* G46 .... 124 A3
Addison Pl *GIF/THBK* G46 .... 124 B2
Addison Rd *GIF/THBK* G46 .... 124 A2
  KVD/HLHD G12 .... 6 A3
Adelphi St *GBLS* G5 .... 46 B4
Admiral St *PLKSD/SHW* G41 .... 43 D2
Advie Pl *GVH/MTFL* G42 .... 116 B2
Affric Av *GIF/THBK* G46 .... 123 C2
Afton Crs *BSDN* G61 .... 67 D3
Afton Dr *RNFRW* PA4 .... 85 C4
Afton St *PLKSD/SHW* G41 .... 115 C2
Agnew La *GVH/MTFL* G42 .... 56 B5
Aikenhead Rd *LNPK/KPK* G44 .... 117 C4
Ailean Dr *CAR/SHTL* G32 .... 108 A2
Ailean Gdns *CAR/SHTL* G32 .... 108 A2
Ailort Av *LNPK/KPK* G44 .... 128 A1
Ailsa Dr *GVH/MTFL* G42 .... 115 D3
  RUTH G73 .... 130 B1
Ailsa Rd *BSHPBGS* G64 .... 69 D4
  RNFRW PA4 .... 84 A4
Ainslie Rd *CARD/HILL/MSPK* G52 ..... 94 B3
Airdale Av *GIF/THBK* G46 .... 126 A4
Airgold Dr *DRUM* G15 .... 63 D2
Airlie Gdns *RUTH* G73 .... 132 B2
Airlie La *KVD/HLHD* G12 .... 4 C5
Airlie Rd *BAIL/MDB/MHD* G69 .... 109 C3
Airlie St *KVD/HLHD* G12 .... 4 C5
  PTCK G11 .... 16 B1

Airlour Rd *PLKSW/MSWD* G43 .... 127 C1
Airth Dr *CARD/HILL/MSPK* G52 .... 51 F1
Airth La *CARD/HILL/MSPK* G52 .... 51 F2
Airthrey Av *SCOT* G14 .... 2 C5
Airthrey La *SCOT* G14 .... 2 C4
Aitken St *DEN/PKHD* G31 .... 37 C4
Albany Av *CAR/SHTL* G32 .... 99 D4
Albany Dr *RUTH* G73 .... 119 D4
Albany Qd *CAR/SHTL* G32 .... 99 D4
Albany St *DMNK/BRGTN* G40 .... 48 A5
Albany Ter *BLTYR/CAMB* G72 .... 133 D3
Albert Av *GVH/MTFL* G42 .... 56 A5
Albert Dr *BSDN* G61 .... 67 D3
  PLKSD/SHW G41 .... 42 B5
  PLKSD/SHW G41 .... 53 F3
  RUTH G73 .... 131 D1
Albert Rd *RNFRW* PA4 .... 84 A3
Albion Ga *CGLE* G1 .... 34 A4
Albion St *BAIL/MDB/MHD* G69 .... 108 B3
  CGLE G1 .... 34 A4
Alcaig Rd *CARD/HILL/MSPK* G52 ..... 51 D3
Alderman Pl *KNTSWD* G13 .... 73 C4
Alderman Rd *KNTSWD* G13 .... 71 D3
  KNTSWD G13 .... 73 C4
Alder Pl *PLKSW/MSWD* G43 .... 125 D1
Alder Rd *PLKSW/MSWD* G43 .... 126 A1
Alexander Crs *GBLS* G5 .... 45 D4
Alexandra Ct *DEN/PKHD* G31 .... 36 C2
Alexandra Dr *RNFRW* PA4 .... 84 B3
Alexandra Pde *DEN/PKHD* G31 .... 35 E1
Alexandra Park St *DEN/PKHD* G31 .... 36 C1
Alford St *SPRGB/BLRNK* G21 .... 10 B5
Alfred La *KVD/HLHD* G12 .... 18 B1
Algie St *PLKSD/SHW* G41 .... 115 D2
Allan Av *RNFRW* PA4 .... 93 C1
Allander Gdns *BSHPBGS* G64 .... 68 B2 ⬛
Allander St *PPK/MIL* G22 .... 9 E4 ⬛
Allan Glen Gdns *BSHPBGS* G64 .... 69 D2 ⬛
Allan Pl *DMNK/BRGTN* G40 .... 60 C3
Allan St *DMNK/BRGTN* G40 .... 60 C3
Allanton Dr *CARD/HILL/MSPK* G52 .. 102 B1
Allender Rd *BSDN* G61 .... 65 D3 ⬛
Allen Wy *RNFRW* PA4 .... 92 B1 ⬛
Allerdyce Dr *DRUM* G15 .... 71 D1
Allerton Gdns *CAR/SHTL* G32 .... 108 B2 ⬛
Alleysbank Rd *RUTH* G73 .... 119 C1
Allison St *GVH/MTFL* G42 .... 57 D5
Alloway Crs *RUTH* G73 .... 130 B1
Alloway Dr *CLYDBK* G81 .... 62 A3 ⬛
  RUTH G73 .... 130 B1
Alloway Rd *PLKSW/MSWD* G43 ...... 114 B4
Alma St *DEN/PKHD* G31 .... 48 C2
Almond Av *RNFRW* PA4 .... 85 C4
Almond Rd *BSDN* G61 .... 65 C4
  STPS/GTHM/RID G33 .... 91 C1
Almond St *STPS/GTHM/RID* G33 .... 96 B1
Alness Crs *CARD/HILL/MSPK* G52 ..... 50 C1
Alsatian Av *CLYDBK* G81 .... 62 B4
Altyre St *CAR/SHTL* G32 .... 105 D3
Alva Gdns *CARD/HILL/MSPK* G52 ..... 51 D3
Alva Ga *CARD/HILL/MSPK* G52 .... 50 C2
Alyth Gdns *CARD/HILL/MSPK* G52 .... 51 D2
Amisfield St *MRYH/FIRH* G20 .... 6 C2
Amulree Pl *CAR/SHTL* G32 .... 106 A1 ⬛
Amulree St *CAR/SHTL* G32 .... 106 A3 ⬛
Ancaster Dr *KNTSWD* G13 .... 74 B4
Ancaster La *KNTSWD* G13 .... 74 B4 ⬛
Anchor La *CGLE* G1 .... 33 E3
Ancroft St *MRYH/FIRH* G20 .... 8 A5
Anderson Dr *RNFRW* PA4 .... 84 B2 ⬛
Anderson St *PTCK* G11 .... 17 D4 ⬛
Anderston Quay *KVGV* G3 .... 31 F5

Andrew Av *RNFRW* PA4 .... 85 C3
Andrew Dr *CLYDBK* G81 .... 70 A2
Angle Ga *SCOT* G14 ....
Angus Av *BSHPBGS* G64 .... 82 B1
  CARD/HILL/MSPK G52 .... 103 C3
Angus Ov *CARD/HILL/MSPK* G52 ... 102 B2
Angus Pl *CARD/HILL/MSPK* G52 .... 102 B2 🔢
Angus St *CLYDBK* G81 .... 71 C2
  SPRGB/BLRNK G21 .... 11 D4
Annandale St *GVH/MTFL* G42 .... 56 C2
Annan Dr *BSDN* G61 .... 65 C3
  RUTH G73 .... 120 B3
Annan St *GVH/MTFL* G42 .... 116 A2 🔢
Annbank Pl *DEN/PKHD* G31 ...... 35 F5 🔢
Annbank St *DEN/PKHD* G31 .... 35 F5
Anne Av *RNFRW* PA4 .... 84 B2
Annes Ct *DMNK/BRGTN* G40 .... 47 D4
Annette St *GVH/MTFL* G42 .... 56 B4
Annfield Pl *DEN/PKHD* G31 .... 35 F4
Annick Dr *DRUM* G15 .... 65 C3
Annick St *CAR/SHTL* G32 .... 106 B1
Anniesland Crs *SCOT* G14 .... 86 A1 🔢
Anniesland Rd *KNTSWD* G13 .... 73 C4
  SCOT G14 .... 86 A1
Anson St *DMNK/BRGTN* G40 .... 47 E4
Anstruther St *CAR/SHTL* G32 ...... 105 D2
Anthony St *CGLW* G2 .... 32 A3 🔢
Anwoth St *CAR/SHTL* G32 .... 106 A3
Appin Crs *DEN/PKHD* G31 .... 37 D3
Appin Rd *DEN/PKHD* G31 .... 37 D3
Appin Ter *RUTH* G73 .... 132 B2
Appleby St *PPK/MIL* G22 .... 8 C5
Applecross St *MRYH/FIRH* G20 ...... 20 C1
Apsley La *PTCK* G11 .... 16 A3 🔢
Apsley St *PTCK* G11 .... 16 A2
Aranthrue Crs *RNFRW* PA4 .... 84 A2
Aranthrue Dr *RNFRW* PA4 .... 84 A2 🔢
Aray St *MRYH/FIRH* G20 .... 76 B4
Arbroath Av *CARD/HILL/MSPK* G52 .. 102 B2
Arcadia St *DMNK/BRGTN* G40 .... 47 D3
Arcan Crs *DRUM* G15 .... 64 B3
Archerfield Av *CAR/SHTL* G32 ...... 106 A4 🔢
Archerfield Crs *CAR/SHTL* G32 ..... 106 A4 🔢
Archerfield Dr *CAR/SHTL* G32 ...... 106 A4
Archerfield Gv *CAR/SHTL* G32 ...... 106 A4 🔢
Archerhill Av *KNTSWD* G13 .... 72 A2
Archerhill Crs *KNTSWD* G13 .... 72 B2
Archerhill Rd *KNTSWD* G13 .... 72 A2
Archerhill Sq *KNTSWD* G13 .... 71 D2
Archerhill Ter *KNTSWD* G13 .... 72 A2
Ardbeg Av *BSHPBGS* G64 .... 82 A1 🔢
  RUTH G73 .... 133 C3
Ardbeg La *GVH/MTFL* G42 .... 56 B3
Ardbeg St *GVH/MTFL* G42 .... 56 B3
Ardconnel St *DMNK/BRGTN* G46 .... 124 B2
Arden Av *GIF/THBK* G46 .... 124 A4
Ardencraig Dr *CSMK* G45 .... 130 B4
Ardencraig Pl *CSMK* G45 .... 130 A3
Ardencraig Qd *CSMK* G45 .... 130 B4
Ardencraig Rd *CSMK* G45 .... 130 B4
Ardencraig St *CSMK* G45 .... 131 C3
Ardencraig Ter *CSMK* G45 .... 130 A4
Arden Dr *GIF/THBK* G46 .... 125 D4
Ardenlea St *DMNK/BRGTN* G40 ..... 60 C2
Arden Pl *GIF/THBK* G46 .... 124 A4
Ardery St *PTCK* G11 .... 16 B3 🔢
Ardessie St *SMSTN* G23 .... 76 B1 🔢
Ardfern St *CAR/SHTL* G32 .... 106 A3
Ardgay Pl *CAR/SHTL* G32 .... 106 A2
Ardgay St *CAR/SHTL* G32 .... 106 A2
Ardgay Wy *RUTH* G73 .... 131 D3
Ardholm St *CAR/SHTL* G32 .... 106 A1 🔢

Ardhu Pl *DRUM* G15 .... 64 A3 🔢
Ardlaw St *GOV/IBX* G51 .... 27 F5
Ardle Rd *PLKSW/MSWD* G43 .... 127 C1
Ardlui St *CAR/SHTL* G32 .... 105 D2
Ardmaleish Crs *CSMK* G45 .... 130 A4 🔢
Ardmaleish Dr *CSMK* G45 .... 129 D4
Ardmaleish Rd *CSMK* G45 .... 129 D4
Ardmaleish St *CSMK* G45 .... 129 D4 🔢
Ardmaleish Ter *CSMK* G45 .... 130 A4 🔢
Ardmay Crs *LNPK/KPK* G44 .... 117 C3
Ardmillan St *STPS/GTHM/RID* G33 .. 97 D2
Ardmory Av *GVH/MTFL* G42 .... 117 D3
Ardmory La *RUTH* G73 .... 118 A3
Ardmory Pl *GVH/MTFL* G42 .... 118 A3 🔢
Ardnahoe Av *GVH/MTFL* G42 .... 117 D3
Ardnahoe Pl *GVH/MTFL* G42 .... 117 D2 🔢
Ardneil Rd *GOV/IBX* G51 .... 27 E5
Ardnish St *GOV/IBX* G51 .... 26 B4
Ardoch Gv *BLTYR/CAMB* G72 .... 121 D4
Ardoch Rd *BSDN* G61 .... 67 D1
Ardoch St *PPK/MIL* G22 .... 9 D5
Ardo Gdns *GOV/IBX* G51 .... 40 B2
Ardshiel Rd *GOV/IBX* G51 .... 27 D4
Ardsloy Pl *SCOT* G14 .... 86 A2
Ard St *CAR/SHTL* G32 .... 106 A2 🔢
Arduthie Rd *GOV/IBX* G51 .... 27 D4
Ardwell Rd *CARD/HILL/MSPK* G52 .. 50 C1
Argyle St *CGLE* C1 .... 33 E4
  CGLW G2 .... 32 C4
  KVGV G3 .... 18 A4
  KVGV G3 .... 30 C3
  KVGV G3 .... 31 E2
Argyll Rd *CLYDBK* G81 .... 70 A1
Arisaig Dr *BSDN* G61 .... 67 D3
  CARD/HILL/MSPK G52 .... 50 B2
Arisaig Pl *CARD/HILL/MSPK* G52 ... 50 C2
Ark La *DEN/PKHD* G31 .... 35 E3
Arkleston Rd *PSLYN/LNWD* PA3 ..... 92 A3
Arkle Ter *BLTYR/CAMB* G72 .... 133 C3 🔢
Arklet Rd *GOV/IBX* G51 .... 27 E4
Arlington St *KVGV* G3 .... 19 F4
Armadale Pl *DEN/PKHD* G31 .... 36 B1
Armadale St *DEN/PKHD* G31 .... 36 B2
Armour St *COWCAD* G4 .... 35 D5
Arngask Rd *GOV/IBX* G51 .... 27 D4
Arnhall Pl *CARD/HILL/MSPK* G52 ... 50 C1
Arnholm Pl *CARD/HILL/MSPK* G52 .. 50 C1
Arnisdale Pl *ESTRH* G34 .... 101 C2 🔢
Arnisdale Rd *ESTRH* G34 .... 101 C3
Arnisdale Wy *RUTH* G73 .... 131 D3 🔢
Arniston St *CAR/SHTL* G32 .... 97 D3
Arnold Av *BSHPBGS* G64 .... 81 C1
Arnol Pl *STPS/GTHM/RID* G33 ...... 100 B3 🔢
Arnprior Crs *CSMK* G45 .... 129 D3 🔢
Arnprior Qd *CSMK* G45 .... 129 D2
Arnprior Rd *CSMK* G45 .... 129 D2
Arnprior St *CSMK* G45 .... 129 D2
Arnside Av *GIF/THBK* G46 .... 126 A3
Arnwood Dr *KVD/HLHD* G12 .... 4 A2
Aron Ter *BLTYR/CAMB* G72 .... 133 D3
Aros Dr *CARD/HILL/MSPK* G52 ..... 50 C3
Arran Dr *CARD/HILL/MSPK* G52 .... 51 F1
  GIF/THBK G46 .... 125 D4
Arran Pl *CLYDBK* G81 .... 62 A4
Arran Rd *RNFRW* PA4 .... 84 B4
Arran Ter *RUTH* G73 .... 130 B1 🔢
Arrochar Ct *SMSTN* G23 .... 76 B2 🔢
Arrochar Dr *SMSTN* G23 .... 76 B1
Arrochar St *MRYH/FIRH* G20 .... 76 B2
  SMSTN G23 .... 76 B1
Arrol St *CARD/HILL/MSPK* G52 ..... 93 C3
Arrowsmith Av *KNTSWD* G13 .... 73 D2

Arthurlie St *GOV/IBX* G51 .... **27** F4
Arthur St *KVCV* G3 .... **18** A5 🗓
Arundel Dr *BSHPBGS* G64 .... **69** D2 🗓
  GVH/MTFL G42 .... **116** A3 🗓
Ascaig Crs *CARD/HILL/MSPK* G52 ... **50** C2
Ascog Rd *BSDN* G61 .... **66** B4
Ascog St *GVH/MTFL* G42 .... **56** B3
Ascot Av *KVD/HLHD* G12 .... **74** B4
Ashburton La *KVD/HLHD* G12 .... **75** D4
Ashburton Rd *KVD/HLHD* G12 .... **75** C4
Ashby Crs *KNTSWD* G13 .... **74** A1
Ashcroft Dr *LNPK/KPK* G44 .... **118** A4
Ashdale Dr *CARD/HILL/MSPK* G52 ... **50** C1
Ashdene Dr *PPK/MIL* G22 .... **78** B3
Ashfield *BSHPBGS* G64 .... **69** C3
Ashfield St *PPK/MIL* G22 .... **9** F3
Ashgill Pl *PPK/MIL* G22 .... **79** C4
Ashgill Rd *PPK/MIL* G22 .... **78** B4
Ash Gv *BSHPBGS* G64 .... **81** D2
Ashgrove St *DMNK/BRGTN* G40 .... **60** B3
Ashkirk Dr *CARD/HILL/MSPK* G52 ... **50** C1
Ashlea Dr *GIF/THBK* G46 .... **126** B2
Ashley La *KVGV* G3 .... **19** F4
Ashley St *KVGV* G3 .... **19** F4
Ashmore Rd *PLKSW/MSWD* G43 .. **127** D1
Ash Rd *BAIL/MDB/MHD* G69 .... **109** C3
Ashton La *KVD/HLHD* G12 .... **18** A2
Ashton La North *KVD/HLHD* G12 ... **18** A2 🗓
Ashton Rd *KVD/HLHD* G12 .... **18** A2
  RUTH G73 .... **119** C1
Ashtree Rd *PLKSW/MSWD* G43 .... **114** A3 🗓
Ashvale Crs *SPRGB/BLRNK* G21 ... **10** C3
Aspen Dr *SPRGB/BLRNK* G21 .... **12** A5 🗓
Aster Dr *CSMK* G45 .... **131** C4 🗓
Aster Gdns *PLK/PH/NH* G53 .... **123** C3
Athelstane Rd *KNTSWD* G13 .... **73** C3
Atholl Av *CARD/HILL/MSPK* G52 ... **93** C3
Atholl Gdns *BSHPBGS* G64 .... **68** B3
  RUTH G73 .... **133** C2 🗓
Atlas Pl *SPRGB/BLRNK* G21 .... **11** F5
Atlas Rd *SPRGB/BLRNK* G21 .... **11** D4
Attlee Av *CLYDBK* G81 .... **70** B1
Attow Rd *PLKSW/MSWD* G43 ...... **125** D1 🗓
Auchentorlie Ter *PTCK* G11 .... **15** F3
Auchentoshan Ter
  SPRGB/BLRNK G21 .... **23** D2
Auchinairn Rd *BSHPBGS* G64 .... **82** B2
  SPRGB/BLRNK G21 .... **82** A3 🗓
Auchinlea Rd *ESTRH* G34 .... **100** B1
Auchinleck Av *STPS/GTHM/RID* G33 .. **83** C4 🗓
Auchinleck Crs
  STPS/GTHM/RID G33 .... **83** C4 🗓
Auchinleck Dr *STPS/GTHM/RID* G33 .. **83** C4 🗓
Auchinleck Gdns
  STPS/GTHM/RID G33 .... **83** C4 🗓
Auchinleck Rd *STPS/GTHM/RID* G33 .. **83** D3
Auchinloch St *SPRGB/BLRNK* G21 ... **23** D1
Auckland St *PPK/MIL* G22 .... **8** C5
Auldbar Rd *CARD/HILL/MSPK* G52 ... **51** C1
Auldburn Pl *PLKSW/MSWD* G43 ... **113** D4
Auldburn Rd *PLKSW/MSWD* G43 ... **113** C4
Auldearn Rd *SPRGB/BLRNK* G21 ... **82** A3
Auldgirth Rd *CARD/HILL/MSPK* G52 ... **51** C1
Auldhouse Av
  PLKSW/MSWD G43 .... **113** D4 🗓
Auldhouse Gdns
  PLKSW/MSWD G43 .... **113** D4
Auldhouse Rd *PLKSW/MSWD* G43 ... **114** A4
Auldhouse Ter
  PLKSW/MSWD G43 .... **114** B4 🗓
Aultbea St *PPK/MIL* G22 .... **78** B2
Aultmore Rd *STPS/GTHM/RID* G33 .. **100** B3

Austen La *KNTSWD* G13 .... **3** D1
Austen Rd *KNTSWD* G13 .... **3** D1
Avenel Rd *KNTSWD* G13 .... **74** A1
Avenue End Rd
  STPS/GTHM/RID G33 .... **90** B2
Avenuepark St *MRYH/FIRH* G20 ...... **6** C3
Avenue St *DMNK/BRGTN* G40 .... **48** A3
  RUTH G73 .... **119** D1
Aviemore Gdns *BSDN* G61 .... **67** C1
Aviemore Rd *CARD/HILL/MSPK* G52 ... **50** C2
Avoch St *ESTRH* G34 .... **101** D1 🗓
Avon Av *BSDN* G61 .... **67** D2
Avonbank Rd *RUTH* G73 .... **118** B3 🗓
Avondale Dr *STPS/GTHM/RID* G33 ... **98** A1
Avon Rd *BSHPBGS* G64 .... **81** C2
  GIF/THBK G46 .... **125** D4 🗓
Avonspark St *SPRGB/BLRNK* G21 ... **12** B5
Aylmer Rd *PLKSW/MSWD* G43 .... **115** D4
Ayr St *SPRGB/BLRNK* G21 .... **11** D5
Aytoun Rd *PLKSD/SHW* G41 .... **54** B1

B

Back Cswy *DEN/PKHD* G31 .... **104** B1 🗓
Backmuir Rd *DRUM* G15 .... **64** B2
Baillieston Rd *CAR/SHTL* G32 ..... **108** A2 🗓
  UD/BTH/TAN G71 .... **109** D4
Bainsford St *CAR/SHTL* G32 .... **97** D4
Bain St *DMNK/BRGTN* G40 .... **46** C1
Baird Av *CARD/HILL/MSPK* G52 .... **93** C2
Baird Brae *MRYH/FIRH* G20 .... **20** C1
Baird Dr *BSDN* G61 .... **65** D1
Baird St *COWCAD* G4 .... **22** A5
Baker St *PLKSD/SHW* G41 .... **115** C1
Bakewell Rd *BAIL/MDB/MHD* G69 ... **109** C1 🗓
Balaclava St *KVGV* G3 .... **32** A4
Balado Rd *STPS/GTHM/RID* G33 .. **100** A3
Balbeggie St *CAR/SHTL* G32 .... **107** C2
Balbeg St *GOV/IBX* G51 .... **38** C1
Balcomie St *STPS/GTHM/RID* G33 ... **98** A1
Baldinnie Rd *ESTRH* G34 .... **101** D2
Baldovan Crs *STPS/GTHM/RID* G33 .. **100** B3
Baldovie Rd *CARD/HILL/MSPK* G52 ... **103** C3
Baldragon Rd *ESTRH* G34 .... **101** D1
Baldric Rd *KNTSWD* G13 .... **73** C4
Baldwin Av *KNTSWD* G13 .... **73** D1
Balerno Dr *CARD/HILL/MSPK* G52 ... **51** D2
Balfluig St *ESTRH* G34 .... **100** B1
Balfour St *MRYH/FIRH* G20 .... **76** B4
Balfron Rd *GOV/IBX* G51 .... **27** D3
Balgair Dr *PPK/MIL* G22 .... **9** D2
Balgair Ter *CAR/SHTL* G32 .... **106** B1 🗓
Balglass St *PPK/MIL* G22 .... **8** C3
Balgonie Rd *CARD/HILL/MSPK* G52 ... **38** C5
Balgownie Crs *GIF/THBK* G46 ..... **125** D4
Balgraybank St *SPRGB/BLRNK* G21 ... **12** A3
Balgrayhill Rd *SPRGB/BLRNK* G21 ... **11** E2
Balintore St *CAR/SHTL* G32 .... **106** A1 🗓
Baliol La *KVGV* G3 .... **19** F5
Baliol St *KVGV* G3 .... **19** F4
Ballaig Av *BSDN* G61 .... **65** D1
Ballaig Crs *STPS/GTHM/RID* G33 ... **91** C1 🗓
Ballantay Qd *CSMK* G45 .... **131** C3
Ballantay Rd *CSMK* G45 .... **131** C3
Ballantay Ter *CSMK* G45 .... **131** C3
Ballantine Av *CARD/HILL/MSPK* G52 ... **94** A3
Ballater Dr *BSDN* G61 .... **66** B4
Ballater Pl *GBLS* G5 .... **46** A4

Ballater St *GBLS* G5 .... 45 E2
Ballindalloch Dr *DEN/PKHD* G31 .... 36 C2
Ballindalloch La *DEN/PKHD* G31 .... 36 B2
Balloch Gdns *CARD/HILL/MSPK* G52 ... 51 E3
Ballochmill Rd *BLTYR/CAMB* G72 ...... 120 B2
Ballogie Rd *LNPK/KPK* G44 .... 116 B3
Balmartin St *SMSTN* G23 .... 76 B1
Balmoral Dr *BLTYR/CAMB* G72 .... 133 C1
      BSDN G61 .... 67 C4
Balmoral St *SCOT* G14 .... 86 B3
Balmore Pl *PPK/MIL* G22 .... 78 B4
Balmore Rd *PPK/MIL* G22 .... 9 D2
      SMSTN G23 .... 78 A3
Balmore Sq *MRYH/FIRH* G20 .... 9 D1
Balmuildy Rd *BSHPBGS* G64 .... 68 A1
Balornock Rd *SPRGB/BLRNK* G21 ...... 12 B4
Balruddery Pl *BSHPBGS* G64 .... 82 B2
Balshagray Av *SCOT* G14 .... 3 E5
Balshagray Crs *PTCK* G11 .... 15 D2
Balshagray Dr *PTCK* G11 .... 15 D2
Balshagray La *PTCK* G11 .... 15 E2
Balshagray Pl *PTCK* G11 .... 15 E1
Baltic Ct *DMNK/BRGTN* G40 .... 60 B2
Baltic La *DMNK/BRGTN* G40 .... 60 B1
Baltic Pl *DMNK/BRGTN* G40 .... 47 F4
Baltic St *DMNK/BRGTN* G40 .... 60 B2
Balure St *DEN/PKHD* G31 .... 37 F4
Balvaird Crs *RUTH* G73 .... 119 C3
Balvaird Dr *RUTH* G73 .... 119 C3
Balveny St *STPS/GTHM/RID* G33 .... 91 D4
Balvicar Dr *GVH/MTFL* G42 .... 55 F5
Balvicar St *GVH/MTFL* G42 .... 55 F5
Balvie Av *DRUM* G15 .... 72 A1
      GIF/THBK G46 .... 126 B4
Banavie Rd *PTCK* G11 .... 16 C1
Banchory Av *PLKSW/MSWD* G43 ..... 125 D1
Banchory Crs *BSDN* G61 .... 67 C4
Banff St *STPS/GTHM/RID* G33 .... 90 B4
Bangorshill St *GIF/THBK* G46 .... 124 B2
Bankbrae Av *PLK/PH/NH* G53 .... 110 A4
Bankend St *STPS/GTHM/RID* G33 ...... 98 A1
Bankfoot Dr
      CARD/HILL/MSPK G52 .... 102 B1
Bankfoot Rd
      CARD/HILL/MSPK G52 .... 102 B2
Bankglen Rd *DRUM* G15 .... 64 B2
Bankhall St *GVH/MTFL* G42 .... 56 C4
Bankhead Av *KNTSWD* G13 .... 72 A4
Bankhead Dr *RUTH* G73 .... 119 C3
Bankhead Rd *RUTH* G73 .... 118 B3
Banknock St *CAR/SHTL* G32 .... 97 C4
Bank St *KVD/HLHD* G12 .... 18 C2
Bannatyne Av *DEN/PKHD* G31 .... 37 D3
Bannercross Av
      BAIL/MDB/MHD G69 .... 109 C1
Bannercross Dr
      BAIL/MDB/MHD G69 .... 101 C4
Bannercross Gdns
      BAIL/MDB/MHD G69 .... 109 C1
Banner Dr *KNTSWD* G13 .... 73 C1
Bannerman Pl *CLYDBK* G81 .... 62 A4
Banner Rd *BSDN* G61 .... 65 D4
Bantaskin St *MRYH/FIRH* G20 .... 76 A3
Barberry Av *PLK/PH/NH* G53 .... 122 B4
Barberry Gdns *PLK/PH/NH* G53 .... 122 B4
Barberry Pl *PLK/PH/NH* G53 .... 122 B4
Barclay St *SPRGB/BLRNK* G21 .... 11 E2
Bard Av *KNTSWD* G13 .... 72 B2
Bardowie St *PPK/MIL* G22 .... 8 C3
      PPK/MIL G22 .... 9 F3
Bardrill Dr *BSHPBGS* G64 .... 80 A1

Barfillan Dr *CARD/HILL/MSPK* G52 .... 38 C2
Bargaran Rd *PLK/PH/NH* G53 .... 102 B3
Bargeddie St *STPS/GTHM/RID* G33 .... 88 B4
Barholm Sq *STPS/GTHM/RID* G33 ...... 99 D1
Barlanark Av *CAR/SHTL* G32 .... 99 C4
Barlanark Crs *CAR/SHTL* G32 .... 99 D3
Barlanark Pl
      STPS/GTHM/RID G33 .... 100 A3
Barlanark Rd *STPS/GTHM/RID* G33 .... 99 D3
Barlanark Wy *CAR/SHTL* G32 .... 99 D3
Barlia Dr *CSMK* G45 .... 130 A3
Barlia St *CSMK* G45 .... 130 A3
Barlia Ter *CSMK* G45 .... 130 B3
Barloch St *PPK/MIL* G22 .... 9 E3
Barlogan Av *CARD/HILL/MSPK* G52 ... 38 C3
Barlogan Qd *CARD/HILL/MSPK* G52 ... 38 C3
Barmulloch Rd *SPRGB/BLRNK* G21 ... 12 B4
Barnbeth Rd *PLK/PH/NH* G53 .... 102 B4
Barnes Rd *MRYH/FIRH* G20 .... 78 B4
Barness Pl *STPS/GTHM/RID* G33 .... 98 A2
Barnflat St *RUTH* G73 .... 119 D1
Barnhill Dr *SPRGB/BLRNK* G21 .... 12 B5
Barnkirk Av *DRUM* G15 .... 64 A3
Barns St *CLYDBK* G81 .... 70 A2
Barnton St *CAR/SHTL* G32 .... 97 C3
Barnwell Ter *GOV/IBX* G51 .... 27 D4
Barochan Rd *PLK/PH/NH* G53 .... 102 B3
Baronald Dr *KVD/HLHD* G12 .... 75 D4
Baronald Ga *KVD/HLHD* G12 .... 75 D4
Baronald St *RUTH* G73 .... 61 D5
Baron Dr *RNFRW* PA4 .... 84 A4
Barony Dr *BAIL/MDB/MHD* G69 ...... 101 D4
Barony Gdns *BAIL/MDB/MHD* G69 .. 109 D1
Barony Wynd
      BAIL/MDB/MHD G69 .... 101 D4
Barra Av *RNFRW* PA4 .... 92 A1
Barrachnie Ct
      BAIL/MDB/MHD G69 .... 108 B1
Barrachnie Crs
      BAIL/MDB/MHD G69 .... 108 B1
Barrachnie Rd
      BAIL/MDB/MHD G69 .... 109 C1
Barrack St *COWCAD* G4 .... 35 D5
Barra St *MRYH/FIRH* G20 .... 76 A2
Barrhead Rd *PLK/PH/NH* G53 .... 110 A3
Barrie Rd *CARD/HILL/MSPK* G52 .... 94 A3
Barrington Dr *KVGV* G3 .... 19 E3
Barrisdale Rd *MRYH/FIRH* G20 .... 76 B3
Barrisdale Wy *RUTH* G73 .... 131 D2
Barrland Dr *GIF/THBK* G46 .... 126 A3
Barrland St *PLKSD/SHW* G41 .... 56 A2
Barrmill Rd *PLKSW/MSWD* G43 ...... 125 C1
Barrowfield St *DMNK/BRGTN* G40 ..... 48 B3
Barr St *MRYH/FIRH* G20 .... 20 B1
Barrwood St
      STPS/GTHM/RID G33 .... 89 C2
Barshaw Rd *CARD/HILL/MSPK* G52 ... 93 C4
Bartholomew St *DMNK/BRGTN* G40 ... 60 A1
Bartiebeith Rd
      STPS/GTHM/RID G33 .... 99 D3
Bassett Av *KNTSWD* G13 .... 72 B2
Bassett Crs *KNTSWD* G13 .... 72 B2
Bathgate St *DEN/PKHD* G31 .... 36 B5
Bath La *CGLW* G2 .... 32 B1
Bath St *CGLW* G2 .... 31 F1
Batson St *GVH/MTFL* G42 .... 57 D3
Battlefield Av *GVH/MTFL* G42 .... 116 A3
Battlefield Gdns *GVH/MTFL* G42 ...... 116 A3
Battlefield Rd *GVH/MTFL* G42 .... 116 A2
Bavelaw St *STPS/GTHM/RID* G33 ...... 91 D4
Bayfield Av *DRUM* G15 .... 64 A3
Bayfield Ter *DRUM* G15 .... 64 A3

Beaconsfield Rd *KVD/HLHD* G12 .... 4 C2
Bearford Dr *CARD/HILL/MSPK* G52 .. 102 B1
Bearsden Rd *BSDN* G61 .... 74 B2
   KNTSWD G13 .... 3 E1
Beaton Rd *PLKSD/SHW* G41 .... 54 C4
Beattock St *DEN/PKHD* G31 .... 104 D1
Beaufort Av *PLKSW/MSWD* G43 .... 114 A4
Beaufort Gdns *BSHPBGS* G64 .... 80 A1
Beauly Pl *MRYH/FIRH* G20 .... 76 B4 🔟
Beauly Rd *BAIL/MDB/MHD* G69 .... 109 C3
Bedale Rd *BAIL/MDB/MHD* G69 .... 108 B2
Bedford Av *CLYDBK* G81 .... 62 B4
Bedford La *GBLS* G5 .... 45 D3
Bedford St *GBLS* G5 .... 44 C3
Beech Av *BAIL/MDB/MHD* G69 .... 109 C1
   BLTYR/CAMB G72 .... 121 D4 🔟
   GOV/IBX G51 .... 41 D3
   PLKSD/SHW G41 .... 41 D4
   RUTH G73 .... 132 A2
Beech Gdns *BAIL/MDB/MHD* G69 .... 109 C1
Beechgrove St *DMNK/BRGTN* G40..... 60 B3
Beechlands Av *LNPK/KPK* G44 .... 127 C4
Beech Pl *BSHPBGS* G64 .... 81 D2
Beech Rd *BSHPBGS* G64 .... 81 D2
Beechwood Av *RUTH* G73.......... 120 A4
Beechwood Ct *BSDN* G61 .... 66 B3 🔟
Beechwood Dr *PTCK* G11 .... 3 F4
Beechwood La *BSDN* G61 .... 66 B3 🔟
Beechwood Pl *PTCK* G11 .... 3 F4 🔟
Beil Dr *KNTSWD* G13 .... 71 D3
Beith St *PTCK* G11.......... 16 B4
Belgrave La *KVD/HLHD* G12 .... 18 C1
Belhaven Ter West *KVD/HLHD* G12 ..... 5 F4
Belhaven Terrace West La
   KVD/HLHD G12.......... 5 E4
Bellahouston Dr
   CARD/HILL/MSPK G52.......... 50 C2
Belleisle St *GVH/MTFL* G42 .... 56 C5
Bellfield St *DEN/PKHD* G31 .... 36 A5
Bellflower Av *PLK/PH/NH* G53.......... 123 C3
Bellflower Gdns *PLK/PH/NH* G53....... 123 C3 🔟
Bellflower Pl *PLK/PH/NH* G53 .... 123 C3 🔟
Bellgrove St *DEN/PKHD* G31.......... 35 F5
Bellrock Ct *STPS/GTHM/RID* G33 ..... 98 A2
Bellrock Crs *STPS/GTHM/RID* G33 ..... 98 A2
Bellrock St *STPS/GTHM/RID* G33 ..... 98 A2
Bellscroft Av *RUTH* G73 .... 118 B3 🔟
Bellshaugh La *KVD/HLHD* G12 .... 5 E2
Bell St *CGLE* G1 .... 34 A4
   CLYDBK G81 .... 70 B3
   COWCAD G4 .... 34 C5
   RNFRW PA4 .... 84 B2
Bell View Ct *RNFRW* PA4 .... 84 B2
Bellwood St *PLKSD/SHW* G41.......... 115 C2
Belmont Crs *KVD/HLHD* G12 .... 19 D1
Belmont Dr *GIF/THBK* G46 .... 125 D3
   RUTH G73 .... 119 D3 🔟
Belmont La *KVD/HLHD* G12.......... 19 D1
Belmont Rd *BLTYR/CAMB* G72 .... 133 C3
Belmont St *KVD/HLHD* G12.......... 19 D1
Belses Dr *CARD/HILL/MSPK* G52...... 103 C1
Belses Gdns *CARD/HILL/MSPK* G52 .. 103 C1
Belsyde Av *DRUM* G15.......... 64 A4
Beltane St *KVGV* G3 .... 31 F1
Beltrees Av *PLK/PH/NH* G53.......... 110 A1
Beltrees Crs *PLK/PH/NH* G53 .... 102 A4
Beltrees Rd *PLK/PH/NH* G53.......... 110 A1
Belvidere Crs *BSHPBGS* G64 .... 69 C4
Bemersyde Av *PLKSW/MSWD* G43 .. 125 D1
Benalder St *PTCK* G11.......... 17 E3 🔟
Bencroft Dr *LNPK/KPK* G44.......... 130 A1
Ben Donich Pl *GIF/THBK* G46 .... 123 D1

Ben Edra Pl *GIF/THBK* G46 .... 123 D2
Bengairn St *DEN/PKHD* G31 .... 37 F4
Bengal Pl *PLKSW/MSWD* G43 .... 114 A3 🔟
Bengal St *PLKSW/MSWD* G43 .... 114 A3
Ben Garrisdale Pl *GIF/THBK* G46 .. 123 D2 🔟
Benholm St *CAR/SHTL* G32 .... 105 D3 🔟
Ben Laga Pl *GIF/THBK* G46 .... 123 D2 🔟
Ben Lui Pl *GIF/THBK* G46 .... 123 D2 🔟
Ben Macdui Gdns *GIF/THBK* G46 .. 123 D2 🔟
Bennan Sq *GVH/MTFL* G42 .... 57 E4
Benthall St *GBLS* G5 .... 46 A5
Bentinck St *KVGV* G3 .... 18 C5
Bents Rd *BAIL/MDB/MHD* G69 .... 109 D1
Ben Uird Pl *GIF/THBK* G46 .... 123 D2
Benview St *MRYH/FIRH* G20.......... 7 F3
Ben Vorlich Dr *GIF/THBK* G46 .... 123 D2
Berelands Crs *RUTH* G73 .... 118 A3
Berelands Rd *RUTH* G73 .... 118 B3
Beresford Av *SCOT* G14 .... 2 C4
Berkeley St *KVGV* G3 .... 31 D1
Berkeley Terrace La *KVGV* G3.......... 31 E1
Bernard St *DMNK/BRGTN* G40 .... 48 B4
Bernard Ter *DMNK/BRGTN* G40 .... 48 A4
Berneray St *PPK/MIL* G22 .... 79 C3
Berridale Av *LNPK/KPK* G44 .... 128 A1
Berriedale Av *BAIL/MDB/MHD* G69 .. 109 C2
Berryburn Rd *SPRGB/BLRNK* G21 ..... 13 E4
Berryhill Dr *GIF/THBK* G46.......... 125 D4
Berryknowes Av
   CARD/HILL/MSPK G52 .... 103 C1
Berryknowes La
   CARD/HILL/MSPK G52 .... 103 C1 🔟
Berryknowes Rd
   CARD/HILL/MSPK G52.......... 103 C1
   GOV/IBX G51 .... 26 A5
Bertram St *PLKSD/SHW* G41 .... 115 C1
Bervie St *GOV/IBX* G51.......... 27 E5
Berwick Dr *CARD/HILL/MSPK* G52 ..... 102 B2
   RUTH G73 .... 120 B3
Beverley Rd *PLKSW/MSWD* G43 .... 114 B4
Bevin Av *CLYDBK* G81 .... 70 B1
Bideford Crs *CAR/SHTL* G32 .... 107 D3
Biggar St *DEN/PKHD* G31 .... 49 D1
Bigton St *STPS/GTHM/RID* G33 .... 90 B4
Bilsland Dr *MRYH/FIRH* G20 .... 8 B1
Binend Rd *PLK/PH/NH* G53.......... 111 C2
Binnie Pl *DMNK/BRGTN* G40 .... 46 C3
Binns Rd *STPS/GTHM/RID* G33 .... 91 C4
Birchend Dr *SPRGB/BLRNK* G21 ..... 24 C2
Birchend Pl *SPRGB/BLRNK* G21 ..... 24 C2
Birchfield Dr *SCOT* G14 .... 86 B2
Birch Knowe *BSHPBGS* G64 .... 81 D2
Birchlea Dr *GIF/THBK* G46.......... 126 B2
Birch St *GBLS* G5 .... 58 A1
Birch Vw *BSDN* G61 .... 67 C1
Birchwood Av *CAR/SHTL* G32 .... 108 A2
Birchwood Pl *CAR/SHTL* G32 .... 108 A2 🔟
Birdston Rd *SPRGB/BLRNK* G21 ..... 82 A4 🔟
Birgidale Rd *CSMK* G45 .... 129 D4
Birgidale Ter *CSMK* G45 .... 129 D4 🔟
Birkenshaw St *DEN/PKHD* G31 .... 37 D3
Birkhall Dr *BSDN* G61 .... 66 B4
Birkhill Av *BSHPBGS* G64.......... 69 D4
Birkhill Gdns *BSHPBGS* G64.......... 69 D4
Birkmyre Rd *GOV/IBX* G51 .... 27 F5
Birkwood St *DMNK/BRGTN* G40......... 60 C3
Birnam Av *BSHPBGS* G64.......... 69 D4
Birnam Crs *BSDN* G61 .... 67 D1
Birnam Rd *DEN/PKHD* G31 .... 104 B3 🔟
Birness Dr *PLKSW/MSWD* G43 .... 114 B3
Birnie Ct *SPRGB/BLRNK* G21 .... 13 E4

Birnie Rd *SPRGB/BLRNK* G21 ...... **13** F4
Birnock Av *RNFRW* PA4 .... **93** C1
Birsay Rd *PPK/MIL* G22 .... **78** B3
Bishop Gdns *BSHPBGS* G64 .... **68** A4
Bishop La *KVGV* G3 .... **32** A3
Bishopmill Pl *SPRGB/BLRNK* G21 .... **13** F3
Bishopsgate Rd *SPRGB/BLRNK* G21 .. **80** A3
Blackburn St *GOV/IBX* G51 .... **42** B1
Blackcraig Av *DRUM* G15 .... **64** A3
Blackcroft Gdns *CAR/SHTL* G32 .... **107** D3
Blackcroft Rd *CAR/SHTL* G32 .... **107** D2
Blackfaulds Rd *RUTH* G73 .... **118** A2
Blackfriars St *CGLE* G1 .... **34** A4
Blackhall Pl *STPS/GTHM/RID* G33 .. **88** B1 ꓸ
Blackie St *KVGV* G3 .... **30** B1
Blackstone Av *PLK/PH/NH* G53 .... **111** C1
Blackstone Crs *PLK/PH/NH* G53 .... **111** C1
Black St *COWCAD* G4 .... **22** B5
Blackthorn St *PPK/MIL* G22 .... **10** C2
Blackwood St *KNTSWD* G13 .... **74** A3
Bladnoch Dr *DRUM* G15 .... **65** C4 ꓸ
Blairatholl Av *PTCK* G11 .... **16** A1
Blairatholl Gdns *PTCK* G11 .... **16** B1 ꓸ
Blairbeth Dr *LNPK/KPK* G44 .... **116** B3
Blairbeth Rd *RUTH* G73 .... **131** C1
Blairbeth Ter *RUTH* G73 .... **132** A1 ꓸ
Blair Crs *BAIL/MDB/MHD* G69 ...... **109** C3 ꓸ
Blairdardie Rd *DRUM* G15 .... **72** B1
Blairgowrie Rd
    CARD/HILL/MSPK G52 .... **103** C2 ꓸ
Blairhall Av *PLKSD/SHW* G41 .... **115** D2
Blairhill St *STPS/GTHM/RID* G33 .... **98** B1
Blairlogie St *STPS/GTHM/RID* G33 .. **91** D2
Blair Rd *PSLY* PA1 .... **93** C4
Blair St *CAR/SHTL* G32 .... **105** D1 ꓸ
Blairtum Dr *RUTH* G73 .... **131** D1
Blairtummock Rd
    STPS/GTHM/RID G33.................. **99** D2
Blaneview *STPS/GTHM/RID* G33 .... **91** D2
Blantyre St *KVGV* G3 .... **18** A5
Blawarthill St *SCOT* G14 .... **85** D1
Blochairn Rd *SPRGB/BLRNK* G21 .... **24** B4
Bluebell Gdns *CSMK* G45 .... **131** C4 ꓸ
Bluevale St *DEN/PKHD* G31 .... **36** B5
Blythe Pl *STPS/GTHM/RID* G33 ...... **99** D4 ꓸ
Blyth Rd *STPS/GTHM/RID* G33 ...... **100** A4
Blythswood Av *RNFRW* PA4 .... **84** B2
Blythswood Dr *RNFRW* PA4 .... **84** B1
Blythswood Sq *CGLW* G2 .... **32** B2 ꓸ
Blythswood St *CGLW* G2 .... **32** C2
Boclair Av *BSDN* G61 .... **66** B2
Boclair Crs *BSDN* G61 .... **67** C2
    BSHPBGS G64.............................. **81** C1
Boclair Rd *BSDN* G61 .... **67** C1
    BSHPBGS G64.............................. **69** C4
Boclair St *KNTSWD* G13 .... **74** A2
Boden St *DMNK/BRGTN* G40 .... **48** B5
Bogany Ter *CSMK* G45 .... **130** A4
Bogbain Rd *ESTRH* G34 .... **101** C2 ꓸ
Boghall Rd *UD/BTH/TAN* G71 ...... **109** C3
Boghall St *STPS/GTHM/RID* G33 .... **98** B1
Boghead Rd *SPRGB/BLRNK* G21 .... **12** A2
Bogleshole Rd *BLTYR/CAMB* G72 .. **121** C3
Bogmoor Pl *GOV/IBX* G51 .... **95** C1
Bogmoor Rd *GOV/IBX* G51 .... **95** C2
Bogside Rd *STPS/GTHM/RID* G33 .... **90** A1
Bogside St *DMNK/BRGTN* G40 ...... **49** D5
Bogton Av *LNPK/KPK* G44 .... **127** D2
Bogton Avenue La *LNPK/KPK* G44.. **127** D2
Boleyn Rd *PLKSD/SHW* G41 .... **55** D4
Bolivar Ter *GVH/MTFL* G42 .... **117** C2
Bolton Dr *GVH/MTFL* G42 .... **116** A2
Bonawe St *MRYH/FIRH* G20 .... **7** F5

Boness St *DMNK/BRGTN* G40 .... **49** D5
Bonhill St *PPK/MIL* G22 .... **8** C5
Bonnar St *DMNK/BRGTN* G40 .... **60** A2
Bonnyholm Av *PLK/PH/NH* G53 .... **102** A3
Bonnyrigg Dr *PLKSW/MSWD* G43 .. **125** C1
Bonyton Av *KNTSWD* G13 .... **71** D4
Boon Dr *DRUM* G15 .... **64** B4
Borden La *KNTSWD* G13 .... **3** D1
Borden Rd *KNTSWD* G13 .... **3** D1
Boreland Dr *KNTSWD* G13 .... **72** B3
Boreland Pl *KNTSWD* G13 .... **72** B4 ꓸ
Borland Rd *BSDN* G61 .... **67** C3
Borron St *COWCAD* G4 .... **21** E1
Borthwick St
    STPS/GTHM/RID G33 .... **98** B1 ꓸ
Boswell Ct *PLKSD/SHW* G41 .... **115** D3 ꓸ
Boswell Sq *CARD/HILL/MSPK* G52 .. **93** D3
Botanic Crs *MRYH/FIRH* G20 .... **6** B4
Bothwell La *CGLW* G2 .... **32** B3
    KVD/HLHD G12.............................. **19** D2
Bothwell St *BLTYR/CAMB* G72 ...... **121** C4
    CGLW G2 .... **32** B3
Bouverie St *RUTH* G73 .... **118** B2
    SCOT G14 .... **71** C4
Bowden Dr *CARD/HILL/MSPK* G52 .. **94** B3
Bower St *KVD/HLHD* G12.................. **18** C1
Bowes Crs *BAIL/MDB/MHD* G69 .... **108** B2
Bowfield Av *CARD/HILL/MSPK* G52 .. **93** D4
Bowfield Crs *CARD/HILL/MSPK* G52 .. **93** D4
Bowfield Dr *CARD/HILL/MSPK* G52 .. **93** D4
Bowfield Pl *CARD/HILL/MSPK* G52 .. **93** D4
Bowling Green La *SCOT* G14 .... **2** A5
Bowling Green Rd *CAR/SHTL* G32 .. **107** D2
    LNPK/KPK G44 .... **128** A1 ꓸ
    SCOT G14 .... **2** A5
Bowman St *GVH/MTFL* G42 .... **56** A3
Bowmore Gdns *RUTH* G73 .... **133** C3 ꓸ
Bowmore Rd *CARD/HILL/MSPK* G52 .. **39** D3
Bowmount Gdns *KVD/HLHD* G12.... **5** F5
Boydstone Rd *GIF/THBK* G46 .... **124** B1
Boydstone Rd *GIF/THBK* G46 .... **124** B2
    PLKSW/MSWD G43 .... **112** A4
Boyd St *GVH/MTFL* G42 .... **57** D5
Boyle St *CLYDBK* G81 .... **70** B2
Boyndie St *ESTRH* G34 .... **101** D2 ꓸ
Brackenbrae Av *BSHPBGS* G64 ...... **68** A4
Brackenbrae Rd *BSHPBGS* G64 ...... **80** B1
Brackenrig Rd *GIF/THBK* G46 ...... **124** A4
Bracken St *PPK/MIL* G22 .... **78** B4
Brackla Av *KNTSWD* G13 .... **71** C2
Bradan Av *KNTSWD* G13 .... **71** C3
Bradda Av *RUTH* G73 .... **132** A2
Bradfield Av *KVD/HLHD* G12............ **5** E1
Braefield Dr *GIF/THBK* G46 .... **125** C3
Braehead Rd *GBLS* G5 .... **58** A2
Braemar Ct *GIF/THBK* G46.............. **127** C2
Braemar Crs *BSDN* G61 .... **66** B4
Braemar Rd *RUTH* G73 .... **132** B3
Braemar St *GVH/MTFL* G42 .... **115** D3 ꓸ
Braemore Gdns *PPK/MIL* G22 .... **10** A3 ꓸ
Braes Av *CLYDBK* G81...................... **70** B2
Braeside Av *RUTH* G73 .... **120** A3
Braeside St *MRYH/FIRH* G20 .... **7** F5
Braidbar Farm Rd *GIF/THBK* G46 .. **126** B3
Braidbar Rd *GIF/THBK* G46 .... **126** A3
Braidcraft Pl *PLK/PH/NH* G53 ...... **111** C2 ꓸ
Braidcraft Rd *PLK/PH/NH* G53 ...... **111** D2
Braidfauld Gdns *CAR/SHTL* G32 .. **105** D3
Braidfauld Pl *CAR/SHTL* G32 .... **105** D4 ꓸ
Braidfauld St *CAR/SHTL* G32 .... **105** D4
Braidfield Rd *CLYDBK* G81 .... **62** A1
Braidholm Crs *GIF/THBK* G46 ...... **126** A2

Braidholm Rd *GIF/THBK* G46 .... 126 B2
Braidpark Dr *GIF/THBK* G46 .... 126 B3
Braid Sq *COWCAD* G4 .... 20 B3
Braid St *COWCAD* G4 .... 20 B3
Brandon Dr *BLTYR/CAMB* G72 .... 133 C1 ◩
Brandon St *DEN/PKHD* G31 .... 35 F5
Brand Pl *GOV/IBX* G51 .... 41 E1
Brand St *GOV/IBX* G51 .... 41 E1
Brassey St *MRYH/FIRH* G20 .... 77 C4
Breadalbane Gdns *RUTH* G73 ...... 132 B2 ◩
Breadalbane St *KVGV* G3 .... 31 E2
Brechin Rd *BSHPBGS* G64 .... 82 A1
Brechin St *KVGV* G3 .... 31 D1
Brenfield Av *LNPK/KPK* G44 .... 127 D2
Brenfield Dr *LNPK/KPK* G44 .... 127 D2 ◩
Brenfield Rd *LNPK/KPK* G44 .... 127 D2
Brent Dr *GIF/THBK* G46 .... 124 B1
Brent Gdns *GIF/THBK* G46 .... 124 B1
Brent Rd *GIF/THBK* G46 .... 124 B1
Brent Wy *GIF/THBK* G46 .... 124 B1 ◩
Brentwood Av *PLK/PH/NH* G53 ... 122 A3
Brentwood Dr *PLK/PH/NH* G53 ... 122 A3
Brentwood Sq *PLK/PH/NH* G53 ... 122 B2 ◩
Brereton St *GVH/MTFL* G42 .... 57 E5
Bressay Rd *STPS/GTHM/RID* G33 ... 100 A4
Briarcroft Dr *STPS/GTHM/RID* G33 .... 82 B3
Briarcroft Pl *STPS/GTHM/RID* G33 .. 82 B4 ◩
Briarcroft Rd
   STPS/GTHM/RID G33 .... 82 B4 ◩
Briar Gdns *PLKSW/MSWD* G43 ..... 126 B1
Briar Gv *PLKSW/MSWD* G43 .... 126 B1 ◩
Briarlea Dr *GIF/THBK* G46 .... 126 A2
Briar Neuk *BSHPBGS* G64 .... 81 D2 ◩
Briar Rd *PLKSW/MSWD* G43 .... 126 B1
Briarwood Ct *CAR/SHTL* G32 ...... 108 A4 ◩
Bridgegate *CGLE* G1 .... 45 F1
Bridge St *GBLS* G5 .... 45 D1
Brigham Pl *SMSTN* G23 .... 77 C2 ◩
Brighton Pl *GOV/IBX* G51 .... 29 D5
Brighton St *GOV/IBX* G51 .... 28 C5
Brisbane Ct *GIF/THBK* G46 .... 126 B3
Brisbane St *LNPK/KPK* G44 .... 116 A3
Briton St *GOV/IBX* G51 .... 28 C5
Broadford St *COWCAD* G4 .... 21 F2
Broadholm St *PPK/MIL* G22 .... 79 C4
Broadleys Av *BSHPBGS* G64 .... 68 B4
Broadlie Dr *KNTSWD* G13 .... 72 A4
Broadloan *RNFRW* PA4 .... 84 A4
Broad St *DMNK/BRGTN* G40 .... 47 F3
Broadwood Dr *LNPK/KPK* G44 ..... 116 B4
Brockburn Crs *PLK/PH/NH* G53 ... 110 B2
Brockburn Rd *PLK/PH/NH* G53 ... 110 B1
Brockburn Ter *PLK/PH/NH* G53 ... 111 C2 ◩
Brock Ov *PLK/PH/NH* G53 .... 111 C4
Brock Pl *PLK/PH/NH* G53 .... 111 C3
Brock Rd *PLK/PH/NH* G53 .... 110 B4
Brock Ter *PLK/PH/NH* G53 .... 111 C4
Brockville St *CAR/SHTL* G32 .... 97 D4 ◩
Brodick St *SPRGB/BLRNK* G21 ..... 24 A4
Brodie Rd *SPRGB/BLRNK* G21 ..... 82 B3
Brooklea Dr *GIF/THBK* G46 .... 126 A1
   PLKSW/MSWD G43 .... 126 A1 ◩
Brookside St *DMNK/BRGTN* G40 ... 48 A3
Brook St *DMNK/BRGTN* G40 .... 47 F2
Broomfield Av *BLTYR/CAMB* G72 .. 120 B3 ◩
Broomfield La *SPRGB/BLRNK* G21 .. 11 F2
Broomfield Rd *SPRGB/BLRNK* G21 .. 11 F1
Broomhill Av *PTCK* G11 .... 15 E3
Broomhill Dr *PTCK* G11 .... 15 E1
   RUTH G73 .... 131 D1
Broomhill Gdns *PTCK* G11 .... 15 F1
Broomhill La *PTCK* G11 .... 15 E1

Broomhill Pl *PTCK* G11 .... 15 E2
Broomhill Ter *PTCK* G11 .... 15 D2
Broomieknowe Dr *RUTH* G73 ..... 119 D4 ◩
Broomieknowe Gdns *RUTH* G73 .. 119 C4 ◩
Broomieknowe Rd *RUTH* G73 ..... 119 D4
Broomielaw *KVGV* G3 .... 32 A5
Broomknowes Rd
   SPRGB/BLRNK G21 .... 12 A3
Broomloan Rd *GOV/IBX* G51 .... 28 B5
Broompark Circ *DEN/PKHD* G31 .. 35 F2
Broompark Dr *DEN/PKHD* G31 .... 35 E3
Broompark La *DEN/PKHD* G31 .... 35 F3
Broompark St *DEN/PKHD* G31 .... 35 F3 ◩
Broom Rd *PLKSW/MSWD* G43 ..... 126 B1
Broomton Rd *SPRGB/BLRNK* G21 .. 82 A3
Brora Dr *BSDN* G61 .... 67 D2
   GIF/THBK G46 .... 126 B4
   RNFRW PA4 .... 85 C3
Brora Gdns *BSHPBGS* G64 .... 81 D1
Brora Rd *BSHPBGS* G64 .... 81 D1
Brora St *STPS/GTHM/RID* G33 ...... 96 B1
Broughton Dr *SMSTN* G23 .... 77 C2 ◩
Broughton Gdns *SMSTN* G23 ...... 77 D1 ◩
Broughton Rd *SMSTN* G23 .... 77 C2
Brown Av *CLYDBK* G81 .... 70 B2
Brownhill Rd *GIF/THBK* G46 .... 125 D2
Brownlie St *GVH/MTFL* G42 .... 116 B2 ◩
Brownsdale Rd *RUTH* G73 .... 118 B3
Brownside Av *BLTYR/CAMB* G72 .. 133 C1 ◩
Brownside Dr *KNTSWD* G13 .... 71 D4
Brownside Rd *RUTH* G73 .... 132 B1
Brown St *KVGV* G3 .... 32 B4
   RNFRW PA4 .... 84 A3
Bruce Rd *PLKSD/SHW* G41 .... 42 C5
Brunstane Rd *ESTRH* G34 .... 101 C1
Brunswick La *CGLE* G1 .... 33 F4 ◩
Brunswick St *CGLE* G1 .... 33 F4
Brunton St *LNPK/KPK* G44 .... 128 A1
Brunton Ter *LNPK/KPK* G44 .... 127 D2
Bruntsfield Av *PLK/PH/NH* G53 .. 122 B3
Bruntsfield Gdns
   PLK/PH/NH G53 .... 122 B3 ◩
Buccleuch Av *CARD/HILL/MSPK* G52 .. 93 C2
Buccleuch La *KVGV* G3 .... 20 B5
Buccleuch St *KVGV* G3 .... 20 A5
Buchanan Crs *SPRGB/BLRNK* G21 .. 82 A3 ◩
Buchanan Dr *BLTYR/CAMB* G72 .. 121 C4
   BSDN G61 .... 67 C2
   BSHPBGS G64 .... 82 A2 ◩
   RUTH G73 .... 119 D4
Buchanan Gv *BAIL/MDB/MHD* G69 .. 109 D1
Buchanan St
   BAIL/MDB/MHD G69 .... 109 D1 ◩
   CGLE G1 .... 33 D4
Buchan Ter *BLTYR/CAMB* G72 ..... 133 C1
Buchlyvie Gdns *BSHPBGS* G64 ...... 80 B2
Buchlyvie Pth *ESTRH* G34 .... 101 D3
Buchlyvie St *ESTRH* G34 .... 101 D3
Buckingham Dr *RUTH* G73 .... 120 B3
Buckingham St *KVD/HLHD* G12 ..... 6 B5
Buckingham Ter *KVD/HLHD* G12 ... 6 B5
Bucklaw Gdns
   CARD/HILL/MSPK G52 .... 103 C2
Bucklaw Pl
   CARD/HILL/MSPK G52 .... 103 C2 ◩
Bucklaw Ter *CARD/HILL/MSPK* G52 .. 103 C2
Buckley St *PPK/MIL* G22 .... 79 D4
Bucksburn Rd *SPRGB/BLRNK* G21 .. 13 F5
Buckthorne Pl *PLK/PH/NH* G53 .. 122 B3
Buddon St *DMNK/BRGTN* G40 ..... 49 E5
Budhill Av *CAR/SHTL* G32 .... 106 A1
Buildale Ct *SCOT* G14 .... 85 C1

Bulldale St *SCOT* G14 .... **71** C4
Bullionslaw Dr *RUTH* G73 .... **120** B4
Bulloch Rd *GIF/THBK* G46 .... **126** B4
Bunessan St *CARD/HILL/MSPK* G52 ... **39** E2
Burghead Dr *GOV/IBX* G51 .... **26** C2
Burghead Pl *GOV/IBX* G51 .... **26** C1
Burgher St *DEN/PKHD* G31 .... **49** F4
Burgh Hall La *PTCK* G11 .... **16** C3
Burgh Hall St *PTCK* G11 .... **16** C3
Burgh La *KVD/HLHD* G12 .... **18** B1
Burleigh St *GOV/IBX* G51 .... **28** B1
Burlington Av *KVD/HLHD* G12 ...... **75** D4
Burmola St *PPK/MIL* G22 .... **9** D3
Burnbank Gdns *MRYH/FIRH* G20 .... **19** F2
Burnbank Pl *MRYH/FIRH* G20 ...... **19** F2
Burnbank Ter *COWCAD* G4 .... **19** F3
Burnbrae Dr *RUTH* G73 .... **132** B1 ▣
Burnbrae St *SPRGB/BLRNK* G21 .... **12** B4
Burndyke Ct *GOV/IBX* G51 .... **29** D3
Burndyke Sq *GOV/IBX* G51 .... **29** E4
Burnett Rd *STPS/GTHM/RID* G33 ... **100** A3 ▣
Burnfield Av *GIF/THBK* G46 .... **125** D2
Burnfield Dr *GIF/THBK* G46 .... **125** D2
Burnfield Gdns *GIF/THBK* G46 ...... **126** A2
Burnfield Rd *GIF/THBK* G46 .... **125** C1
Burnfoot Crs *RUTH* G73 .... **132** B1
Burnfoot Dr *CARD/HILL/MSPK* G52 ... **38** A2
Burnham Rd *SCOT* G14 .... **64** A2
Burnhead Rd *PLKSW/MSWD* G43 ... **127** C1 ▣
Burnhill Qd *RUTH* G73 .... **118** B2 ▣
Burnhill St *RUTH* G73 .... **118** B2
Burnhouse St *MRYH/FIRH* G20 ...... **76** B4
Burnmouth Pl *BSDN* G61 .... **67** C1
Burnmouth Rd
 STPS/GTHM/RID G33 .... **100** B4
Burn Pl *BLTYR/CAMB* G72 .... **121** C3 ▣
Burns Gv *GIF/THBK* G46 .... **125** C4
Burnside Ct *RUTH* G73 .... **132** A1 ▣
Burnside La *RUTH* G73 .... **132** A1 ▣
Burnside Rd *RUTH* G73 .... **132** A1 ▣
Burns St *COWCAD* G4 .... **20** C2
Burntbroom Dr
 BAIL/MDB/MHD G69 .... **108** B3
Burntbroom Gdns *CAR/SHTL* G32 .... **108** B3
Burntbroom Rd
 UD/BTH/TAN G71 .... **108** B4 ▣
Burntbroom St
 STPS/GTHM/RID G33 .... **99** D2 ▣
Burn Ter *BLTYR/CAMB* G72 .... **121** C3
Burrell Ct *PLKSD/SHW* G41 .... **53** E4
Burrell's La *COWCAD* G4 .... **34** C3
Burrelton Rd *PLKSW/MSWD* G43 .... **115** D4
Burton La *GVH/MTFL* G42 .... **56** A5
Bute Av *RNFRW* PA4 .... **92** B1
Bute Crs *BSDN* G61 .... **66** B4
Bute Gdns *KVD/HLHD* G12 .... **18** B2
 LNPK/KPK G44 .... **127** D3
Bute La *KVD/HLHD* G12 .... **18** B2
Bute Ter *RUTH* G73 .... **131** C1
Butterbiggins Rd *GVH/MTFL* G42 .... **56** B2
Butterfield Pl *GVH/MTFL* G42 ...... **56** B2 ▣
Byrebush Rd *PLK/PH/NH* G53 ...... **111** C1 ▣
Byres Rd *PTCK* G11 .... **17** F3
Byron St *PTCK* G11 .... **15** E3
Byshot St *PPK/MIL* G22 .... **10** A4

Cadder Rd *BSHPBGS* G64 .... **69** D1
  MRYH/FIRH G20 .... **77** C3
Cadder Wy *BSHPBGS* G64 .... **69** D1
Cadogan St *CCGLW* G2 .... **32** B3
Cadzow St *CCGLW* G2 .... **32** A4
Caird Dr *PTCK* G11 .... **17** D2
Cairn Av *RNFRW* PA4 .... **93** C1
Cairnban St *GOV/IBX* G51 .... **26** B5
Cairndow Av *LNPK/KPK* G44 ...... **127** D2 ▣
Cairndow Avenue La
 LNPK/KPK G44 .... **127** D2 ▣
Cairndow Ct *LNPK/KPK* G44 ...... **127** D2 ▣
Cairngorm Rd *PLKSW/MSWD* G43 ... **126** A1
Cairnhill Rd *BSDN* G61 .... **74** B1
Cairnlea Dr *GOV/IBX* G51 .... **40** C1
Cairnsmore Rd *DRUM* G15 .... **63** D4
Cairn St *SPRGB/BLRNK* G21 ...... **80** B4 ▣
Cairntoul Dr *KNTSWD* G13 .... **72** A4
Cairntoul Pl *SCOT* G14 .... **86** A1
Caithness St *MRYH/FIRH* G20 ...... **7** E3
Caldarvan St *PPK/MIL* G22 .... **8** C5
Calderbank Vw
 BAIL/MDB/MHD G69 .... **109** D3
Caldercuilt Rd *MRYH/FIRH* G20 .... **76** A2
Calder Ga *BSHPBGS* G64 .... **68** B2 ▣
Calderpark Av *UD/BTH/TAN* G71 .... **109** D4
Calderpark Crs
 UD/BTH/TAN G71 .... **109** D4 ▣
Calder Pl *BAIL/MDB/MHD* G69 .... **109** D2 ▣
Calder St *GVH/MTFL* G42 .... **56** B3
 GVH/MTFL G42 .... **57** F4
Calderwood Av
 BAIL/MDB/MHD G69 .... **109** C3
Calderwood Dr
 BAIL/MDB/MHD G69 .... **109** C3
Calderwood Gdns
 BAIL/MDB/MHD G69 .... **109** C3 ▣
Calderwood Rd *PLKSW/MSWD* G43.. **114** B4
 RUTH G73 .... **120** A3
Caldwell Av *KNTSWD* G13 .... **72** A4
Caledonia Av *GBLS* G5 .... **57** F2
 RUTH G73 .... **119** D2 ▣
Caledonia Dr
 BAIL/MDB/MHD G69 .... **109** D3 ▣
Caledonian Crs *KVD/HLHD* G12 .... **19** D2 ▣
Caledonia Rd *GBLS* G5 .... **45** D4 ▣
 UD/BTH/TAN G71 .... **109** C3
Caledonia St *GBLS* G5 .... **57** F2
Calfhill Rd *PLK/PH/NH* G53 .... **102** B3
Calgary St *COWCAD* G4 .... **21** F5
Callander St *MRYH/FIRH* G20 ...... **20** B1
Callieburn Rd *BSHPBGS* G64 ...... **81** C2
Cally Av *DRUM* G15 .... **64** A3
Calvay Crs *STPS/GTHM/RID* G33 .... **99** D3
Calvay Rd *STPS/GTHM/RID* G33 ... **100** A3 ▣
Cambridge Av *CLYDBK* G81 .... **62** A4 ▣
Cambridge Rd *RNFRW* PA4 .... **84** A4
Cambridge St *CCGLW* G2 .... **32** C1
Camburn St *CAR/SHTL* G32 .... **105** D1
Cambusdoon Rd
 STPS/GTHM/RID G33................ **91** C4
Cambuskenneth Gdns
 CAR/SHTL G32 .... **107** D1 ▣
Cambuslang Rd *BLTYR/CAMB* G72.. **121** C2
 CAR/SHTL G32 .... **121** D2
 RUTH G73 .... **120** A1
Cambus Pl *STPS/GTHM/RID* G33 ... **91** C4 ▣
Camden St *GBLS* G5 .... **45** E5
Camelon St *CAR/SHTL* G32 .... **97** D4
Cameron Ct *CLYDBK* G81 .... **70** A2 ▣
Cameron Dr *BSDN* G61 .... **67** C3
Cameron St *CARD/HILL/MSPK* G52 .... **93** C3

Camlachie St *DEN/PKHD* G31 .... 48 C2
   DMNK/BRGTN G40 .... 48 B1 🔢
Campbell Dr *BSDN* G61 .... 65 D1
Campbell St *MRYH/FIRH* G20 .... 76 B3
   RNFRW PA4 .... 84 B2
Camphill Av *PLKSD/SHW* G41 .... 115 D2 🔢
Camp Rd *BAIL/MDB/MHD* G69 .... 109 D1
   RUTH G73 .... 59 E3
Camps Crs *RNFRW* PA4 .... 85 C4
Campsie Crs *SPRGB/BLRNK* G21 .... 11 F3
Campsie Vw *STPS/GTHM/RID* G33 .. 91 D2 🔢
Campston Pl
   STPS/GTHM/RID G33 .... 98 B1 🔢
Camsbusmore Pl
   STPS/GTHM/RID G33 .... 91 C4 🔢
Camstradden Dr East *BSDN* G61 .... 65 C4
Camstradden Dr West *BSDN* G61 .... 65 C2
Camus Pl *DRUM* G15 .... 63 D2 🔢
Canal St *COWCAD* G4 .... 21 F4
   RNFRW PA4 .... 84 B2
Cander Rigg *BSHPBGS* G64 .... 69 C2
Candleriggs *CGLE* G1 .... 34 A5
Canmore Pl *DEN/PKHD* G31 .... 104 B2 🔢
Canmore St *DEN/PKHD* G31 .... 104 B2 🔢
Canniesburn Rd *BSDN* G61 .... 65 C4
Canting Wy *GOV/IBX* G51 .... 29 E4
Capelrig St *GIF/THBK* G46 .... 124 A2
Caprington St
   STPS/GTHM/RID G33 .... 98 A1 🔢
Cara Dr *GOV/IBX* G51 .... 26 C2
Carberry Rd *PLKSD/SHW* G41 .... 54 B4
Carbeth St *PPK/MIL* G22 .... 9 D3
Carbisdale St *PPK/MIL* G22 .... 10 C1
Carbrook St *SPRGB/BLRNK* G21 .... 24 A5
Cardarrach St *SPRGB/BLRNK* G21 .... 12 A3
Cardonald Dr
   CARD/HILL/MSPK G52 .... 102 A2
Cardonald Gdns
   CARD/HILL/MSPK G52 .... 102 B2 🔢
Cardonald Place Rd
   CARD/HILL/MSPK G52 .... 102 B2
Cardowan Dr *STPS/GTHM/RID* G33 .... 91 D1
Cardowan Rd *CAR/SHTL* G32 .... 97 D2
Cardow Rd *SPRGB/BLRNK* G21 .... 13 F4
Cardrona St *STPS/GTHM/RID* G33 .. 90 B3
Cardross St *DEN/PKHD* G31 .... 35 F4
Cardwell St *PLKSD/SHW* G41 .... 44 B5
Cardyke St *SPRGB/BLRNK* G21 .... 12 B4
Careston Pl *BSHPBGS* G64 .... 82 B1
Carfin St *GVH/MTFL* G42 .... 56 C3
Cargill Sq *BSHPBGS* G64 .... 81 D2 🔢
Carham Crs *CARD/HILL/MSPK* G52 .... 103 C2
Carillon Rd *GOV/IBX* G51 .... 41 D2
Carisbrooke Crs *BSHPBGS* G64 .... 69 D2 🔢
Carlaverock Rd *PLKSW/MSWD* G43.. 114 B2
Carleith Qd *GOV/IBX* G51 .... 26 A3
Carleston St *SPRGB/BLRNK* G21 .... 11 E3
Carleton Ct *GIF/THBK* G46 .... 126 A2 🔢
Carleton Dr *GIF/THBK* G46 .... 126 A2
Carleton Ga *GIF/THBK* G46 .... 126 A2
Carlibar Av *KNTSWD* G13 .... 71 D4 🔢
Carlisle St *SPRGB/BLRNK* G21 .... 10 B5
Carlton Ct *GBLS* G5 .... 44 C1
Carlton Pl *GBLS* G5 .... 45 D1
Carlyle Av *CARD/HILL/MSPK* G52 .... 93 D3
Carmaben Rd *STPS/GTHM/RID* G33.... 99 D2
Carment Dr *PLKSD/SHW* G41 .... 114 B2
Carmichael Pl *GVH/MTFL* G42 .... 115 D3
Carmichael St *GOV/IBX* G51 .... 41 D1
Carmunnock Rd *CSMK* G45.............. 129 C3
   LNPK/KPK G44 .... 116 B3

Carmyle Av *CAR/SHTL* G32 .... 106 B4
Carna Dr *LNPK/KPK* G44 .... 129 C1
Carnarvon St *KVGV* G3.............. 19 F4
Carnegie Rd
   CARD/HILL/MSPK G52 .... 94 A3 🔢
Carnoch St *SMSTN* G23 .... 76 B1 🔢
Carnock Rd *PLK/PH/NH* G53.............. 111 C2
Carnoustie Crs *BSHPBGS* G64 .... 82 A1 🔢
Carnoustie Pl *GBLS* G5 .... 43 F3
Carntynehall Rd *CAR/SHTL* G32 .... 97 D3 🔢
Carntyne Pl *CAR/SHTL* G32 .... 96 B3
Carntyne Rd *CAR/SHTL* G32 .... 96 B3
   CAR/SHTL G32 .... 98 B3 🔢
   DEN/PKHD G31 .... 37 F5
Carnwadric Rd *GIF/THBK* G46 .... 124 A2
Carnwath Av *PLKSW/MSWD* G43 .... 115 D2
Caroline St *DEN/PKHD* G31 .... 105 C1
Caroleside Dr *DRUM* G15.............. 64 B3
Carrbridge Dr *MRYH/FIRH* G20 ...... 76 B4 🔢
Carrickarden Rd *BSDN* G61.............. 66 B3
Carrick Dr *CAR/SHTL* G32 .... 108 A2
   RUTH G73 .... 131 C1
Carrick Gv *CAR/SHTL* G32 .... 108 A2 🔢
Carrick Rd *BSHPBGS* G64 .... 82 A1 🔢
   RUTH G73 .... 130 B1
Carrick St *KVGV* G3 .... 32 B5
Carrington St *COWCAD* G4 .... 19 F3
Carroglen Gdns *CAR/SHTL* G32.......... 107 D1
Carroglen Gv *CAR/SHTL* G32 .... 107 D1 🔢
Carron Crs *BSDN* G61.............. 65 C3
   BSHPBGS G64.............. 81 D1
   PPK/MIL G22 .... 10 B1
Carron Pl *PPK/MIL* G22 .... 10 C1
Carron St *PPK/MIL* G22 .... 10 C1
Carrour Gdns *BSHPBGS* G64 .... 68 B4
Carsaig Dr *CARD/HILL/MSPK* G52 .... 39 D2
Carstairs St *DMNK/BRGTN* G40.......... 60 A3
Carswell Gdns *PLKSD/SHW* G41 .... 55 D4
Cartcraigs Rd
   PLKSW/MSWD G43 .... 113 D4 🔢
Cartha St *PLKSW/MSWD* G43 .... 114 B3
Cartside Qd *PLKSW/MSWD* G43 .... 116 A3
Cartside St *GVH/MTFL* G42 .... 115 D3
Cartvale Rd *GVH/MTFL* G42 .... 115 D3
Cassiltoun Gdns *CSMK* G45 .... 129 C4 🔢
Cassley Av *RNFRW* PA4 .... 85 D4
Castlebank Ct *KNTSWD* G13 .... 74 A1 🔢
Castlebank Crs *PTCK* G11 .... 16 B4
Castlebank Gdns *KNTSWD* G13 .... 74 A4 🔢
Castlebank St *PTCK* G11 .... 15 F4
   PTCK G11 .... 17 D4
Castlebank Vls *KNTSWD* G13 .... 74 A1 🔢
Castlebay Dr *PPK/MIL* G22 .... 79 C1
Castlebay Pl *PPK/MIL* G22 .... 79 C2 🔢
Castlebay St *PPK/MIL* G22 .... 79 C2
Castlefern Rd *RUTH* G73 .... 131 C3
Castlehill Crs *RNFRW* PA4 .... 84 B2
Castlelaw Gdns *CAR/SHTL* G32 .... 98 B4 🔢
Castlelaw St *CAR/SHTL* G32 .... 98 B4 🔢
Castlemilk Crs *LNPK/KPK* G44.......... 130 A1
Castlemilk Dr *CSMK* G45 .... 130 A4
Castlemilk Rd *LNPK/KPK* G44 .... 118 A3
   RUTH G73 .... 130 B1 🔢
Castle St *BAIL/MDB/MHD* G69 .... 108 B3
   COWCAD G4 .... 23 D5
   COWCAD G4 .... 34 C2
   PTCK G11 .... 17 E4
   RUTH G73 .... 119 C2 🔢
Castleton Av *SPRGB/BLRNK* G21 .... 80 A3 🔢
Cathay St *PPK/MIL* G22 .... 79 C2
Cathcart Pl *RUTH* G73 .... 118 B3
Cathcart Rd *GBLS* G5 .... 45 D4

GVH/MTFL G42	57 D3
GVH/MTFL G42	116 B5 🔲
LNPK/KPK G44	116 B3
RUTH G73	118 B3
Cathedral Sq COWCAD C4	34 C5 🔲
Cathedral St CGLE G1	33 F2
Cathkin Av BLTYR/CAMB G72	121 C4
RUTH G73	120 A3 🔲
Cathkin By-pass RUTH G73	132 B3
Cathkin Pl BLTYR/CAMB G72	121 C4 🔲
Cathkin Rd GVH/MTFL G42	115 D3
Cathkinview Pl GVH/MTFL G42	116 B3 🔲
Cathkinview Rd GVH/MTFL G42	116 A3
Catrine Ct PLK/PH/NH G53	110 A2 🔲
Catrine Gdns PLK/PH/NH G53	110 A2
Catrine Pl PLK/PH/NH G53	110 A2 🔲
Catrine Rd PLK/PH/NH G53	110 A2
Causewayside Crs	
CAR/SHTL G32	106 A3 🔲
Causewayside St CAR/SHTL G32	106 A4
Cavendish Pl GBLS G5	44 C4
Cavendish St GBLS G5	44 C4
Cavin Dr CSMK G45	130 A2
Cavin Rd CSMK G45	130 A2
Cayton Gdns	
BAIL/MDB/MHD G69	108 B2 🔲
Cecil St KVD/HLHD G12	18 B1
Cedar Ct MRYH/FIRH G20	20 B2
Cedar Gdns RUTH G73	132 A3
Cedar Rd BSHPBGS G64	81 D2
Cedar St MRYH/FIRH G20	20 B2
Cedric Pl KNTSWD G13	73 D3 🔲
Cedric Rd KNTSWD G13	73 D3
Celtic St MRYH/FIRH G20	76 A3
Cemetery Rd CARD/HILL/MSPK G52	38 B4
Central Av BLTYR/CAMB G72	121 D4
CAR/SHTL G32	107 D3
PTCK G11	15 E2 🔲
Central Gv CAR/SHTL G32	107 D2
Central Pth CAR/SHTL G32	108 A3
Centre St GBLS G5	44 C1
Ceres Gdns BSHPBGS G64	82 B1
Cessnock St STPS/GTHM/RID G33	90 A1
Chalmers Ga DMNK/BRGTN G40	47 D1
Chalmers St DMNK/BRGTN G40	47 D1
Chamberlain La KNTSWD G13	2 C1
Chamberlain Rd KNTSWD G13	74 A4 🔲
Chancellor St PTCK G11	17 D3
Chapel Ct RUTH G73	118 B2 🔲
Chapel St MRYH/FIRH G20	6 C1
RUTH G73	118 B2
Chapelton Av BSDN G61	66 B2
Chapelton Gdns BSDN G61	66 B2
Chapelton St PPK/MIL G22	79 C4
Chaplet Av KNTSWD G13	73 C2
Charing Cross La KVGV G3	31 F1 🔲
Charles Av RNFRW PA4	84 B2
Charles St SPRGB/BLRNK G21	23 E4
Charlotte St CGLE G1	46 B1
Chatelherault Av	
BLTYR/CAMB G72	133 C1 🔲
Chatton St SMSTN G23	76 B1
Cheapside St KVGV G3	31 F4
Chelmsford Dr KVD/HLHD G12	4 C1
Cherrybank Rd PLKSW/MSWD G43	127 D1
Cherry Pl BSHPBGS G64	81 D2
Chesterfield Av KVD/HLHD G12	4 B1
Chesters Pl RUTH G73	119 C3 🔲
Chesters Rd BSDN G61	65 C2
Chester St CAR/SHTL G32	106 A1 🔲
Cheviot Rd PLKSW/MSWD G43	126 A1
Chirmorie Pl PLK/PH/NH G53	110 A1
Chirnside Pl CARD/HILL/MSPK G52	94 A4
Chirnside Rd CARD/HILL/MSPK G52	94 A4
Chisolm St CGLE G1	34 A5 🔲
Christian St PLKSW/MSWD G43	114 A2
Christopher St SPRGB/BLRNK G21	24 A4
Church Av RUTH G73	132 A1 🔲
Churchill Dr PTCK G11	3 E3
Church St GIF/THBK G46	126 A4
Circus Dr DEN/PKHD G31	35 F3
Circus Pl DEN/PKHD G31	35 F3
Circus Place La DEN/PKHD G31	35 F2
Citizen La CGLE G1	33 E3
Cityford Dr RUTH G73	118 B4
Civic St COWCAD C4	20 C4
Clachan Dr GOV/IBX G51	27 D1
Claddens Qd PPK/MIL G22	79 C4
Claddens St PPK/MIL G22	78 B4
Clairinch Gdns RNFRW PA4	92 A1 🔲
Clairmont Gdns KVGV G3	19 E5
Clair Rd BSHPBGS G64	82 B1
Claremont Pas KVGV G3	19 E5 🔲
Claremont Pl KVGV G3	19 E5 🔲
Claremont St KVGV G3	31 D1
Claremont Ter KVGV G3	19 D5
Claremount Av GIF/THBK G46	126 A4
Claremount Terrace La KVGV G3	19 D5
Clarence Dr PTCK G11	16 A1
Clarence Gdns PTCK G11	16 A1
Clarence La KVD/HLHD G12	4 C5
Clarence St CLYDBK G81	62 A4
Clarendon Pl COWCAD C4	20 A3
Clarendon St MRYH/FIRH G20	20 A3
Clare St SPRGB/BLRNK G21	24 A4
Clarion Crs KNTSWD G13	72 A2
Clarion Rd KNTSWD G13	72 A3
Clarkston Av LNPK/KPK G44	127 D2
Clarkston Rd LNPK/KPK G44	127 D1
Clathic Av BSDN G61	67 C3
Clavens Rd CARD/HILL/MSPK G52	93 C4
Claverhouse Rd	
CARD/HILL/MSPK G52	93 D3
Claypotts Pl STPS/GTHM/RID G33	98 A1 🔲
Claypotts Rd	
STPS/GTHM/RID G33	98 A1 🔲
Clayslaps Rd KVGV G3	18 B5
Claythorn Av DMNK/BRGTN G40	46 C2
Claythorn Circ DMNK/BRGTN G40	46 C2
Claythorn Pk DMNK/BRGTN G40	46 C2
Claythorn Ter DMNK/BRGTN G40	47 D1
Clayton Ter DEN/PKHD G31	35 F3
Cleddans Rd CLYDBK G81	62 A1
Cleddens Ct BSHPBGS G64	81 C1 🔲
Cleeves Qd PLK/PH/NH G53	122 A1
Cleeves Rd PLK/PH/NH G53	122 A1
Cleghorn St PPK/MIL G22	8 C5
Cleland La GBLS G5	45 D3
Cleland St GBLS G5	45 E3
Clelland Av BSHPBGS G64	81 C2
Clerwood St CAR/SHTL G32	96 B4
Cleveden Crs KVD/HLHD G12	5 D2
Cleveden Crescent La	
KVD/HLHD G12	5 D2
Cleveden Dr KVD/HLHD G12	5 D2
RUTH G73	120 A4
Cleveden Gdns KVD/HLHD G12	5 E2
Cleveden La KVD/HLHD G12	75 D4 🔲
Cleveden Pl KVD/HLHD G12	75 D4
Cleveden Rd KVD/HLHD G12	5 E2
Cleveland La CGLW G2	31 F1
Cleveland St KVGV G3	31 F1
Clifford Gdns GOV/IBX G51	40 C2
Clifford La GOV/IBX G51	41 F2

Clifford Pl GOV/IBX G51 .... 42 A2
Clifford St GOV/IBX G51 .... 41 E2
Cliff Rd KVGV G3 .... 19 E4
Clifton Pl KVGV G3 .... 31 D1
Clifton Rd GIF/THBK G46 .... 125 D3
Clifton St KVGV G3 .... 19 D5
Clifton Ter BLTYR/CAMB G72 ...... 133 C3
Clincarthill Rd RUTH G73 .... 119 D3 🔢
    RUTH G73 .... 119 C3 🔢
Clincart Rd GVH/MTFL G42 .... 116 B2 🔢
Cloan Av DRUM G15 .... 64 B4
Cloan Crs BSHPBGS G64 .... 69 D2
Cloberhill Rd KNTSWD G13 .... 73 C1
Cloch St STPS/GTHM/RID G33 .... 98 A2 🔢
Closeburn St PPK/MIL G22 .... 9 E2
Clouston La MRYH/FIRH G20 .... 6 C4
Clouston St MRYH/FIRH G20 .... 6 B3
Clova St GIF/THBK G46 .... 124 B2
Cloverbank St SPRGB/BLRNK G21 .. 24 B4
Clovergate BSHPBGS G64 .... 80 A1
Clunie Rd CARD/HILL/MSPK G52 ... 38 C5
Cluny Av BSDN G61 .... 67 C4
Cluny Dr BSDN G61 .... 67 C4
Cluny Gdns BAIL/MDB/MHD G69 . 109 C2
    SCOT G14 .... 3 D3
Clutha St GOV/IBX G51 .... 42 A2
Clydebrae St GOV/IBX G51 .... 29 D2
Clydeford Dr CAR/SHTL G32 .... 105 C3
Clydeholm Rd SCOT G14 .... 14 B2 🔢
Clydeholm Ter CLYDBK G81 .... 70 B3 🔢
Clyde Pl GBLS G5 .... 32 B5
Clydeside Rd RUTH G73 .... 59 E3
Clyde St CCGLE G1 .... 33 D5
    CLYDBK G81 .... 70 A3
    RNFRW PA4 .... 84 B1
Clynder St GOV/IBX G51 .... 29 D5
Clyth Dr GIF/THBK G46 .... 126 B4
Coalhill St DEN/PKHD G31 .... 49 D2
Coats Crs BAIL/MDB/MHD G69 .... 109 C1
Cobington Pl
    STPS/GTHM/RID G33 .... 98 B1 🔢
Cobinshaw St CAR/SHTL G32 .... 98 A4
Coburg St GBLS G5 .... 44 C2
Cochno St CLYDBK G81 .... 70 A2
Cochrane St CCLE G1 .... 33 F3
Cockels Loan RNFRW PA4 .... 92 A2
Cockenzie St CAR/SHTL G32 .... 106 A1
Cockmuir St SPRGB/BLRNK G21 .... 12 A3
Cogan Rd PLKSW/MSWD G43 ...... 114 A4 🔢
Cogan St PLKSW/MSWD G43 .... 114 A3
Colbert St DMNK/BRGTN G40 .... 59 E1
Colchester Dr KVD/HLHD G12 .... 75 C4
Coldingham Av SCOT G14 .... 71 C4
Coldstream Dr RUTH G73 .... 120 B4
Coldstream Pl COWCAD G4 .... 21 F1
Colebrooke Pl KVD/HLHD G12 ...... 19 D1
Colebrooke St KVD/HLHD G12 ...... 19 D1
Colebrooke Ter KVD/HLHD G12 .... 19 D1
Colgrain St MRYH/FIRH G20 .... 78 A4
Colgrave Crs CAR/SHTL G32 .... 105 D3 🔢
Colinslie Rd PLK/PH/NH G53 .... 111 C3
Colinton Pl CAR/SHTL G32 .... 98 B3
Colintraive Av STPS/GTHM/RID G33 .. 89 C3
Colintraive Crs STPS/GTHM/RID G33 .. 89 C3
Coll Av RNFRW PA4 .... 92 B1
College La CCGLE G1 .... 34 A3
College St CCGLE G1 .... 34 A4
Collessie Dr STPS/GTHM/RID G33 .. 91 C4
Collina St MRYH/FIRH G20 .... 76 A4
Collins St COWCAD G4 .... 34 C3
Coll Pl SPRGB/BLRNK G21 .... 25 D2
Coll St SPRGB/BLRNK G21 .... 24 C2

Collylinn Rd BSDN G61 .... 66 A2
Colmonell Av KNTSWD G13 .... 71 D3 🔢
Colonsay Av RNFRW PA4 .... 92 A1
Colonsay Rd CARD/HILL/MSPK G52 .. 39 D2
Colquhoun Av
    CARD/HILL/MSPK G52 .... 94 A3
Colquhoun Dr BSDN G61 .... 65 D1
Colston Av SPRGB/BLRNK G21 ...... 80 B3
Colston Dr BSHPBGS G64 .... 80 B3
Colston Gdns BSHPBGS G64 .... 80 A3
Colston Pth SPRGB/BLRNK G21 ... 80 A3 🔢
Colston Pl SPRGB/BLRNK G21 ...... 80 A3 🔢
Colston Rd PPK/MIL G22 .... 80 A3
    SPRGB/BLRNK G21 .... 80 B3
Coltmuir Crs BSHPBGS G64 .... 80 A2 🔢
Coltmuir Dr PPK/MIL G22 .... 80 A2 🔢
Coltmuir Gdns PPK/MIL G22 .... 80 A2 🔢
Coltmuir St PPK/MIL G22 .... 78 B4
Coltness La STPS/GTHM/RID G33 .. 99 C3
Coltness St STPS/GTHM/RID G33 .. 99 C2
Coltpark Av BSHPBGS G64 .... 80 A2
Coltpark La BSHPBGS G64 .... 80 B2 🔢
Coltsfoot Dr PLK/PH/NH G53 ...... 122 B3
Columba St GOV/IBX G51 .... 28 C4
Colvend Dr RUTH G73 .... 131 D3 🔢
Colvend St DMNK/BRGTN G40 ...... 59 F2
Colville Dr RUTH G73 .... 120 B3
Colwood Av PLK/PH/NH G53 .... 122 A2
Colwood Gdns PLK/PH/NH G53 ... 122 A3 🔢
Colwood Pl PLK/PH/NH G53 .... 122 A3 🔢
Colwood Sq PLK/PH/NH G53 .... 122 A2 🔢
Comelypark St DEN/PKHD G31 ...... 47 F1
Commerce St GBLS G5 .... 44 C2
Commercial Rd GBLS G5 .... 45 F4
Commore Dr KNTSWD G13 .... 72 A3
Comrie Rd STPS/GTHM/RID G33 ... 91 C1 🔢
Comrie St CAR/SHTL G32 .... 106 B1
Cona St GIF/THBK G46 .... 124 A2 🔢
Congress Rd KVGV G3 .... 30 B3
Congress Wy KVGV G3 .... 30 C3
Conistone Crs BAIL/MDB/MHD G69.. 108 B2
Connal St DMNK/BRGTN G40 .... 60 B3
Conniston St CAR/SHTL G32 .... 97 C3 🔢
Conon Av BSDN G61 .... 65 D3
Consett La STPS/GTHM/RID G33 ... 99 C2 🔢
Cook St GBLS G5 .... 44 B3
Cooperage Ct KNTSWD G13 .... 70 B4
Cooper's Well St PTCK G11 .... 17 E5 🔢
Copland Pl GOV/IBX G51 .... 29 D5
Copland Qd GOV/IBX G51 .... 29 D5
Copland Rd GOV/IBX G51 .... 40 C2
Coplaw St GVH/MTFL G42 .... 56 B2
Corbett Ct CAR/SHTL G32 .... 105 D3 🔢
Corbett St CAR/SHTL G32 .... 106 A3
Cordiner St LNPK/KPK G44 .... 116 B3 🔢
Corkerhill Gdns
    CARD/HILL/MSPK G52 .... 38 C4
Corkerhill Pl CARD/HILL/MSPK G52 .. 50 B3
Corkerhill Rd CARD/HILL/MSPK G52 .. 50 B2
Corlaich Av GVH/MTFL G42 .... 118 A3
Corlaich Dr RUTH G73 .... 118 A3
Cornaig Rd PLK/PH/NH G53 .... 110 B2
Cornalee Gdns PLK/PH/NH G53 ... 110 A3
Cornalee Pl PLK/PH/NH G53 .... 110 A2
Cornalee Rd PLK/PH/NH G53 ...... 110 B2
Cornhill St SPRGB/BLRNK G21 ...... 12 A2
Corn St COWCAD G4 .... 32 C3
Cornwall Av RUTH G73 .... 132 B1 🔢
Cornwall St GOV/IBX G51 .... 42 A3
Cornwall St South PLKSD/SHW G41 .. 42 B3
Coronation Wy BSDN G61 .... 66 B4
Corran St STPS/GTHM/RID G33 ..... 97 D2

Corrie Gv LNPK/KPK G44 .... 127 D2
Corrour Rd PLKSW/MSWD G43..... 114 B3
Corselet Rd PLK/PH/NH G53........ 122 B3
Corse Rd CARD/HILL/MSPK G52 ... 93 C4
Corsewall Av CAR/SHTL G32 .... 108 A3 🔢
Corsford Dr PLK/PH/NH G53........ 111 C4
Corsock St DEN/PKHD G31........... 37 E3
Corston St STPS/GTHM/RID G33 ... 96 B2
Cortachy Pl BSHPBGS G64 .... 82 B1
Corunna St KVGV G3 .... 30 C1
Coshneuk Rd STPS/GTHM/RID G33 ... 90 B1
Cottar St MRYH/FIRH G20 .... 77 C3
Coulin Gdns PPK/MIL G22 .... 10 A3
County Av BLTYR/CAMB G72 .... 120 B3
Couper St COWCAD G4................ 22 A5
Courthill Av LNPK/KPK G44.......... 128 B1
Coustonholm Rd
    PLKSW/MSWD G43 .... 114 B3
Coventry Dr DEN/PKHD G31.......... 36 C1
Cowal St MRYH/FIRH G20 .... 76 A3
Cowan La KVD/HLHD G12 .... 19 D2
Cowan St KVD/HLHD G12 .... 19 D2
Cowcaddens Rd COWCAD G4 .... 20 C5
Cowcaddens St CGLW G2 .... 33 D1
Cowdenhill Circ KNTSWD G13....... 73 D2
Cowdenhill Pl KNTSWD G13 .... 73 D2 🔢
Cowdenhill Rd KNTSWD G13......... 73 C2
Cowden St GOV/IBX G51 .... 26 A4
Cowdray Crs RNFRW PA4 .... 84 B3 🔢
Cowglen Rd PLK/PH/NH G53 .... 111 C3
Cowlairs St SPRGB/BLRNK G21 .... 10 C4
Coxhill St COWCAD G4 .... 22 A1
Coxton Pl STPS/GTHM/RID G33 .... 99 D1
Coylton Rd PLKSW/MSWD G43...... 127 C1
Craggan Dr KNTSWD G13............. 71 D4
Craiganour La PLKSW/MSWD G43 ... 114 A4
Craigard Pl RUTH G73 .... 132 B3
Craigbank Dr PLK/PH/NH G53 ...... 110 A4
Craigbarnet Crs
    STPS/GTHM/RID G33 .... 90 B2 🔢
Craigbo Av SMSTN G23 .... 76 B1 🔢
Craigbo Rd SMSTN G23 .... 76 B1
Craigbo St SMSTN G23 .... 76 B1 🔢
Craigellan Rd
    PLKSW/MSWD G43 .... 114 B4 🔢
Craigenbay St SPRGB/BLRNK G21 ... 12 C4
Craigendmuir St
    STPS/GTHM/RID G33.............. 88 B4
Craigend Pl KNTSWD G13 .... 74 A4 🔢
Craigend St KNTSWD G13 .... 74 A4 🔢
Craigflower Gdns
    PLK/PH/NH G53 .... 122 A2 🔢
Craigflower Rd PLK/PH/NH G53 ... 122 A2
Craighall Rd COWCAD G4.............. 21 D3
Craighead Av STPS/GTHM/RID G33 ... 88 A3
Craighouse St STPS/GTHM/RID G33 ... 98 A1
Craigiebburn Gdns MRYH/FIRH G20 ... 75 D2
Craigiehall Pl GOV/IBX G51 .... 30 B5
Craigiehall St GOV/IBX G51 .... 42 B1
Craigielea Pk RNFRW PA4 .... 84 A3 🔢
Craigielea Rd RNFRW PA4............ 84 A3
Craigielea St DEN/PKHD G31........ 36 B3
Craigie St GVH/MTFL G42 .... 56 A4
Craigleith St CAR/SHTL G32 .... 97 C4 🔢
Craiglockhart St
    STPS/GTHM/RID G33 .... 91 D4 🔢
    STPS/GTHM/RID G33 .... 99 D1 🔢
Craigmaddie Terrace La KVGV G3 ... 18 C5 🔢
Craigmillar Rd GVH/MTFL G42 ..... 116 A3 🔢
Craigmont Dr MRYH/FIRH G20...... 6 C1
Craigmont St MRYH/FIRH G20...... 77 C4
Craigmore St DEN/PKHD G31........ 37 E5

Craigmuir Crs CARD/HILL/MSPK G52.. 93 D4
Craigmuir Pl CARD/HILL/MSPK G52 ... 93 C4
Craigmuir Rd CARD/HILL/MSPK G52 .. 93 C4
Craignure Rd RUTH G73 .... 131 D3
Craigpark DEN/PKHD G31 .... 36 A3
Craigpark Dr DEN/PKHD G31 .... 36 A3
Craig Rd LNPK/KPK G44................ 128 A1
Craigton Dr GOV/IBX G51 .... 39 E1
Craigton Pl GOV/IBX G51 .... 27 D5
Craigton Rd GOV/IBX G51 .... 27 E4
Craigvicar Gdns CAR/SHTL G32 ... 107 D2 🔢
Craigwell Av RUTH G73 .... 120 B4
Crail St DEN/PKHD G31 .... 104 B1
Cramond Av RNFRW PA4 .... 85 C4
Cramond St GBLS G5 .... 58 B3
Cramond Ter CAR/SHTL G32 .... 106 B1 🔢
Cranborne Rd KVD/HLHD G12 ...... 4 A1
Cranbrooke Dr MRYH/FIRH G20 ... 76 B3
Cranston St KVGV G3 .... 31 E3 🔢
Cranworth La KVD/HLHD G12 .... 18 B1
Cranworth St KVD/HLHD G12....... 18 A1
Crarae Av BSDN G61 .... 66 A4
Crathes Ct LNPK/KPK G44............ 127 C2 🔢
Crathie Dr PTCK G11 .... 16 A2
Crawford Dr DRUM G15................ 72 A1
Crawford St PTCK G11.................. 16 B3
Crawfurd Av RUTH G73 .... 131 D1
Crawfurd Gdns RUTH G73............ 132 A2
Crawfurd Rd RUTH G73................ 131 D2
Crebar St GIF/THBK G46 .... 124 A2
Credon Gdns RUTH G73................ 132 A2
Cree Av BSHPBGS G64 .... 82 B1
Cree Gdns CAR/SHTL G32 .... 105 D1
Crescent Rd SCOT G14 .... 86 B1
Cresswell La KVD/HLHD G12 .... 18 A1
Cresswell St KVD/HLHD G12 .... 18 A1
Cressy St GOV/IBX G51 .... 27 D1
Crest Av KNTSWD G13 .... 72 B2
Crichton St SPRGB/BLRNK G21..... 10 C4
Criffell Gdns CAR/SHTL G32 .... 107 D3 🔢
Criffell Rd CAR/SHTL G32............. 107 D2
Crimea St CGLW G2 .... 32 A4
Crinan Gdns BSHPBGS G64 .... 82 A1
Crinan St DEN/PKHD G31 .... 36 C1
Cripps Av CLYDBK G81.................. 70 B1
Croftbank St SPRGB/BLRNK G21 ... 11 F4
Croftburn Dr LNPK/KPK G44........ 129 D2
Croftcroighn Rd
    STPS/GTHM/RID G33................ 98 B1
Croftend Av LNPK/KPK G44 .... 118 A4
Croftend La RUTH G73 .... 130 B1 🔢
Croftfoot Crs CSMK G45 .... 131 C2 🔢
Croftfoot Pl CSMK G45 .... 130 B2
Croftfoot Qd CSMK G45 .... 130 A2
Croftfoot Rd CSMK G45 .... 129 D2
    LNPK/KPK G44 .... 129 D2
Croftfoot St CSMK G45 .... 131 C2 🔢
Croftfoot Ter CSMK G45 .... 130 B2
Crofthill Rd LNPK/KPK G44 .... 130 A2 🔢
Crofthouse Dr LNPK/KPK G44...... 130 A2 🔢
Croftmont Av LNPK/KPK G44 .... 130 A2
Crofton Av LNPK/KPK G44 .... 129 D2
Croftpark Av LNPK/KPK G44 .... 130 A1
Croftside Av LNPK/KPK G44 .... 130 A2
Croftspar Av CAR/SHTL G32 .... 99 D4
Croftspar Dr CAR/SHTL G32 .... 99 D4
Croftspar Gv CAR/SHTL G32 .... 99 D4
Croftspar Pl CAR/SHTL G32.......... 99 D4
Croft Wy RNFRW PA4................... 92 B1
Croftwood Av LNPK/KPK G44 ...... 129 D2
Cromarty Av PLKSW/MSWD G43 ... 115 D3

Crombie Gdns
  BAIL/MDB/MHD G69 .... **108** B3 🔟
Cromdale St *GOV/IBX* G51 .... **26** C5
Cromer St *MRYH/FIRH* G20 .... **7** F1
Crompton Av *LNPK/KPK* G44 .... **128** B1
Cromwell La *COWCAD* G4 .... **20** A3 🔟
Cromwell St *COWCAD* G4 .... **20** A3
Crookston Av
  CARD/HILL/MSPK G52 .... **102** A2
Crookston Ct
  CARD/HILL/MSPK G52 .... **102** A2 🔟
Crookston Gv
  CARD/HILL/MSPK G52 .... **102** A2 🔟
Crookston Ter
  CARD/HILL/MSPK G52 .... **102** A2 🔟
Crosbie La *MRYH/FIRH* G20 .... **76** A2
Crosbie St *MRYH/FIRH* G20 .... **76** A2
Crossbank Av *GVH/MTFL* G42 ...... **118** A1
Crossbank Dr *GVH/MTFL* G42 ...... **117** D1 🔟
Crossbank Rd *GVH/MTFL* G42 ...... **117** D1 🔟
Crossford Dr *SMSTN* G23 .... **77** C1 🔟
Crosshill Av *GVH/MTFL* G42 .... **116** B1 🔟
Crosshill Dr *RUTH* G73 .... **119** D4
Crosslees Dr *GIF/THBK* G46 .... **124** B3
Crosslees Pk *GIF/THBK* G46 .... **124** B3
Crosslees Rd *GIF/THBK* G46 .... **124** B4
Crosslee St *CARD/HILL/MSPK* G52 ..... **38** B3
Crossloan Rd *GOV/IBX* G51 .... **27** F3
Crossloan Ter *GOV/IBX* G51 .... **27** F3
Crossmyloof Gdns *PLKSD/SHW* G41 ... **54** A5
Crosspoint Dr *SMSTN* G23 .... **77** C1 🔟
Crossstobs Rd *PLK/PH/NH* G53 ..... **110** A1
Crovie Rd *PLK/PH/NH* G53 .... **110** A3 🔟
Crowhill Rd *BSHPBGS* G64 .... **80** B2
Crowhill St *PPK/MIL* G22 .... **79** C4
Crow La *KNTSWD* G13 .... **3** E2
Crowlin Crs *STPS/GTHM/RID* G33 ..... **98** B2
Crown Circ *KVD/HLHD* G12 .... **17** E1
Crown Gdns *KVD/HLHD* G12 .... **17** E1
Crownhall Pl *CAR/SHTL* G32 .... **107** C1
Crownhall Rd *CAR/SHTL* G32 .... **107** C1 🔟
Crownpoint Rd
  DMNK/BRGTN G40 .... **48** B2 🔟
Crown Rd North *KVD/HLHD* G12 ..... **17** D1
Crown Rd South *KVD/HLHD* G12 ..... **17** D1
Crown St *BAIL/MDB/MHD* G69 ...... **108** B3 🔟
  GBLS G5 .... **45** E4
Crown Ter *KVD/HLHD* G12 .... **17** D1
Crow Rd *KNTSWD* G13 .... **3** E2
  KNTSWD G13 .... **74** B3
  PTCK G11 .... **3** E4
Croy Rd *SPRGB/BLRNK* G21 .... **13** E1
Cruachan Av *RNFRW* PA4 .... **92** A1
Cruachan Rd *RUTH* G73 .... **132** B3
Cruachan St *GIF/THBK* G46 .... **124** B3
Cruden St *GOV/IBX* G51 .... **27** E5
Crum Av *GIF/THBK* G46 .... **125** C5
Crusader Av *KNTSWD* G13 .... **73** D1
Cubie St *DMNK/BRGTN* G40 .... **47** F2
Culbin Dr *KNTSWD* G13 .... **71** D2
Cullen St *CAR/SHTL* G32 .... **106** A2
Cullins Rd *RUTH* G73 .... **132** B3
Culloden St *DEN/PKHD* G31 .... **36** C1
Culrain Gdns *CAR/SHTL* G32 .... **106** A1 🔟
Culrain St *CAR/SHTL* G32 .... **106** A1
Culross St *CAR/SHTL* G32 .... **107** C2
Cults St *GOV/IBX* G51 .... **27** F5
Culzean Crs
  BAIL/MDB/MHD G69 .... **109** C2 🔟
Culzean Dr *CAR/SHTL* G32 .... **107** D2 🔟
Cumberland Pl *GBLS* G5 .... **45** F5 🔟
Cumberland St *GBLS* G5 .... **44** C3

  GBLS G5 .... **45** E4 🔟
  GBLS G5 .... **46** A5
Cumbernauld Rd *DEN/PKHD* G31 ..... **36** C4
  DMNK/BRGTN G40 .... **48** A5
  STPS/GTHM/RID G33 .... **90** A2
  STPS/GTHM/RID G33 .... **96** B1
Cumbrae Rd *RNFRW* PA4 .... **92** B1 🔟
Cumbrae St *STPS/GTHM/RID* G33 ..... **98** A1
Cumlodden Dr *MRYH/FIRH* G20 .... **76** A3
Cumming Dr *GVH/MTFL* G42 .... **116** B2
Cumnock Rd *STPS/GTHM/RID* G33 ..... **83** C4
Cunningham Dr *GIF/THBK* G46 ...... **127** C3
Cunninghame Rd *RUTH* G73 .... **120** A2
Cunningham Rd
  CARD/HILL/MSPK G52 .... **93** D2 🔟
Curfew Rd *KNTSWD* G13 .... **73** D1
Curle St *SCOT* G14 .... **14** A2
Curling Crs *GVH/MTFL* G42 .... **117** C2
Currie St *MRYH/FIRH* G20 .... **77** C4
Curtis Av *LNPK/KPK* G44 .... **117** D3
Curzon St *MRYH/FIRH* G20 .... **77** C4
Cuthbertson St *GVH/MTFL* G42 .... **56** A2
Cuthelton Dr *DEN/PKHD* G31 .... **105** C2 🔟
Cuthelton Rd *DEN/PKHD* G31 .... **104** B2
Cuthelton Ter *DEN/PKHD* G31 .... **104** B2

Daer Av *RNFRW* PA4 .... **93** C1
Dairsie Gdns *BSHPBGS* G64 .... **82** B2
Dairsie St *LNPK/KPK* G44 .... **127** D2 🔟
Daisy St *GVH/MTFL* G42 .... **56** C5
Dalbeth Rd *CAR/SHTL* G32 .... **105** D4
Dalcross St *PTCK* G11 .... **17** E3
Dalcharn Pl *ESTRH* G34 .... **101** C2 🔟
Daldowie Av *CAR/SHTL* G32 .... **107** D3 🔟
Daldowie Rd *UD/BTH/TAN* G71 ...... **109** C4
Dale St *DMNK/BRGTN* G40 .... **47** F5
Daleview Av *KVD/HLHD* G12 .... **75** D4 🔟
Dale Wy *RUTH* G73 .... **131** C2
Dalgarroch Av *KNTSWD* G13 .... **71** C2
Dalhousie Gdns *BSHPBGS* G64 .... **68** B4
Dalhousie La *KVGV* G3 .... **20** B5
Dalhousie St *CCLW* G2 .... **32** B1
  COWCAD G4 .... **20** C5
Dalintober St *GBLS* G5 .... **44** A1 🔟
Dalkeith Av *BSHPBGS* G64 .... **69** D3
  PLKSD/SHW G41 .... **40** C2
Dalkeith Rd *BSHPBGS* G64 .... **69** D2 🔟
Dalmahoy St *CAR/SHTL* G32 .... **97** C3 🔟
Dalmally St *MRYH/FIRH* G20 .... **7** F5
Dalmarnock Rd *DMNK/BRGTN* G40 ..... **47** F5
  RUTH G73 .... **60** C5
Dalmellington Rd *PLK/PH/NH* G53 ..... **110** A2
Dalmeny Av *GIF/THBK* G46 .... **126** A3
Dalmeny St *GBLS* G5 .... **58** C3
Dalnair St *KVGV* G3 .... **17** F5
Dalness St *CAR/SHTL* G32 .... **106** A3
Dalriada St *DMNK/BRGTN* G40 .... **49** E4
Dalry St *CAR/SHTL* G32 .... **106** B2
Dalserf St *DEN/PKHD* G31 .... **48** C3
Dalsetter Av *DRUM* G15 .... **63** D4
Dalsetter Pl *DRUM* G15 .... **64** A4 🔟
Dalsholm Rd *MRYH/FIRH* G20 .... **75** D3
Dalton Av *CLYDBK* G81 .... **71** C1
Dalton St *DEN/PKHD* G31 .... **105** C1
Dalveen St *CAR/SHTL* G32 .... **105** D1 🔟
Dalveen Wy *RUTH* G73 .... **132** A3
Dalziel Dr *PLKSD/SHW* G41 .... **53** F1
Dalziel Rd *CARD/HILL/MSPK* G52 ..... **93** D2

Damshot Crs *PLK/PH/NH* G53 .... 111 D2
Damshot Rd *PLK/PH/NH* G53 .... 111 D3
Danby Rd *BAIL/MDB/MHD* G69 .... 108 B2
Danes Av *SCOT* G14 .... 87 C2
Danes Crs *SCOT* G14 .... 86 B1 🟦
Danes Dr *SCOT* G14 .... 2 A4
Danes La North *SCOT* G14 .... 87 C2
Danes La South *SCOT* G14 .... 87 C2
Dargarvel Av *PLKSD/SHW* G41 .... 40 C5
Dargarvel Pth *PLKSD/SHW* G41 .... 52 B1 🟦
Darleith St *CAR/SHTL* G32 .... 105 D1
Darnaway Av *STPS/GTHM/RID* G33.... 91 D4
Darnaway Dr *STPS/GTHM/RID* G33 ... 91 D4
Darnaway St *STPS/GTHM/RID* G33 ... 91 D4
Darnick St *SPRGB/BLRNK* G21 .... 24 B1
Darnley Crs *BSHPBGS* G64 .... 68 B3
Darnley Gdns *PLKSD/SHW* G41 .... 55 D4
Darnley Mains Rd *PLK/PH/NH* G53 .. 123 C3
Darnley Rd *PLKSD/SHW* G41 .... 54 C4
Darnley St *PLKSD/SHW* G41 .... 55 F2
Dartford St *PPK/MIL* G22 .... 8 C5
Davaar Rd *RNFRW* PA4 .... 92 B1
Davaar St *DMNK/BRGTN* G40 .... 49 D4
Dava St *GOV/IBX* G51 .... 28 B4
Daventry Dr *KVD/HLHD* G12 .... 4 B1
David Pl *BAIL/MDB/MHD* G69 .... 108 B2
Davidson Pl *CAR/SHTL* G32 .... 99 C4 🟦
Davidson St *CLYDBK* G81 .... 71 C2
DMNK/BRGTN G40......................... 60 B3
David St *DMNK/BRGTN* G40 .... 48 B2
Daviot St *GOV/IBX* G51 .... 26 A5
Dawson Pl *COWCAD* G4 .... 21 D1
Dawson Rd *COWCAD* G4 .... 21 D1
Deanfield Qd *CARD/HILL/MSPK* G52 . 93 D4
Deanfield Quaudrant
CARD/HILL/MSPK G52.................... 93 D4
Dean Park Rd *RNFRW* PA4 .... 84 B4
Deanside Rd *CARD/HILL/MSPK* G52.... 94 A2
Deanston Dr *PLKSD/SHW* G41 .... 115 C2
Dean St *CLYDBK* G81 .... 70 A1
Deanwood Av *GIF/THBK* G46 .... 127 D3
Deanwood Rd *GIF/THBK* G46 .... 127 D3
Dechmont St *DEN/PKHD* G31 .... 49 F4
Dee Av *RNFRW* PA4 .... 85 C3
Deepdene Rd *BSDN* G61 .... 65 D3
Dee St *STPS/GTHM/RID* G33 .... 96 B2
Delny Pl *STPS/GTHM/RID* G33 .... 100 A3 🟦
Delvin Rd *LNPK/KPK* G44 .... 116 A4
Denbeck St *CAR/SHTL* G32 .... 105 D1
Denbrae St *CAR/SHTL* G32 .... 105 D1
Denham St *PPK/MIL* G22 .... 8 C5
Denmark St *PPK/MIL* G22 .... 9 E3
Derby St *KVGV* G3 .... 30 C1
Derby Terrace La *KVGV* G3 .... 18 B5
Derwent St *PPK/MIL* G22 .... 8 C4
Despard Av *CAR/SHTL* G32 .... 107 D2
Despard Gdns *CAR/SHTL* G32 .... 108 A2 🟦
Deveron Av *GIF/THBK* G46 .... 126 B4
Deveron Rd *BSDN* G61 .... 65 C4
Deveron St *STPS/GTHM/RID* G33 .... 96 B1
Devol Crs *PLK/PH/NH* G53 .... 110 B2
Devon Gdns *BSHPBGS* G64 .... 68 B3
Devon Pl *GVH/MTFL* G42 .... 44 C5
Devonshire Gardens La
KVD/HLHD G12 .... 5 D3
Devonshire Ter *KVD/HLHD* G12 .... 5 D3
Devonshire Terrace La
KVD/HLHD G12 .... 4 C3
Devon St *GBLS* G5 .... 44 C5
Diana Av *KNTSWD* G13 .... 72 B2
Dick St *MRYH/FIRH* G20 .... 19 F1
Dilwara Av *SCOT* G14 .... 14 C3

Dinard Dr *GIF/THBK* G46 .... 126 A2
Dinart St *STPS/GTHM/RID* G33 .... 96 B1
Dinmont Rd *PLKSD/SHW* G41 .... 114 B1
Dinwiddie St *SPRGB/BLRNK* G21 .... 25 E2
Dipple Pl *DRUM* G15 .... 64 B4
Dirleton Dr *PLKSD/SHW* G41 .... 115 C2
Dirleton Ga *BSDN* G61 .... 65 D3
Dixon Av *GVH/MTFL* G42 .... 56 C5
Dixon Rd *GVH/MTFL* G42 .... 57 D5
Dixon St *CGLE* G1 .... 33 D5
Dobbie's Loan *CGLW* G2 .... 21 F4
COWCAD G4 .... 21 F5 🟦
Dobbie's Loan Pl *COWCAD* G4 .... 34 A1
Dochart Av *RNFRW* PA4 .... 93 C1
Dochart St *STPS/GTHM/RID* G33 .... 89 C4
Dock St *CLYDBK* G81 .... 70 B3
Dodhill Pl *KNTSWD* G13 .... 72 B4
Dodside Gdns *CAR/SHTL* G32 .... 107 C2 🟦
Dodside Pl *CAR/SHTL* G32 .... 107 C2 🟦
Dodside St *CAR/SHTL* G32 .... 107 C2 🟦
Dolan St *BAIL/MDB/MHD* G69 .... 109 D1
Dollar Ter *MRYH/FIRH* G20 .... 76 A2 🟦
Dolphin Rd *PLKSD/SHW* G41 .... 54 B4
Donaldson Dr *RNFRW* PA4 .... 84 B3 🟦
Don Av *RNFRW* PA4 .... 85 C4
Doncaster St *MRYH/FIRH* G20 .... 8 A5
Don St *STPS/GTHM/RID* G33 .... 96 B2
Doon Crs *BSDN* G61 .... 65 C3
Doonfoot Rd *PLKSW/MSWD* G43 ..... 114 A4
Doon St *CLYDBK* G81 .... 62 A3 🟦
Dora St *DMNK/BRGTN* G40 .... 60 A2
Dorchester Av *KVD/HLHD* G12 .... 75 C4
Dorchester Ct *KVD/HLHD* G12 .... 75 C4
Dormanside Ct *PLK/PH/NH* G53 ...... 102 B3 🟦
Dormanside Ga *PLK/PH/NH* G53 ...... 102 B3 🟦
Dormanside Gv *PLK/PH/NH* G53 ...... 102 B3 🟦
Dormanside Rd *PLK/PH/NH* G53 ...... 102 B2 🟦
Dornal Av *KNTSWD* G13 .... 71 C3
Dornford Av *CAR/SHTL* G32 .... 107 D4
Dornford Rd *CAR/SHTL* G32 .... 107 D4 🟦
Dornoch Rd *BSDN* G61 .... 65 D4
Dornoch St *DMNK/BRGTN* G40 .... 47 E2
Dorset St *KVGV* G3 .... 31 E2
Dosk Av *KNTSWD* G13 .... 71 C2
Dosk Pl *KNTSWD* G13 .... 71 D2
Dougalston Rd *SMSTN* G23 .... 77 C1
Douglas Av *RUTH* G73 .... 132 A1
Douglas Dr *BAIL/MDB/MHD* G69 ..... 108 B1
BLTYR/CAMB G72 .... 133 D1
DRUM G15 .... 71 D1
Douglas Gdns *BSDN* G61 .... 66 B2
Douglas La *CGLW* G2 .... 32 B2 🟦
Douglas Pl *BSDN* G61 .... 66 A1 🟦
Douglas St *CGLW* G2 .... 32 B2
Douglas Ter *PLKSD/SHW* G41 .... 55 E3
Dougrie Dr *CSMK* G45 .... 129 D3
Dougrie Pl *CSMK* G45 .... 130 A3
Dougrie Rd *CSMK* G45 .... 129 D3
Dougrie St *CSMK* G45 .... 129 D3
Dougrie Ter *CSMK* G45 .... 129 D3
Dougrie Gdns *CSMK* G45 .... 129 D4
Doune Crs *BSHPBGS* G64 .... 69 D2
Doune Gdns *MRYH/FIRH* G20 .... 7 D5
Doune Gardens La *MRYH/FIRH* G20 .... 7 D5
Doune Qd *MRYH/FIRH* G20 .... 7 D5
Dovecot *PLKSW/MSWD* G43 .... 114 A2 🟦
Dover St *KVGV* G3 .... 31 E2
Dove St *PLK/PH/NH* G53 .... 122 A1
Dowanhill St *PTCK* G11 .... 17 E3
Dowanside Rd *KVD/HLHD* G12 .... 17 F1
Downcraig Dr *CSMK* G45 .... 129 C4
Downcraig Gv *CSMK* G45 .... 129 C4 🟦

Downcraig Rd *CSMK* G45 .... 129 C4
Downcraig Ter *CSMK* G45 .... 129 D4
Downfield St *CAR/SHTL* G32 .... 105 C3
Downhill St *KVD/HLHD* G12 .... 17 F2
Downiebrae Rd *RUTH* G73 .... 61 E4
Downs St *SPRGB/BLRNK* G21 ...... 11 F3
Dowrie Crs *PLK/PH/NH* G53 .... 110 B1
Drakemire Av *CSMK* G45 .... 129 C2
Drakemire Dr *CSMK* G45 .... 128 B4
Drake St *DMNK/BRGTN* G40 .... 47 D2
Dreghorn St *DEN/PKHD* G31 .... 37 E4
Drive Rd *GOV/IBX* G51 .... 27 D2
Drochil St *ESTRH* G34 .... 101 C1
Drumbeg Dr *PLK/PH/NH* G53 ..... 110 A4
Drumbottie Rd *SPRGB/BLRNK* G21 .... 12 A2
Drumchapel Gdns *DRUM* G15 ...... 64 A4 🔢
Drumchapel Pl *DRUM* G15 .... 64 B4
Drumchapel Rd *DRUM* G15 .... 64 B4
Drumclog Gdns
  STPS/GTHM/RID G33 .... 83 D4 🔢
Drumcross Rd *PLK/PH/NH* G53 .... 111 C1
Drumhead Pl *CAR/SHTL* G32 .... 121 D1
Drumhead Rd *CAR/SHTL* G32 ...... 121 D1
Drumilaw Rd *RUTH* G73 .... 131 C1
Drumilaw Wy *RUTH* G73 .... 131 C1 🔢
Drumlaken Av *MRYH/FIRH* G20 .... 76 A1 🔢
Drumlaken Ct *MRYH/FIRH* G20 .... 76 A1 🔢
Drumlaken St *MRYH/FIRH* G20 .... 76 A1
Drumlochy Rd *STPS/GTHM/RID* G33 .... 98 A1
Drummond Av *RUTH* G73 .... 118 B2 🔢
Drummore Rd *DRUM* G15 .... 64 A1
Drumover Dr *DEN/PKHD* G31 ...... 105 C2
Drumoyne Av *GOV/IBX* G51 .... 27 D3
Drumoyne Circ *GOV/IBX* G51 ...... 27 D5
Drumoyne Dr *GOV/IBX* G51 .... 27 D3
Drumoyne Pl *GOV/IBX* G51 .... 39 D1
Drumoyne Qd *GOV/IBX* G51 .... 27 D5 🔢
Drumoyne Rd *GOV/IBX* G51 .... 27 D4
  GOV/IBX G51 .... 38 C1
Drumoyne Sq *GOV/IBX* G51 .... 26 C4
Drumpark St *GIF/THBK* G46 .... 124 B2 🔢
Drumpellier Av
  BAIL/MDB/MHD G69 .... 109 D3
Drumpellier Pl
  BAIL/MDB/MHD G69 .... 109 D2 🔢
Drumpellier Rd
  BAIL/MDB/MHD G69 .... 109 D3
Drumpellier St *STPS/GTHM/RID* G33 .. 88 B4
Drumreoch Dr *GVH/MTFL* G42 ..... 118 A3
Drumreoch Pl *GVH/MTFL* G42 ..... 118 A2
Drumry Rd *CLYDBK* G81 .... 62 A3
Drumry Rd East *DRUM* G15 .... 63 D4
Drumsargard Rd *RUTH* G73 .... 132 B1
Drums Rd *PLK/PH/NH* G53 .... 102 A3
Drury St *CGLW* G2 .... 33 D3
Dryad St *GIF/THBK* G46 .... 124 A1
Dryburgh Av *RUTH* G73 .... 119 D3
Dryburgh Gdns *MRYH/FIRH* G20 .. 7 E5
Dryburn Av *CARD/HILL/MSPK* G52 .. 102 A1
Drygate *COWCAD* G4 .... 34 C3
Drygrange Rd *STPS/GTHM/RID* G33 .. 91 D4
Drymen Rd *BSDN* G61 .... 66 A1
Drymen St *CARD/HILL/MSPK* G52 .. 39 D3
Drynoch Pl *PPK/MIL* G22 .... 78 B3
Drysdale St *SCOT* G14 .... 85 D1
Duart St *MRYH/FIRH* G20 .... 76 A1
Dubton St *ESTRH* G34 .... 101 D1
Duchall Pl *SCOT* G14 .... 86 B2 🔢
Duchess Palace *RUTH* G73 .... 120 A2
Duchess Rd *RUTH* G73 .... 120 A1
Duchray La *STPS/GTHM/RID* G33 .. 96 B1 🔢
Duchray St *STPS/GTHM/RID* G33 .. 96 B1

Dudhope St *STPS/GTHM/RID* G33 .. 91 D4
Dudley Dr *KVD/HLHD* G12 .... 4 B5
  PTCK G11 .... 4 B5
Dudley La *KVD/HLHD* G12 .... 4 B5
Duffus St *ESTRH* G34 .... 100 B1
Duich Gdns *SMSTN* G23 .... 77 C1
Duke's Rd *RUTH* G73 .... 132 B1
Duke St *COWCAD* G4 .... 34 C4
  DEN/PKHD G31 .... 37 E5
Dulsie Rd *SPRGB/BLRNK* G21 ...... 82 A4 🔢
Dumbarton Rd *PTCK* G11 .... 15 F3
  SCOT G14 .... 71 C4
Dumbreck Av *CARD/HILL/MSPK* G52 .. 52 A1
  PLKSD/SHW G41 .... 40 B5
Dumbreck Ct *PLKSD/SHW* G41 .... 52 B1
Dumbreck Pth *PLKSD/SHW* G41 ... 40 B5 🔢
Dumbreck Pl *PLKSD/SHW* G41 ..... 52 B1
Dumbreck Rd *GOV/IBX* G51 .... 40 B3
  PLKSD/SHW G41 .... 40 B4
Dumbreck Sq *PLKSD/SHW* G41 ... 40 B5 🔢
Dunagoil Rd *CSMK* G45 .... 129 D3
Dunagoil St *CSMK* G45 .... 130 A4
Dunalastair Dr *STPS/GTHM/RID* G33 .. 90 B1
Dunan Pl *STPS/GTHM/RID* G33 .... 100 A3 🔢
Dunard Rd *RUTH* G73 .... 119 D3
Dunard St *MRYH/FIRH* G20 .... 7 F4
Dunaskin St *PTCK* G11 .... 17 E4
Dunbar Av *RUTH* G73 .... 120 A3
Dunblane St *CGLW* G2 .... 21 D5
  COWCAD G4 .... 21 D4
Duncan Av *SCOT* G14 .... 87 C3
Duncan La North *SCOT* G14 .... 87 C2 🔢
Duncan La South *SCOT* G14 .... 87 C2 🔢
Duncansby Rd
  STPS/GTHM/RID G33 .... 99 D4 🔢
Dunchattan Pl *DEN/PKHD* G31 .... 35 E5
Dunchattan St *DEN/PKHD* G31 .... 35 E3
Dunclutha St *DMNK/BRGTN* G40 .. 60 C3
Duncombe St *MRYH/FIRH* G20 .... 76 B3
Duncrub Dr *BSHPBGS* G64 .... 80 A1
Duncruin St *MRYH/FIRH* G20 ...... 76 A3
Duncruin Ter *MRYH/FIRH* G20 ..... 76 B3
Duncryne Av *CAR/SHTL* G32 .... 107 D2
Duncryne Gdns *CAR/SHTL* G32 .... 108 A2 🔢
Duncryne Pl *BSHPBGS* G64 .... 80 A2
Duncryne Rd *CAR/SHTL* G32 .... 107 D2 🔢
Dundashill *COWCAD* G4 .... 21 D3
Dundas La *CGLE* G1 .... 33 E2
Dundas St *CGLE* G1 .... 33 E2
Dundee Dr *CARD/HILL/MSPK* G52 .. 102 B3
Dundonald Rd *KVD/HLHD* G12 ..... 5 F4 🔢
Dundrennan Rd *GVH/MTFL* G42 ... 115 D3
Dunearn St *COWCAD* G4 .... 19 F3
Dunellan St *CARD/HILL/MSPK* G52 .. 39 D3
Dunglass Av *SCOT* G14 .... 87 C2 🔢
Dunglass La *SCOT* G14 .... 87 C2 🔢
Dunglass La North *SCOT* G14 ...... 87 C2 🔢
Dunglass La South *SCOT* G14 ...... 87 C2 🔢
Dungoyne St *MRYH/FIRH* G20 ..... 76 A2 🔢
Dunira St *CAR/SHTL* G32 .... 105 D3
Dunivaig St *STPS/GTHM/RID* G33 .. 99 D2
Dunkeld Av *RUTH* G73 .... 119 D3
Dunkeld Dr *BSDN* G61 .... 67 D2
Dunkeld St *DEN/PKHD* G31 .... 49 F4
Dunkenny Rd *DRUM* G15 .... 63 D2
Dunlop St *CGLE* G1 .... 45 E1
  RNFRW PA4 .... 84 B2 🔢
Dunmore St *CLYDBK* G81 .... 70 A2
Dunnichen Gdns *BSHPBGS* G64 ... 82 B1
Dunning St *DEN/PKHD* G31 .... 104 B2 🔢
Dunnottar St *STPS/GTHM/RID* G33 .. 90 B4
Dunn St *DMNK/BRGTN* G40 .... 59 F1
Dunolly St *SPRGB/BLRNK* G21 .... 24 A4

Dunragit St *DEN/PKHD* G31 ....37 E4
Dunrobin St *DEN/PKHD* G31..............49 D1
Dunrod Rd *CAR/SHTL* G32 ....106 B2
Dunside Dr *PLK/PH/NH* G53 ....110 A4
Dunsmuir St *GOV/IBX* G51...............28 C4
Dunsyre Pl *SMSTN* G23 ....77 C1 ⬚
Dunsyre St *STPS/GTHM/RID* G33 ....97 C2 ⬚
Duntarvie Pl *ESTRH* G34 ....101 D2 ⬚
Duntarvie Cl *ESTRH* G34 ....101 D2 ⬚
Duntarvie Rd *ESTRH* G34 ....101 D2
Dunterlie Av *KNTSWD* G13 ....72 A4
Duntreath Av *DRUM* G15 ....63 D4
   KNTSWD G13 ....71 C2
Duntreath Dr *DRUM* G15 ....71 D1
Duntreath Gdns *DRUM* G15 ....63 D4
Duntreath Gv *DRUM* G15 ....71 D1 ⬚
Duntroon St *DEN/PKHD* G31 ....36 C1
Dunure Dr *RUTH* G73 ....130 B1
Dunure St *MRYH/FIRH* G20 ....76 B3
Dunvegan Dr *BSHPBGS* G64 ....69 C2
Dunwan Av *KNTSWD* G13 ....71 D3
Dunwan Pl *KNTSWD* G13 ....71 D3
Durham St *PLKSD/SHW* G41 ....42 B3
Durness Av *BSDN* G61 ....67 D1
Duror St *CAR/SHTL* G32 ....98 A4
Durris Gdns *CAR/SHTL* G32 ....107 D3 ⬚
Durward Av *PLKSD/SHW* G41 ....114 B1
Durward Ct *PLKSD/SHW* G41 ....54 B5
Duthil St *GOV/IBX* G51 ....26 B5
Dyce La *PTCK* G11..............16 B2
Dyer's La *CGLE* G1..............46 A1
Dykebar Av *KNTSWD* G13 ....72 A4
Dykehead La *STPS/GTHM/RID* G33 ....99 D3
Dykehead St *STPS/GTHM/RID* G33 ....99 D3
Dykemuir Pl *SPRGB/BLRNK* G21 ....12 C4
Dykemuir Qd *SPRGB/BLRNK* G21 ....12 A4 ⬚
Dykemuir St *SPRGB/BLRNK* G21 ....12 B4
Dyke Rd *KNTSWD* G13 ....71 D4

E

Eaglesham Ct *GOV/IBX* G51 ....42 C1 ⬚
Eaglesham Pl *GOV/IBX* G51 ....42 C1 ⬚
Eagle St *COWCAD* G4 ....21 E2
Earlbank Av *SCOT* G14..............87 C2
Earlbank La North *SCOT* G14 ....87 C2 ⬚
Earlbank La South *SCOT* G14 ....87 C2
Earl Haig Rd *CARD/HILL/MSPK* G52 ....93 D3
Earl La *SCOT* G14..............87 C3
Earl Pl *SCOT* G14 ....87 C2 ⬚
Earlspark Av *PLKSW/MSWD* G43 ....115 D4
Earl St *SCOT* G14 ....86 B2
Earn Av *BSDN* G61 ....67 D2
   RNFRW PA4 ....85 C4
Earnock St *STPS/GTHM/RID* G33 ....88 B2
Earnside St *CAR/SHTL* G32 ....106 B1 ⬚
Earn St *STPS/GTHM/RID* G33 ....97 C1
Easdale Dr *CAR/SHTL* G32 ....105 D2
East Av *RNFRW* PA4 ....84 B3
Eastbank Dr *CAR/SHTL* G32 ....107 C1 ⬚
East Barns St *CLYDBK* G81 ....70 B2
East Bath La *CGLE* G1 ....33 E2
Eastburn Crs *SPRGB/BLRNK* G21 ....81 D4 ⬚
East Campbell St *COWCAD* G4 ....34 C5
Eastcote Av *SCOT* G14 ....3 D4
Eastcroft *RUTH* G73 ....119 D2
Eastcroft Ter *SPRGB/BLRNK* G21 ....12 A4
Easter Craigs *DEN/PKHD* G31..............37 D3
Easterhill Pl *CAR/SHTL* G32 ....105 D3 ⬚
Easterhill St *CAR/SHTL* G32 ....105 D3

Easterhouse Rd
   BAIL/MDB/MHD G69 ....109 D1
Easter Queenslie Rd
   STPS/GTHM/RID G33 ....100 A2
Eastfield Av *BLTYR/CAMB* G72 ....133 C1
Eastfield Rd *SPRGB/BLRNK* G21 ....11 D3
East Hallhill Rd
   BAIL/MDB/MHD G69 ....100 B4
Easthall Pl *STPS/GTHM/RID* G33 ....100 B3 ⬚
East Kilbride Rd *RUTH* G73 ....132 A1
Eastmuir St *CAR/SHTL* G32 ....106 B1
East Springfield Ter *BSHPBGS* G64 ....81 D2
Eastvale Pl *KVGV* G3..............29 E1
East Wellington St
   DEN/PKHD G31 ....104 B1 ⬚
Eastwood Av *GIF/THBK* G46 ....126 A4
   PLKSD/SHW G41 ....114 B2
Eastwood Crs *GIF/THBK* G46 ....124 B2 ⬚
Eccles St *PPK/MIL* G22 ....11 D1
Eckford St *CAR/SHTL* G32 ....106 A2 ⬚
Eday St *PPK/MIL* G22 ....79 D4
Edderton Pl
   STPS/GTHM/RID G33 ....101 C3 ⬚
Eddlewood Ct
   STPS/GTHM/RID G33 ....101 C3 ⬚
Eddlewood Pth
   STPS/GTHM/RID G33 ....100 B3 ⬚
Eddlewood Pl
   STPS/GTHM/RID G33 ....100 B3
Eddlewood Rd
   STPS/GTHM/RID G33..............100 B3
Eden La *STPS/GTHM/RID* G33 ....96 B1
Eden Pl *RNFRW* PA4 ....85 C4
Eden St *STPS/GTHM/RID* G33 ....96 B1
Edenwood St *DEN/PKHD* G31 ....105 C1 ⬚
Edgam Dr *CARD/HILL/MSPK* G52 ....103 C1
Edgefauld Av *SPRGB/BLRNK* G21 ....11 F5
Edgefauld Dr *SPRGB/BLRNK* G21..............11 F4
Edgefauld Pl *SPRGB/BLRNK* G21 ....11 E2
Edgefauld Rd *SPRGB/BLRNK* G21 ....11 F3
Edgehill La *PTCK* G11 ....4 A4
Edgehill Rd *PTCK* G11 ....3 F4
Edgemont St *PLKSD/SHW* G41..............115 D4
Edinbeg Av *GVH/MTFL* G42 ....118 A2
Edinbeg Pl *GVH/MTFL* G42 ....118 A2 ⬚
Edinburgh Rd *CAR/SHTL* G32 ....98 A3
   STPS/GTHM/RID G33 ....97 C3 ⬚
Edington St *COWCAD* G4..............20 C3
Edison St *CARD/HILL/MSPK* G52..............93 C3
Edmiston Dr *GOV/IBX* G51 ....40 B1
Edrom Ct *CAR/SHTL* G32 ....105 D1
Edrom St *CAR/SHTL* G32 ....105 D2
Edward Av *RNFRW* PA4 ....84 B2
Edward St *CLYDBK* G81 ....70 B3
Edwin St *GOV/IBX* G51 ....42 B2
Edzell Ct *SCOT* G14 ....14 A2
Edzell Gdns *BSHPBGS* G64..............82 A2
Edzell Pl *SCOT* G14 ....14 A2
Edzell St *SCOT* G14 ....14 A2
Egidia Av *GIF/THBK* G46 ....126 A4 ⬚
Egilsay Crs *PPK/MIL* G22 ....79 C2
Egilsay Pl *PPK/MIL* G22 ....79 C2
Egilsay St *PPK/MIL* G22 ....79 C2
Egilsay Ter *PPK/MIL* G22 ....79 C2 ⬚
Eglinton Ct *GBLS* G5..............44 C3
Eglinton Dr *GIF/THBK* G46..............126 A4
Eglinton St *GBLS* G5..............44 C5
Eileen Gdns *BSHPBGS* G64 ....69 D4
Elcho St *DMNK/BRGTN* G40..............47 E1
Elderbank *BSDN* G61 ....66 A3
Elderpark Gdns *GOV/IBX* G51 ....27 F3
Elderpark Gv *GOV/IBX* G51 ....27 F3

Elderpark St *GOV/IBX* G51.................... 27 F3
Elderslie St *KVGV* G3............................ 31 E1
Elder St *GOV/IBX* G51........................... 27 F3
Eldon Gdns *BSHPBGS* G64.................... 80 A1
Eldon St *KVGV* G3................................. 19 D3
Elibank St *STPS/GTHM/RID* G33......... 98 A1
Elie St *PTCK* G11.................................... 17 F3
Elizabeth Crs *GIF/THBK* G46................ 125 C4
Elizabeth St *GOV/IBX* G51.................... 41 E2
Ellangowan Rd *PLKSD/SHW* G41 .... 114 A4
Ellergreen Rd *BSDN* G61........................ 66 A2
Ellesmere St *PPK/MIL* G22 .... 8 B4
Elliot Av *GIF/THBK* G46....................... 126 A4
Elliot Dr *GIF/THBK* G46................. 126 A3 🖸
Elliot Pl *KVGV* G3................................. 31 D3
Elliot St *KVGV* G3................................. 31 D4
Ellisland Av *CLYDBK* G81..................... 62 A3
Ellisland Crs *CSMK* G45................. 130 B1 🖸
Ellisland Rd *PLKSW/MSWD* G43......... 114 B4
Elliston Av *PLK/PH/NH* G53................. 123 C1
Elliston Crs *PLK/PH/NH* G53................ 123 C1
Elliston Dr *PLK/PH/NH* G53.................. 123 C1
Elm Av *RNFRW* PA4................................ 84 A2
Elm Bank *BSHPBGS* G64........................ 81 D2
Elmbank Crs *CGLW* G2.......................... 32 A2
Elmbank St *CGLW* G2............................ 32 A2
Elmbank Street La *KVGV* G3................. 32 A2
Elmfoot St *GBLS* G5............................... 58 B3
Elmore Av *LNPK/KPK* G44.................... 128 B1
Elm Rd *RUTH* G73................................. 131 D2
Elm St *SCOT* G14................................... 14 B1
Elmvale Rw *SPRGB/BLRNK* G21 .... 10 C3
Elmvale St *PPK/MIL* G22 .... 10 C2
Elmwood Av *PTCK* G11............................ 3 E4
Elmwood La *PTCK* G11............................ 3 E4
Elphinstone Pl *GOV/IBX* G51................ 29 E3
Elphin St *SMSTN* G23............................ 76 B1
Elrig Rd *LNPK/KPK* G44....................... 127 D1
Eltham St *PPK/MIL* G22........................... 8 C5
Elvan St *CAR/SHTL* G32...................... 105 D1
Embo Dr *KNTSWD* G13................... 72 B4 🖸
Emerson Rd *BSHPBGS* G64.................... 81 C2
Emerson Rd West *BSHPBGS* G64.......... 81 C1
Emerson St *MRYH/FIRH* G20................. 78 A4
Endfield Av *KVD/HLHD* G12.................. 75 D3
Endrick Bank *BSHPBGS* G64........... 69 C2 🖸
Endrick Dr *BSDN* G61............................ 66 B2
Endrick St *SPRGB/BLRNK* G21 .... 10 B5
Ensay St *PPK/MIL* G22.................... 79 D3 🖸
Enterkin St *CAR/SHTL* G32.................. 105 D2 🖸
Eriboll Pl *PPK/MIL* G22.......................... 78 B3
Eriboll St *PPK/MIL* G22.......................... 78 B3
Ericht Rd *PLKSW/MSWD* G43.............. 126 A1
Eriska Av *SCOT* G14............................... 86 A1
Erradale St *PPK/MIL* G22....................... 78 A3
Errogie St *ESTRH* G34......................... 101 D2
Erskine Av *PLKSD/SHW* G41................. 41 D5
Erskine Sq *CARD/HILL/MSPK* G52....... 93 D3
Esk Av *RNFRW* PA4................................ 85 C4
Eskbank St *CAR/SHTL* G32.................... 98 A4
Eskdale Dr *RUTH* G73........................... 120 B3
Eskdale Rd *BSDN* G61........................... 65 C4
Esk St *SCOT* G14................................... 85 D1
Esmond St *KVGV* G3.............................. 17 F5
Essenside Av *DRUM* G15....................... 65 C4
Essex Dr *SCOT* G14................................. 2 C4
Essex La *SCOT* G14................................. 2 C4
Esslemont Av *SCOT* G14........................ 86 B2
Etive Av *BSDN* G61................................ 67 D2
Etive Ct *CLYDBK* G81............................ 62 A4
Etive Crs *BSHPBGS* G64........................ 81 D1
Etive St *CAR/SHTL* G32....................... 106 A1

Eton La *KVD/HLHD* G12........................ 18 C2
Ettrick Av *RNFRW* PA4.......................... 85 D4
Ettrick Crs *RUTH* G73.......................... 120 A3
Ettrick Pl *PLKSW/MSWD* G43............. 114 B3
Evan Crs *GIF/THBK* G46...................... 126 B4
Evanton Dr *GIF/THBK* G46.................. 124 A3
Evanton Pl *GIF/THBK* G46.................. 124 A3
Everard Ct *SPRGB/BLRNK* G21............. 80 A3
Everard Dr *SPRGB/BLRNK* G21............ 80 A4
Everard Pl *SPRGB/BLRNK* G21....... 80 A3 🖸
Everard Qd *SPRGB/BLRNK* G21............ 80 A3
Eversley St *CAR/SHTL* G32................. 106 A3 🖸
Everton Rd *PLK/PH/NH* G53................ 103 C3 🖸
Ewing Pl *DEN/PKHD* G31...................... 49 F3
Ewing St *RUTH* G73............................. 119 C3
Exeter Dr *PTCK* G11.............................. 16 A3
Eynort St *PPK/MIL* G22......................... 78 A3
Eyrepoint Ct
    STPS/GTHM/RID G33.................... 98 A2 🖸

F

Fairbairn Crs *GIF/THBK* G46............... 125 C4
Fairburn St *CAR/SHTL* G32................. 105 D2
Fairfax Av *LNPK/KPK* G44................... 129 C1
Fairfield Dr *RNFRW* PA4....................... 92 B1
Fairfield Gdns *GOV/IBX* G51................ 27 F2
Fairfield Pl *GOV/IBX* G51..................... 27 F2
Fairfield St *GOV/IBX* G51..................... 27 F2
Fairhaven Rd *SMSTN* G23..................... 76 B2
Fairhill Av *PLK/PH/NH* G53................. 111 C3
Fairholm St *CAR/SHTL* G32................. 105 D2 🖸
Fairley St *GOV/IBX* G51........................ 41 D1
Fairlie Park Dr *PTCK* G11..................... 16 B3
Fairway *BSDN* G61................................ 64 B1
Falcon Ter *MRYH/FIRH* G20................. 76 A2
Falcon Terrace La *MRYH/FIRH* G20 ... 76 A2
Falfield St *GBLS* G5............................... 44 B4
Falkland Crs *BSHPBGS* G64.................. 82 B2
Falklandcrs *BSHPBGS* G64.................... 82 B1
Falkland La *KVD/HLHD* G12................... 5 D5
Falkland St *KVD/HLHD* G12.................... 4 C5
Falloch Rd *BSDN* G61............................ 65 C4
    GVH/MTFL G42................................ 116 A3
Falside Rd *CAR/SHTL* G32................... 106 A4
Fara St *SMSTN* G23................................ 77 D2
Farie St *RUTH* G73............................... 118 B2
Farmeloan Rd *RUTH* G73...................... 119 D2
Farmington Av *CAR/SHTL* G32 .... 107 D1 🖸
Farmington Gdns
    CAR/SHTL G32................................ 107 D1 🖸
Farmington Gv *CAR/SHTL* G32 .... 107 D1 🖸
Farm Rd *PLKSD/SHW* G41.................... 40 C3
Farne Dr *LNPK/KPK* G44...................... 128 B2
Farnell St *COWCAD* G4......................... 20 C2
Faskally Av *BSHPBGS* G64.................... 68 A3
Fasque Pl *DRUM* G15............................ 63 C2
Fauldhouse St *GBLS* G5........................ 58 A2
Fauldshead Rd *RNFRW* PA4................. 84 A3
Fearnmore Rd *MRYH/FIRH* G20........... 76 B3
Felton Pl *KNTSWD* G13......................... 71 D3
Fendoch St *CAR/SHTL* G32................. 106 A2
Fenella St *CAR/SHTL* G32................... 106 B1 🖸
Fennsbank Av *RUTH* G73..................... 132 B3
Fenwick Rd *GIF/THBK* G46................. 126 A3
Fereneze Crs *KNTSWD* G13.................. 71 D3
Fergus Dr *MRYH/FIRH* G20.................... 7 D4
Fergus La *MRYH/FIRH* G20..................... 7 E4
Ferguson Av *RNFRW* PA4..................... 84 B3
Ferguson St *RNFRW* PA4...................... 84 B3

Ferguston Rd *BSDN* G61 .... **66** B2
Fernan St *CAR/SHTL* G32 .... **105** D1
Fern Av *BSHPBGS* G64 .... **81** D2
Fernbank St *PPK/MIL* G22 .... **11** D2
Fernbrae Av *RUTH* G73 .... **131** D4
Fernbrae Wy *RUTH* G73 .... **131** D3 ⓘ
Ferncroft Dr *LNPK/KPK* G44 .... **129** D1
Ferndale Dr *SMSTN* G23 .... **76** B2
Ferndale Gdns *SMSTN* G23 .... **76** A2
Ferndale Gdns *SMSTN* G23 .... **76** B2
Ferndale Pl *SMSTN* G23 .... **76** B2
Ferness Ov *SPRGB/BLRNK* G21 .... **82** A3
Ferness Pl *SPRGB/BLRNK* G21 .... **82** A3 ⓘ
Ferness Rd *SPRGB/BLRNK* G21 .... **82** A4
Ferngrove Av *KVD/HLHD* G12 .... **75** D4 ⓘ
Fernhill Rd *RUTH* G73 .... **131** C1
Fernie Gdns *MRYH/FIRH* G20 .... **77** C3 ⓘ
Fern La *KNTSWD* G13 .... **3** E1
Fernlea *BSDN* G61 .... **66** A3
Fernleigh Rd *PLKSW/MSWD* G43 ... **126** B1
Ferryden St *SCOT* G14 .... **14** C3
Ferry Rd *KVGV* G3 .... **17** E5
 RNFRW PA4 .... **84** B2
Fersit St *PLKSW/MSWD* G43 .... **114** A4 ⓘ
Fetlar Dr *LNPK/KPK* G44 .... **129** C1
Fettercairn Av *DRUM* G15 .... **63** C2
Fettes St *STPS/GTHM/RID* G33 .... **97** D2
Fidra St *STPS/GTHM/RID* G33 .... **97** D2 ⓘ
Fielden Pl *DMNK/BRGTN* G40 .... **48** B3
Fielden St *DMNK/BRGTN* G40 .... **48** B3
Fieldhead Dr *PLKSW/MSWD* G43 ... **125** C1
Fieldhead Sq *PLKSW/MSWD* G43 .. **125** C1 ⓘ
Fife Av *CARD/HILL/MSPK* G52 ...... **102** B2
Fife Wy *BSHPBGS* G64 .... **82** B2
Fifth Av *KVD/HLHD* G12 .... **3** F1
 RNFRW PA4 .... **84** A4
 STPS/GTHM/RID G33 .... **90** B1 ⓘ
Fifty Pitches Pl *GOV/IBX* G51 .... **95** C3
Fifty Pitches Rd *GOV/IBX* G51 .... **94** B4
Finch Dr *KNTSWD* G13 .... **71** D2
Findhorn Av *RNFRW* PA4 .... **85** C3
Findhorn St *STPS/GTHM/RID* G33 ... **96** B3 ⓘ
Findochty St *STPS/GTHM/RID* G33 .. **100** A1
Fingal La *MRYH/FIRH* G20 .... **76** A3 ⓘ
Fingal St *MRYH/FIRH* G20 .... **76** B3
Fingask St *CAR/SHTL* G32 .... **107** C2
Finglen Pl *PLK/PH/NH* G53 .... **122** B2
Finhaven St *CAR/SHTL* G32 .... **105** C3
Finlas Pl *PPK/MIL* G22 .... **10** A3
Finlay Dr *DEN/PKHD* G31 .... **36** B4
Finnart Sq *DMNK/BRGTN* G40 .... **59** F1
Finnart St *DMNK/BRGTN* G40 .... **59** F1
Finnieston Sq *KVGV* G3 .... **31** D2
Finnieston St *KVGV* G3 .... **31** D3
Finsbay St *GOV/IBX* G51 .... **26** B5
Fintry Crs *BSHPBGS* G64 .... **82** A1
Fintry Dr *LNPK/KPK* G44 .... **117** C3
Firdon Crs *DRUM* G15 .... **72** A1
Firhill Rd *MRYH/FIRH* G20 .... **8** A3
Firhill St *MRYH/FIRH* G20 .... **8** A4
Firpark Rd *BSHPBGS* G64 .... **81** D2
Firpark St *DEN/PKHD* G31 .... **35** E2
Firpark Ter *DEN/PKHD* G31 .... **35** E3
Fir Pl *BAIL/MDB/MHD* G69 .... **109** C3 ⓘ
First Av *BSDN* G61 .... **67** C3
 LNPK/KPK G44 .... **127** D4
 RNFRW PA4 .... **84** A4 ⓘ
 STPS/GTHM/RID G33 .... **90** B1
First Gdns *PLKSW/SHW* G41 .... **40** B5
Firwood Dr *LNPK/KPK* G44 .... **117** C4
Fishescoates Av *RUTH* G73 .... **132** A2 ⓘ
 RUTH G73 .... **132** B1 ⓘ

Fishescoates Gdns *RUTH* G73 ...... **132** B1 ⓘ
Fitzroy La *KVGV* G3 .... **30** C1
Fleet Av *RNFRW* PA4 .... **93** C1
Fleet St *CAR/SHTL* G32 .... **106** B2
Fleming Av *CLYDBK* G81 .... **70** B2
Fleming St *DEN/PKHD* G31 .... **37** D5
Flemington St *SPRGB/BLRNK* G21 ... **11** E5
Fleurs Av *PLKSD/SHW* G41 .... **52** C1
Fleurs Rd *PLKSD/SHW* G41 .... **40** C5
Florence Dr *GIF/THBK* G46 .... **126** A4
Florence Gdns *RUTH* G73 .... **132** A3
Florence St *GBLS* G5 .... **45** F3
Florida Av *GVH/MTFL* G42 .... **116** B2
Florida Crs *GVH/MTFL* G42 .... **116** B2
Florida Dr *GVH/MTFL* G42 .... **116** A2 ⓘ
Florida Gdns
 BAIL/MDB/MHD G69 .... **109** C1 ⓘ
Florida Sq *GVH/MTFL* G42 .... **116** B2
Florida St *GVH/MTFL* G42 .... **116** B2
Flowerdale Pl *PLK/PH/NH* G53 ..... **122** B3 ⓘ
Fochabers Dr *CARD/HILL/MSPK* G52.. **95** C4
Fogo Pl *MRYH/FIRH* G20 .... **76** B3 ⓘ
Forbes Dr *DMNK/BRGTN* G40 .... **47** E2 ⓘ
Forbes St *DMNK/BRGTN* G40 .... **47** E1
Fordneuk St *DMNK/BRGTN* G40... **48** A2
Ford Rd *KVD/HLHD* G12 .... **6** A3
Fordyce St *PTCK* G11 .... **17** D3
Foresthall Crs *SPRGB/BLRNK* G21 .. **12** A5
Foresthall Dr *SPRGB/BLRNK* G21 ... **12** A5
Fore St *SCOT* G14 .... **87** C3
Forfar Av *CARD/HILL/MSPK* G52 ... **102** B2
Forfar Crs *BSHPBGS* G64 .... **82** A2
Forgan Gdns *BSHPBGS* G64 .... **82** B2
Forge Pl *SPRGB/BLRNK* G21 .... **25** D1
Forge St *SPRGB/BLRNK* G21 .... **24** C3
Forglen St *ESTRH* G34 .... **101** D1
Formby Dr *SMSTN* G23 .... **76** B2
Forres Av *GIF/THBK* G46 .... **126** B3
Forres Ga *GIF/THBK* G46 .... **126** A4
Forres St *SMSTN* G23 .... **77** C1 ⓘ
Forrester Ct *BSHPBGS* G64 .... **80** B2 ⓘ
Forrestfield St *SPRGB/BLRNK* G21... **24** A5
Forrest St *DMNK/BRGTN* G40 .... **48** A3 ⓘ
Forth Rd *BSDN* G61 .... **65** D4
Forth St *CLYDBK* G81 .... **70** A2
 PLKSD/SHW G41 .... **55** F2
Forties Ct *GIF/THBK* G46 .... **124** B3 ⓘ
Forties Crs *GIF/THBK* G46 .... **124** B1
Forties Gdns *GIF/THBK* G46 .... **125** C1 ⓘ
Forties Wy *GIF/THBK* G46 .... **125** C1 ⓘ
Fortingall Av *KVD/HLHD* G12 .... **76** A4 ⓘ
Fortingall Pl *KVD/HLHD* G12 .... **76** A4
Fortrose St *PTCK* G11 .... **16** C2
Foswell Pl *DRUM* G15 .... **63** D1
Fotheringay La *PLKSD/SHW* G41 .... **54** A3
Fotheringay Rd *PLKSD/SHW* G41 .... **54** B3
Foulis La *KNTSWD* G13 .... **74** B4
Foulis St *KNTSWD* G13 .... **74** B4 ⓘ
Fountainwell Av *COWCAD* G4 .... **22** B2
Fountainwell Dr *COWCAD* G4 .... **22** B2
Fountainwell Pl *COWCAD* G4 .... **22** B2
Fountainwell Rd *COWCAD* G4 .... **22** B2
Fountainwell Sq *COWCAD* G4 .... **22** C2
Fountainwell Ter
 SPRGB/BLRNK G21 .... **22** C2
Fourth Av *RNFRW* PA4 .... **84** A4
 STPS/GTHM/RID G33 .... **90** B1
Fourth Gdns *PLKSD/SHW* G41 .... **40** B5
Foxbar Dr *KNTSWD* G13 .... **72** B4
Foxglove Pl *PLK/PH/NH* G53 .... **122** B3
Foxhills Pl *SMSTN* G23 .... **77** C1
Fox St *CGLE* G1 .... **33** D5

Foyers Ter *SPRGB/BLRNK* G21 .... 12 A4
Francis St *GBLS* G5 .... 44 B4
Frankfield St *STPS/GTHM/RID* G33 ...... 88 B4
Frankfort St *PLKSD/SHW* G41 .... 115 C1
Franklin St *DMNK/BRGTN* G40 .... 59 E1
Fraser Av *RUTH* G73 .... 120 A3
Fraser St *BLTYR/CAMB* G72 .... 121 C4
Frazer St *DMNK/BRGTN* G40 .... 48 C3
Freeland Ct *PLK/PH/NH* G53 .... 111 C4 ⊡
Freeland Crs *PLK/PH/NH* G53 .... 110 B4
Freeland Dr *PLK/PH/NH* G53 .... 110 B4
French St *DMNK/BRGTN* G40 .... 59 E2
Freuchie St *ESTRH* G34 .... 101 D3
Friar Av *BSHPBGS* G64 .... 69 D2
Friarscourt Av *KNTSWD* G13 .... 73 D2
Friars Pl *KNTSWD* G13 .... 73 D2 ⊡
Fruin Rd *DRUM* G15 .... 71 D1
Fruin St *PPK/MIL* G22 .... 9 F3
Fulbar Av *RNFRW* PA4 .... 84 A2
Fulbar Ct *RNFRW* PA4 .... 84 A2 ⊡
Fulbar La *RNFRW* PA4 .... 84 B2 ⊡
Fulbar Rd *GOV/IBX* G51 .... 95 C3
Fulbar St *RNFRW* PA4 .... 84 B2
Fullarton Av *CAR/SHTL* G32 .... 106 A4
Fullarton La *CAR/SHTL* G32 .... 106 A4
Fulton St *KNTSWD* G13 .... 74 A3
Fulwood Av *KNTSWD* G13 .... 71 D3
Fulwood Pl *KNTSWD* G13 .... 71 D3
Fyvie Av *PLKSW/MSWD* G43 .... 125 C1

G

Gadie Av *RNFRW* PA4 .... 85 C4
Gadie St *STPS/GTHM/RID* G33 .... 96 B2
Gadloch St *PPK/MIL* G22 .... 79 C4
Gadsburn Ct *SPRGB/BLRNK* G21 .... 82 A4 ⊡
Gadshill St *SPRGB/BLRNK* G21 .... 23 E4
Gailes St *DMNK/BRGTN* G40 .... 49 D5
Gairbraid Av *MRYH/FIRH* G20 .... 76 A4
Gairbraid Ct *MRYH/FIRH* G20 .... 76 A4 ⊡
Gairbraid Pl *MRYH/FIRH* G20 .... 76 B4 ⊡
Gala Av *RNFRW* PA4 .... 85 C4
Gala St *STPS/GTHM/RID* G33 .... 89 C4
Galbraith Dr *GOV/IBX* G51 .... 26 B2
Galdenoch St *STPS/GTHM/RID* G33 .... 90 B4
Gallan Av *SMSTN* G23 .... 77 C1
Galloway Dr *RUTH* G73 .... 131 D3
Galloway St *SPRGB/BLRNK* G21 .... 80 B4
Gallowflat St *RUTH* G73 .... 119 D2 ⊡
Gallowgate *CGLE* G1 .... 34 B5
 COWCAD G4 .... 46 C1
 DEN/PKHD G31 .... 49 D2
 DMNK/BRGTN G40 .... 47 F1
Gamrie Dr *PLK/PH/NH* G53 .... 110 A3
Gamrie Gdns *PLK/PH/NH* G53 .... 110 A3
Gamrie Rd *PLK/PH/NH* G53 .... 110 A2
Gannochy Dr *BSHPBGS* G64 .... 82 A1
Gantock Crs *STPS/GTHM/RID* G33 ...... 98 B3
Gardner St *PTCK* G11 .... 17 D2
Gardyne St *ESTRH* G34 .... 101 C1 ⊡
Garfield St *DEN/PKHD* G31 .... 36 A5
Garforth Rd *BAIL/MDB/MHD* G69 ...... 108 B2
Gargrave Av *BAIL/MDB/MHD* G69 ...... 108 B2
Garion Dr *KNTSWD* G13 .... 86 B1 ⊡
Garlieston Rd *STPS/GTHM/RID* G33.. 100 A4
Garmouth Ct *GOV/IBX* G51 .... 28 A2
Garmouth Gdns *GOV/IBX* G51 .... 27 F2
Garmouth St *GOV/IBX* G51 .... 27 F2
Garnethill St *KVGV* G3 .... 20 B5

Garnet St *CGLW* G2 .... 20 A5
Garnock St *SPRGB/BLRNK* G21 .... 23 F3
Garrioch Crs *MRYH/FIRH* G20 .... 6 B2
Garrioch Dr *MRYH/FIRH* G20 .... 6 B2
Garriochmill Rd *MRYH/FIRH* G20 .... 6 B4
Garrioch Qd *MRYH/FIRH* G20 .... 6 B2
Garrioch Rd *MRYH/FIRH* G20 .... 6 B3
Garrowhill Dr *BAIL/MDB/MHD* G69 .. 108 B1
Garry Av *BSDN* G61 .... 67 C4
Garry St *LNPK/KPK* G44 .... 116 A3
Garscadden Rd *DRUM* G15 .... 63 D4
Garscadden Rd South *DRUM* G15 .. 71 D3 ⊡
 KNTSWD G13 .... 72 A2
Garscube Rd *COWCAD* G4 .... 20 C5
Gartconnell Rd *BSDN* G61 .... 66 A1 ⊡
Gartcraig Pl *STPS/GTHM/RID* G33 ...... 97 D1
Gartcraig Rd *STPS/GTHM/RID* G33 .... 97 C2
 STPS/GTHM/RID G33 .... 98 A1 ⊡
Gartferry St *SPRGB/BLRNK* G21 .... 12 A3
Garthamlock Rd
 STPS/GTHM/RID G33 .... 100 A1
Garthland Dr *DEN/PKHD* G31 .... 36 B4
Garth St *CGLE* G1 .... 33 F4
Gartloch Rd *STPS/GTHM/RID* G33 ...... 97 D1
Gartly St *LNPK/KPK* G44 .... 127 D2 ⊡
Gartmore Ter *BLTYR/CAMB* G72 .... 133 C3
Gartocher Dr *CAR/SHTL* G32 .... 107 C1
Gartocher Rd *CAR/SHTL* G32 .... 107 C1
Gartocher Ter *CAR/SHTL* G32 .... 107 C1
Gartons Rd *SPRGB/BLRNK* G21 .... 13 E2
Garturk St *GVH/MTFL* G42 .... 56 C4
Garvald Ct *DMNK/BRGTN* G40 .... 60 B2
Garvald St *DMNK/BRGTN* G40............ 60 C2
Garve Av *LNPK/KPK* G44 .... 128 A2
Garvel Crs *STPS/GTHM/RID* G33 ...... 100 A4
Garvel Rd *STPS/GTHM/RID* G33 .... 100 A4
Garvock Dr *PLKSW/MSWD* G43 .... 125 D1
Gask Pl *KNTSWD* G13 .... 71 D2
Gatehouse St *CAR/SHTL* G32 .... 106 B1
Gateside St *DEN/PKHD* G31 .... 36 C5
Gauldry Av *CARD/HILL/MSPK* G52 .... 103 C3
Gavinton St *LNPK/KPK* G44................ 127 D1
Geary St *SMSTN* G23 .... 76 B1
Geddes Rd *SPRGB/BLRNK* G21 .... 82 A3
Gelston St *CAR/SHTL* G32 .... 106 B2
George Av *CLYDBK* G81 .... 62 A3 ⊡
George Crs *CLYDBK* G81 .... 62 A3 ⊡
George Gray St *RUTH* G73 .... 120 A2
George Mann Ter *RUTH* G73 .... 131 C2 ⊡
George Reith Av *KVD/HLHD* G12 .... 3 F1
George Sq *CGLE* G1 .... 33 E3
George St *BAIL/MDB/MHD* G69 .... 109 D2
 CGLE G1 .... 34 A3
Gibson St *DMNK/BRGTN* G40 .... 46 C1
 KVD/HLHD G12.............................. 18 C2
Giffnock Park Av *GIF/THBK* G46........ 126 A2
Gifford Dr *CARD/HILL/MSPK* G52 ...... 102 A1
Gilbertfield Pl
 STPS/GTHM/RID G33 .... 90 B4 ⊡
Gilbertfield St *STPS/GTHM/RID* G33 .. 90 B4
Gilhill St *MRYH/FIRH* G20 .... 76 B3
Gilmerton St *CAR/SHTL* G32 .... 106 A2
Gilmour Rd *RUTH* G73 .... 118 B2
Gilmour Pl *GBLS* G5 .... 45 F5
Gilmour St *CLYDBK* G81 .... 62 A2
Girthon St *CAR/SHTL* G32 .... 107 C2
Girvan St *STPS/GTHM/RID* G33........ 96 B1
Gladney Av *KNTSWD* G13 .... 71 C2
Gladsmuir Rd *CARD/HILL/MSPK* G52.. 94 A4
Gladstone St *COWCAD* G4 .... 20 A3
Glaive Rd *KNTSWD* G13 .... 73 D1
Glamis Rd *DEN/PKHD* G31 .... 104 B2

Glanderston Ct *KNTSWD* G13 .... 72 A3 ☒
Glanderston Dr *KNTSWD* G13 .... 72 A3 ☒
Glasgow Rd *BAIL/MDB/MHD* G69 ...... 108 B2
   RNFRW PA4 .... 85 C4
   RUTH G73 .... 59 E5
Glasgow St *KVD/HLHD* G12 .... 18 C1
Glasserton Pl
   PLKSW/MSWD G43 .... 127 D1 ☒
Glasserton Rd *PLKSW/MSWD* G43 .. 127 D1
Glassford St *CGLE* G1 .... 33 F4
Glebe Ct *COWCAD* G4 .... 34 B1
Glebe Pl *RUTH* G73 .... 118 B2 ☒
Glebe St *COWCAD* G4 .... 22 B5
   RNFRW PA4 .... 84 B1
Gleddoch Rd *CARD/HILL/MSPK* G52 .. 93 C4
Glenacre Dr *CSMK* G45 .... 129 C3
Glenacre Rd *CSMK* G45 .... 129 D3
Glenacre Ter *CSMK* G45 .... 129 D3
Glen Alby Pl *GIF/THBK* G46 .... 123 C2 ☒
Glenalmond St *CAR/SHTL* G32 .... 106 A2
Glenapp St *PLKSD/SHW* G41 .... 55 F2
Glen Av *CAR/SHTL* G32 .... 98 B4
Glenavon Rd *MRYH/FIRH* G20 .... 76 B3
Glenbank Dr *GIF/THBK* G46 .... 124 B4
Glenbarr St *SPRGB/BLRNK* G21 .... 23 D4
Glenbervie Pl *SMSTN* G23 .... 76 B1 ☒
Glenbuck Av *STPS/GTHM/RID* G33.... 83 D4 ☒
Glenbuck Dr *STPS/GTHM/RID* G33 .. 83 D4 ☒
Glenburn Av *BLTYR/CAMB* G72........ 132 B1
Glenburn Gdns *BSHPBGS* G64............ 68 B4
Glenburnie Pl
   STPS/GTHM/RID G33 .... 100 B3 ☒
Glenburn La *MRYH/FIRH* G20 .... 77 D3
Glenburn Rd *BSDN* G61 .... 65 D1
Glenburn St *MRYH/FIRH* G20 .... 77 C3
Glencairn Ct *RUTH* G73 .... 118 B2 ☒
Glencairn Dr *PLKSD/SHW* G41 .... 54 C3
   RUTH G73 .... 118 B2
Glencairn Gdns *PLKSD/SHW* G41 ...... 54 C3
Glencairn La *PLKSD/SHW* G41 .... 55 D3
Glencloy St *MRYH/FIRH* G20 .... 76 A3 ☒
Glen Clunie Av *GIF/THBK* G46............ 123 C2
Glen Clunie Dr *GIF/THBK* G46 .... 123 C2
Glen Clunie Pl *GIF/THBK* G46 .... 123 C2 ☒
Glencoe Pl *KNTSWD* G13 .... 74 A3
Glencoe Rd *RUTH* G73 .... 132 B1 ☒
Glencoe St *KNTSWD* G13 .... 74 B3
Glen Cona Dr *GIF/THBK* G46 .... 123 C1
Glencorse St *STPS/GTHM/RID* G33.... 97 C3
Glen Crs *KNTSWD* G13 .... 71 C3
Glencroft Rd *LNPK/KPK* G44 .... 129 C1
Glendale Crs *BSHPBGS* G64 .... 82 A2 ☒
Glendale Dr *BSHPBGS* G64 .... 82 A2
Glendale Pl *DEN/PKHD* G31 .... 36 C5
   SPRGB/BLRNK G21 .... 82 A3 ☒
Glendale St *DEN/PKHD* G31 .... 36 C5
Glendaruel Av *BSDN* G61 .... 67 D2
Glendaruel Rd
   CRMNK/CLK/EAG G76 .... 133 C4
Glendarvel Gdns *PPK/MIL* G22 .... 10 A3 ☒
Glendee Gdns *RNFRW* PA4 .... 84 B4
Glendee Rd *RNFRW* PA4 .... 84 B4
Glendevon Sq
   STPS/GTHM/RID G33 .... 90 B4 ☒
Glendinning Rd *KNTSWD* G13 .... 74 A1
Glendore St *SCOT* G14 .... 14 C2
Glenduffhill Rd
   BAIL/MDB/MHD G69 .... 108 B1
Gleneagles Gdns *BSHPBGS* G64 .... 68 B3
Gleneagles La North *SCOT* G14 .... 87 C3
Gleneagles La South *SCOT* G14 .... 87 C3
Glenesk Crs *GIF/THBK* G46 .... 123 C2

Glen Esk Dr *GIF/THBK* G46.................. 123 C2
Glenesk Pl *GIF/THBK* G46.................... 123 C2
Glen Etive Pl
   CRMNK/CLK/EAG G76 .... 133 C4 ☒
Glenfarg Crs *BSDN* G61 .... 67 D2
Glenfarg Rd *RUTH* G73 .... 131 D2
Glenfarg St *MRYH/FIRH* G20.............. 20 A3
Glenfinnan Dr *BSDN* G61 .... 67 D3
   MRYH/FIRH G20 .... 76 B4
Glenfinnan Pl *MRYH/FIRH* G20 .... 76 B4 ☒
Glengarry Dr
   CARD/HILL/MSPK G52 .... 103 C1 ☒
Glengavel Crs
   STPS/GTHM/RID G33 .... 83 D4 ☒
Glenhead Crs *PPK/MIL* G22 .... 79 C4 ☒
Glenhead St *PPK/MIL* G22 .... 79 C4
Gleniffer Av *KNTSWD* G13 .... 72 A4
Glenisla St *CAR/SHTL* G32 .... 104 B3 ☒
   DEN/PKHD G31 .... 104 B3
Glenkirk Dr *DRUM* G15 .... 64 B4
Glen Livet Pl *GIF/THBK* G46 .... 123 C2 ☒
Glenlora Dr *PLK/PH/NH* G53 .... 110 A4
Glenlora Ter *PLK/PH/NH* G53 .... 110 B3 ☒
Glen Loy Pl *GIF/THBK* G46.................. 123 C2
Glen Luce Dr *CAR/SHTL* G32 .... 107 D3
Glenlui Av *RUTH* G73 .... 131 D1 ☒
Glenlyon Pl *RUTH* G73 .... 132 A3
Glen Markie Dr *GIF/THBK* G46 .... 123 C2
Glenmavis St *COWCAD* G4 .... 21 D5
Glenmore Av *GVH/MTFL* G42 .... 118 A2
Glen Moriston Rd *GIF/THBK* G46 .. 123 C1 ☒
Glenmuir Dr *PLK/PH/NH* G53 .... 122 B1
Glen Nevis Pl *RUTH* G73 .... 132 A4
Glen Ogle St *CAR/SHTL* G32 .... 107 C2
Glen Orchy Dr *GIF/THBK* G46 .... 123 C2
Glen Orchy Pl *GIF/THBK* G46 .... 123 D2
Glenpark Av *GIF/THBK* G46 .... 124 B4
Glenpark Gdns *BLTYR/CAMB* G72 .... 121 C3 ☒
Glenpark Rd *DEN/PKHD* G31 .... 48 C1
Glenpark St *DEN/PKHD* G31 .... 36 C5
Glenpark Ter *BLTYR/CAMB* G72 ...... 121 C3 ☒
Glenraith Rd *STPS/GTHM/RID* G33.... 90 B3
Glen Rd *CAR/SHTL* G32........................ 98 B3
Glen Sax Dr *RNFRW* PA4 .... 93 C1
Glenshee St *DEN/PKHD* G31 .... 104 B3
Glenside Av *PLK/PH/NH* G53 .... 102 B4
Glenside Dr *BLTYR/CAMB* G72 .... 120 B4
Glenspean St *PLKSW/MSWD* G43 .... 114 B4
Glentanar Pl *PPK/MIL* G22 .... 78 B3
Glentanar Rd *PPK/MIL* G22 .... 78 B3
Glentarbert Rd *RUTH* G73 .... 132 B3
Glentrool Gdns *PPK/MIL* G22 .... 10 A3
Glenturret St *CAR/SHTL* G32 .... 106 A2
Glentyan Dr *PLK/PH/NH* G53 .... 110 A3
Glentyan Ter *PLK/PH/NH* G53 .... 110 A4
Glenville Av *GIF/THBK* G46 .... 125 D3
Glenwood Dr *GIF/THBK* G46 .... 124 B4
Glenwood Pth *CSMK* G45 .... 130 A3 ☒
Glenwood Rd *CSMK* G45 .... 130 A3
Gloucester Av *RUTH* G73 .... 132 B1 ☒
Gloucester St *GBLS* G5........................ 43 F2
Gogar Pl *STPS/GTHM/RID* G33 .... 97 C3
Gogar St *STPS/GTHM/RID* G33 .... 97 C3 ☒
Goldberry Av *SCOT* G14 .... 86 B3
Golf Dr *DRUM* G15 .... 71 D1
Golfhill Dr *DEN/PKHD* G31 .... 36 A2
Golf Rd *RUTH* G73 .... 131 D2
Golfview *BSDN* G61 .... 64 B1
Golspie St *GOV/IBX* G51 .... 28 B2
Goosedubbs *CGLE* G1 .... 45 F1
Gorbals St *GBLS* G5 .... 45 E2
Gordon Av *BAIL/MDB/MHD* G69 ...... 108 B1

CARD/HILL/MSPK G52 .... 93 C3
LNPK/KPK G44 .... 127 C4
Gordon Dr GIF/THBK G46 .... 127 C3
Gordon La CGLE G1 .... 33 D3 🔢
Gordon Rd LNPK/KPK G44 .... 127 C4
Gordon St CGLE G1 .... 33 D3
CGLW G2 .... 32 C3
Gorebridge St CAR/SHTL G32 ..... 97 C3 🔢
Gorget Av KNTSWD G13 .... 73 C1
Gorget Pl KNTSWD G13 .... 73 C1
Gorget Qd DRUM G15 .... 72 B1
Gorsewood BSHPBGS G64 .... 80 A1
Gorstan Pl MRYH/FIRH G20 .... 5 F1 🔢
Gorstan St SMSTN G23 .... 76 B2
Gosford La SCOT G14 .... 86 A2 🔢
Gough St STPS/GTHM/RID G33 ...... 96 B2
Gourlay St SPRGB/BLRNK G21 ..... 10 B5
Gourock St GBLS G5 .... 44 B5 🔢
Govanhill St GVH/MTFL G42 .... 56 C3 🔢
Govan Rd GOV/IBX G51 .... 14 B5
GOV/IBX G51 .... 42 B1
Gowanlea Av DRUM G15 .... 72 A1
Gowanlea Dr GIF/THBK G46 .... 126 B2
Gower St PLKSD/SHW G41 .... 41 E3
Gower Ter PLKSD/SHW G41 .... 41 E3
Goyle Av DRUM G15 .... 65 C3
Grace St KVGV G3 .... 31 E3
Graffham Av GIF/THBK G46 .... 126 B3
Grafton Pl CGLE G1 .... 33 F2
Graham Sq DMNK/BRGTN G40 ..... 47 E1
Graham Ter BSHPBGS G64 .... 81 D3
Graigneston Pl
DMNK/BRGTN G40 .... 47 D3 🔢
Graignestock St DMNK/BRGTN G40 .. 47 D2
Grainger Rd BSHPBGS G64 .... 82 B1
Grampian Crs CAR/SHTL G32 ...... 106 B2
Grampian Pl CAR/SHTL G32 .... 106 B2 🔢
Grampian St CAR/SHTL G32 .... 106 B2
Granby La KVD/HLHD G12 .... 18 B1
Grandtuly Dr KVD/HLHD G12 .... 76 A4
Grange Rd BSDN G61 .... 66 B1
GVH/MTFL G42 .... 116 A2
Gran St CLYDBK G81 .... 71 C2
Grantlea Gv CAR/SHTL G32 .... 107 D2
Grantlea Ter CAR/SHTL G32 .... 107 D2 🔢
Grantley Gdns PLKSD/SHW G41 ... 114 B2
Grantley St PLKSW/MSWD G43 .... 114 B2
Granton St GBLS G5 .... 58 C3
Grant St KVGV G3 .... 19 F4
Granville St KVGV G3 .... 31 F1
Gray Dr BSDN G61 .... 66 B3
Gray St KVGV G3 .... 18 C5
Great Dovehill COWCAD G4 .... 34 B5
Great George La KVD/HLHD G12 .... 18 A1
Great George St KVD/HLHD G12 .... 18 A1
Great Kelvin La KVD/HLHD G12 .... 18 C2
Great Western Rd CLYDBK G81 .... 62 A2
KNTSWD G13 .... 73 C2
KVD/HLHD G12 .... 4 C2 🔢
KVD/HLHD G12 .... 6 A5
Great Western Ter KVD/HLHD G12 .. 5 E3
Great Western Terrace La
KVD/HLHD G12 .... 5 E3
Greenan Av LNPK/KPK G44 .... 118 A3 🔢
Greendyke St CGLE G1 .... 46 A1
Greenend Pl CAR/SHTL G32 .... 99 C3 🔢
Greenfield Rd CAR/SHTL G32 ...... 99 C4
Greenfield St GOV/IBX G51 .... 27 F3
Greengairs Av GOV/IBX G51 .... 26 B3
Greenhead Rd BSDN G61 .... 66 B2 🔢
Greenhead St DMNK/BRGTN G40 .. 47 D3 🔢
Greenhill BSHPBGS G64 .... 82 A2

Greenhill Ct RUTH G73 .... 119 C2
Greenhill Rd RUTH G73 .... 119 C3
Greenhill St RUTH G73 .... 119 C3 🔢
Greenholme St LNPK/KPK G44 .... 116 B4 🔢
Greenknowe Rd
PLKSW/MSWD G43 .... 113 D4 🔢
Greenlaw Rd SCOT G14 .... 70 B4
Greenlea St KNTSWD G13 .... 74 A4 🔢
Greenlees Gdns BLTYR/CAMB G72 .. 133 C3
Greenlees Rd BLTYR/CAMB G72 ... 133 D4
Greenloan Av GOV/IBX G51 .... 26 B2
Greenmount PPK/MIL G22 .... 78 A3 🔢
Greenock Av LNPK/KPK G44 .... 128 B1
Greenrig St STPS/GTHM/RID G33 .. 88 B3
Greenshields Rd
BAIL/MDB/MHD G69 .... 109 D1
Greenside Crs STPS/GTHM/RID G33 .. 89 C3
Greenside St STPS/GTHM/RID G33 .. 89 C3
Green St DMNK/BRGTN G40 .... 47 D2
The Green DMNK/BRGTN G40 ...... 47 D4
Greentree Dr BAIL/MDB/MHD G69 .. 108 B3
Greenview St
PLKSW/MSWD G43 .... 114 A2 🔢
Greenwood Dr BSDN G61 .... 67 C2
Greenwood Qd CLYDBK G81 .... 70 B1
Grenville Dr BLTYR/CAMB G72 .... 133 D2
Gretna St DMNK/BRGTN G40 .... 49 D3
Greyfriars St CAR/SHTL G32 .... 97 D3
Greystone Av RUTH G73 .... 120 A4
Greywood St KNTSWD G13 .... 74 A3 🔢
Grierson La STPS/GTHM/RID G33 .. 96 B2 🔢
Grierson St STPS/GTHM/RID G33 .. 96 B2 🔢
Grogarry Rd DRUM G15 .... 64 A2
Grosvenor Crs KVD/HLHD G12 ...... 6 A5
Grosvenor Crescent La
KVD/HLHD G12 .... 6 A5 🔢
Grosvenor La KVD/HLHD G12 .... 6 A5
Grosvenor Ter KVD/HLHD G12 ...... 6 A5
Groveburn Av GIF/THBK G46 ...... 125 C2
Grovepark Ct MRYH/FIRH G20 ..... 20 B2 🔢
Grove Park Gdns MRYH/FIRH G20 .. 20 A2
Grovepark St MRYH/FIRH G20 ..... 20 A1
The Groves SPRGB/BLRNK G21 .... 82 A3 🔢
Grudie St ESTRH G34 .... 101 C2 🔢
Gryffe St LNPK/KPK G44 .... 116 A4
Guildford St STPS/GTHM/RID G33 .. 99 C1
Gullane St PTCK G11 .... 17 D4
Guthrie St MRYH/FIRH G20 .... 76 B4

H

Haberlea Av PLK/PH/NH G53 ...... 123 C3
Haberlea Gdns PLK/PH/NH G53 ... 123 C4 🔢
Haggs La PLKSD/SHW G41 .... 53 E4
Haggs Rd PLKSD/SHW G41 .... 53 F5
Haggswood Av PLKSD/SHW G41 .... 53 E4
Haghill Rd DEN/PKHD G31 .... 37 E5
Haig Dr BAIL/MDB/MHD G69 ...... 108 B2
Haig St SPRGB/BLRNK G21 .... 12 A4
Hailes Av CAR/SHTL G32 .... 107 D1
Haining Rd RNFRW PA4 .... 84 B3
The Haining RNFRW PA4 .... 84 B4 🔢
Hairmyres St GVH/MTFL G42 .... 57 E4 🔢
Hairst St RNFRW PA4 .... 84 B2
Halbeath Av DRUM G15 .... 63 D3
Halbert St PLKSD/SHW G41 .... 115 C1
Haldane La SCOT G14 .... 14 A1
Haldane St SCOT G14 .... 14 B1
Halgreen Av DRUM G15 .... 63 C3
Hallbrae St STPS/GTHM/RID G33 .. 89 C2 🔢

Halley Dr *KNTSWD* G13 .... **71** C3
Halley Pl *KNTSWD* G13 .... **71** C4
Halley St *KNTSWD* G13 .... **71** C3
Hallforest St
  STPS/GTHM/RID G33 .... **90** B4 ▣
Hallhill Crs *STPS/GTHM/RID* G33 .. **100** A4 ▣
Hallhill Rd *BAIL/MDB/MHD* G69 ...... **101** C4
Hallside Rd
  CAR/SHTL G32 .... **99** C4
Halliburton Crs *ESTRH* G34 .... **100** B3 ▣
Halliburton Ter *ESTRH* G34 .... **101** C3 ▣
Halldale Crs *RNFRW* PA4................ **85** D4
Hallrule Dr *CARD/HILL/MSPK* G52 .. **103** C1
Hallside St *GBLS* G5 .... **45** F5
Hallydown Dr *KNTSWD* G13 .... **87** C1
Halton Gdns
  BAIL/MDB/MHD G69 .... **108** B2 ▣
Hamilton Av *PLKSD/SHW* G41 .... **53** D1
Hamilton Crs *RNFRW* PA4................ **84** B1
Hamilton Dr *GIF/THBK* G46 .... **126** B4
  KVD/HLHD G12................................ **6** C5
Hamiltonhill Crs *PPK/MIL* G22 .... **9** D4 ▣
Hamiltonhill Rd *PPK/MIL* G22............ **9** D5
Hamilton Park Av *KVD/HLHD* G12 .... **7** D5
Hamilton Rd *CAR/SHTL* G32 .... **107** C4
  RUTH G73 .... **119** D3
  UD/BTH/TAN G71.......................... **108** B4
Hamilton St *CLYDBK* G81................ **70** B3
  GVH/MTFL G42 .... **57** F5
Hamilton Ter *CLYDBK* G81................ **70** B3
Hampden Dr *LNPK/KPK* G44............ **116** B3
Hampden La *GVH/MTFL* G42............ **116** B2
Hampden Ter *GVH/MTFL* G42 .... **116** B2
Hangingshaw Pl *GVH/MTFL* G42 .... **117** C2
Hanover Cl *GVH/MTFL* G42 .... **116** A2 ▣
Hanover Ct *CGLE* G1........................ **33** F2
Hanover St *CGLE* G1........................ **33** E3
Hanson St *DEN/PKHD* G31 .... **35** F3
Hapland Av *PLK/PH/NH* G53 .... **103** C4 ▣
Hapland Rd *PLK/PH/NH* G53 .... **103** C4 ▣
Harburn Pl *SCOT* G14 .... **71** D4
Harcourt Dr *DEN/PKHD* G31 .... **36** C1
Hardgate Dr *GOV/IBX* G51 .... **95** C2
Hardgate Gdns *GOV/IBX* G51 .... **95** C3
Hardgate Pl *GOV/IBX* G51 .... **95** C2 ▣
Hardgate Rd *GOV/IBX* G51 .... **95** C2
Hardie Av *RUTH* G73 .... **120** A2
Hardridge Av *CARD/HILL/MSPK* G52 .. **50** B4
Hardridge Pl *CARD/HILL/MSPK* G52.... **50** C4
Hardridge Rd *CARD/HILL/MSPK* G52 .. **50** B3
Harefield Dr *SCOT* G14.................... **86** B1
Harelaw Av *LNPK/KPK* G44 .... **127** C2
Harhill St *GOV/IBX* G51.................... **27** F3
Harland St *SCOT* G14 .... **87** C1
Harmetray St *PPK/MIL* G22 .... **79** D4
Harmony Pl *GOV/IBX* G51 .... **28** A3
Harmony Rw *GOV/IBX* G51 .... **28** A3
Harmony Sq *GOV/IBX* G51.............. **28** A3
Harmsworth St *PTCK* G11 .... **15** D3
Harport St *GIF/THBK* G46 .... **124** A2
Harriet Pl *PLKSW/MSWD* G43 .... **113** D4 ▣
Harriet St *RUTH* G73........................ **119** C2
Harrison Dr *GOV/IBX* G51 .... **40** C1
Harris Rd *SMSTN* G23...................... **76** B1 ▣
Harrow Ct *DRUM* G15 .... **63** D3 ▣
Harrow Pl *DRUM* G15 .... **63** D3 ▣
Hartlaw Crs *CARD/HILL/MSPK* G52 .. **94** A4
Hartree Av *KNTSWD* G13 .... **71** C2
Hartstone Rd *PLK/PH/NH* G53 .... **110** B3
Hart St *DEN/PKHD* G31 .... **105** C1
Harvey St *COWCAD* G4 .... **21** E2
Harvie St *GOV/IBX* G51 .... **42** B3 ▣
Harwood St *CAR/SHTL* G32 .... **97** C3 ▣

Hastie St *KVGV* G3.......................... **18** A5
Hatfield Dr *KVD/HLHD* G12 .... **4** A1
Hathaway Dr *GIF/THBK* G46 .... **125** D4
Hathaway St *MRYH/FIRH* G20 .... **6** C2
Hathersage Av
  BAIL/MDB/MHD G69.................. **109** D1
Hathersage Dr
  BAIL/MDB/MHD G69.................. **109** D1
Hathersage Gdns
  BAIL/MDB/MHD G69.................. **109** D1 ▣
Hatton Gdns *CARD/HILL/MSPK* G52.. **102** A2
Haughburn Pl *PLK/PH/NH* G53 ...... **110** B3 ▣
Haughburn Rd *PLK/PH/NH* G53........ **110** B3
Haughburn Ter *PLK/PH/NH* G53 ...... **110** B3
Haugh Rd *KVGV* G3.......................... **30** A1
Havelock La *PTCK* G11.................... **17** E2
Havelock St *PTCK* G11.................... **17** E2
Hawick St *KNTSWD* G13.................. **71** C3
Hawthorn Av *BSHPBGS* G64 .... **81** D2
Hawthorn St *PPK/MIL* G22 .... **9** E2
  PPK/MIL G22 .... **11** D2
  SPRGB/BLRNK G21 .... **11** D2
Hawthorn Wk *BLTYR/CAMB* G72 .... **132** B1
Hayburn Crs *PTCK* G11 .... **16** B1
Hayburn Ga *PTCK* G11 .... **16** C2
Hayburn La *KVD/HLHD* G12 .... **4** B5
  PTCK G11 .... **16** B1
Hayburn St *PTCK* G11...................... **16** C4
Hayfield St *GBLS* G5 .... **46** A4
Haylynn St *SCOT* G14 .... **15** D2
Haymarket St *CAR/SHTL* G32 .... **97** D3
Haywood St *PPK/MIL* G22 .... **78** B4
Hazel Av *LNPK/KPK* G44 .... **127** D2 ▣
Hazel Dene *BSHPBGS* G64 .... **81** D1
Hazellea Dr *GIF/THBK* G46.............. **127** C2
Hazelwood Gdns *RUTH* G73 .... **132** A2 ▣
Hazelwood Rd *PLKSD/SHW* G41 .... **41** E4
Hazlitt Gdns *MRYH/FIRH* G20 .... **78** A4 ▣
Hazlitt Pl *MRYH/FIRH* G20 .... **78** A4 ▣
Heath Av *BSHPBGS* G64 .... **81** D2 ▣
Heathcot Av *DRUM* G15 .... **63** C4
Heathcot Pl *DRUM* G15 .... **62** B4 ▣
Heatherbrae *BSHPBGS* G64 .... **80** A1
Heathfield St
  STPS/GTHM/RID G33 .... **99** C2 ▣
Heathside Rd *GIF/THBK* G46 .... **126** B3 ▣
Heathwood Dr *GIF/THBK* G46 .... **125** C1
Hecla Av *DRUM* G15 .... **63** D3
Hecla Pl *DRUM* G15 .... **63** D3
Hecla Sq *DRUM* G15 .... **63** D3
Hector Rd *PLKSD/SHW* G41.............. **114** B2
Helensburgh Dr *KNTSWD* G13 .... **73** D4
Helen St *CARD/HILL/MSPK* G52 ...... **39** F3
  GOV/IBX G51 .... **28** A5
Helenvale Ct *DEN/PKHD* G31 .... **104** B1 ▣
Helenvale St *DEN/PKHD* G31 .... **49** F4
Hemlock St *KNTSWD* G13 .... **74** B3
Henderland Dr *BSDN* G61 .... **66** A4
Henderland Rd *BSDN* G61 .... **66** A4 ▣
  BSDN G61 .... **74** B1
Henderson St *KNTSWD* G13 .... **71** C2
  MRYH/FIRH G20.......................... **19** E1
Henrietta St *SCOT* G14 .... **87** C3 ▣
Hepburn Rd *CARD/HILL/MSPK* G52 .. **94** A3
Herald Av *KNTSWD* G13 .... **73** D1
Herbert Rd *MRYH/FIRH* G20 .... **19** E1
Herbert St *MRYH/FIRH* G20 .... **19** F1
Heriot Crs *BSHPBGS* G64 .... **69** C3
Herma St *SMSTN* G23...................... **77** C2
Hermiston Av *CAR/SHTL* G32 .... **98** B4
Hermiston Pl *CAR/SHTL* G32 .... **99** C4 ▣
Hermiston Rd *CAR/SHTL* G32 .... **98** B4

Hermitage Av *KNTSWD* G13 .... **73** C3
Herries Rd *PLKSD/SHW* G41 .... **53** F5
Herriet St *PLKSD/SHW* G41 .... **55** E1
Herschell St *KNTSWD* G13 .... **74** B4 🔢
Hertford Av *KVD/HLHD* G12 .... **75** D4 🔢
Hexham Gdns *PLKSD/SHW* G41 .... **54** A5
Hickman St *GVH/MTFL* G42 .... **57** D5
Hickman Ter *GVH/MTFL* G42 .... **57** E3
Hickory St *PPK/MIL* G22 .... **10** C2
Highburgh Dr *RUTH* G73 .... **131** D1
Highburgh Rd *KVD/HLHD* G12 .... **17** E1
Highcroft Av *LNPK/KPK* G44 .... **130** A1 🔢
Highfield Dr *KVD/HLHD* G12 .... **75** D4
   RUTH G73 .... **132** A3
Highfield Pl *KVD/HLHD* G12 .... **75** D4 🔢
High Graighall Rd *COWCAD* G4 .... **21** D3
Highland La *GOV/IBX* G51 .... **29** E3
High St *COWCAD* G4 .... **34** B4
   RNFRW PA4 .... **84** B3
   RUTH G73 .... **119** C2 🔢
Hilary Dr *BAIL/MDB/MHD* G69 .... **108** B1
Hilary Av *RUTH* G73 .... **120** B4 🔢
Hillcrest Av *LNPK/KPK* G44 .... **127** C3
Hillcrest Rd *BSDN* G61 .... **66** B2
Hillcroft Ter *BSHPBGS* G64 .... **80** B2 🔢
Hillhead Av *RUTH* G73 .... **131** D2
Hillhead Pl *RUTH* G73 .... **131** D2 🔢
Hillhead Rd *SPRGB/BLRNK* G21 .... **82** B3
Hillhead St *KVD/HLHD* G12 .... **18** B3
Hillhouse St *SPRGB/BLRNK* G21 .... **12** A3
Hillington Gdns
   CARD/HILL/MSPK G52 .... **103** C2
Hillington Park Circ
   CARD/HILL/MSPK G52 .... **103** C1 🔢
Hillington Qd
   CARD/HILL/MSPK G52 .... **102** A1
Hillington Rd *CARD/HILL/MSPK* G52 .. **93** D1
   CARD/HILL/MSPK G52 .... **94** A2 🔢
Hillington Rd South
   CARD/HILL/MSPK G52 .... **94** A4
Hillington Ter
   CARD/HILL/MSPK G52 .... **102** A1
Hillkirk Pl *SPRGB/BLRNK* G21 .... **11** E4
Hillkirk St *SPRGB/BLRNK* G21 .... **11** E3
Hillneuk Av *BSDN* G61 .... **66** B1
Hillneuk Dr *BSDN* G61 .... **67** C1
Hillpark Dr *PLKSW/MSWD* G43 .... **113** D4
Hillsborough Rd
   BAIL/MDB/MHD G69 .... **108** D1
Hillside Av *BSDN* G61 .... **66** B1
Hillside Ct *GIF/THBK* G46 .... **124** B3 🔢
Hillside Rd *BSDN* G61 .... **67** C1
   BSHPBGS G64 .... **69** C4
Hillside Gardens La *PTCK* G11 .... **17** D1 🔢
Hillside Qd *PLKSW/MSWD* G43 .... **125** D1 🔢
Hillside Rd *PLKSW/MSWD* G43 .... **125** D1
Hill St *KVGV* G3 .... **20** B5
Hillswick Crs *PPK/MIL* G22 .... **78** B2
Hillview Gdns *SPRGB/BLRNK* G21 ...... **82** B3 🔢
Hillview St *CAR/SHTL* G32 .... **105** D1
Hilton Gdns *KNTSWD* G13 .... **74** B3
Hilton Pk *BSHPBGS* G64 .... **68** B3
Hilton Rd *BSHPBGS* G64 .... **68** B3
Hilton Ter *BLTYR/CAMB* G72 .... **133** C3 🔢
   BSHPBGS G64 .... **68** B3
   KNTSWD G13 .... **74** A3
Hinshaw St *MRYH/FIRH* G20 .... **8** A5

Hinshelwood Dr *GOV/IBX* G51 .... **40** B2
Hinshelwood Pl *GOV/IBX* G51 .... **40** C2 🔢
Hobart St *PPK/MIL* G22 .... **8** C3
Hobden St *SPRGB/BLRNK* G21 .... **24** B1
Hoddam Av *CSMK* G45 .... **130** B3
Hoddam Ter *CSMK* G45 .... **131** C3
Hogarth Av *CAR/SHTL* G32 .... **96** B3
Hogarth Gdns *CAR/SHTL* G32 .... **96** B3
Hogganfield St
   STPS/GTHM/RID G33 .... **88** B4
Holeburn La *PLKSW/MSWD* G43 ...... **114** A4
Holeburn Rd *PLKSW/MSWD* G43 ...... **114** A4
Holehouse Dr *KNTSWD* G13 .... **72** A4
Holland St *CGLW* G2 .... **32** A2
Hollinwell Rd *SMSTN* G23 .... **76** B2
Hollowglen Rd *CAR/SHTL* G32 .... **98** B4
Hollybank St *SPRGB/BLRNK* G21 ...... **24** A5
Hollybrook St *GVH/MTFL* G42 .... **57** D3
Holly Dr *SPRGB/BLRNK* G21 .... **24** A1
Hollymount *BSDN* G61 .... **66** B4
Holmbank Av *PLKSW/MSWD* G43 .... **114** B3
Holmbyre Ter *CSMK* G45 .... **129** C4 🔢
Holmes Av *RNFRW* PA4 .... **92** A1
Holmfauldhead Dr *GOV/IBX* G51 ...... **26** C2
Holmfauldhead Pl *GOV/IBX* G51 ...... **26** C2
Holmfauld Rd *GOV/IBX* G51 .... **14** C5
Holmhead Crs *LNPK/KPK* G44 .... **116** A4
Holmhead Pl *LNPK/KPK* G44 .... **116** A4 🔢
Holmhead Rd *LNPK/KPK* G44 .... **128** A1
Holmhills Dr *BLTYR/CAMB* G72 ...... **133** D3
Holmhills Gdns *BLTYR/CAMB* G72 .... **133** D2
Holmhills Gv *BLTYR/CAMB* G72 ...... **133** D3
Holmhills Pl *BLTYR/CAMB* G72 ...... **133** D2 🔢
Holmhills Rd *BLTYR/CAMB* G72 ...... **133** D3
Holmhills Ter *BLTYR/CAMB* G72 ...... **133** D2
Holmlea Rd *GVH/MTFL* G42 .... **116** A3
Holm St *CGLW* G2 .... **32** C4
Holyrood Crs *MRYH/FIRH* G20 .... **19** F2
Holyrood Qd *MRYH/FIRH* G20 .... **19** E2
Holywell St *DEN/PKHD* G31 .... **49** D2
Honeybog Rd *CARD/HILL/MSPK* G52 .. **93** C4
Hood St *CLYDBK* G81 .... **62** A4
Hopefield Av *KVD/HLHD* G12 .... **5** E1
Hopehill Gdns *MRYH/FIRH* G20 .... **20** A1
Hopehill Rd *MRYH/FIRH* G20 .... **20** A1
Hopeman Av *GIF/THBK* G46 .... **124** A2
Hopeman Dr *GIF/THBK* G46 .... **124** A2
Hopeman Rd *GIF/THBK* G46 .... **124** A2
Hopeman St *GIF/THBK* G46 .... **124** A2
Hope St *CGLW* G2 .... **33** D3
Hopetoun Pl *SMSTN* G23 .... **77** C1 🔢
Hopetoun Ter *SPRGB/BLRNK* G21 .... **12** B5
Horndean Crs *STPS/GTHM/RID* G33 .. **99** D2
Hornshill St *SPRGB/BLRNK* G21 .... **12** A4
Horsburgh St
   STPS/GTHM/RID G33 .... **91** D4 🔢
Horse Shoe Rd *BSDN* G61 .... **66** A2 🔢
Hospital St *GBLS* G5 .... **45** D5
Hotspur St *MRYH/FIRH* G20 .... **6** C3
Houldsworth La *KVGV* G3 .... **31** D2
Houldsworth St *KVGV* G3 .... **31** D2
Househillmuir Crs *PLK/PH/NH* G53 .. **111** C4
Househillmuir Pl
   PLK/PH/NH G53 .... **111** C3 🔢
Househillmuir Rd *PLK/PH/NH* G53 .. **122** A1
Househillwood Crs
   PLK/PH/NH G53 .... **110** B3
Househillwood Rd
   PLK/PH/NH G53 .... **110** B4
Housel Av *KNTSWD* G13 .... **72** B4
Houston Pl *GBLS* G5 .... **43** E1
Houston St *PLKSD/SHW* G41 .... **43** E2

RNFRW PA4 .... **84** B2 🔢
Howard St *CGLE* G1 .... **33** E5
Howat St *GOV/IBX* G51 .... **28** A1
Howford Rd *CARD/HILL/MSPK* G52 .. **102** B2
Howgate Av *GOV/IBX* G15 .... **63** D3
Howth Dr *KNTSWD* G13 .... **74** B2
Howth Ter *KNTSWD* G13 .... **74** B2 🔢
Hoylake Pl *SMSTN* G23 .... **77** C1
Hughenden Dr *KVD/HLHD* G12 ..... **4** C3
Hughenden Gdns *KVD/HLHD* G12 .... **4** B4
Hughenden La *KVD/HLHD* G12 ..... **4** C3
Hughenden Rd *KVD/HLHD* G12 ..... **4** C3
Hunterfield Dr *BLTYR/CAMB* G72 .. **133** C1
Hunter Rd G73 .... **61** E5
Hunters Hill Ct *SPRGB/BLRNK* G21 .. **80** B4 🔢
Huntershill Rd *BSHPBGS* G64 ...... **81** C2 🔢
Huntershill St *SPRGB/BLRNK* G21 .. **80** A4 🔢
Huntershill Wy *BSHPBGS* G64 ...... **80** B3 🔢
Hunter St *COWCAD* G4 .... **34** C5
Huntingdon Rd *COWCAD* G4 .... **22** C3
Huntingdon Sq
   SPRGB/BLRNK G21 .... **22** C2 🔢
Huntingtower Rd
   BAIL/MDB/MHD G69 .... **108** B2
Huntley Gdns *KVD/HLHD* G12 ...... **6** A5
Huntly Av *GIF/THBK* G46 .... **126** B3
Huntly Ct *BSHPBGS* G64 .... **81** C2
Huntly Rd *CARD/HILL/MSPK* G52 .. **93** D2
Hurlford Av *KNTSWD* G13 .... **71** D3
Hurly Hawkin *BSHPBGS* G64 .... **82** B2
Hutcheson Rd *GIF/THBK* G46 ...... **125** C4
Hutcheson St *CGLE* G1 .... **33** F5
Hutchison Dr *BSDN* G61 .... **67** C4
Hutton *KVD/HLHD* G12 .... **75** C4
Hutton Dr *GOV/IBX* G51 .... **27** D2
Huxley St *MRYH/FIRH* G20 .... **77** D4
Hydepark St *KVGV* G3 .... **31** E4
Hyndal Av *PLK/PH/NH* G53 .... **111** C1
Hyndland Av *PTCK* G11 .... **17** D2
Hyndland Rd *KVD/HLHD* G12 .... **17** D1
   PTCK G11 .... **17** E2
Hyndland St *PTCK* G11 .... **17** E3
Hyndlee Dr *CARD/HILL/MSPK* G52 .... **103** C1

I

Ian Smith Ct *CLYDBK* G81 .... **70** B2 🔢
Ibroxholm Av *GOV/IBX* G51 .... **41** D2
Ibroxholm Ov *GOV/IBX* G51 .... **41** D1
Ibroxholm Pl *GOV/IBX* G51 .... **41** D2 🔢
Ibrox St *GOV/IBX* G51 .... **41** E1
Ibrox Ter *GOV/IBX* G51 .... **41** D1
Ilay Av *BSDN* G61 .... **75** C2 🔢
Ilay Ct *BSDN* G61 .... **75** C2
Ilay Rd *BSDN* G61 .... **75** C2
Inchbrae Rd *CARD/HILL/MSPK* G52 .. **103** C2
Inchfad Dr *DRUM* G15 .... **63** C3
Inchfad Pl *DRUM* G15 .... **63** C3 🔢
Inchholm La *PTCK* G11 .... **15** D3
Inchholm St *PTCK* G11 .... **15** D3
Inchkeith Pl *CAR/SHTL* G32 .... **98** B3 🔢
Inchlaggan Pl *DRUM* G15 .... **63** C2 🔢
Inchlee St *SCOT* G14 .... **14** C2
Inchmurrin Dr
   CRMNK/CLK/EAG G76 .... **132** B4
Inchmurrin Gdns
   CRMNK/CLK/EAG G76 .... **132** B4 🔢
Inchmurrin Pl
   CRMNK/CLK/EAG G76 .... **132** B4 🔢
Inchrory Pl *DRUM* G15 .... **63** C2

India St *CGLW* G2 .... **32** A1
Inga St *MRYH/FIRH* G20 .... **77** C3
Ingerbreck Av *RUTH* G73 .... **132** B1 🔢
Ingleby Dr *DEN/PKHD* G31 .... **36** C3
Inglefield St *GVH/MTFL* G42 .... **56** C3
Ingleneuk Av *STPS/GTHM/RID* G33 .. **90** B1
Inglestone Av *GIF/THBK* G46 ...... **125** C4
Inglis St *DEN/PKHD* G31 .... **36** B5
Ingram St *CGLE* G1 .... **34** A4
Inishail Rd *STPS/GTHM/RID* G33 ... **99** C1
Innerwick Dr
   CARD/HILL/MSPK G52 .... **102** B1
Inverary Dr *BSHPBGS* G64 .... **69** D2
Invercanny Dr *DRUM* G15 .... **64** A2
Invercanny Pl *DRUM* G15 .... **64** A2
Inverclyde Gdns *RUTH* G73 .... **132** B3
Inveresk Qd *CAR/SHTL* G32 .... **98** A4
Inveresk St *CAR/SHTL* G32 .... **98** A4
Inverewe Av *GIF/THBK* G46 .... **123** D4
Inverewe Dr *GIF/THBK* G46 .... **123** D4
Inverewe Gdns *GIF/THBK* G46 ... **123** D4
Inverewe Pl *GIF/THBK* G46 .... **123** D3
Invergarry Ct *GIF/THBK* G46 ..... **124** A4
Invergarry Dr *GIF/THBK* G46 ..... **123** D4
Invergarry Gdns *GIF/THBK* G46 .. **123** D4
Invergarry Gv *GIF/THBK* G46 ..... **123** D4
Invergarry Pl *GIF/THBK* G46 ...... **124** A4 🔢
Invergarry Quad *GIF/THBK* G46 .. **124** A4
Invergarry Vw *GIF/THBK* G46 .... **124** A4
Inverglas Av *RNFRW* PA4 .... **93** D1 🔢
Invergordon Av
   PLKSW/MSWD G43 .... **115** D3
Invergyle Dr *CARD/HILL/MSPK* G52 . **102** D3
Inverlair Av *PLKSW/MSWD* G43 ... **115** D4
Inverleith St *CAR/SHTL* G32 .... **97** C3
Inverlochy St *STPS/GTHM/RID* G33 . **99** D1
Inverness St *GOV/IBX* G51 .... **26** A3
Inveroran Dr *BSDN* G61 .... **67** D2
Inver Rd *STPS/GTHM/RID* G33 .... **100** A3
Invershiel Rd *SMSTN* G23 .... **76** B1
Invershin Dr *MRYH/FIRH* G20 ..... **6** A1
Inverurie St *SPRGB/BLRNK* G21 .. **10** B5
Iona Rd *RNFRW* PA4 .... **92** A1
   RUTH G73 .... **133** C3 🔢
Iona St *GOV/IBX* G51 .... **28** C4
Iris Av *CSMK* G45 .... **131** C3
Irongray St *DEN/PKHD* G31 .... **37** F3
Irvine St *DMNK/BRGTN* G40 ...... **60** C1
Islay Av *RUTH* G73 .... **133** C3
Ivanhoe Rd *KNTSWD* G13 .... **73** D2

J

Jagger Gdns *BAIL/MDB/MHD* G69 .... **108** B2
Jamaica St *CGLE* G1 .... **33** D5
James Dunlop Gdns
   BSHPBGS G64 .... **81** D3 🔢
James Gray St *PLKSD/SHW* G41 .. **115** C2 🔢
James Morrison St *CGLE* G1 .... **46** A1 🔢
James Nisbet St *SPRGB/BLRNK* G21 . **35** E1
James St *DMNK/BRGTN* G40 ...... **47** D4
James Watt St *KVGV* G3 .... **32** B4
Jamieson Ct *GVH/MTFL* G42 ...... **57** D3 🔢
Jamieson St *GVH/MTFL* G42 ...... **57** D3
Janefield St *DEN/PKHD* G31 .... **49** D2
   DMNK/BRGTN G40 .... **49** E4
Jane Rae Gdns *CLYDBK* G81 ...... **70** B2 🔢
Jardine St *MRYH/FIRH* G20 .... **19** E1 🔢
Jean Armour Dr *CLYDBK* G81 ..... **62** A3
Jean Maclean Pl *BSHPBGS* G64 ... **69** D2 🔢
Jedburgh Av *RUTH* G73 .... **119** D3

Jedburgh Gdns *MRYH/FIRH* G20 .... 7 E5 ⑤
Jedworth Av *DRUM* G15 .... 64 B3
Jedworth Rd *DRUM* G15 .... 64 B3 ⑥
Jerviston Rd *STPS/GTHM/RID* G33...... 91 C4
Jocelyn Sq *CGLE* G1 .... 45 F1 ⑤
John Knox St *CLYDBK* G81 .... 70 B3
        COWCAD G4 .... 35 D3
John Marshall Dr *PPK/MIL* G22 ...... 80 A2
Johnsburn Dr *PLK/PH/NH* G53 ...... 110 B4 ⑧
Johnsburn Rd *PLK/PH/NH* G53 ...... 110 B3 ⑤
Johnshaven St
        PLKSW/MSWD G43 .... 114 A3 ⑥
Johnstone Ct *CARD/HILL/MSPK* G52... 94 B3
        CLYDBK G81 .... 70 B2
Johnstone Dr *RUTH* G73 .... 119 C3
John St *CGLE* G1 .... 33 F4
Joppa St *STPS/GTHM/RID* G33 ...... 97 C3 ⑦
Jordanhill Crs *KNTSWD* G13 .... 2 A1
Jordanhill Dr *KNTSWD* G13 .... 2 A1
Jordanhill La *KNTSWD* G13 .... 3 D1 ⑤
Jordan St *SCOT* G14 .... 14 B2
Jordanvale Av *SCOT* G14 .... 14 A2
Jowitt Av *CLYDBK* G81 .... 70 B1
Jubilee Ct *CARD/HILL/MSPK* G52 ...... 93 D3
Jubilee Gdns *BSDN* G61 .... 66 A2
Julian Av *KVD/HLHD* G12 .... 5 F3
Julian La *KVD/HLHD* G12 .... 5 E3
Juniper Pl *CAR/SHTL* G32 .... 108 B2 ⑥
Juniper Ter *CAR/SHTL* G32 .... 108 A3
Jura Av *RNFRW* PA4 .... 92 B1
Jura St *CARD/HILL/MSPK* G52 .... 39 E2

K

Kaim Dr *PLK/PH/NH* G53 .... 111 C4
Katewell Av *DRUM* G15 .... 63 C2
Katewell Pl *DRUM* G15 .... 63 C2 ⑧
Katrine Av *BSHPBGS* G64 .... 81 D1
Kaystone Rd *DRUM* G15 .... 72 A1
Kay St *SPRGB/BLRNK* G21 .... 11 E3
Keal Av *DRUM* G15 .... 72 B1 ⑤
Keal Crs *DRUM* G15 .... 72 A2
Keal Dr *DRUM* G15 .... 72 A2
Keal Pl *DRUM* G15 .... 72 A2
Kearn Av *DRUM* G15 .... 72 B1
Kearn Pl *DRUM* G15 .... 72 B1
Keir Dr *BSHPBGS* G64 .... 68 B4
Keir St *PLKSD/SHW* G41 .... 55 E2
Keith Av *GIF/THBK* G46 .... 126 A3
Keith Ct *PTCK* G11 .... 17 E3
Keith St *PTCK* G11 .... 17 E3
Kelbourne St *MRYH/FIRH* G20 ...... 6 C3
Kelburne Gdns
        BAIL/MDB/MHD G69 .... 109 C3 ⑤
Kellas St *GOV/IBX* G51 .... 28 B4
Kells Pl *DRUM* G15 .... 63 C2
Kelso Av *RUTH* G73 .... 119 D3 ⑥
Kelso Pl *SCOT* G14 .... 71 C4
Kelso St *KNTSWD* G13 .... 71 D2
        SCOT G14 .... 71 C4
Kelton St *CAR/SHTL* G32 .... 106 B2
Kelvin Av *CARD/HILL/MSPK* G52...... 93 D2
Kelvin Crs *BSDN* G61 .... 66 B4
Kelvindale Gdns *MRYH/FIRH* G20 ...... 76 A4
Kelvindale Pl *MRYH/FIRH* G20 ...... 76 B4 ⑧
Kelvin Dr *BSHPBGS* G64 .... 69 C4
        MRYH/FIRH G20 .... 6 B4
Kelvingrove St *KVGV* G3 .... 30 C1
Kelvinhaugh Ga *KVGV* G3 .... 30 A1
Kelvinhaugh Pl *KVGV* G3 .... 30 B1 ⑤
Kelvinhaugh St *KVGV* G3 .... 30 A1
Kelvinside Av *MRYH/FIRH* G20 ...... 7 E5 ⑤
Kelvinside Dr *MRYH/FIRH* G20 ...... 7 E4
Kelvinside Gdns *MRYH/FIRH* G20.... 7 D4
Kelvinside Gdns East
        MRYH/FIRH G20 .... 7 E5
Kelvinside Gdns La *MRYH/FIRH* G20 ... 7 D4
Kelvinside Ter South
        MRYH/FIRH G20 .... 6 C5
Kelvinside Ter West
        MRYH/FIRH G20 .... 6 C5 ⑤
Kelvin Wy *KVGV* G3 .... 18 B5
Kempock St *MRYH/BRGTN* G40 ...... 49 E5
Kempsthorn Crs *PLK/PH/NH* G55 ... 110 A1
Kempsthorn Rd *PLK/PH/NH* G53.... 110 A1
Kemp St *SPRGB/BLRNK* G21 .... 11 D4
Kendal Av *GIF/THBK* G46 .... 126 A3 ⑤
        KVD/HLHD G12 .... 75 C4 ⑤
Kendal Dr *KVD/HLHD* G12 .... 75 C4
Kendoon Av *DRUM* G15 .... 63 C3
Kenilworth Av *PLKSD/SHW* G41 ...... 114 B2
Kenmore Gdns *BSDN* G61 .... 67 D1 ⑤
Kenmore St *CAR/SHTL* G32 .... 106 A1
Kenmuir Av *CAR/SHTL* G32 .... 108 A3
Kenmuirhill Rd *CAR/SHTL* G32 ...... 107 D4
Kenmure Av *BSHPBGS* G64 .... 80 A1
Kenmure Crs *BSHPBGS* G64 .... 80 B1
Kenmure Dr *BSHPBGS* G64 .... 80 B1
Kenmure Gdns *BSHPBGS* G64 ...... 80 A1
Kenmure La *BSHPBGS* G64 .... 80 B1
Kenmure Rd *PLKSD/SHW* G41 ...... 55 E2
Kenmure Wy *RUTH* G73 .... 131 D3 ⑤
Kennedar Dr *GOV/IBX* G51 .... 26 C2
Kennedy St *COWCAD* G4 .... 22 B5
Kennishead Av *GIF/THBK* G46 ...... 124 A1
Kennishead Pl *GIF/THBK* G46 ...... 124 A1
Kennishead Rd *GIF/THBK* G46 ...... 122 B2
        GIF/THBK G46 .... 124 B2 ⑧
Kennisholm Av *GIF/THBK* G46 ...... 124 A1
Kennoway Dr *PTCK* G11 .... 15 F3
Kennyhill Sq *DEN/PKHD* G31 ...... 37 D2
Kensington Ga *KVD/HLHD* G12...... 5 E4
Kensington Gate La
        KVD/HLHD G12 .... 5 E4 ⑤
        KVD/HLHD G12 .... 5 F4 ⑧
Kensington Rd *KVD/HLHD* G12 ...... 5 E4
Kentallen Rd *STPS/GTHM/RID* G33 ... 99 D4
Kent Dr *RUTH* G73 .... 132 B1
Kentigern Ter *BSHPBGS* G64 ...... 81 C2
Kent Rd *KVGV* G3 .... 31 D1
Kent St *CGLE* G1 .... 46 C1
Keppel Dr *LNPK/KPK* G44 .... 118 A3
Keppochhill Dr *COWCAD* G4 ...... 22 A1
Keppochhill Rd *COWCAD* G4 ...... 21 F1
Keppoch St *SPRGB/BLRNK* G21 ...... 10 B5
Kerfield Pl *DRUM* G15 .... 63 C2 ⑧
Kerr Dr *DMNK/BRGTN* G40 .... 47 E3
Kerrera Pl *STPS/GTHM/RID* G33 ...... 99 D4 ⑤
Kerrera Rd *STPS/GTHM/RID* G33 ...... 99 D4
Kerr Pl *DMNK/BRGTN* G40 .... 47 E3
Kerr St *DMNK/BRGTN* G40 .... 47 E3
Kerrycroy Av *GVH/MTFL* G42 ...... 117 D2
Kerrycroy Pl *GVH/MTFL* G42 ...... 117 D2 ⑧
Kerrycroy St *GVH/MTFL* G42 ...... 117 D2
Kerrydale St *DMNK/BRGTN* G40...... 49 D3
Kerrylamont Av *GVH/MTFL* G42 .. 117 D3 ⑤
Kerry Pl *DRUM* G15 .... 63 C3
Kersland La *KVD/HLHD* G12 .... 18 B1
Kersland St *KVD/HLHD* G12 .... 18 B1
Kessington Dr *BSDN* G61 .... 67 C2
Kessington Rd *BSDN* G61 .... 67 C3
Kessock Dr *PPK/MIL* G22 .... 9 D5

Kessock Pl *PPK/MIL* G22 .... 9 D5
Kestrel Pl *KNTSWD* G13 .... 73 C4
Kew La *KVD/HLHD* G12 .... 6 A5
Kew Ter *KVD/HLHD* G12 .... 6 A4
Kilbarchan St *CBLS* G5 .... 44 C3 ⓘ
Kilbeg Ter *GIF/THBK* G46 ...... 123 D3
Kilberry St *SPRGB/BLRNK* G21 .... 24 A5
Kilbirnie St *GBLS* G5 .... 44 B4
Kilbride St *GBLS* G5 .... 58 B3
Kilburn Pl *KNTSWD* G13 .... 72 B4
Kilchattan Dr *LNPK/KPK* G44 ...... 117 C3
Kilchoan Rd *STPS/GTHM/RID* G33 .. 91 C4
Kilcloy Av *DRUM* G15 .... 64 A2
Kildale Wy *RUTH* G73 .... 118 B3 ⓘ
Kildary Av *LNPK/KPK* G44 .... 128 A1 ⓘ
Kildary Rd *LNPK/KPK* G44 .... 128 A1
Kildermorie Rd *ESTRH* G34 ...... 100 B2
Kildonan Dr *PTCK* G11 .... 16 A3
Kildrostan St *PLKSD/SHW* G41 .... 55 E3 ⓘ
Kilfinan St *PPK/MIL* G22 .... 78 B5 ⓘ
Kilkerran Dr *STPS/GTHM/RID* G33 .. 83 D4
Killearn St *PPK/MIL* G22 .... 9 F4
Killermont Av *BSDN* G61 .... 67 D4
Killermont Rd *BSDN* G61 .... 66 B3
Killermont St *CGLE* G1 .... 33 E1
Killermont Vw *MRYH/FIRH* G20 .... 67 C4
Killiegrew Rd *PLKSD/SHW* G41 .... 54 A4
Killin St *CAR/SHTL* G32 .... 106 B3
Killoch Dr *KNTSWD* G13 .... 72 A3
Kilmailing Rd *LNPK/KPK* G44 .... 128 B1
Kilmaluag Ter *GIF/THBK* G46 ... 123 D3 ⓘ
Kilmany Dr *CAR/SHTL* G32 .... 105 D1
Kilmany Gdns *CAR/SHTL* G32 ... 105 D1 ⓘ
Kilmardinny Ga *BSDN* G61 .... 66 B1 ⓘ
Kilmarnock Rd *PLKSW/MSWD* G43 .. 114 B4
Kilmartin Pl *GIF/THBK* G46 ...... 124 A2
Kilmaurs Dr *GIF/THBK* G46 .... 127 C3
Kilmaurs St *GOV/IBX* G51 .... 27 E5
Kilmorie Dr *RUTH* G73 .... 118 A3
Kilmuir Crs *GIF/THBK* G46 .... 123 D2
Kilmuir Dr *GIF/THBK* G46 .... 124 A2
Kilmuir Rd *GIF/THBK* G46 .... 123 D3
Kilmun St *MRYH/FIRH* G20 .... 76 B3
Kiloran St *GIF/THBK* G46 .... 124 B2
Kiltearn Rd *STPS/GTHM/RID* G33 .. 100 B3 ⓘ
Kilvaxter Dr *GIF/THBK* G46 .... 124 A3
Kinalty Rd *PLKSW/MSWD* G43 ... 128 A1
Kinbuck St *PPK/MIL* G22 .... 10 A4
Kincardine Dr *BSHPBGS* G64 ...... 81 D2
Kincardine Pl *SPRGB/BLRNK* G21 .... 82 A3 ⓘ
Kincardine Sq
   STPS/GTHM/RID G33 .... 99 D1 ⓘ
Kincath Av *RUTH* G73 .... 132 A3
Kinclaven Av *DRUM* G15 .... 64 A3
Kincraig St *GOV/IBX* G51 .... 26 B5
Kinellan Rd *BSDN* G61 .... 74 B1
Kinellar Dr *SCOT* G14 .... 72 A4
Kinfauns Dr *DRUM* G15 .... 63 D3
   DRUM G15 .... 65 C3
Kingarth La *GVH/MTFL* G42 ...... 56 B3
Kingarth St *PLKSD/SHW* G41 ..... 56 A3
King Edward La *KNTSWD* G13 ...... 3 E2
King Edward Rd *KNTSWD* G13 ...... 3 E2
Kingfisher Dr *KNTSWD* G13 .... 71 D3
King George Ct *RNFRW* PA4 ...... 93 C1 ⓘ
King George Gdns *RNFRW* PA4 ... 85 C4 ⓘ
King George Park Av *RNFRW* PA4 ... 93 C1
King George Pl *RNFRW* PA4 .... 93 C1 ⓘ
King George Wy *RNFRW* PA4 ...... 93 C1 ⓘ
Kinghorn Dr *LNPK/KPK* G44 ..... 117 C4
Kinglas Rd *BSDN* G61 .... 65 C4
Kingsacre Rd *LNPK/KPK* G44 ... 117 C3

RUTH G73 .... 118 A3
Kingsbarns Dr *LNPK/KPK* G44 .... 116 B3
Kingsborough Gdns *KVD/HLHD* G12 .... 5 D4
Kingsborough Ga *KVD/HLHD* G12 .. 17 D1
Kingsborough La *KVD/HLHD* G12 .... 5 D5
Kingsborough La East
   KVD/HLHD G12 .... 5 D5
Kingsbrae Av *LNPK/KPK* G44 .... 117 C3
Kingsbridge Crs *LNPK/KPK* G44 .. 117 D4
Kingsbridge Dr *LNPK/KPK* G44 .. 117 C4 ⓘ
   RUTH G73 .... 118 A4
Kingsburn Dr *RUTH* G73 .... 119 C3
Kingsburn Gv *RUTH* G73 .... 119 C4
Kingscliffe Av *LNPK/KPK* G44 ... 117 C3
Kingscourt Av *LNPK/KPK* G44 ... 117 D4 ⓘ
Kingsdale Av *LNPK/KPK* G44 .... 117 C3 ⓘ
King's Dr *DMNK/BRGTN* G40 ...... 46 C5
Kingsdyke Av *LNPK/KPK* G44 .... 117 D3
Kingsford Av *LNPK/KPK* G44 .... 127 C2
Kingsheath Av *RUTH* G73 .... 118 A4
Kingshill Dr *LNPK/KPK* G44 ..... 117 C4
Kingshouse Av *LNPK/KPK* G44 .. 117 C3
Kingshurst Av *LNPK/KPK* G44 ... 117 C4
King's Inch Rd *RNFRW* PA4 .... 85 D2
Kingsknowe Dr *RUTH* G73 .... 118 A4
Kingsland Dr *CARD/HILL/MSPK* G52 .. 94 B4
Kingsley Av *GVH/MTFL* G42 ...... 116 B1 ⓘ
Kingslynn Dr *LNPK/KPK* G44 .... 117 D4
King's Park Av *LNPK/KPK* G44 .. 116 B4
   RUTH G73 .... 118 A4
King's Park Rd *LNPK/KPK* G44 .. 116 B3
King's Pl *PPK/MIL* G22 .... 78 B4
Kingston St *GBLS* G5 .... 44 B1
King St *CGLE* G1 .... 45 F1
   CLYDBK G81 .... 70 B2
   RUTH G73 .... 119 C2
King Street La *RUTH* G73 ...... 119 C2 ⓘ
Kingsway *SCOT* G14 .... 86 B1
Kingsway Ct *SCOT* G14 .... 86 B1 ⓘ
Kingswood Dr *LNPK/KPK* G44 ... 117 C4
Kingussie Dr *LNPK/KPK* G44 .... 117 C4
Kiniver Dr *DRUM* G15 .... 72 A1
Kinloch St *DMNK/BRGTN* G40 .... 49 E4
Kinmount Av *LNPK/KPK* G44 .... 116 B3
Kinnaird Crs *BSDN* G61 .... 67 D1
Kinnaird Pl *BSHPBGS* G64 .... 81 D2
Kinnear Rd *DMNK/BRGTN* G40 .... 60 C1
Kinnell Av *CARD/HILL/MSPK* G52 .. 103 C3
Kinnell Crs *CARD/HILL/MSPK* G52 .. 103 C3
Kinnell Pl *CARD/HILL/MSPK* G52 .. 50 A2
Kinning St *GBLS* G5 .... 43 F2
Kinnoul La *KVD/HLHD* G12 .... 17 E1
Kinross Av *CARD/HILL/MSPK* G52 .. 102 B2
Kinsail Dr *CARD/HILL/MSPK* G52 ... 93 D4
Kinstone Av *SCOT* G14 .... 86 A1
Kintillo Dr *KNTSWD* G13 .... 72 B4
Kintore Rd *PLKSW/MSWD* G43 ... 115 D3
Kintra St *GOV/IBX* G51 .... 28 C4
Kintyre St *SPRGB/BLRNK* G21 .... 24 A5
Kippen St *PPK/MIL* G22 .... 79 D4
Kippford St *CAR/SHTL* G32 ...... 107 C2
Kirkaig Av *RNFRW* PA4 .... 85 D4
Kirkbean Av *RUTH* G73 .... 131 C2
Kirkbriggs Gdns *RUTH* G73 .... 131 D1
Kirkcaldy Rd *PLKSD/SHW* G41 ... 54 A4
Kirkconnel Av *KNTSWD* G13 ...... 71 D4
Kirkconnel Dr *RUTH* G73 .... 130 B1
Kirkdale Dr *CARD/HILL/MSPK* G52 .. 38 C4
Kirkhill Dr *MRYH/FIRH* G20 .... 6 B1
Kirkhope Dr *DRUM* G15 .... 64 B4
Kirkinner Rd *CAR/SHTL* G32 ..... 107 C3
Kirkintilloch Rd *BSHPBGS* G64 ... 69 D3

Kirklandneuk Rd *RNFRW* PA4............ 84 A2
Kirkland St *MRYH/FIRH* G20........... 7 F5
Kirk La *BSDN* G61................................. 66 A1
   PLKSW/MSWD G43.................. 114 A3
Kirklee Circ *KVD/HLHD* G12............... 6 A3
Kirklee Pl *KVD/HLHD* G12................... 6 A3
Kirklee Qd *KVD/HLHD* G12.................. 6 A3
Kirklee Quadrant La *KVD/HLHD* G12.... 6 A4
Kirklee Rd *KVD/HLHD* G12................... 6 A4
Kirklee Terrace La *KVD/HLHD* G12...... 6 A4
Kirkliston St *CAR/SHTL* G32 .... 97 D4
Kirkmichael Av *PTCK* G11.................. 16 B1
Kirkmichael Gdns *PTCK* G11............. 16 B1
Kirkmuir Dr *RUTH* G73..................... 131 D3
Kirknewton St *CAR/SHTL* G32 .... 98 B4
Kirkoswald Dr *CLYDBK* G81.............. 62 B3
Kirkoswald Rd *PLKSW/MSWD* G43 ... 114 B4
Kirkpatrick St *DMNK/BRGTN* G40 .... 48 A4
Kirk Pl *BSDN* G61............................... 66 A1
Kirkriggs Av *RUTH* G73.................... 131 D1
Kirk Rd *BSDN* G61.............................. 66 A1
Kirkstall Gdns *BSHPBGS* G64............ 69 D2
Kirkton Av *KNTSWD* G13................... 72 A4
Kirkton Crs *KNTSWD* G13.................. 72 A4
Kirkville Pl *DRUM* G15....................... 72 B1
Kirkwell Rd *LNPK/KPK* G44.............. 128 B1
Kirkwood Av *CLYDBK* G81................. 71 C1
Kirkwood St *GOV/IBX* G51................ 41 E2
   RUTH G73....................................... 119 C2
Kirn St *MRYH/FIRH* G20................... 76 A2
Kirriemuir Av
   CARD/HILL/MSPK G52................. 103 C3
Kirriemuir Pl
   CARD/HILL/MSPK G52................. 103 C3
Kirriemuir Rd *BSHPBGS* G64............. 82 A1
Kirtle Dr *RNFRW* PA4......................... 85 C4
Kishorn Pl *STPS/GTHM/RID* G33...... 99 C1
Knapdale St *PPK/MIL* G22................ 78 A3
Knightsbridge St *KNTSWD* G13 .... 73 D4
Knightscliffe Av *KNTSWD* G13 .... 73 D2
Knightswood Rd *KNTSWD* G13 .... 73 D2
Knockhall St *STPS/GTHM/RID* G33... 91 D4
Knockhill Dr *LNPK/KPK* G44............. 116 B3
Knowehead Gdns
   PLKSD/SHW G41........................... 55 E1
Knowehead Ter *PLKSD/SHW* G41 ..... 55 D1
Knowetap St *MRYH/FIRH* G20........... 77 C3
Kyleakin Rd *GIF/THBK* G46.............. 123 D3
Kyleakin Ter *GIF/THBK* G46.............. 123 D3
Kyle Dr *GIF/THBK* G46....................... 127 C3
Kylerhea Rd *GIF/THBK* G46.............. 123 D3
Kyle Sq *CSMK* G45............................ 130 B1
Kyle St *COWCAD* G4.......................... 22 A5

L

La Belle Allee *KVGV* G3...................... 19 D5
La Belle Pl *KVGV* G3.......................... 19 D5
Laburnum Rd *PLKSD/SHW* G41....... 41 E4
Lade Ter *CARD/HILL/MSPK* G52....... 102 A2
Ladhope Pl *KNTSWD* G13................... 71 C2
Lady Anne St *SCOT* G14.................... 85 D1
Ladybank Dr *CARD/HILL/MSPK* G52 .. 38 C5
Ladyhill Dr *BAIL/MDB/MHD* G69..... 109 C2
Ladykirk Crs
   CARD/HILL/MSPK G52................. 94 B4
Ladykirk Dr *CARD/HILL/MSPK* G52... 94 B4
Ladyloan Av *DRUM* G15..................... 63 D2
Ladyloan Ct *DRUM* G15...................... 63 C2
Ladyloan Gdns *DRUM* G15................ 63 D2

Ladymuir Crs *PLK/PH/NH* G53......... 103 C4
Ladywell St *COWCAD* G4..................... 35 D3
Laggan Rd *BSHPBGS* G64.................. 81 D1
   PLKSW/MSWD G43...................... 127 C1
Laidlaw St *GBLS* G5............................ 44 A3
Lainshaw Dr *CSMK* G45................... 128 B4
   LNPK/KPK G44............................ 128 A4
Laird Pl *DMNK/BRGTN* G40.............. 47 E5
Lamberton Dr
   CARD/HILL/MSPK G52................. 94 B4
Lambhill Qd *PLKSD/SHW* G41.......... 42 B2
Lambhill St *PLKSD/SHW* G41.......... 42 B2
Lamb St *PPK/MIL* G22........................ 78 B4
Lamington Rd
   CARD/HILL/MSPK G52................. 102 B2
Lamlash Crs *STPS/GTHM/RID* G33 ... 98 B2
Lamlash Pl *STPS/GTHM/RID* G33 .... 98 B2
Lammermoor Av
   CARD/HILL/MSPK G52................. 103 C3
Lamont Rd *SPRGB/BLRNK* G21......... 81 D4
Lancaster Crs *KVD/HLHD* G12........... 5 E3
Lancaster Crescent La
   KVD/HLHD G12............................. 5 E3
Lancaster Rd *BSHPBGS* G64............. 69 D2
Lancaster Ter *KVD/HLHD* G12........... 5 E3
Lancaster Terrace La
   KVD/HLHD G12............................. 5 E3
Lancefield Quay *KVGV* G3................. 30 C4
Lancefield St *KVGV* G3...................... 31 E4
Landemer Dr *RUTH* G73.................. 118 B4
Landressy Pl *DMNK/BRGTN* G40 ...... 47 D4
Landressy St *DMNK/BRGTN* G40 ...... 47 E4
Langa St *MRYH/FIRH* G20................. 77 C3
Lang Av *RNFRW* PA4........................... 92 B1
Langbar Crs
   STPS/GTHM/RID G33................. 100 B3
Langcroft Pl *GOV/IBX* G51................. 95 C3
Langcroft Rd *GOV/IBX* G51............... 26 A3
Langcroft Ter *GOV/IBX* G51.............. 26 A4
Langdale Av *STPS/GTHM/RID* G33... 89 C3
Langdale St *STPS/GTHM/RID* G33 ... 89 C3
Langford Dr *PLK/PH/NH* G53.......... 122 A3
Langford Pl *PLK/PH/NH* G53........... 122 B3
Langlands Av *GOV/IBX* G51............... 26 B3
Langlands Ct *GOV/IBX* G51............... 27 E2
Langlands Dr *GOV/IBX* G51............... 95 C2
Langlands Rd *GOV/IBX* G51.............. 26 A4
Langlea Av *BLTYR/CAMB* G72.......... 132 B2
Langlea Ct *BLTYR/CAMB* G72.......... 133 C2
Langlea Dr *BLTYR/CAMB* G72.......... 133 C1
Langlea Gdns *BLTYR/CAMB* G72 ..... 133 C1
Langlea Gv *BLTYR/CAMB* G72.......... 133 C2
Langlea Rd *BLTYR/CAMB* G72.......... 133 C1
Langley Av *KNTSWD* G13................... 72 B3
Langness Rd *STPS/GTHM/RID* G33 .. 98 B2
Langrig Rd *SPRGB/BLRNK* G21......... 12 B3
Langshot St *GOV/IBX* G51................. 42 A2
Langside Av *PLKSD/SHW* G41......... 115 C1
Langside Dr *PLKSW/MSWD* G43...... 115 C4
   PLKSW/MSWD G43...................... 127 C2
Langside Gdns *GVH/MTFL* G42....... 116 A3
Langside La *GVH/MTFL* G42............. 56 A5
Langside Pl *PLKSD/SHW* G41.......... 115 D2
Langside Rd *GVH/MTFL* G42............. 56 B5
Langton Crs *PLK/PH/NH* G53.......... 111 C1
Langton Gdns
   BAIL/MDB/MHD G69................. 108 B2
Langton Rd *PLK/PH/NH* G53........... 111 C2
Lansdowne Crs *MRYH/FIRH* G20 ..... 19 E2
Lansdowne Crescent La
   COWCAD G4................................. 19 E2
Lanton Dr *CARD/HILL/MSPK* G52 .... 102 B1

Lanton Rd PLKSW/MSWD G43 .... 127 C1
Lappin St CLYDBK G81 .... 70 B2
Larbert St CGLW G2 .... 21 D5
Larch Av BSHPBGS G64 .... 81 D2
Larchfield Av SCOT G14 .... 86 B2
Larchfield Dr RUTH G73 .... 132 A3
Larchfield Pl SCOT G14 .... 86 B2
Larchfield Rd BSDN G61 .... 74 B1
Larchgrove Av CAR/SHTL G32 .... 99 C4
Larchgrove Pl CAR/SHTL G32 .... 99 C3
Larchgrove Rd CAR/SHTL G32 .... 99 C3
Larch Rd PLKSD/SHW G41 .... 41 D4
Largie Rd LNPK/KPK G44 .... 127 C1
Largo Pl GOV/IBX G51 .... 27 D3
Larkfield St GVH/MTFL G42 .... 57 D2 ⑤
Lasswade St SCOT G14 .... 71 C4 ⑥
Latherton Dr MRYH/FIRH G20 .... 6 B1 ⑦
Latimer Gdns
  CARD/HILL/MSPK G52 .... 102 A2 ④
Lauderdale Gdns PTCK G11 .... 16 C1
Lauderdale La KVD/HLHD G12 .... 4 C5
Lauder Dr RUTH G73 .... 120 B3 ⑨
  RUTH G73 .... 120 B4 ⑩
Lauder St GBLS G5 .... 44 B5 ⑪
Laundry La STPS/GTHM/RID G33 .... 91 C1
Laurel Park Gdns KNTSWD G13 .... 87 C1 ①
Laurel Pl PTCK G11 .... 16 A2
Laurel St PTCK G11 .... 16 A2
Laurieston Rd GBLS G5 .... 45 D4
Laurieston Wy RUTH G73 .... 131 C2 ③
Laverockhall St SPRGB/BLRNK G21 ... 23 E1
Lawers Rd PLKSW/MSWD G43 .... 125 D1
Lawhill Av CSMK G45 .... 129 D2 ⑧
Lawmoor Av GBLS G5 .... 57 F2
Lawmoor Pl GVH/MTFL G42 .... 57 F3
Lawmoor Rd GBLS G5 .... 57 F2
Lawmoor St GBLS G5 .... 57 E1
Lawrence Av PTCK G11 .... 17 E2
Lawrie St PTCK G11 .... 17 D3
Law St DEN/PKHD G31 .... 48 B3
Laxford Av LNPK/KPK G44 .... 128 A2
Leadburn Rd SPRGB/BLRNK G21 ...... 13 E4
Leadburn St CAR/SHTL G32 .... 97 C3 ⑥
Leader St STPS/GTHM/RID G33 .... 96 B1 ⑧
Leander Crs RNFRW PA4 .... 85 C4
Leckie St PLKSW/MSWD G43 .... 114 A2 ⑥
Ledaig St DEN/PKHD G31 .... 37 F3
Ledard Rd GVH/MTFL G42 .... 115 D3
Ledcameroch Crs BSDN G61 .... 65 D2
Ledcameroch Pk BSDN G61 .... 65 D2 ⑧
Ledcameroch Rd BSDN G61 .... 65 D2
Ledgowan Pl MRYH/FIRH G20 .... 76 B2
Ledi Rd PLKSW/MSWD G43 .... 126 A1
Ledmore Dr DRUM G15 .... 63 D2
Lednock Rd CARD/HILL/MSPK G52 .. 102 A1
  STPS/GTHM/RID G33 .... 91 C1
Lee Av STPS/GTHM/RID G33 .... 97 C1
Lee Crs BSHPBGS G64 .... 80 B2
Leefield Dr LNPK/KPK G44 .... 127 D4 ①
Leehill Rd SPRGB/BLRNK G21 .... 80 A3
Leewood Dr LNPK/KPK G44 .... 128 A4 ⑧
Leglen Wood Rd
  STPS/GTHM/RID G33 .... 82 B4
Leicester Av KVD/HLHD G12 .... 4 C2
Leighton St MRYH/FIRH G20 .... 77 C4
Leithland Av PLK/PH/NH G53 .... 110 B1 ①
Leithland Rd PLK/PH/NH G53 .... 110 B1
Leith St STPS/GTHM/RID G33 .... 96 B3
Lendale La BSHPBGS G64 .... 69 C3
Lendel Pl GOV/IBX G51 .... 42 A2
Lenihall Dr CSMK G45 .... 130 A4
Lenihall Ter CSMK G45 .... 130 A3 ⑧

Lennox Av SCOT G14 .... 87 C3
Lennox Crs BSHPBGS G64 .... 80 B2
Lennox Gdns SCOT G14 .... 2 A4
Lennox La West SCOT G14 .... 2 A4
Lennox St MRYH/FIRH G20 .... 76 A3 ⑧
Leny St MRYH/FIRH G20 .... 7 F3
Lenzie St SPRGB/BLRNK G21 .... 11 E2
Lenzie Wy SPRGB/BLRNK G21 .... 80 A1
Leslie Rd PLKSD/SHW G41 .... 55 D2
Leslie St PLKSD/SHW G41 .... 55 E2
Lesmuir Dr SCOT G14 .... 86 A1
Lesmuir Pl SCOT G14 .... 85 D1
Letham Ct PLKSW/MSWD G43 .... 127 C1 ⑥
Letham Dr BSHPBGS G64 .... 82 A2
  PLKSW/MSWD G43 .... 127 C1
Lethamhill Pl
  STPS/GTHM/RID G33 .... 97 C1 ⑤
Lethamhill Rd STPS/GTHM/RID G33 .. 97 C1
Letham Ov BSHPBGS G64 .... 82 B2 ②
Letherby Dr LNPK/KPK G44 .... 116 B3
Lethington Av PLKSD/SHW G41 .... 115 C2
Lethington Pl PLKSD/SHW G41 .... 115 C2
Lettoch St GOV/IBX G51 .... 28 B5
Leven Av BSHPBGS G64 .... 81 D1
Leven Dr BSDN G61 .... 66 B2
Leven St PLKSD/SHW G41 .... 55 E2
Levernside Av PLK/PH/NH G53 .... 111 C2 ③
Levernside Crs PLK/PH/NH G53 .... 110 B1
Levernside Rd PLK/PH/NH G53 .... 110 B1
Lewis Av RNFRW PA4 .... 92 B1
Lewiston Dr SMSTN G23 .... 76 B1 ⑩
Lewiston Pl SMSTN G23 .... 76 B1 ⑪
Lewiston Rd SMSTN G23 .... 76 B1 ⑪
Leyden Ct MRYH/FIRH G20 .... 7 D2
Leyden Gdns MRYH/FIRH G20 .... 7 D2
Leyden St MRYH/FIRH G20 .... 7 D2
The Leys BSHPBGS G64 .... 81 C1
Liberton St STPS/GTHM/RID G33 .... 97 C2
Libo Av PLK/PH/NH G53 .... 111 D1
Library Gdns BLTYR/CAMB G72 .... 121 D4 ②
Library La GIF/THBK G46 .... 124 B3
Liddells Ct BSHPBGS G64 .... 81 C3 ⑤
Liddesdale Pl PPK/MIL G22 .... 80 A3 ③
Liddesdale Rd PPK/MIL G22 .... 79 C3
Liddesdale Sq PPK/MIL G22 .... 80 A3 ⑥
Liddesdale Ter PPK/MIL G22 .... 80 A3 ②
Liddoch Wy RUTH G73 .... 118 B2
Liff Gdns BSHPBGS G64 .... 82 B2 ⑧
Lightburn Pl CAR/SHTL G32 .... 98 B3 ⑤
Lightburn Rd DEN/PKHD G31 .... 49 F1
Lilac Gdns BSHPBGS G64 .... 81 D2 ⑥
Lillyburn Pl DRUM G15 .... 63 C2
Lilybank Gdns KVD/HLHD G12 .... 18 A2
Lilybank Gardens La KVD/HLHD G12 .. 18 A2 ②
Lilybank La KVD/HLHD G12 .... 18 A2 ②
Lilybank Ter KVD/HLHD G12 .... 18 A2 ⑧
Lilybank Terrace La KVD/HLHD G12 .. 18 B2
Lily St DMNK/BRGTN G40 .... 60 C1
Limeside Av RUTH G73 .... 120 A3
Limeside Gdns RUTH G73 .... 120 A3 ⑧
Lime St SCOT G14 .... 14 A1
Linacre Dr CAR/SHTL G32 .... 107 C1
Linacre Gdns CAR/SHTL G32 .... 107 D1 ⑧
Linburn Pl CARD/HILL/MSPK G52 ..... 94 A4
Linburn Rd CARD/HILL/MSPK G52 ... 93 D3
Lincoln Av KNTSWD G13 .... 72 B4
Linden Pl KNTSWD G13 .... 74 B3 ⑧
Linden St KNTSWD G13 .... 74 B3
Lindores Av RUTH G73 .... 119 D3 ⑧
Lindores St GVH/MTFL G42 .... 116 B1
Lindrick Dr SMSTN G23 .... 76 B1
Lindsay Dr KVD/HLHD G12 .... 75 D4 ②

Lindsay Pl *KVD/HLHD* G12 .... **75** D4
Linfern Rd *KVD/HLHD* G12 .... **5** E5
Linhead Dr *PLK/PH/NH* G53 .... **111** C4
Links Rd *CAR/SHTL* G32 .... **107** D3 ☐
LNPK/KPK G44 .... **128** B2 ☐
Linkwood Av *DRUM* G15 .... **63** D3 ☐
Linkwood Crs *DRUM* G15 .... **64** A3
Linkwood Dr *DRUM* G15 .... **63** D3
Linkwood Gdns *DRUM* G15 .... **64** B3 ☐
Linkwood Pl *DRUM* G15 .... **63** D3 ☐
Linlithgow Gdns *CAR/SHTL* G32 ... **107** D1 ☐
Linn Dr *LNPK/KPK* G44 .... **127** D3
Linnet Pl *KNTSWD* G13 .... **71** D3
Linnhead Dr *PLK/PH/NH* G53 .... **122** B1
Linnhead Pl *SCOT* G14 .... **86** B2 ☐
Linnhe Av *BSHPBGS* G64 .... **81** D1
LNPK/KPK G44 .... **128** A2
Linnpark Av *LNPK/KPK* G44 .... **127** D4
Linthaugh Rd *PLK/PH/NH* G53 .... **50** A5
Linthaugh Ter *PLK/PH/NH* G53 ...... **50** A5 ☐
Linthouse Buildings *GOV/IBX* G51 ... **26** C1
Linthouse Rd *GOV/IBX* G51 .... **14** C5
Lintlaw Dr *CARD/HILL/MSPK* G52 ... **94** B4
Linton St *STPS/GTHM/RID* G33 .... **97** C2
Lismore Av *RNFRW* PA4 .... **92** B1
Lismore Rd *KVD/HLHD* G12 .... **4** C2
Lister Pl *CARD/HILL/MSPK* G52 .... **94** A3
Lister Rd *CARD/HILL/MSPK* G52 ...... **93** D3
Lister St *COWCAD* G4 .... **22** B5
Little Dovehill *COWCAD* G4 .... **34** B5
Littlehill St *SPRGB/BLRNK* G21 .... **12** A4
Little St *KVGV* G3 .... **31** E3
Littleton St *MRYH/FIRH* G20 .... **76** B1
Livingstone Av
CARD/HILL/MSPK G52 .... **94** A2
Livingstone St *CLYDBK* G81 .... **70** B1
Lloyd Av *CAR/SHTL* G32 .... **106** A4 ☐
Lloyd St *DEN/PKHD* G31 .... **36** A2
RUTH G73 .... **119** D1
Loanbank Pl *GOV/IBX* G51 .... **28** A4
Loanbank Qd *GOV/IBX* G51 .... **27** F4
Loancroft Pl *BAIL/MDB/MHD* G69 ... **109** D3
Loanfoot Av *KNTSWD* G13 .... **72** A3
Loanhead Av *RNFRW* PA4 .... **84** B3 ☐
Loanhead St *CAR/SHTL* G32 .... **97** D3 ☐
Lobnitz Av *RNFRW* PA4 .... **84** B3
Lochaber Dr *RUTH* G73 .... **132** B2 ☐
Lochaber Rd *BSDN* G61 .... **67** D4
Loch Achray St *CAR/SHTL* G32 ...... **107** C2
Lochaline Dr *LNPK/KPK* G44 .... **128** A2
Lochar Crs *PLK/PH/NH* G53 .... **50** A4
Lochay St *CAR/SHTL* G32 .... **107** C2
Lochbrae Dr *RUTH* G73 .... **132** B2
Lochbridge Rd *ESTRH* G34 .... **101** C3 ☐
Lochburn Crs *MRYH/FIRH* G20 .... **77** C3 ☐
Lochburn Pas *MRYH/FIRH* G20 .... **77** C3 ☐
Lochburn Rd *MRYH/FIRH* G20 .... **77** C3
Lochend Crs *BSDN* G61 .... **65** D3
Lochend Dr *BSDN* G61 .... **65** D3
Lochend Rd *BSDN* G61 .... **66** A3
ESTRH G34 .... **101** D3
Lochgilp St *MRYH/FIRH* G20 .... **76** A3
Lochgoin Av *DRUM* G15 .... **63** C2
Lochgreen St
STPS/GTHM/RID G33 .... **88** B3 ☐
Lochiel Rd *GIF/THBK* G46 .... **124** B2
Lochinver Dr *LNPK/KPK* G44 .... **128** A1
Loch Laidon St *CAR/SHTL* G32 ...... **107** D2
Lochlea Av *CLYDBK* G81 .... **62** A3 ☐
Lochlea Rd *PLKSW/MSWD* G43 ...... **114** B4
RUTH G73 .... **130** B1
Lochleven La *GVH/MTFL* G42 .... **116** A3 ☐

Lochleven Rd *GVH/MTFL* G42 .... **116** A3
Lochlibo Av *KNTSWD* G13 .... **71** D4
Lochmaddy Av *LNPK/KPK* G44 ..... **128** A2
Loch Rd *STPS/GTHM/RID* G33 .... **91** D1
Lochside *BSDN* G61 .... **66** B3 ☐
Lochside St *PLKSD/SHW* G41 .... **54** C5
Lochview Crs *STPS/GTHM/RID* G33 ... **89** D3
Lochview Dr *STPS/GTHM/RID* G33 ... **89** D3
Lochview Gdns
STPS/GTHM/RID G33 .... **89** D3
Lochview Pl *STPS/GTHM/RID* G33 ... **89** D3 ☐
Lochview Rd *BSDN* G61 .... **66** A3 ☐
Loch Voil St *CAR/SHTL* G32 .... **107** D2 ☐
Lochwood St
STPS/GTHM/RID G33 .... **89** C4 ☐
Lochy Av *RNFRW* PA4 .... **93** D1
Lockerbie Av *PLKSW/MSWD* G43 ... **115** D4
Lockhart Pl *UD/BTH/TAN* G71 .... **109** D4 ☐
Lockhart St *SPRGB/BLRNK* G21 ...... **25** D2
Locksley Av *KNTSWD* G13 .... **73** C2
Logan St *GBLS* G5 .... **58** B3
Loganswell Dr *GIF/THBK* G46 ...... **124** A4 ☐
Loganswell Gdns *GIF/THBK* G46 ... **124** A4 ☐
Loganswell Pl *GIF/THBK* G46 .... **124** A4 ☐
Loganswell Rd *GIF/THBK* G46 ...... **124** A4
Lomax St *STPS/GTHM/RID* G33 .... **96** B2 ☐
Lomond Av *BSHPBGS* G64 .... **68** B3
Lomond Pl *STPS/GTHM/RID* G33 .... **91** D2
Lomond Rd *BSDN* G61 .... **66** A4
Lomond St *PPK/MIL* G22 .... **9** D1
London Rd *CAR/SHTL* G32 .... **105** D4
DEN/PKHD G31 .... **104** B3
DMNK/BRGTN G40 .... **46** C1
DMNK/BRGTN G40 .... **48** A4
London St *RNFRW* PA4 .... **84** B1
Longay Pl *PPK/MIL* G22 .... **79** D3
Longay St *PPK/MIL* G22 .... **79** C2
Longden St *CLYDBK* G81 .... **70** B2
Longford St *STPS/GTHM/RID* G33 .. **96** B2 ☐
Longlee *BAIL/MDB/MHD* G69 .... **109** D2 ☐
Longstone Rd *STPS/GTHM/RID* G33 ... **98** B2
Lonmay Rd *STPS/GTHM/RID* G33 ..... **99** D2
Lonsdale Av *GIF/THBK* G46 .... **126** A3
Lora Dr *CARD/HILL/MSPK* G52 .... **39** D5
Loretto Pl *STPS/GTHM/RID* G33 ...... **97** D2 ☐
Loretto St *STPS/GTHM/RID* G33 ...... **97** D2
Lorne Rd *CARD/HILL/MSPK* G52 ..... **93** D2
Lorne St *GOV/IBX* G51 .... **42** B1
Lorne Ter *BLTYR/CAMB* G72 .... **133** D3
Lorraine Gardens La
KVD/HLHD G12 .... **5** E4 ☐
Lorraine Rd *KVD/HLHD* G12 .... **5** E4
Loskin Dr *PPK/MIL* G22 .... **78** B3
Lossie Crs *RNFRW* PA4 .... **85** D4
Lossie St *STPS/GTHM/RID* G33 .... **96** B1
Lothian Gdns *MRYH/FIRH* G20 .... **7** D5 ☐
Lothian St *CARD/HILL/MSPK* G52 ... **93** C2
Louden Hill Pl
STPS/GTHM/RID G33 .... **83** C4 ☐
Louden Hill Rd *STPS/GTHM/RID* G33 ... **83** C4 ☐
Louden Rd *STPS/GTHM/RID* G33 ..... **90** B2 ☐
Lounsdale Pl *SCOT* G14 .... **86** B2 ☐
Lourdes Av *CARD/HILL/MSPK* G52 ... **38** B4
Lovat Pl *CARD/HILL/MSPK* G52 .... **93** C3
RUTH G73 .... **132** B2 ☐
Low Crs *CLYDBK* G81 .... **71** C2
Lower Bourtree Dr *RUTH* G73 ...... **132** A2
Lowther Ter *KVD/HLHD* G12 .... **5** F4
Loyne Dr *RNFRW* PA4 .... **85** D4
Luath St *GOV/IBX* G51 .... **27** F1
Lubas Av *GVH/MTFL* G42 .... **117** D3

Lubas Pl *GVH/MTFL* G42 .... **117** D3
Lubnaig Rd *PLKSW/MSWD* G43 .... **127** C1
Luffness Gdns *CAR/SHTL* G32 .... **106** B4
Lugar Dr *CARD/HILL/MSPK* G52 .... **39** D5
Lugar Pl *LNPK/KPK* G44 .... **130** A1 🖼
Luing Rd *CARD/HILL/MSPK* G52 .... **38** C2
Luma Gdns *GOV/IBX* G51 .... **95** C3
Lumloch St *SPRGB/BLRNK* G21 .... **12** A3
Lumsden La *KVGV* G3 .... **18** A5 🖼
Lumsden St *KVGV* G3 .... **30** A1
Lunan Dr *BSHPBGS* G64 .... **82** A2
Lunan Pl *GOV/IBX* G51 .... **27** D4
Luncarty Pl *CAR/SHTL* G32 .... **106** A3 🖼
Luncarty St *CAR/SHTL* G32 .... **106** A3 🖼
Lunderston Dr *PLK/PH/NH* G53 .... **110** A3
Lundie Gdns *BSHPBGS* G64 .... **82** B2 🖼
Lundie St *CAR/SHTL* G32 .... **105** C3 🖼
Lusshill Ter *UD/BTH/TAN* G71 .... **109** D4
Luss Rd *GOV/IBX* G51 .... **27** E4
Lymburn St *KVGV* G3 .... **18** B5
Lyndale Pl *MRYH/FIRH* G20 .... **76** B2 🖼
Lyndale Rd *MRYH/FIRH* G20 .... **76** B2
Lyndhurst Gdns *MRYH/FIRH* G20 .... **7** D5
Lyndhurst Gardens La
  MRYH/FIRH G20 .... **7** D5
Lyne Cft *BSHPBGS* G64 .... **69** C2
Lynedoch Crs *KVGV* G3 .... **19** E4
Lynedoch Crescent La *KVGV* G3 .... **19** E4
Lynedoch Pl *KVGV* G3 .... **19** E5
Lynedoch St *KVGV* G3 .... **19** E5
Lynedoch Ter *KVGV* G3 .... **19** E5 🖼
Lynne Dr *SMSTN* G23 .... **77** C1 🖼
Lyoncross Rd *PLK/PH/NH* G53 .... **102** B4
Lytham Dr *SMSTN* G23 .... **77** C1 🖼

M

Macbeth Pl *DEN/PKHD* G31 .... **104** B2 🖼
Macbeth St *DEN/PKHD* G31 .... **104** B2 🖼
Macdonald St *RUTH* G73 .... **119** C3 🖼
Macdougall St
  PLKSW/MSWD G43 .... **114** A3 🖼
Macduff Pl *DEN/PKHD* G31 .... **104** B2 🖼
Macduff St *DEN/PKHD* G31 .... **104** B2
Mace Rd *KNTSWD* G13 .... **73** C1
Macfarlane Rd *BSDN* G61 .... **66** B3
Machrie Dr *CSMK* G45 .... **130** B2
Machrie Rd *CSMK* G45 .... **130** B2
Machrie St *CSMK* G45 .... **130** B3 🖼
Macintyre St *KVGV* G3 .... **31** F3
Mackeith St *DMNK/BRGTN* G40 .... **47** C4
Mackinlay St *GBLS* G5 .... **44** C5
Maclean Sq *GOV/IBX* G51 .... **30** B5
Maclean St *CLYDBK* G81 .... **71** C2 🖼
  GOV/IBX G51 .... **42** B1
Maclellan St *PLKSD/SHW* G41 .... **42** A3
Macleod St *COWCAD* G4 .... **34** C3
Madison Av *LNPK/KPK* G44 .... **128** B1
Madras St *DMNK/BRGTN* G40 .... **59** E1
Mafeking St *GOV/IBX* G51 .... **40** C1
Magnus Crs *LNPK/KPK* G44 .... **128** B2
Maidland Rd *PLK/PH/NH* G53 .... **111** C3
Mailing Av *BSHPBGS* G64 .... **69** D4
Main St *BLTYR/CAMB* G72 .... **121** D4
  DMNK/BRGTN G40 .... **59** E1
  GIF/THBK G46 .... **124** B3
  RUTH G73 .... **119** C2
Mair St *GOV/IBX* G51 .... **42** C1
Maitland St *COWCAD* G4 .... **21** D4
Malborough La North *PTCK* G11 .... **3** E5

Malborough La South *PTCK* G11 .... **15** E1
Malin Pl *STPS/GTHM/RID* G33 .... **97** D2
Mallaig Pl *GOV/IBX* G51 .... **26** B3
Mallaig Rd *GOV/IBX* G51 .... **26** B4
Malloch St *MRYH/FIRH* G20 .... **6** C2
Maltbarns St *MRYH/FIRH* G20 .... **8** A5
Mambeg Dr *GOV/IBX* G51 .... **26** C2
Mamore Pl *PLKSW/MSWD* G43 .... **114** A4
Mamore St *PLKSW/MSWD* G43 .... **114** A4
Manchester Dr *KVD/HLHD* G12 .... **75** C4
Mannering Ct *PLKSD/SHW* G41 .... **114** A2 🖼
Mannering Rd *PLKSD/SHW* G41 .... **114** A2 🖼
Mannofield *BSDN* G61 .... **65** D2 🖼
Manor Rd *DRUM* G15 .... **71** D1
  SCOT G14 .... **3** D4
Manor Wy *RUTH* G73 .... **132** A2
Manresa Pl *COWCAD* G4 .... **20** C3
Manse Av *BSDN* G61 .... **66** B1
Manse Brae *LNPK/KPK* G44 .... **116** B4
Mansel St *SPRGB/BLRNK* G21 .... **11** F2
Manse Rd *BSDN* G61 .... **66** B1
  CAR/SHTL G32 .... **107** D2
Manse St *RNFRW* PA4 .... **84** B2
Mansewood Rd *GIF/THBK* G46 .... **125** D2
  PLKSW/MSWD G43 .... **125** D1
Mansfield Rd *CARD/HILL/MSPK* G52 .... **93** D3
Mansfield St *PTCK* G11 .... **17** E3
Mansionhouse Gdns
  PLKSD/SHW G41 .... **115** C3
Mansionhouse Gv
  CAR/SHTL G32 .... **108** A3 🖼
Mansionhouse Rd *CAR/SHTL* G32 .... **108** A3 🖼
  PLKSD/SHW G41 .... **115** C3
Mansion St *PPK/MIL* G22 .... **9** E2
Maple Rd *PLKSD/SHW* G41 .... **41** D4
Marchglen Pl *GOV/IBX* G51 .... **26** B3 🖼
Marchmont Gdns *BSHPBGS* G64 .... **68** B3
March St *PLKSD/SHW* G41 .... **55** F3
Maree Dr *CARD/HILL/MSPK* G52 .... **39** D4
Maree Gdns *BSHPBGS* G64 .... **81** C1 🖼
Marfield St *CAR/SHTL* G32 .... **97** C3
Mar Gdns *RUTH* G73 .... **132** B2 🖼
Marine Crs *GOV/IBX* G51 .... **43** D1 🖼
Marine Gdns *GOV/IBX* G51 .... **43** D1
Mariscat Rd *PLKSD/SHW* G41 .... **55** D3
Marlborough Av *PTCK* G11 .... **3** E5
Marldon La *PTCK* G11 .... **15** E1
Marlow St *PLKSD/SHW* G41 .... **43** D4
Marne St *DEN/PKHD* G31 .... **36** C3
Martha St *CGLE* G1 .... **33** F2
Martin St *DMNK/BRGTN* G40 .... **59** F2
Mart St *CGLE* G1 .... **45** F1 🖼
Martyrs Pl *BSHPBGS* G64 .... **81** C2
Marwick St *DEN/PKHD* G31 .... **37** D3
Maryhill Rd *BSDN* G61 .... **67** C4
  COWCAD G4 .... **20** A4
  MRYH/FIRH G20 .... **7** F5
Maryland Dr *CARD/HILL/MSPK* G52 .... **38** C3
Maryland Gdns
  CARD/HILL/MSPK G52 .... **38** C3
Maryston St *STPS/GTHM/RID* G33 .... **88** B4
Maryville Av *GIF/THBK* G46 .... **126** A4
Maryville Gdns *GIF/THBK* G46 .... **126** A4 🖼
Marywood Sq *PLKSD/SHW* G41 .... **55** E4
Masterton St *COWCAD* G4 .... **21** F1
Mathieson Rd *RUTH* G73 .... **120** A1
Matilda Rd *PLKSD/SHW* G41 .... **42** C5
Maukinfauld Ct *DEN/PKHD* G31 .... **104** B3 🖼
Maukinfauld Rd *CAR/SHTL* G32 .... **105** C3 🖼
Mauldslie St *DMNK/BRGTN* G40 .... **48** C4 🖼
Maule Dr *PTCK* G11 .... **16** A3

Mavis Bank *BSHPBGCS* G64.............. **80** B2
Mavisbank Gdns *GOV/IBX* G51 .... **30** C5
Mavisbank Rd *GOV/IBX* G51 .... **30** B5
Maxton Ter *BLTYR/CAMB* G72 .... **133** D3
Maxwell Av *BAIL/MDB/MHD* G69 .... **109** C2
   BSDN G61 .... **66** A4
   PLKSD/SHW G41 .... **43** D5
Maxwell Dr *BAIL/MDB/MHD* G69 .... **108** B1
   PLKSD/SHW G41 .... **41** E5
Maxwell Gdns *PLKSD/SHW* G41 .... **42** A4
Maxwell Gv *PLKSD/SHW* G41 .... **42** B4
Maxwell La *PLKSD/SHW* G41 .... **43** D5
Maxwell Ov *PLKSD/SHW* G41 .... **43** E5
Maxwell Pl *PLKSD/SHW* G41 .... **56** B1
Maxwell Rd *PLKSD/SHW* G41 .... **43** E5
Maxwell St *BAIL/MDB/MHD* G69 ...... **109** D2 ▣
   CGLE G1 .... **33** E5
Maxwelton Rd *STPS/GTHM/RID* G33... **88** B4
Maybank La *GVH/MTFL* G42 .... **56** A5
Maybank St *GVH/MTFL* G42 .... **56** A5
Mayberry Crs *CAR/SHTL* G32 .... **107** C1
Mayberry Gdns *CAR/SHTL* G32 .... **107** D1 ▣
Mayberry Gv *CAR/SHTL* G32 .... **107** D1 ▣
Mayfield St *MRYH/FIRH* G20 .... **77** D4
May Ter *GIF/THBK* G46 .... **126** A3 ▣
   GVH/MTFL G42 .... **116** B2
Mcalpine St *KVGV* G3 .... **32** A5
Mcarthur St *PLKSW/MSWD* G43 ..... **114** A3 ▣
Mcaslin Ct *COWCAD* G4 .... **34** B1
Mcaslin St *COWCAD* G4 .... **34** C1
Mccallum Av *RUTH* G73 .... **119** D2 ▣
Mccreery St *CLYDBK* G81 .... **70** B2
Mcculloch St *PLKSD/SHW* G41 .... **43** E5
Mcdonald Crs *CLYDBK* G81 .... **70** B2
Mcfarlane St *COWCAD* G4 .... **46** C1
Mcgregor St *CLYDBK* G81 .... **70** B2
   GOV/IBX G51 .... **27** E5
Mcintosh St *DEN/PKHD* G31 .... **35** E4
Mckechnie St *GOV/IBX* G51 .... **28** A1
Mclaren Av *RNFRW* PA4 .... **92** A1 ▣
Mclaren Crs *MRYH/FIRH* G20 .... **77** C3
Mclaren Gdns *MRYH/FIRH* G20 .... **77** C3 ▣
Mclennan St *GVH/MTFL* G42 .... **116** B2 ▣
Mcnair St *CAR/SHTL* G32 .... **106** A1 ▣
Mcneil Av *CLYDBK* G81 .... **71** C1
Mcneil Gdns *GBLS* G5 .... **46** B4
Mcneil St *GBLS* G5 .... **46** B4
Mcphail St *DMNK/BRGTN* G40 .... **47** D4
Mcphater St *CGLW* G2 .... **21** D5
Meadowburn *BSHPBGCS* G64 .... **69** C2
Meadow La *RNFRW* PA4 .... **84** B1
Meadowpark St *DEN/PKHD* G31 ...... **36** C2
Meadow Rd *PTCK* G11 .... **16** A4
Meadowside St *GOV/IBX* G51 .... **16** B5
   RNFRW PA4 .... **84** B1
Meadowwell St *CAR/SHTL* G32 .... **106** B1 ▣
Medwyn St *SCOT* G14 .... **14** B1
Megan Ga *DMNK/BRGTN* G40 .... **47** E4
Megan St *DMNK/BRGTN* G40 .... **47** E4
Meikle Av *RNFRW* PA4 .... **84** A4
Meiklerig Crs *PLK/PH/NH* G53 .... **103** C4
Meikle Rd *PLK/PH/NH* G53 .... **111** C2 ▣
Meiklewood Rd *GOV/IBX* G51 .... **26** A5
Melbourne Ct *GIF/THBK* G46............. **126** B3
Melbourne St *DEN/PKHD* G31 .... **35** E5
Meldon Pl *GOV/IBX* G51 .... **26** B3
Meldrum St *CLYDBK* G81 .... **70** B2
Melford Av *GIF/THBK* G46 .... **126** B4
Melfort Av *CLYDBK* G81 .... **62** A3
   PLKSD/SHW G41 .... **40** C5
Mellerstain Dr *SCOT* G14 .... **71** C4
Melness Pl *GOV/IBX* G51 .... **26** B3 ▣

Melrose Av *RUTH* G73 .... **119** D3
Melrose Gdns *MRYH/FIRH* G20.......... **7** E5
Melrose St *COWCAD* G4 .... **19** F4
Melvick Pl *GOV/IBX* G51 .... **26** B3 ▣
Melville Ct *CGLE* G1 .... **33** F5 ▣
Melville Gdns *BSHPBGCS* G64 .... **69** C4
Melville St *PLKSD/SHW* G41 .... **55** E2
Memel St *PPK/MIL* G22 .... **10** C2
Memus Av *CARD/HILL/MSPK* G52..... **103** C2
Mennock Dr *BSHPBGCS* G64 .... **69** C2 ▣
Menock Rd *LNPK/KPK* G44 .... **116** B4
Menteith Av *BSHPBGCS* G64 .... **81** D1
Menteith Dr *RUTH* G73 .... **132** B4
Menteith Pl *RUTH* G73 .... **132** B4
Menzies Dr *SPRGB/BLRNK* G21 .... **12** B1
Menzies Pl *SPRGB/BLRNK* G21 .... **12** B1
Menzies Rd *SPRGB/BLRNK* G21 .... **12** B1
Merchant La *CGLE* G1 .... **45** F1
Merchiston St *CAR/SHTL* G32 .... **97** C3
Merkland St *PTCK* G11 .... **16** C3
Merlinford Av *RNFRW* PA4 .... **85** C3
Merlinford Crs *RNFRW* PA4 .... **85** C3 ▣
Merlinford Dr *RNFRW* PA4 .... **85** C3
Merlinford Wy *RNFRW* PA4 .... **85** C3 ▣
Merrick Gdns *GOV/IBX* G51 .... **40** C2
Merrick Wy *RUTH* G73 .... **131** D3 ▣
Merryburn Av *PLKSW/MSWD* G43 ... **126** B2
Merrycrest Av *GIF/THBK* G46 .... **126** B2
Merrycroft Av *GIF/THBK* G46 .... **126** B2
Merryland Pl *GOV/IBX* G51 .... **29** D4
Merryland St *GOV/IBX* G51 .... **29** D4
Merrylee Crs *PLKSW/MSWD* G43 ..... **126** A1 ▣
Merrylee Pk *GIF/THBK* G46 .... **126** A1 ▣
Merrylee Park Av *GIF/THBK* G46 ...... **126** B2
Merrylee Rd *PLKSW/MSWD* G43 ...... **127** C1
Merryton Av *DRUM* G15 .... **64** B3
   GIF/THBK G46 .... **126** A2
Merryton Pl *DRUM* G15 .... **64** B3
Merryvale Av *PLKSW/MSWD* G43 ..... **126** B2
Merryvale Pl *PLKSW/MSWD* G43 ..... **126** B1 ▣
Merton Dr *CARD/HILL/MSPK* G52..... **102** A1
Meryon Gdns *CAR/SHTL* G32............ **107** D4
Meryon Rd *CAR/SHTL* G32 .... **107** D3 ▣
Methil St *SCOT* G14 .... **87** C3
Methven Av *BSDN* G61 .... **67** D1
Methven St *DEN/PKHD* G31 .... **104** B3
Metropole La *CGLE* G1 .... **45** E1
Micklehouse Ov
   BAIL/MDB/MHD G69 .... **101** D4 ▣
Micklehouse Pl
   BAIL/MDB/MHD G69 .... **101** D4 ▣
Micklehouse Rd
   BAIL/MDB/MHD G69 .... **101** D4
Micklehouse Wynd
   BAIL/MDB/MHD G69 .... **101** D4 ▣
Midcroft Av *LNPK/KPK* G44 .... **129** D1
Middlesex Gdns *PLKSD/SHW* G41 .... **42** C2
Middlesex St *PLKSD/SHW* G41 .... **42** C2
Middleton St *GOV/IBX* G51 .... **41** F1
Midfaulds Av *RNFRW* PA4 .... **85** C4 ▣
Midland St *CGLE* G1 .... **32** C4
Midlem Dr *CARD/HILL/MSPK* G52..... **103** C1
Midlem Ov
   CARD/HILL/MSPK G52 .... **103** C1 ▣
Midlock St *GOV/IBX* G51 .... **41** E1
Midlothian Dr *PLKSD/SHW* G41 .... **114** B1 ▣
Midton St *SPRGB/BLRNK* G21 .... **23** E1
Mid-wharf St *COWCAD* G4 .... **21** F3
Milford St *STPS/GTHM/RID* G33 .... **98** A2
Millarbank St *SPRGB/BLRNK* G21 ..... **11** D4
Millbeg Crs *STPS/GTHM/RID* G33 .... **108** B1 ▣
Millbeg Pl *STPS/GTHM/RID* G33 ...... **108** A1

Millbrae Crs *GVH/MTFL* G42	**115**	C3
KNTSWD G13	**70**	B3 🖫
Millbrae Gdns *PLKSD/SHW* G41	**115**	D3 🖫
Millbrae Rd *GVH/MTFL* G42	**115**	C3
Millbrix Av *SCOT* G14	**86**	A1
Millburn Av *KNTSWD* G13	**71**	C2
RNFRW PA4	**84**	B3 🖫
RUTH G73	**119**	C4
Millburn Dr *RNFRW* PA4	**85**	C3 🖫
Millburn Rd *RNFRW* PA4	**84**	B3
Millburn St *SPRGB/BLRNK* G21	**24**	A5
Millburn Wy *RNFRW* PA4	**85**	C3 🖫
Mill Ct *RUTH* G73	**119**	C2 🖫
Mill Crs *DMNK/BRGTN* G40	**59**	E1
Millcroft Rd *RUTH* G73	**59**	E4
Millerfield Pl *DMNK/BRGTN* G40	**61**	D2
Millerfield Rd *DMNK/BRGTN* G40	**60**	C3
Millersneuk Crs		
STPS/GTHM/RID G33	**90**	A1
Millerston St *DEN/PKHD* G31	**48**	B1
Miller St *BAIL/MDB/MHD* G69	**109**	D2
CGLE G1	**33**	E4
Millholm Rd *LNPK/KPK* G44	**128**	B2
Millhouse Crs *MRYH/FIRH* G20	**76**	A3 🖫
Millhouse Dr *MRYH/FIRH* G20	**75**	D3
Millport Av *LNPK/KPK* G44	**117**	C3
Mill Rd *KNTSWD* G13	**70**	B3
Millroad Dr *DMNK/BRGTN* G40	**47**	D1
Millroad St *DMNK/BRGTN* G40	**46**	C1
Mill St *DMNK/BRGTN* G40	**59**	E1
RUTH G73	**119**	C2
Millview Pl *PLK/PH/NH* G53	**122**	B2 🖫
Millwood St *PLKSD/SHW* G41	**115**	C2
Milnbank St *DEN/PKHD* G31	**36**	A2
Milncroft Pl *STPS/GTHM/RID* G33	**98**	A1 🖫
Milncroft Rd *STPS/GTHM/RID* G33	**98**	A1
Milner La *KNTSWD* G13	**3**	D3
Milner Rd *KNTSWD* G13	**3**	D2
Milngavie Rd *BSDN* G61	**66**	B3
Milnpark Gdns *GOV/IBX* G51	**42**	B2
Milnpark St *PLKSD/SHW* G41	**42**	C2
Milovaig Av *SMSTN* G23	**76**	B1 🖫
Milovaig St *SMSTN* G23	**76**	B1
Milrig Rd *RUTH* G73	**118**	B3
Milton Av *BLTYR/CAMB* G72	**133**	C1
Milton Dr *BSHPBGS* G64	**80**	B3 🖫
Milton St *CGLW* G2	**21**	E5
Minard Rd *PLKSD/SHW* G41	**54**	C5
Minerva St *KVGV* G3	**30**	C2
Minerva Wy *KVGV* G3	**30**	B2
Mingarry La *MRYH/FIRH* G20	**6**	C4
Mingarry St *MRYH/FIRH* G20	**6**	C4
Mingulay Crs *PPK/MIL* G22	**79**	D2
Mingulay Pl *PPK/MIL* G22	**80**	A2
Mingulay St *PPK/MIL* G22	**79**	D2
Minstrel Rd *KNTSWD* G13	**73**	D1
Minto Av *RUTH* G73	**132**	B2 🖫
Minto Crs *CARD/HILL/MSPK* G52	**39**	E3
Minto St *CARD/HILL/MSPK* G52	**39**	E3
Mireton St *PPK/MIL* G22	**8**	C2
Mitchell Dr *RUTH* G73	**119**	D4 🖫
Mitchell Hill Rd *CSMK* G45	**130**	B4
Mitchell La *CGLE* G1	**33**	D3
Mitchell St *CGLE* G1	**33**	D4
Mitre Ct *PTCK* G11	**3**	E5
Mitre La *SCOT* G14	**2**	B4
Mitre La West *SCOT* G14	**2**	B4
Mitre Rd *PTCK* G11	**3**	E4
SCOT G14	**2**	C4
Moat Av *KNTSWD* G13	**73**	C2
Mochrum Rd *PLKSW/MSWD* G43	**115**	C4
Moffat St *GBLS* G5	**46**	A4

Moidart Crs *CARD/HILL/MSPK* G52	**39**	D3
Moidart Pl *CARD/HILL/MSPK* G52	**39**	E3 🖫
Moidart Rd *CARD/HILL/MSPK* G52	**39**	D3
Moir St *CGLE* G1	**46**	B1
Molendinar St *CGLE* G1	**34**	B5
Mollinsburn St *SPRGB/BLRNK* G21	**11**	D5
Monach Rd *STPS/GTHM/RID* G33	**99**	C2
Monar Dr *PPK/MIL* G22	**9**	D5
Monar St *PPK/MIL* G22	**9**	D5
Monart Pl *MRYH/FIRH* G20	**7**	E2
Moncur St *DMNK/BRGTN* G40	**46**	C1
Moness Dr *CARD/HILL/MSPK* G52	**38**	C4
Monifieth Av *CARD/HILL/MSPK* G52	**50**	A1
Monikie Gdns *BSHPBGS* G64	**82**	B1 🖫
Monksbridge Av *KNTSWD* G13	**73**	D2 🖫
Monkscroft Av *PTCK* G11	**16**	B1
Monkscroft Ct *PTCK* G11	**16**	B2
Monkscroft Gdns *PTCK* G11	**16**	B2 🖫
Monkton Dr *DRUM* G15	**72**	B1
Monmouth Av *KVD/HLHD* G12	**4**	A1
Monreith Av *BSDN* G61	**65**	D4
Monreith Rd *PLKSW/MSWD* G43	**114**	B4
Monreith Rd East *LNPK/KPK* G44	**128**	A1
Montague La *KVD/HLHD* G12	**5**	D4
Montague St *KVGV* G3	**19**	E3
Monteith Pl *DMNK/BRGTN* G40	**46**	C2 🖫
Monteith Rw *CGLE* G1	**46**	B1
DMNK/BRGTN G40	**46**	C2
Montford Av *LNPK/KPK* G44	**117**	D3
RUTH G73	**118**	A3
Montgomery St *DMNK/BRGTN* G40	**48**	A4
Montraive St *RUTH* G73	**120**	A1 🖫
Montrave St *CARD/HILL/MSPK* G52	**38**	A4
Montrose Av *CARD/HILL/MSPK* G52	**93**	D3
Montrose St *CGLE* G1	**34**	A4
CLYDBK G81	**62**	A4
Montrose Ter *SPRGB/BLRNK* G21	**82**	A3
Monymusk Pl *CLYDBK* G81	**63**	C1
Moodiesburn St		
STPS/GTHM/RID G33	**88**	B4 🖫
Moorburn Av *GIF/THBK* G46	**125**	D3
Moore Dr *BSDN* G61	**66**	B3
Moore St *DMNK/BRGTN* G40	**35**	E5
Moorfoot Av *GIF/THBK* G46	**125**	D3
Moorfoot St *CAR/SHTL* G32	**97**	C4
Moorhouse Av *KNTSWD* G13	**71**	D4
Moorpark Av *CARD/HILL/MSPK* G52	**93**	D4
Moorpark Dr *CARD/HILL/MSPK* G52	**94**	A1
Moraine Av *DRUM* G15	**72**	B1
Moraine Circ *DRUM* G15	**72**	A1
Moraine Dr *DRUM* G15	**72**	A1
Moraine Pl *DRUM* G15	**72**	B1 🖫
Morar Crs *BSHPBGS* G64	**68**	A3
Morar Dr *BSDN* G61	**67**	D3
RUTH G73	**131**	D3
Morar Rd *CARD/HILL/MSPK* G52	**39**	D3
Morar Ter *RUTH* G73	**132**	B2 🖫
Moray Pl *BSHPBGS* G64	**82**	A1
PLKSD/SHW G41	**55**	D4
Mordaunt St *DMNK/BRGTN* G40	**60**	B1
Moredun Crs *CAR/SHTL* G32	**99**	C3
Moredun St *CAR/SHTL* G32	**99**	C3
Morefield Rd *GOV/IBX* G51	**26**	B4
Morgan Ms *GVH/MTFL* G42	**57**	D2
Morina Gdns *PLK/PH/NH* G53	**123**	C3 🖫
Morion Rd *KNTSWD* G13	**73**	D2
Morley St *LNPK/KPK* G44	**116**	A3
Morna La *SCOT* G14	**14**	C2
Morningside St		
STPS/GTHM/RID G33	**96**	B2
Morrin St *SPRGB/BLRNK* G21	**10**	C5 🖫
Morrison Qd *CLYDBK* G81	**71**	C1

Morrison St *GBLS* G5 .... **44** A1
Morriston Cr *RNFRW* PA4 .... **93** D1
Morton Gdns *PLKSD/SHW* G41 ...... **53** F5
Morven Av *BSHPBGS* G64 .... **82** A1
Morven Rd *BLTYR/CAMB* G72 ...... **133** D3
Morven St *CARD/HILL/MSPK* G52 ..... **39** D3
Mosesfield St *SPRGB/BLRNK* G21 ..... **11** E1
Mosque Av *GBLS* G5 .... **45** E2
Mossbank Av *STPS/GTHM/RID* G33 ... **89** D2
Mossbank Dr *STPS/GTHM/RID* G33 .. **89** D3
Mosscastle Rd
  STPS/GTHM/RID G33 .... **91** C4 🔢
Mossend La *STPS/GTHM/RID* G33 ... **99** D2
Mossend St *STPS/GTHM/RID* G33 ... **99** D3 🔢
Mossgiel Av *RUTH* G73 .... **131** C1
Mossgiel Dr *CLYDBK* G81 .... **62** A3
Mossgiel Pl *RUTH* G73 .... **131** C1 🔢
Mossgiel Rd *PLKSW/MSWD* G43 ...... **114** B3
Moss Heights Av
  CARD/HILL/MSPK G52 .... **38** A3
Mossland Rd *CARD/HILL/MSPK* G52 .. **92** B2
Mosspark Av *CARD/HILL/MSPK* G52 .. **51** E2
Mosspark Bvd
  CARD/HILL/MSPK G52 .... **38** B4
Mosspark Dr *CARD/HILL/MSPK* G52 .. **50** B2
Mosspark Ov *CARD/HILL/MSPK* G52 .. **51** D1
Mosspark Sq *CARD/HILL/MSPK* G52 .. **51** D3
Moss Rd *GOV/IBX* G51 .... **26** B1
Moss-side Rd *PLKSD/SHW* G41 ...... **115** C1
Mossvale La
  STPS/GTHM/RID G33 .... **90** B4 🔢
Mossvale Rd *STPS/GTHM/RID* G33 ... **91** C4 🔢
Mossvale Sq *STPS/GTHM/RID* G33 .. **90** B4 🔢
Mossview La
  CARD/HILL/MSPK G52 .... **103** C1 🔢
Moulin Circ
  CARD/HILL/MSPK G52 .... **102** B2 🔢
Moulin Pl *CARD/HILL/MSPK* G52 ...... **102** A2
Moulin Rd *CARD/HILL/MSPK* G52 .... **102** A2
Moulin Ter *CARD/HILL/MSPK* G52 .... **102** A3
Mountainblue St *DMNK/BRGTN* G40 .. **48** B2
Mount Annan Dr *LNPK/KPK* G44 .... **116** B3
Mountgarrie Rd *GOV/IBX* G51 .... **26** B4
Mount Lockhart *UD/BTH/TAN* G71 .. **109** D4
Mount St *MRYH/FIRH* G20 .... **19** F1
Mount Stuart St *PLKSD/SHW* G41 .. **115** C2
Mount Vernon Av *CAR/SHTL* G32 .. **108** A3
Moyne Rd *PLK/PH/NH* G53 .... **102** A1
Muirbank Av *RUTH* G73 .... **118** B3
Muirbank Gdns *RUTH* G73 .... **118** B3 🔢
Muirbrae Rd *RUTH* G73 .... **131** D2
Muirbrae Wy *RUTH* G73 .... **131** D2 🔢
Muirdrum Av *CARD/HILL/MSPK* G52 .. **50** A1
Muirdykes Av
  CARD/HILL/MSPK G52 .... **102** A1 🔢
Muirdykes Rd
  CARD/HILL/MSPK G52 .... **102** A1
Muiredge Ter
  BAIL/MDB/MHD G69 .... **109** D2 🔢
Muirend Av *LNPK/KPK* G44 .... **127** C1
Muirend Rd *LNPK/KPK* G44 .... **127** C2
Muirfield Ct *LNPK/KPK* G44 .... **127** D2 🔢
Muirfield Crs *SMSTN* G23 .... **77** C1
Muirhead Rd *BAIL/MDB/MHD* G69 .. **109** D3
Muirhead Wy *BSHPBGS* G64 .... **82** B1
Muirhill Av *LNPK/KPK* G44 .... **127** C2
Muirhill Crs *KNTSWD* G13 .... **71** D3
Muirhouse St *PLKSD/SHW* G41 ...... **56** B1 🔢
Muirkirk Dr *KNTSWD* G13 .... **74** B3 🔢
Muirpark Av *RNFRW* PA4 .... **84** A4 🔢
Muirpark Dr *BSHPBGS* G64 .... **81** C2
Muirpark St *PTCK* G11 .... **16** C3

Muirpark Ter *BSHPBGS* G64 .... **81** C2 🔢
Muirshiel Crs *PLK/PH/NH* G53 .... **111** C4
Muirside Av *CAR/SHTL* G32 .... **108** A3
Muirside Rd *BAIL/MDB/MHD* G69 ... **109** D2
Muirside St *BAIL/MDB/MHD* G69 .... **109** D2
Muirskeith Crs
  PLKSW/MSWD G43 .... **116** A4 🔢
Muirskeith Pl
  PLKSW/MSWD G43 .... **115** D4 🔢
Muirskeith Rd *PLKSW/MSWD* G43 .. **115** D4
Muir St *BSHPBGS* G64 .... **81** C1
  RNFRW PA4 .... **84** B2 🔢
Muirton Dr *BSHPBGS* G64 .... **68** B3
Muiryfauld Dr *CAR/SHTL* G32 .... **105** C2
Mulberry Rd *PLKSW/MSWD* G43 .... **126** B1
Mullardoch St *SMSTN* G23 .... **76** B3 🔢
Mull Av *RNFRW* PA4 .... **92** A1
Mull St *SPRGB/BLRNK* G21 .... **24** C2
Munlochy Rd *GOV/IBX* G51 .... **26** B3
Munro Ct *KNTSWD* G13 .... **2** C1
Munro La *East KNTSWD* G13 .... **3** D1
Munro Pl *KNTSWD* G13 .... **74** A3
Munro Rd *KNTSWD* G13 .... **2** C1
Murano St *MRYH/FIRH* G20 .... **7** E3
Murrayfield Dr *BSDN* G61 .... **74** A1
Murrayfield St *CAR/SHTL* G32 .... **97** C3 🔢
Murray St *RNFRW* PA4 .... **84** A3 🔢
Murrin Av *BSHPBGS* G64 .... **82** B1 🔢
Murroes Rd *GOV/IBX* G51 .... **26** B3
Muslin St *DMNK/BRGTN* G40 .... **47** E5
Mybster Pl *GOV/IBX* G51 .... **26** B3 🔢
Myreside Pl *CAR/SHTL* G32 .... **96** B4 🔢
Myreside St *CAR/SHTL* G32 .... **97** C4
Myres Rd *PLK/PH/NH* G53 .... **111** D2
Myrie Gdns *BSHPBGS* G64 .... **81** D1
Myrtle Hill La *GVH/MTFL* G42 .... **117** C2
Myrtle Pk *GVH/MTFL* G42 .... **116** B1
Myrtle Pl *GVH/MTFL* G42 .... **117** C2 🔢
Myrtle Sq *BSHPBGS* G64 .... **81** C2
Myrtle St *BLTYR/CAMB* G72 .... **121** D4
Myrtle View Rd *GVH/MTFL* G42 ...... **117** C2
Myrtle Wk *BLTYR/CAMB* G72 .... **121** D4

N

Nairnside Rd *SPRGB/BLRNK* G21 ..... **82** A3
Nairn St *KVGV* G3 .... **18** A5
Nansen St *MRYH/FIRH* G20 .... **20** A1
Napier Dr *GOV/IBX* G51 .... **29** D2
Napier Pl *GOV/IBX* G51 .... **28** C2
Napier Rd *CARD/HILL/MSPK* G52 .... **93** D1
  GOV/IBX G51 .... **28** C2
Napiershall La *COWCAD* G4 .... **19** F2
Napiershall Pl *MRYH/FIRH* G20 .... **19** F2
Napiershall St *COWCAD* G4 .... **19** F2
  MRYH/FIRH G20 .... **19** F1
Napier St *CLYDBK* G81 .... **70** A3
  GOV/IBX G51 .... **29** D2
Napier Ter *GOV/IBX* G51 .... **28** C1
Naseby Av *PTCK* G11 .... **3** F5
Naseby La *PTCK* G11 .... **3** F5
Nasmyth Rd
  CARD/HILL/MSPK G52 .... **94** A3 🔢
Nasmyth Rd North
  CARD/HILL/MSPK G52 .... **94** B3
Nasmyth Rd South
  CARD/HILL/MSPK G52 .... **94** A3
National Bank La *CGLE* G1 .... **33** D3 🔢
Naver St *STPS/GTHM/RID* G33 .... **97** C1 🔢
Neilsland Ov *PLK/PH/NH* G53 .... **111** D2
Neilsland Sq *PLK/PH/NH* G53 .... **111** D1 🔢

Neilston Av *PLK/PH/NH* G53 .... **123** C1
Neil St *RNFRW* PA4 .... **84** B1
Neilvaig Dr *RUTH* G73 .... **132** A3 🔢
Neistpoint Dr
   STPS/GTHM/RID G33 .... **98** A3 🔢
Nelson Mandela Pl *CGLW* G2 ...... **33** E2 🔢
Nelson Pl *BAIL/MDB/MHD* G69 ...... **109** D2
Nelson St *BAIL/MDB/MHD* G69 ...... **109** D2
   GBLS G5 .... **44** B1
Neptune St *GOV/IBX* G51 .... **28** C3
Ness Gdns *BSHPBGS* G64 .... **81** D1 🔢
Ness St *STPS/GTHM/RID* G33 .... **97** C1
Nether Auldhouse Rd
   PLKSW/MSWD G43 .... **114** A4
Netherburn Av *PLK/KPK* G44 ...... **127** D4
Netherby Dr *PLKSD/SHW* G41 .... **42** A5
Nethercairn Rd *GIF/THBK* G46 ...... **126** A2
Nethercliffe Av *LNPK/KPK* G44 .... **127** D4
Netherfield St *DEN/PKHD* G31 .... **37** E5 🔢
Netherlee Pl *LNPK/KPK* G44 .... **128** A2
Netherlee Rd *LNPK/KPK* G44 .... **128** A2
Netherplace Crs
   PLK/PH/NH G53 .... **110** B2 🔢
Netherplace Rd *PLK/PH/NH* G53 .... **110** B2
Netherton Rd *KNTSWD* G13 .... **74** A2
Netherton St *KNTSWD* G13 .... **74** B3 🔢
Nevis Rd *PLKSW/MSWD* G43 .... **125** D1 🔢
Newark Dr *PLKSD/SHW* G41 .... **54** B2
Newbattle Rd *CAR/SHTL* G32 ...... **106** B4 🔢
Newbattle Gdns *CAR/SHTL* G32 .... **106** B4 🔢
Newbattle Pl *CAR/SHTL* G32 .... **106** B4 🔢
Newbold Av *SPRGB/BLRNK* G21 .... **80** B3 🔢
Newburgh St *PLKSW/MSWD* G43 .. **114** B3
Newcastleton Dr *SMSTN* G23 .... **77** C1 🔢
New City Rd *COWCAD* C4 .... **20** B4
Newcroft Dr *LNPK/KPK* G44 .... **129** D1
Newfield Pl *GIF/THBK* G46 .... **124** B4 🔢
   RUTH G73 .... **118** A3
Newfield Sq *PLK/PH/NH* G53 .... **110** A4
Newhall St *DMNK/BRGTN* G40 .... **59** D1
Newhaven Rd *STPS/GTHM/RID* G33 .. **98** B2
Newhaven St *CAR/SHTL* G32 .... **98** A3 🔢
Newhills Rd *STPS/GTHM/RID* G33 .. **100** A3
Newington St *CAR/SHTL* G32 .... **97** D4
New Kirk Rd *BSDN* G61 .... **66** A1
Newlandsfield Rd
   PLKSW/MSWD G43 .... **114** B3
Newlands Pl *PLKSW/MSWD* G43 .... **115** C4
New Luce Dr *CAR/SHTL* G32 .... **107** D3
Newmains Rd *RNFRW* PA4 .... **92** A1
Newstead Gdns *SMSTN* G23 .... **77** D3 🔢
Newtongrange Av *CAR/SHTL* G32 .. **106** B4
Newtongrange Gdns
   CAR/SHTL G32 .... **106** B4 🔢
Newton Pl *KVGV* G3 .... **19** E5
Newton Terrace La *KVGV* G3 .... **31** E1
Newtyle Pl *BSHPBGS* G64 .... **82** B1 🔢
New Wynd *CGLE* G1 .... **33** F5 🔢
Nicholas St *CGLE* G1 .... **34** B3
Nicholson St *GBLS* G5 .... **45** D1
Nicolson Ct *STPS/GTHM/RID* G33 .. **91** D1
Niddrie Sq *GVH/MTFL* G42 .... **55** F5
Nigel Gdns *PLKSD/SHW* G41 .... **114** B1
Nigg Pl *ESTRH* G34 .... **101** C2
Nimmo Dr *GOV/IBX* G51 .... **27** D3
Nisbet St *DEN/PKHD* G31 .... **104** B1 🔢
Nith Dr *RNFRW* PA4 .... **85** C4
Nithsdale Dr *PLKSD/SHW* G41 .... **55** F3
Nithsdale Rd *PLKSD/SHW* G41 .... **40** C5
   PLKSD/SHW G41 .... **55** F3
Nithsdale St *PLKSD/SHW* G41 .... **55** F3
Nith St *STPS/GTHM/RID* G33 .... **96** B1 🔢

Nitshill Rd *GIF/THBK* G46 .... **123** C2
   GIF/THBK G46 .... **124** A4 🔢
   PLK/PH/NH G53 .... **110** A4
   PLK/PH/NH G53 .... **123** C3 🔢
Niven St *MRYH/FIRH* G20 .... **76** A4
Norbreck Dr *GIF/THBK* G46 .... **126** A2
Norby Rd *PTCK* G11 .... **15** E1
Norfield Dr *LNPK/KPK* G44 .... **116** B3
Norfolk Ct *GBLS* G5 .... **45** D2
Norfolk Crs *BSHPBGS* G64 .... **68** A3
Norfolk St *GBLS* G5 .... **45** D2
Norham St *PLKSD/SHW* G41 .... **54** C5
Norman St *DMNK/BRGTN* G40 .... **59** F2
Norse La North *SCOT* G14 .... **87** C2
Norse La South *SCOT* G14 .... **87** C2 🔢
Norse Pl *SCOT* G14 .... **87** C2 🔢
Norse Rd *SCOT* G14 .... **87** C2
Northampton Dr *KVD/HLHD* G12 .... **75** D4
North Av *BLTYR/CAMB* G72 .... **121** D4 🔢
North Bank Pl *CLYDBK* G81 .... **70** A2
North Bank St *CLYDBK* G81 .... **70** A2 🔢
Northbrae Pl *KNTSWD* G13 .... **72** B4 🔢
North Calder Gv
   UD/BTH/TAN G71 .... **109** D4 🔢
North Canal Bank *COWCAD* C4 .... **21** F3
North Canal Bank St *COWCAD* C4 .. **21** E3
North Claremont St *KVGV* G3 .... **19** D5
North Ct *CGLE* G1 .... **33** E3
North Court La *CGLE* G1 .... **33** E3
North Douglas St *CLYDBK* G81 .... **70** A2 🔢
North Elgin Pl *CLYDBK* G81 .... **70** A3
North Elgin St *CLYDBK* G81 .... **70** B2
North Erskine Pk *BSDN* G61 .... **65** D1
North Frederick St *CGLE* G1 .... **33** F2 🔢
North Gardner St *PTCK* G11 .... **17** D2
Northgate Qd *SPRGB/BLRNK* G21 .. **82** A4
Northgate Rd *SPRGB/BLRNK* G21 .. **82** A3
North Gower St *GOV/IBX* G51 .... **41** F2
North Hanover St *CGLE* G1 .... **33** F2
Northinch St *SCOT* G14 .... **14** B2 🔢
Northland Av *SCOT* G14 .... **87** C1 🔢
Northland Dr *SCOT* G14 .... **87** C2 🔢
Northland Gdns *SCOT* G14 .... **87** C1 🔢
Northland La *SCOT* G14 .... **87** C2
North Lodge Rd *RNFRW* PA4 .... **84** A2
Northmuir Rd *DRUM* G15 .... **64** B2
North Park Av *GIF/THBK* G46 ...... **124** B2 🔢
Northpark St *MRYH/FIRH* G20 .... **7** F4
North Portland St *CGLE* G1 .... **34** A3
North St *CGLW* G2 .... **31** F2
Northumberland St
   MRYH/FIRH G20 .... **6** C3 🔢
North Vw *BSDN* G61 .... **65** D4
North Wallace St *COWCAD* C4 .... **22** A5
North Woodside Rd *COWCAD* C4 .... **19** E2
   MRYH/FIRH G20 .... **19** F1
Norval St *PTCK* G11 .... **16** B3
Norwich Dr *KVD/HLHD* G12 .... **5** D1
Norwood Pk *BSDN* G61 .... **66** B3
Nottingham Av *KVD/HLHD* G12 .... **75** D4 🔢
Nottingham La *KVD/HLHD* G12 ...... **75** D4 🔢
Novar Dr *KVD/HLHD* G12 .... **4** C4
Novar Gdns *BSHPBGS* G64 .... **80** A1
Nuneaton St *DMNK/BRGTN* G40 .... **60** B1
Nurseries Rd *BAIL/MDB/MHD* G69 .. **100** B1
Nursery La *PLKSD/SHW* G41 .... **55** F3
Nursery St *PLKSD/SHW* G41 .... **56** A2 🔢
Nutberry Ct *GVH/MTFL* G42 .... **116** B1

O

Oak Crs *BAIL/MDB/MHD* G69 .... 109 C2 🔢
Oakfield Av *KVD/HLHD* G12 .... 18 C1 🔢
Oakfield La *KVD/HLHD* G12 .... 18 C3
Oakhill Av *CAR/SHTL* G32 .... 108 B3
Oakley Dr *LNPK/KPK* G44 .... 127 D3
Oakley Ter *DEN/PKHD* G31 .... 35 F4
Oak Pk *BSHPBGS* G64 .... 81 D2
Oak St *KVGV* G3 .... 32 A3
Oaktree Gdns *CSMK* G45 .... 130 B2
Oatfield St *SPRGB/BLRNK* G21 .... 12 C4
Oban Dr *MRYH/FIRH* G20 .... 7 D4
Oban La *MRYH/FIRH* G20 .... 7 D4
Obiston Gdns *CAR/SHTL* G32 .... 106 A1 🔢
Observatory Rd *KVD/HLHD* G12 .... 6 A5 🔢
Ochil Pl *CAR/SHTL* G32 .... 106 A2
Ochil Rd *BSHPBGS* G64 .... 82 A1
Ochil St *CAR/SHTL* G32 .... 106 A2
Ochiltree Av *KNTSWD* G13 .... 74 B2
Ogilvie Pl *DEN/PKHD* G31 .... 104 B2 🔢
Ogilvie St *DEN/PKHD* G31 .... 104 B2
Old Castle Rd *LNPK/KPK* G44 .... 116 A4 🔢
LNPK/KPK G44 .... 128 B2
Old Dalmarnock Rd
DMNK/BRGTN G40 .... 60 A1 🔢
Old Dumbarton Rd *KVGV* G3 .... 18 A5 🔢
Old Govan Rd *RNFRW* PA4 .... 85 D3
Old Manse Rd *CAR/SHTL* G32 .... 107 D2
Old Renfrew Rd *RNFRW* PA4 .... 86 A4
Old Rutherglen Rd *GBLS* G5 .... 45 E3 🔢
Old Shettleston Rd *CAR/SHTL* G32 .... 106 A1
Old Wood Rd *BAIL/MDB/MHD* G69 .... 109 C3
Old Wynd *CGLE* G1 .... 33 F5 🔢
Olive St *STPS/GTHM/RID* G33 .... 88 B2
Olympia St *DMNK/BRGTN* G40 .... 47 E3
O'neill Av *BSHPBGS* G64 .... 81 D2
Onslow Dr *DEN/PKHD* G31 .... 36 B3
Onslow Rd *CLYDBK* G81 .... 62 A4
Onslow Sq *DEN/PKHD* G31 .... 36 A3
Oran Gdns *MRYH/FIRH* G20 .... 7 D2
Oran Ga *MRYH/FIRH* G20 .... 7 D2
Oran Pl *MRYH/FIRH* G20 .... 7 D3
Oran St *MRYH/FIRH* G20 .... 6 C3
Orcades Dr *LNPK/KPK* G44 .... 128 B2
Orchard Ct *GIF/THBK* G46 .... 125 C3 🔢
Orchard Dr *GIF/THBK* G46 .... 125 D3
RUTH G73 .... 118 B3 🔢
Orchard Gv *GIF/THBK* G46 .... 125 D2
Orchard Pk *GIF/THBK* G46 .... 126 A3 🔢
Orchard Park Av *GIF/THBK* G46 .... 125 C3
Orchard St *BAIL/MDB/MHD* G69 .. 108 B3 🔢
RNFRW PA4 .... 84 B2
Orchy Cl *CLYDBK* G81 .... 62 A1 🔢
Orchy Crs *BSDN* G61 .... 73 D1
Orchy St *LNPK/KPK* G44 .... 116 A4
Oregon Pl *GBLS* G5 .... 45 F5 🔢
Orkney Pl *GOV/IBX* G51 .... 28 C3 🔢
Orkney St *GOV/IBX* G51 .... 28 C3
Orleans Av *SCOT* G14 .... 3 D5
Orleans La *SCOT* G14 .... 3 D5
Ormiston Av *SCOT* G14 .... 87 C2
Ormiston La *SCOT* G14 .... 87 C2 🔢
Ormiston La North *SCOT* G14 .... 87 C2 🔢
Ormiston La South *SCOT* G14 .... 87 C2 🔢
Ormonde Av *LNPK/KPK* G44 .... 127 C3
Ormonde Ct *LNPK/KPK* G44 .... 127 C3
Ormonde Crs *LNPK/KPK* G44 .... 127 D3
Ormonde Dr *LNPK/KPK* G44 .... 127 D3
Ornsay St *PPK/MIL* G22 .... 79 D3

Oronsay Crs *BSDN* G61 .... 67 D3
Orr St *DMNK/BRGTN* G40 .... 47 E3
DMNK/BRGTN G40 .... 47 F1
Orton Pl *GOV/IBX* G51 .... 28 B5
Osborne St *CGLE* G1 .... 33 E5
Ossian Rd *PLKSW/MSWD* G43 .... 115 C4
Oswald St *CGLE* G1 .... 32 C5
Otago La *KVD/HLHD* G12 .... 19 D2
Otago La North *KVD/HLHD* G12 ..... 19 D2 🔢
Otago St *KVD/HLHD* G12 .... 19 D2
Otterburn Dr *GIF/THBK* G46 .... 126 A4
Otterswick Pl *STPS/GTHM/RID* G33... 91 C4 🔢
Overbrae Pl *DRUM* G15 .... 63 D1
Overdale Av *GVH/MTFL* G42 .... 115 D2 🔢
Overdale Gdns *GVH/MTFL* G42 ..... 115 D2 🔢
Overdale St *GVH/MTFL* G42 .... 115 D2
Overlea Av *RUTH* G73 .... 120 B4
Overnewton Pl *KVGV* G3 .... 18 B5
Overnewton Sq *KVGV* G3 .... 18 A5
Overnewton St *KVGV* G3 .... 18 A5
Overtoun Dr *RUTH* G73 .... 119 C3
Overtown Av *PLK/PH/NH* G53 ...... 110 A4
Overtown St *DEN/PKHD* G31 .... 48 B3
Overwood Dr *LNPK/KPK* G44 .... 117 C4
Oxford La *GBLS* G5 .... 45 D2
RNFRW PA4 .... 84 A3 🔢
Oxford St *RNFRW* PA4 .... 84 A3
Oxford St *GBLS* G5 .... 44 C1
Oxton Dr *CARD/HILL/MSPK* G52 ..... 102 B1

P

Paisley Rd *GBLS* G5 .... 43 F1
PLKSD/SHW G41 .... 43 E1
RNFRW PA4 .... 84 A3
Paisley Rd West
CARD/HILL/MSPK G52 .... 38 A4
GOV/IBX G51 .... 40 C2
Paladin Av *KNTSWD* G13 .... 72 B2
Palermo St *SPRGB/BLRNK* G21 .... 11 D4
Palladium Pl *SCOT* G14 .... 14 A1
Palmer Av *KNTSWD* G13 .... 73 D1
Palmerston Pl *KVGV* G3 .... 30 B1 🔢
Panmure St *MRYH/FIRH* G20 .... 8 A3
Park Av *BSHPBGS* G64 .... 69 C3
KVGV G3 .... 19 E3
Parkbrae Gdns *MRYH/FIRH* G20 ..... 78 A4 🔢
Parkbrae Pl *MRYH/FIRH* G20 .... 78 A4 🔢
Park Circ *KVGV* G3 .... 19 D4
Park Circus La *KVGV* G3 .... 19 D4
Park Circus Pl *KVGV* G3 .... 19 E4
Park Ct *BSHPBGS* G64 .... 69 D3
GIF/THBK G46 .... 125 D3
Park Crs *BSDN* G61 .... 65 C1
BSHPBGS G64 .... 69 C3
Park Dr *RUTH* G73 .... 119 C3
Park Gdns *KVGV* G3 .... 19 D5
Park Gardens La *KVGV* G3 .... 19 D5
Park Ga *KVGV* G3 .... 19 D4
Parkgrove Av *GIF/THBK* G46 .... 126 B3
Parkgrove Ter *KVGV* G3 .... 18 C5
Parkgrove Terrace La *KVGV* G3 ..... 18 C5
Parkhill Dr *RUTH* G73 .... 119 C3
Parkhill Rd *PLKSW/MSWD* G43 ...... 114 A2
Parkholm La *GBLS* G5 .... 43 E1
Parklands Rd *LNPK/KPK* G44 .... 127 D3
Park La *DMNK/BRGTN* G40 .... 47 F3
Parkneuk Rd *PLKSW/MSWD* G43 ..... 125 D2
Park Qd *KVGV* G3 .... 19 D4
Park Rd *BSHPBGS* G64 .... 69 C4

GIF/THBK G46 .... 126 A4
KVGV G3 .... 19 D3
Parkside Gdns *MRYH/FIRH* G20 .... 78 A4
Parkside Pl *MRYH/FIRH* G20 .... 78 A4 ▣
Park St South *KVGV* G3 .... 19 D4
Park Ter *KVGV* G3 .... 19 D4
Park Terrace East La *KVGV* G3 .... 19 D4
Park Terrace La *KVGV* G3 .... 19 D4
Parnie St *CGLE* G1 .... 34 A5 ▣
Parsonage Rw *COWCAD* G4 .... 34 B4
Parsonage Sq *COWCAD* G4 .... 34 B4
Partick Bridge St *PTCK* G11 .... 17 E3
Partickhill Av *PTCK* G11 .... 16 C1
Partickhill Ct *PTCK* G11 .... 16 C1
Partickhill Rd *PTCK* G11 .... 16 C2
Paterson St *GBLS* G5 .... 44 A3
Pathhead Gdns
STPS/GTHM/RID G33 .... 83 D4 ▣
Patna St *DMNK/BRGTN* G40 .... 60 C1
Paton St *DEN/PKHD* G31 .... 36 C4
Payne St *COWCAD* G4 .... 21 E4
Pearce La *GOV/IBX* G51 .... 28 B1
Pearce St *GOV/IBX* G51 .... 28 B1
Pearson Dr *RNFRW* PA4 .... 84 B4
Peathill St *PPK/MIL* G22 .... 21 F1
Peat Rd *PLK/PH/NH* G53 .... 110 A4
Peebles Dr *RUTH* G73 .... 120 B3
Peel Glen Gdns *DRUM* G15 .... 64 A1
Peel La *PTCK* G11 .... 16 B2
Peel St *PTCK* G11 .... 16 C2
Pembroke St *KVGV* G3 .... 31 E2 ▣
Pencaitland Dr *CAR/SHTL* G32 .... 106 A3
Pencaitland Gv *CAR/SHTL* G32 .... 106 A3 ▣
Pencaitland Pl *SMSTN* G23 .... 77 C1 ▣
Pendeen Crs *STPS/GTHM/RID* G33 .... 108 A1
Pendeen Pl
STPS/GTHM/RID G33 .... 100 B4 ▣
Pendeen Rd *STPS/GTHM/RID* G33 .... 108 A1
Pendicle Crs *BSDN* G61 .... 65 D3
Pendicle Rd *BSDN* G61 .... 65 D3
Penicuik St *CAR/SHTL* G32 .... 96 B4 ▣
Penilee Rd *PSLYN/LNWD* PA3 .... 92 B2
Penilee Ter *CARD/HILL/MSPK* G52 ...... 93 C3
Peninver Dr *GOV/IBX* G51 .... 26 B1
Penman Av *RUTH* G73 .... 118 B2
Pennan Pl *SCOT* G14 .... 86 A1
Penneld Rd *PLKSD/SHW* G41 .... 114 B1
RUTH G73 .... 132 A1
Pharonhill St *DEN/PKHD* G31 .... 104 B1 ▣
Piccadilly St *KVGV* G3 .... 31 F4
Piershill St *CAR/SHTL* G32 .... 97 D3 ▣
Pikeman Rd *KNTSWD* G13 .... 73 C4
Pilmuir Av *LNPK/KPK* G44 .... 127 D2
Pilrig St *CAR/SHTL* G32 .... 97 C3
Pilton Rd *DRUM* G15 .... 64 A3
Pine Pl *GBLS* G5 .... 45 F4
Pinkerton Av *RUTH* G73 .... 118 B2
Pinkerton La *RNFRW* PA4 .... 92 B1 ▣
Pinkston Dr *COWCAD* G4 .... 22 C3

Pinkston Rd *COWCAD* G4 .... 22 A2
Pinwherry Dr
STPS/GTHM/RID G33 .... 83 D4 ▣
Pitcairn St *DEN/PKHD* G31 .... 105 C2 ▣
Pitcaple Dr *PLKSW/MSWD* G43 .... 113 D4 ▣
Pitlochry Dr *CARD/HILL/MSPK* G52 .... 102 B2
Pitmilly Rd *DRUM* G15 .... 65 C2
Pitreavie Pl *STPS/GTHM/RID* G33 ...... 91 C4
Pitt St *KVGV* G3 .... 32 B2
Pladda Rd *RNFRW* PA4 .... 92 B1 ▣
Plantation Park Gdns *GOV/IBX* G51 .... 42 B2
Plantation Sq *GOV/IBX* G51 .... 42 C1
Plant St *DEN/PKHD* G31 .... 37 E5
Playfair St *DMNK/BRGTN* G40 .... 60 A1
Plean St *SCOT* G14 .... 86 A1
Pleasance St *PLKSW/MSWD* G43 ...... 114 A2
Pointhouse Rd *KVGV* G3 .... 29 E1
Pollock Rd *BSDN* G61 .... 67 C3
Pollok Dr *BSHPBGS* G64 .... 80 A1
Pollokshaws Rd *PLKSD/SHW* G41 ...... 44 C5
PLKSD/SHW G41 .... 56 A3
PLKSW/MSWD G43 .... 113 D3
Pollokshields Sq *PLKSD/SHW* G41 .... 55 D3 ▣
Polmadie Rd *GBLS* G5 .... 58 C2
GVH/MTFL G42 .... 58 A5
Polmadie St *GVH/MTFL* G42 .... 57 F5
Polnoon Av *KNTSWD* G13 .... 72 A4
Polquhap Ct *PLK/PH/NH* G53 .... 110 A2 ▣
Polquhap Gdns *PLK/PH/NH* G53 ...... 110 A2
Polquhap Pl *PLK/PH/NH* G53 .... 110 A2
Polquhap Rd *PLK/PH/NH* G53 .... 110 A2
Polwarth La *KVD/HLHD* G12 .... 4 C4
Polwarth St *KVD/HLHD* G12 .... 4 C4
Poplar Av *PTCK* G11 .... 3 E4 ▣
Poplin St *DMNK/BRGTN* G40 .... 59 F1
Porchester St *STPS/GTHM/RID* G33 .. 91 D4
Portal Rd *KNTSWD* G13 .... 73 C2
Port Dundas Pl *CGLW* G2 .... 33 E1
Port Dundas Rd *COWCAD* G4 .... 21 D4
Porter St *GOV/IBX* G51 .... 41 E3
Portman St *PLKSD/SHW* G41 .... 43 D2
Portmarnock Dr *SMSTN* G23 .... 77 C3 ▣
Portsoy Av *KNTSWD* G13 .... 71 D2 ▣
Portsoy Pl *KNTSWD* G13 .... 71 D2
Port St *KVGV* G3 .... 31 E3
Portugal St *GBLS* G5 .... 45 D3
Possil Rd *COWCAD* G4 .... 20 C2
Potter Cl *CAR/SHTL* G32 .... 105 C3 ▣
Potter Gv *CAR/SHTL* G32 .... 105 C3 ▣
Potterhill Rd *PLK/PH/NH* G53 .... 102 A4
Potter Pl *CAR/SHTL* G32 .... 105 C3 ▣
Potter St *CAR/SHTL* G32 .... 105 C3
Powfoot St *DEN/PKHD* G31 .... 104 B1 ▣
Powrie St *STPS/GTHM/RID* G33 .... 91 C3
Preston Pl *GVH/MTFL* G42 .... 57 D3
Preston St *GVH/MTFL* G42 .... 56 C3 ▣
Prestwick St *PLK/PH/NH* G53 .... 110 A4
Priesthill Av *PLK/PH/NH* G53 .... 111 C4 ▣
Priesthill Crs *PLK/PH/NH* G53 .... 111 C4
Priesthill Rd *PLK/PH/NH* G53 .... 110 B4
Primrose St *SCOT* G14 .... 87 C3
Prince Albert Rd *KVD/HLHD* G12 .... 5 D5
Prince Edward St *GVH/MTFL* G42 ...... 56 A4
Prince of Wales Gdns
MRYH/FIRH G20 .... 76 A2
Prince's Gdns *KVD/HLHD* G12 .... 17 D1
Princes Ga *RUTH* G73 .... 119 C2 ▣
Prince's Pl *KVD/HLHD* G12 .... 17 D1
Princes St *RUTH* G73 .... 119 C2
Prince's Ter *KVD/HLHD* G12 .... 5 E5
Princes Terrace La *KVD/HLHD* G12 ...... 5 E5
Priory Pl *KNTSWD* G13 .... 73 C3 ▣

Priory Rd *KNTSWD* G13 .... **73** D3
Prosen St *CAR/SHTL* G32 .... **105** C3
Prospect Av *BLTYR/CAMB* G72 .... **121** D4
Prospecthill Circ *GVH/MTFL* G42 .... **117** D1
Prospecthill Crs *GVH/MTFL* G42 .... **118** A2
Prospecthill Dr *GVH/MTFL* G42 .... **117** C2
Prospecthill Pl *RUTH* G73 .... **118** A2
Prospecthill Rd *GVH/MTFL* G42 .... **116** B2
    GVH/MTFL G42 .... **118** A2
Prospecthill Sq *GVH/MTFL* G42 .... **117** D2
Prospect Rd *PLKSW/MSWD* G43 .. **114** B2
Provand Hall Crs
    BAIL/MDB/MHD G69 .... **109** D3
Provanhill St *SPRGB/BLRNK* G21 ..... **23** E4
Provanmill Rd *STPS/GTHM/RID* G33 .. **88** B3
Provan Rd *DEN/PKHD* G31 .... **25** F5
Provost Driver Ct *RNFRW* PA4 .... **85** C4
Purdon St *PTCK* G11 .... **17** D3

Quentin St *PLKSD/SHW* G41 .... **54** C5
Quinton Gdns
    BAIL/MDB/MHD G69 .... **109** C1

R

Raasay Pl *PPK/MIL* G22 .... **79** C2
Raasay St *PPK/MIL* G22 .... **79** C2
Raeberry St *MRYH/FIRH* G20 .... **19** E1
Rafford St *GOV/IBX* G51 .... **28** B4
Raglan St *COWCAD* G4 .... **20** B3
Raith Av *CSMK* G45 .... **129** D2
Raithburn Av *CSMK* G45 .... **129** C2
Raithburn Rd *CSMK* G45 .... **129** C3
Ralston Rd *BSDN* G61 .... **66** A1
Rampart Av *KNTSWD* G13 .... **72** A2
Ram St *CAR/SHTL* G32 .... **105** D1
Ranald Gdns *RUTH* G73 .... **132** B3
Randolph *PTCK* G11 .... **3** F5
Randolph La *PTCK* G11 .... **3** F5
Randolph Rd *PTCK* G11 .... **3** E4
    SCOT G14 .... **3** E3
Rannoch Av *BSHPBGS* G64 .... **81** D3
Rannoch Dr *BSDN* G61 .... **67** C4
    RNFRW PA4 .... **84** A2
Rannoch St *LNPK/KPK* G44 .... **116** A4
Raploch Av *SCOT* G14 .... **86** B2
Raploch La *SCOT* G14 .... **86** B2
Rathlin St *GOV/IBX* G51 .... **28** A1
Ratho Dr *SPRGB/BLRNK* G21 .... **11** D3
Rattray St *CAR/SHTL* G32 .... **105** C3
Ravel Rw *DEN/PKHD* G31 .... **104** B1
Ravelston Rd *BSDN* G61 .... **66** A4
Ravelston St *CAR/SHTL* G32 .... **96** B4
Ravenscliffe Dr *GIF/THBK* G46 ...... **125** D3
Ravenscraig Dr *PLK/PH/NH* G53 .... **110** B4
Ravenscraig Ter
    PLK/PH/NH G53 .... **123** C1
Ravenshall Rd *PLKSD/SHW* G41 .... **114** A2
Ravenstone Dr *GIF/THBK* G46 .... **126** A1
Ravenswood Dr *PLKSD/SHW* G41 .. **114** B1
Rayne Pl *DRUM* G15 .... **64** B2
Redan St *DMNK/BRGTN* G40 .... **47** F2
Redcastle Sq
    STPS/GTHM/RID G33 .... **99** D1
Redford St *STPS/GTHM/RID* G33 .... **96** B2
Redgate Pl *SCOT* G14 .... **86** B2
Redlands Ter *KVD/HLHD* G12 .... **5** E3
Redlands Terrace La *KVD/HLHD* G12.. **5** E3
Redmoss St *MRYH/FIRH* G20 .... **8** C2
Rednock St *PPK/MIL* G22 .... **9** F4
Redpath Dr *CARD/HILL/MSPK* G52 .. **94** B4
Red Rd *SPRGB/BLRNK* G21 .... **13** D4
Red Road Ct *SPRGB/BLRNK* G21 ... **13** D5
Redwood Dr *SPRGB/BLRNK* G21 ... **12** A5
Rayne Pl *DRUM* G15 .... **64** B2
Regent Dr *RUTH* G73 .... **119** C2
Regent Moray St *KVGV* G3 .... **18** A5
Regent Park Sq *GVH/MTFL* G42 .... **55** F4
    PLKSD/SHW G41 .... **55** E3
Regwood St *PLKSD/SHW* G41 .... **114** B2
Reid Pl *DMNK/BRGTN* G40 .... **47** F5
Reid St *DMNK/BRGTN* G40 .... **59** F1
    RUTH G73 .... **119** D2
Reidvale St *DEN/PKHD* G31 .... **35** F5
Renfield La *CGLW* G2 .... **33** D3
Renfield St *CGLW* G2 .... **33** D1
    RNFRW PA4 .... **84** B2
Renfrew Ct *CGLW* G2 .... **33** E1

Quadrant Rd *PLKSW/MSWD* G43 ... **127** C1
Quarrybrae St *DEN/PKHD* G31 .... **105** C1
Quarryknowe *RUTH* G73 .... **118** B3
Quarryknowe Gdns
    DEN/PKHD G31 .... **105** C1
Quarryknowe St *DEN/PKHD* G31 ... **105** C1
Quarry Pl *BLTYR/CAMB* G72 .... **121** C4
Quarrywood Av *SPRGB/BLRNK* G21 .. **13** F3
Quarrywood Rd *SPRGB/BLRNK* G21 .. **88** B2
Quay Rd *RUTH* G73 .... **119** C2
Quay Rd North *RUTH* G73 .... **119** C1
Queen Elizabeth Av
    CARD/HILL/MSPK G52 .... **93** C3
Queen Margaret Dr
    KVD/HLHD G12 .... **6** B5
Queen Margaret Rd *MRYH/FIRH* G20 .. **6** C4
Queen Mary Av *CLYDBK* G81 .... **62** B4
    GVH/MTFL G42 .... **56** B5
Queen Mary St *DMNK/BRGTN* G40 .. **47** F5
Queensborough Gdns
    KVD/HLHD G12 .... **4** B2
Queensby Av *BAIL/MDB/MHD* G69 .. **109** D1
Queensby Rd *BAIL/MDB/MHD* G69 .. **101** D4
Queen's Crs *COWCAD* G4 .... **19** F3
Queen's Dr *GVH/MTFL* G42 .... **55** F4
Queen's Drive La *GVH/MTFL* G42 ... **56** B5
Queensferry St *GBLS* G5 .... **59** D3
Queen's Gdns *KVD/HLHD* G12 .... **5** E5
Queensland Ct
    CARD/HILL/MSPK G52 .... **95** C4
Queensland Dr
    CARD/HILL/MSPK G52 .... **95** C4
Queensland Gdns
    CARD/HILL/MSPK G52 .... **95** C4
Queensland La East
    CARD/HILL/MSPK G52 .... **95** C4
Queensland La West
    CARD/HILL/MSPK G52 .... **95** C4
Queenslie St *STPS/GTHM/RID* G33 .. **88** B3
Queen's Park Av *GVH/MTFL* G42 ... **116** B1
Queen's Pl *KVD/HLHD* G12 .... **17** E1
Queen Sq *PLKSD/SHW* G41 .... **55** E4
Queen St *CGLE* G1 .... **33** E4
    RNFRW PA4 .... **84** B1
    RUTH G73 .... **119** C2
Queen Victoria Dr *SCOT* G14 .... **87** C2
Queen Victoria Ga *SCOT* G14 .... **87** C1
Quendale Dr *CAR/SHTL* G32 .... **105** D3

Renfrew Rd *GOV/IBX* G51 .... 95 C1
　RNFRW PA4 .... 94 A1
Renfrew St *CGLW* G2 .... 20 B5
Renshaw Dr *CARD/HILL/MSPK* G52 .. 94 B4
Renton St *COWCAD* G4 .... 21 E4
Reston Dr *CARD/HILL/MSPK* G52 .... 94 B4
Reuther Av *RUTH* G73 .... 119 D3 🇧
Revoch Dr *KNTSWD* G13 .... 72 A3
Rhannan Rd *LNPK/KPK* G44 .... 128 A1
Rhannan Ter *LNPK/KPK* G44 .... 128 A1 🇧
Rhymer St *SPRGB/BLRNK* G21 .... 23 D5
Rhymie Rd *CAR/SHTL* G32 .... 107 D3 🇧
Rhynie Dr *GOV/IBX* G51 .... 40 C2
Riccarton St *GVH/MTFL* G42 .... 57 E4
Richmond Ct *RUTH* G73 .... 120 A2 🇧
Richmond Dr *BLTYR/CAMB* G72 ..... 133 C1 🇧
　RUTH G73 .... 120 B3
Richmond Gv *RUTH* G73 .... 120 A3
Richmond Pl *RUTH* G73 .... 120 A2
Richmond Rd *RUTH* G73 .... 120 B3 🇧
Richmond St *CGLE* G1 .... 34 A3
　CLYDBK G81 .... 70 A1
Riddell St *CLYDBK* G81 .... 62 A3
Riddon Av *KNTSWD* G13 .... 71 C2
Riddon Pl *KNTSWD* G13 .... 71 C2
Riddrie Crs *STPS/GTHM/RID* G33 ... 97 C2
Riddrie Knowes
　STPS/GTHM/RID G33 .... 97 C2
Riddrievale Ct *STPS/GTHM/RID* G33 .. 97 C1
Riddrievale St
　STPS/GTHM/RID G33 .... 97 C1 🇧
Rigby St *CAR/SHTL* G32 .... 96 B4
Riggside Rd *STPS/GTHM/RID* G33 .... 91 C4
Riglaw Pl *KNTSWD* G13 .... 72 A3
Rigmuir Rd *GOV/IBX* G51 .... 95 C4 🇧
Rimsdale St *DMNK/BRGTN* G40 .... 48 A3
Ringford St *SPRGB/BLRNK* G21 .... 11 E5
Ripon Dr *KVD/HLHD* G12 .... 75 C4
Ritchie St *GBLS* G5 .... 44 B4
Riverbank St *PLKSW/MSWD* G43 .... 114 A3
Riverford Rd *PLKSW/MSWD* G43 .... 114 A3
　RUTH G73 .... 120 A3 🇧
Riversdale La *SCOT* G14 .... 86 A2 🇧
Riverside Ct *LNPK/KPK* G44 .... 127 D4
Riverside Rd *PLKSW/MSWD* G43 .... 115 C3
Riverview Dr *GBLS* G5 .... 32 A5
Riverview Gdns *KVGV* G3 .... 32 A5
Riverview Pl *GBLS* G5 .... 32 A5
Robert Burns Av *CLYDBK* G81 .... 62 A3
Roberton Av *PLKSD/SHW* G41 .... 53 E4
Robertson La *CGLW* G2 .... 32 B4
Robertson St *KVGV* G3 .... 32 B5
Robert St *GOV/IBX* G51 .... 28 B2
Robroyston Av
　STPS/GTHM/RID G33 .... 89 C3
Robroyston Rd *BSHPBGS* G64 .... 83 D1
　STPS/GTHM/RID G33 .... 83 C3
　STPS/GTHM/RID G33 .... 88 B2
Roblsee Crs *GIF/THBK* G46 .... 125 C3 🇧
Roblee Dr *GIF/THBK* G46 .... 125 D3
Roblslee Rd *GIF/THBK* G46 .... 125 C3
Robson Gv *GVH/MTFL* G42 .... 57 D5
Rockall Dr *LNPK/KPK* G44 .... 128 B2
Rockbank Pl *DMNK/BRGTN* G40 ...... 48 A3
Rockbank St *DMNK/BRGTN* G40 ...... 48 A3
Rockcliffe St *DMNK/BRGTN* G40 ...... 59 F2
Rockfield Rd *SPRGB/BLRNK* G21 ..... 13 F1
Rockmount Av *GIF/THBK* G46 .... 125 C3
Rock St *PPK/MIL* G22 .... 21 E1
Rodger Dr *RUTH* G73 .... 119 C2
Rodger Pl *RUTH* G73 .... 119 C2 🇧
Rodil Av *LNPK/KPK* G44 .... 129 C2

Rodney St *COWCAD* G4 .... 20 C2
Roebank St *DEN/PKHD* G31 .... 36 C2
Rogart St *DMNK/BRGTN* G40 .... 47 F3
Rokeby La *KVD/HLHD* G12 .... 18 C1
Roman Av *BSDN* G61 .... 66 B1 🇧
　DRUM G15 .... 72 A1
Roman Ct *BSDN* G61 .... 66 A1
Roman Dr *BSDN* G61 .... 66 B1
Roman Gdns *BSDN* G61 .... 66 B1 🇧
Roman Rd *BSDN* G61 .... 66 B1 🇧
Romney Av *LNPK/KPK* G44 .... 129 C1 🇧
Ronaldsay St *PPK/MIL* G22 .... 79 D3
Rona St *SPRGB/BLRNK* G21 .... 24 C2
Rona Ter *BLTYR/CAMB* G72 .... 133 D3
Ronay St *PPK/MIL* G22 .... 79 D3
Ropework La *CGLE* G1 .... 45 E1
Rosebank Gdns
　UD/BTH/TAN G71 .... 109 D4 🇧
Roseberry St *GBLS* G5 .... 58 C3
Rose Dl *BSHPBGS* G64 .... 81 D2 🇧
Rosedale Dr *BAIL/MDB/MHD* G69 .. 109 C2
Rosedale Gdns *MRYH/FIRH* G20 .. 76 A2 🇧
Rose Knowe Rd *GVH/MTFL* G42 .... 117 D2
Roselea Gdns *KNTSWD* G13 .... 74 B3
Rosemount St *SPRGB/BLRNK* G21 .. 23 F5
Roseness Pl *STPS/GTHM/RID* G33 .. 98 A2 🇧
Rose St *CGLW* G2 .... 32 C1
Rosevale Rd *BSDN* G61 .... 66 A2
Rosevale St *PTCK* G11 .... 16 B3
Rosewood St *KNTSWD* G13 .... 74 A3
Roslea Dr *DEN/PKHD* G31 .... 36 B4
Rosneath St *GOV/IBX* G51 .... 28 A1
Rossendale Ct
　PLKSW/MSWD G43 .... 114 A2 🇧
Rossendale Rd
　PLKSW/MSWD G43 .... 114 A2 🇧
Ross Hall Pl *RNFRW* PA4 .... 84 B3
Rossie Crs *BSHPBGS* G64 .... 82 A2
Rosslea Dr *GIF/THBK* G46 .... 126 A4
Rosslyn Av *RUTH* G73 .... 120 A3
Ross Pl *RUTH* G73 .... 132 B2
Ross St *CGLE* G1 .... 46 B1
Rostan Rd *PLKSW/MSWD* G43 ..... 126 A1
Rosyth Rd *GBLS* G5 .... 58 C4
Rosyth St *GBLS* G5 .... 58 C4
Rotherwood Av *KNTSWD* G13 .... 73 C1
Rotherwood La *KNTSWD* G13 .... 65 C4 🇧
Rotherwood Pl *KNTSWD* G13 .... 73 D2 🇧
Rothes Dr *SMSTN* G23 .... 76 B2
Rothes Pl *MRYH/FIRH* G20 .... 76 A1
Rottenrow *CGLE* G1 .... 34 A2
　COWCAD G4 .... 34 C3
Rottenrow East *COWCAD* G4 .... 34 B3
Roukenburn St *GIF/THBK* G46 ..... 124 A2
Rouken Glen Rd *GIF/THBK* G46 .... 124 B4
Rowallan Gdns *PTCK* G11 .... 3 F5
Rowallan La *PTCK* G11 .... 3 F5
Rowallan La East *PTCK* G11 .... 4 A5
Rowallan Rd *GIF/THBK* G46 .... 124 B4
Rowallan Ter
　STPS/GTHM/RID G33 .... 90 B2 🇧
Rowan Av *RNFRW* PA4 .... 84 A2
Rowandale Av
　BAIL/MDB/MHD G69 .... 109 C2
Rowand Av *GIF/THBK* G46 .... 126 A4
Rowan Gdns *PLKSD/SHW* G41 .... 40 C3
Rowanlea Dr *GIF/THBK* G46 .... 126 B2
Rowan Rd *PLKSD/SHW* G41 .... 40 C4
The Rowans *BSHPBGS* G64 .... 68 B4 🇧
Rowantree Av *RUTH* G73 .... 131 D1 🇧
Rowantree Gdns *RUTH* G73 .... 131 D1 🇧
Rowena Av *KNTSWD* G13 .... 73 D1
Roxburgh St *KVD/HLHD* G12 .... 18 A1

Royal Crs *KVGV* G3 .... 30 C1
Royal Exchange Ct *CGLE* G1 .... 33 E3
Royal Exchange Sq *CGLE* G1 .... 33 E3
Royal Inch Ter *RNFRW* PA4 ...... 84 B1
Royal Ter *KVGV* G3 .... 18 C5
Royal Terrace La *KVGV* G3 .... 18 C5
Roystonhill *SPRGB/BLRNK* G21 .... 23 E5
Royston Rd *COWCAD* G4 .... 23 D5
  SPRGB/BLRNK G21 .... 23 F4
  STPS/GTHM/RID G33 .... 89 C3
Royston Sq *SPRGB/BLRNK* G21 .... 23 D4
Roy St *SPRGB/BLRNK* G21 .... 22 A1
Rozelle Av *DRUM* G15 .... 64 B3 ⏹
Rubislaw Dr *BSDN* G61 .... 66 A3
Ruby St *DMNK/BRGTN* G40 .... 48 A5
Ruchazie Pl *STPS/GTHM/RID* G33 .. 97 D2 ⏹
Ruchazie Rd *STPS/GTHM/RID* G33 .. 97 D2
Ruchill St *MRYH/FIRH* G20 .... 7 E1
Ruel St *LNPK/KPK* G44 .... 116 A3
Rugby Av *KNTSWD* G13 .... 72 B2
Rullion Pl *STPS/GTHM/RID* G33 .... 97 D2 ⏹
Rumford St *DMNK/BRGTN* G40 .... 59 E1
Rupert St *COWCAD* G4 .... 19 F3
Rushyhill St *SPRGB/BLRNK* G21 .. 12 A3
Ruskin La *KVD/HLHD* G12 .... 6 C5
Ruskin Ter *KVD/HLHD* G12 .... 18 C1
Rutherglen Rd *GBLS* G5 .... 58 C2
Ruthven Pl *BSHPBGS* G64 .... 82 A2 ⏹
Ruthven St *KVD/HLHD* G12 .... 18 A1
Rutland Crs *GOV/IBX* G51 .... 43 D1
Rutland Pl *GOV/IBX* G51 .... 42 C1
Ryan Rd *BSHPBGS* G64 .... 81 D1 ⏹
Ryan Wy *RUTH* G73 .... 132 A3
Ryecroft Dr *BAIL/MDB/MHD* G69 .. 109 D1
Ryedale Pl *DRUM* G15 .... 64 A2
Ryefield Rd *SPRGB/BLRNK* G21 .... 13 D2
Ryehill Rd *SPRGB/BLRNK* G21 ...... 13 E4
Ryemount Rd *SPRGB/BLRNK* G21 .. 13 F2
Rye Rd *SPRGB/BLRNK* G21 .... 13 E3
Ryeside Rd *SPRGB/BLRNK* G21 .... 13 D2
Rylands Dr *CAR/SHTL* G32 .... 107 D2
Rylands Gdns *CAR/SHTL* G32 ...... 108 A2 ⏹
Rylees Crs *CARD/HILL/MSPK* G52 .. 93 C3
Rylees Rd *CARD/HILL/MSPK* G52 .. 93 C3
Ryvra Rd *KNTSWD* G13 .... 73 D3

Sackville Av *KNTSWD* G13 .... 3 E1
Sackville La *KNTSWD* G13 .... 3 E1
Saddell Rd *DRUM* G15 .... 64 B2
St Andrew's Av *BSHPBGS* G64 ...... 68 A4
St Andrews Crs *PLKSD/SHW* G41 .. 43 D4
St Andrew's Dr *PLKSD/SHW* G41 .. 53 F4
St Andrew's La *CGLE* G1 .... 34 A5 ⏹
St Andrew's Rd *PLKSD/SHW* G41 .. 43 E5
  RNFRW PA4 .... 84 A3
St Andrew's Sq *CGLE* G1 .... 46 A1
St Andrew's St *CGLE* G1 .... 34 A1
St Ann's Dr *GIF/THBK* G46 .... 126 A4
St Blane's Dr *RUTH* G73 .... 118 A4
St Bride's Rd *PLKSW/MSWD* G43 .. 114 B4
St Catherine's Rd *GIF/THBK* G46 .. 126 A4
St Clair Av *GIF/THBK* G46 .... 126 A3
St Clair St *MRYH/FIRH* G20 .... 19 F2
St Cyrus Gdns *BSHPBGS* G64 ...... 82 A1
St Cyrus Rd *BSHPBGS* G64 .... 82 A1
St Enoch Pl *CGLE* G1 .... 33 D5
St Fillans Rd *STPS/GTHM/RID* G33 .. 91 C1
St George's Rd *CGLW* G2 .... 31 F1

  COWCAD G4 .... 20 A3
  KVGV G3 .... 19 F5
St Germains *BSDN* G61 .... 66 A2
St James Rd *COWCAD* G4 .... 34 B2
St John's Ct *PLKSD/SHW* G41 ...... 42 C5
St John's Qd *PLKSD/SHW* G41 .... 43 D5
St John's Rd *PLKSD/SHW* G41 .... 42 C5
St Joseph's Ct *SPRGB/BLRNK* G21 .. 23 F5
St Joseph's Vw *SPRGB/BLRNK* G21 .. 35 F1
St Kenneth Dr *GOV/IBX* G51 ...... 26 C2
St Kilda Dr *SCOT* G14 .... 2 C4
St Leonard's Dr *GIF/THBK* G46 .. 126 A3 ⏹
St Margaret's Pl *CGLE* G1 .... 45 F1 ⏹
St Mark Gdns *CAR/SHTL* G32 ...... 105 D1 ⏹
St Mark St *CAR/SHTL* G32 .... 105 C1
St Marnock St *DMNK/BRGTN* G40 .. 48 A5
St Mary's La *CGLW* G2 .... 33 D3
St Mary's Rd *BSHPBGS* G64 .... 68 A4
St Mungo Av *CGLE* G1 .... 33 F1
  COWCAD G4 .... 34 B1
St Mungo Pl *COWCAD* G4 .... 34 B1
St Mungo St *BSHPBGS* G64 .... 80 B2
St Ninian Ter *GBLS* G5 .... 45 E3
St Peter's La *CGLW* G2 .... 32 B3
St Ronan's Dr *PLKSD/SHW* G41 .. 114 B1
  RUTH G73 .... 120 A4
St Stephens Av *RUTH* G73 .... 132 A3
St Stephen's Crs *RUTH* G73 ...... 132 B3
St Vincent Crs *KVGV* G3 .... 30 B1
St Vincent Crescent La *KVGV* G3 .. 30 C1
St Vincent La *CGLW* G2 .... 32 B2 ⏹
St Vincent Pl *CGLE* G1 .... 33 E3
St Vincent St *CGLW* G2 .... 32 B2
  KVGV G3 .... 31 F2
St Vincent Ter *KVGV* G3 .... 31 F2
Salamanca St *DEN/PKHD* G31 ...... 104 B1 ⏹
Salasaig Ct *STPS/GTHM/RID* G33 .. 98 A3
Salen St *CARD/HILL/MSPK* G52 .... 93 F3
Salisbury St *GBLS* G5 .... 45 D4
Salkeld St *GBLS* G5 .... 44 C4
Salmona St *PPK/MIL* G22 .... 8 C4
Saltmarket *CGLE* G1 .... 45 F1
Saltmarket Pl *CGLE* G1 .... 45 F1
St Mungo Av *CGLE* G1 .... 33 F1
Saltoun La *KVD/HLHD* G12 .... 18 A1
Saltoun St *KVD/HLHD* G12 .... 18 A1
Salvia St *BLTYR/CAMB* G72 ...... 121 C4
Sandaig Rd *STPS/GTHM/RID* G33 .. 108 A1
Sanda St *MRYH/FIRH* G20 .... 6 C4
Sandbank Av *MRYH/FIRH* G20 .... 76 B3
Sandbank Crs *MRYH/FIRH* G20 .... 76 B4
Sandbank Dr *MRYH/FIRH* G20 .... 76 B3
Sandbank St *MRYH/FIRH* G20 .... 76 B4
Sandbank Ter *MRYH/FIRH* G20 .... 76 B3
Sandend Rd *PLK/PH/NH* G53 ...... 110 A3
Sandfield St *MRYH/FIRH* G20 ...... 7 D2 ⏹
Sandgate Av *CAR/SHTL* G32 ...... 107 D3
Sandhaven Rd *PLK/PH/NH* G53 .. 110 A3 ⏹
Sandhaven Rd *PLK/PH/NH* G53 .. 110 A3
Sandholm Pl *SCOT* G14 .... 85 D1
Sandholm Ter *SCOT* G14 .... 85 D1
Sandiefield Rd *GBLS* G5 .... 45 E4
Sandilands St *CAR/SHTL* G32 ...... 106 B1
Sandmill St *SPRGB/BLRNK* G21 .. 24 A4
Sandringham La *KVD/HLHD* G12 .. 6 B5 ⏹
Sandwood Rd
  CARD/HILL/MSPK G52 .... 94 A4
Sandyfaulds Sq *GBLS* G5 .... 45 F4
Sandyfaulds St *GBLS* G5 .... 46 A5
Sandyford Place La *KVGV* G3 ...... 31 D1
Sandyford St *KVGV* G3 .... 29 F1
Sandyhills Crs *CAR/SHTL* G32 .... 106 B3 ⏹
Sandyhills Dr *CAR/SHTL* G32 ...... 106 B3

Sandyhills Gv *CAR/SHTL* G32 .... **107** C4
Sandyhills Pl *CAR/SHTL* G32 .... **106** B3 ⬛
Sandyhills Rd *CAR/SHTL* G32 .... **106** B3
Sandy Rd *PTCK* G11 .... **16** B4
  RNFRW PA4 .... **92** A1
Sannox Gdns *DEN/PKHD* G31 .... **37** D2
Sanquhar Dr *PLK/PH/NH* G53 .... **110** A2
Sanquhar Gdns *PLK/PH/NH* G53 .... **110** A2
Sanquhar Pl *PLK/PH/NH* G53 .... **110** A2
Saracen Head Rd *COWCAD* G4 .... **34** C5
Saracen St *PPK/MIL* G22 .... **9** E3
Sardinia La *KVD/HLHD* G12 .... **18** B1
Sauchiehall La *CGLW* G2 .... **32** A1
Sauchiehall St *CGLW* G2 .... **32** C1
  KVGV G3 .... **18** B5
Saughs Av *STPS/GTHM/RID* G33 .... **83** D4
Saughs Dr *STPS/GTHM/RID* G33 .... **83** D4
Saughs Ga *STPS/GTHM/RID* G33 .... **83** D4
Saughs Pl *STPS/GTHM/RID* G33 .... **83** D4 ⬛
Saughs Rd *STPS/GTHM/RID* G33 .... **83** D4
Saughton St *CAR/SHTL* G32 .... **97** C5 ⬛
Savoy St *DMNK/BRGTN* G40 .... **47** E5
Sawmillfield St *COWCAD* G4 .... **20** C2
Sawmill Rd *PTCK* G11 .... **15** F3 ⬛
Saxon Rd *KNTSWD* G13 .... **73** D3
Scalpay Pl *PPK/MIL* G22 .... **79** D3
Scalpay St *PPK/MIL* G22 .... **79** D3
Scapa St *SMSTN* G23 .... **77** C2
Scaraway Dr *PPK/MIL* G22 .... **79** D2
Scaraway Pl *PPK/MIL* G22 .... **79** D2
Scaraway St *PPK/MIL* G22 .... **79** D2
Scaraway Ter *PPK/MIL* G22 .... **79** D2
Scarba Dr *PLKSW/MSWD* G43 .... **113** D2
Scarrel Dr *CSMK* G45 .... **131** C2
Scarrel Rd *CSMK* G45 .... **131** C2
Scarrel Ter *CSMK* G45 .... **131** C2
Scioncroft Av *RUTH* G73 .... **120** A3 ⬛
Scone St *PPK/MIL* G22 .... **21** F1
Sconser St *SMSTN* G23 .... **77** C1 ⬛
Scorton Gdns *CAR/SHTL* G32 .... **108** B2 ⬛
Scotland St *GBLS* G5 .... **43** F3
Scotland St West *PLKSD/SHW* G41 ...... **42** C2
Scotsburn Rd *SPRGB/BLRNK* G21 .... **13** E3
Scotstoun St *SCOT* G14 .... **87** C3
Scott Rd *CARD/HILL/MSPK* G52 .... **93** D2
Scott St *BAIL/MDB/MHD* G69 .... **109** D2 ⬛
  KVGV G3 .... **20** B5
Seafield Dr *RUTH* G73 .... **132** B3
Seaforth Rd
  CARD/HILL/MSPK G52 .... **94** A3 ⬛
  CLYDBK G81 .... **62** A4
Seaforth Rd North
  CARD/HILL/MSPK G52 .... **94** A3
Seaforth Rd South
  CARD/HILL/MSPK G52 .... **94** A3
Seagrove St *CAR/SHTL* G32 .... **97** C4 ⬛
Seamore St *MRYH/FIRH* G20 .... **19** F2
Seath Rd *RUTH* G73 .... **119** C1
Seath St *GVH/MTFL* G42 .... **57** E3
Seaward La *PLKSD/SHW* G41 .... **43** D1
Seaward Pl *PLKSD/SHW* G41 .... **43** D3
Seaward St *GOV/IBX* G51 .... **31** E5
  PLKSD/SHW G41 .... **43** E2
Second Av *BSDN* G61 .... **67** C3
  LNPK/KPK G44 .... **116** B4
  RNFRW PA4 .... **92** A1
  STPS/GTHM/RID G33 .... **90** B1
Second Gdns *PLKSD/SHW* G41 .... **40** B5
Seggielea La *KNTSWD* G13 .... **73** D4 ⬛
Seggielea Rd *KNTSWD* G13 .... **73** D4 ⬛
Seil Dr *LNPK/KPK* G44 .... **128** B2
Selborne Pl *KNTSWD* G13 .... **3** D2 ⬛

Selborne Place La *KNTSWD* G13 .... **3** D2
Selborne Rd *KNTSWD* G13 .... **3** D2
Selby Gdns *CAR/SHTL* G32 .... **107** D3
Selkirk Av *CARD/HILL/MSPK* G52 .... **103** C2
Selkirk Dr *RUTH* G73 .... **120** A3 ⬛
Seton Ter *DEN/PKHD* G31 .... **35** F4
Settle Gdns *CAR/SHTL* G32 .... **108** B2 ⬛
Shaftesbury St *KVGV* G3 .... **31** F2 ⬛
Shafton Pl *KNTSWD* G13 .... **74** A2
Shafton Rd *KNTSWD* G13 .... **74** A2
Shakespeare St *MRYH/FIRH* G20 .... **6** C2 ⬛
Shamrock St *COWCAD* G4 .... **20** B4 ⬛
Shandwick St *ESTRH* G34 .... **101** C2
Shanks St *MRYH/FIRH* G20 .... **6** C2
Shannon St *MRYH/FIRH* G20 .... **7** F1
Shapinsay St *PPK/MIL* G22 .... **79** D2
Shawbridge St *PLKSW/MSWD* G43 .... **114** A3
Shawfield Dr *GBLS* G5 .... **59** E2
Shawfield Rd *GBLS* G5 .... **59** E2
Shawhill Ct *PLKSD/SHW* G41 .... **114** B2 ⬛
Shawhill Rd *PLKSW/MSWD* G43 .... **114** B2
Shawholm Crs
  PLKSW/MSWD G43 .... **113** D3 ⬛
Shawmoss Rd *PLKSD/SHW* G41 .... **114** A1
Shawpark St *MRYH/FIRH* G20 .... **77** C4
Shaw St *GOV/IBX* G51 .... **28** A1
Sheddens Pl *CAR/SHTL* G32 .... **97** D4
Sheila St *STPS/GTHM/RID* G33 .... **89** C2
Sheldaig Rd *PPK/MIL* G22 .... **79** C2
Shelley Rd *KVD/HLHD* G12 .... **3** F2
Sherbrooke Av *PLKSD/SHW* G41 .... **53** E2
Sherbrooke Dr *PLKSD/SHW* G41 .... **41** E5
Sherbrooke Gdns *PLKSD/SHW* G41 ..... **53** E1
Sherburn Gdns *CAR/SHTL* G32 .... **108** B2
Sheriff Park Av *RUTH* G73 .... **119** C3 ⬛
Sherwood Dr *GIF/THBK* G46 .... **125** C3
Sherwood Pl *DRUM* G15 .... **64** B3
Shetland Dr *LNPK/KPK* G44 .... **128** B2
Shettleston Rd *DEN/PKHD* G31 .... **105** C4
Shielbridge Gdns *SMSTN* G23 .... **77** C1
Shieldaig Dr *RUTH* G73 .... **131** D2
Shieldburn Rd *GOV/IBX* G51 .... **95** C4
Shieldhall Gdns *GOV/IBX* G51 .... **95** C3 ⬛
Shieldhall Rd *GOV/IBX* G51 .... **94** B2
Shields Rd *PLKSD/SHW* G41 .... **43** E3
  PLKSD/SHW G41 .... **55** D3
Shiel Rd *BSHPBGS* G64 .... **81** D1
Shilford Av *KNTSWD* G13 .... **72** A3
Shillay St *PPK/MIL* G22 .... **80** A2 ⬛
Shilton Dr *PLK/PH/NH* G53 .... **123** C1
Shinwell Av *CLYDBK* G81 .... **70** B1
Shiskine Dr *MRYH/FIRH* G20 .... **76** A2
Shiskine Pl *MRYH/FIRH* G20 .... **76** A2 ⬛
Shiskine St *MRYH/FIRH* G20 .... **76** A2
Shortridge St *MRYH/FIRH* G20 .... **6** C2 ⬛
Shotts St *STPS/GTHM/RID* G33 .... **99** D2
Shuna Pl *MRYH/FIRH* G20 .... **7** D1
Shuna St *MRYH/FIRH* G20 .... **77** C4
Shuttle St *CGLE* G1 .... **34** B3
Sielga Pl *ESTRH* G34 .... **101** C2
Siemens Pl *SPRGB/BLRNK* G21 .... **24** C3
Siemens St *SPRGB/BLRNK* G21 .... **24** C3
Sievewright St *RUTH* G73 .... **61** E5
Silkin Av *CLYDBK* G81 .... **70** B1
Silverburn St
  STPS/GTHM/RID G33 .... **97** C2 ⬛
Silverdale St *DEN/PKHD* G31 .... **49** F5
Silverfir St *GBLS* G5 .... **58** A1
Silvergrove St *DMNK/BRGTN* G40 .... **47** D4
Simons Crs *RNFRW* PA4 .... **84** B1
Simpson St *MRYH/FIRH* G20 .... **19** F1
Simshill Rd *LNPK/KPK* G44 .... **128** B3

Sinclair Dr GVH/MTFL G42 .... 115 D3
Sinclair Gdns BSHPBGS G64 .... 81 D2 🔟
Sinclair St GBLS G81 .... 70 B2
Sixth Av RNFRW PA4 .... 92 A1
Skaethorn Rd MRYH/FIRH G20 ...... 75 D3
Skaterigg Dr KNTSWD G13 .... 3 E2
Skaterigg Gdns KNTSWD G13 .... 3 E1
Skaterigg La KNTSWD G13 .... 2 C1
Skene Rd GOV/IBX G51 .... 40 B2
Skerray Qd PPK/MIL G22 .... 79 C2 🔟
Skerray St PPK/MIL G22 .... 79 C2
Skerryvore Pl
  STPS/GTHM/RID G33 .... 98 B2 🔟
Skerryvore Rd STPS/GTHM/RID G33 .. 98 B2
Skipness Dr GOV/IBX G51 .... 26 B2
Skirsa Ct SMSTN G23 .... 78 A2
Skirsa Pl SMSTN G23 .... 77 D3
Skirsa Sq SMSTN G23 .... 78 A3
Skirsa St SMSTN G23 .... 77 D2
Skirving St PLKSD/SHW G41 .... 115 C2
Skye Av RNFRW PA4 .... 92 A1
Skye Rd RUTH G73 .... 132 B3
Slatefield St DEN/PKHD G31 .... 48 A1
Slenavon Av RUTH G73 .... 132 B3
Sloy St PPK/MIL G22 .... 10 A3
Smeaton St MRYH/FIRH G20 .... 77 D4
Smith St SCOT G14 .... 14 C2
Smithycroft Rd
  STPS/GTHM/RID G33 .... 97 C1
Snaefell Av RUTH G73 .... 132 A2 🔟
  RUTH G73 .... 132 A1 🔟
Snaefell Crs RUTH G73 .... 132 A1
Snowdon St GBLS G5 .... 46 A5
Snuff Mill Rd LNPK/KPK G44 .... 128 B1 🔟
  LNPK/KPK G44 .... 128 A1 🔟
Society St DEN/PKHD G31 .... 49 D2
Sollas Pl KNTSWD G13 .... 71 C2 🔟
Solway St DMNK/BRGTN G40 .... 59 F3
Somerford Rd BSDN G61 .... 74 B1
Somerset Pl KVGV G3 .... 19 E5
Somerset Place Ms KVGV G3 .... 19 E5 🔟
Somervell St BLTYR/CAMB G72 ..... 121 D4
Somerville Dr GVH/MTFL G42 .... 116 B2
Sorby St DEN/PKHD G31 .... 104 B1 🔟
Sorley St PTCK G11 .... 15 F3
Sorn St DMNK/BRGTN G40 .... 60 C1
Southampton Dr KVD/HLHD G12 .... 75 D4
Southampton La KVD/HLHD G12 .... 75 D4
South Annandale St GVH/MTFL G42 .. 56 C3
South Av RNFRW PA4 .... 84 B3
South Bank St CLYDBK G81 .... 70 A3 🔟
Southbank St DEN/PKHD G31 ..... 104 B1 🔟🔟
Southbar Av KNTSWD G13 .... 72 A3 🔟
Southbrae Dr KNTSWD G13 .... 2 C3
Southbrae La KNTSWD G13 .... 3 D2
South Chester St CAR/SHTL G32 .. 106 A1 🔟
Southcroft Rd RUTH G73 .... 59 C5
Southcroft St GOV/IBX G51 .... 29 D3
South Crosshill Rd BSHPBGS G64 .. 81 C1
Southdeen Av DRUM G15 .... 64 B3
Southdeen Rd DRUM G15 .... 64 A3
South Douglas St CLYDBK G81 .... 70 A2 🔟
South Elgin Pl CLYDBK G81 .... 70 A3
South Elgin St CLYDBK G81 .... 70 A3
Southern Av RUTH G73 .... 131 D1
South Erskine Pk BSDN G61 .... 65 D1
Southesk Av BSHPBGS G64 .... 68 B3
South Exchange Ct CGLE G1 .... 33 E4
Southfield Crs PLK/PH/NH G53 ..... 111 C2
South Frederick St CGLE G1 .... 33 F4
Southhill Av RUTH G73 .... 132 A1 🔟
Southinch Av KNTSWD G13 .... 71 C4

Southinch La SCOT G14 .... 71 C4
Southlea Av GIF/THBK G46 .... 125 C3
Southloch Gdns SPRGB/BLRNK G21 .. 23 F1
Southloch St SPRGB/BLRNK G21 ... 23 F1
Southpark Av KVD/HLHD G12 ..... 18 C1 🔟
Southpark La KVD/HLHD G12 .... 18 C2
South Portland St GBLS G5 .... 45 D2
South Scott St
  BAIL/MDB/MHD G69 .... 109 D2 🔟
South St SCOT G14 .... 86 A1
South Vesalius St CAR/SHTL G32 .. 106 A1 🔟
Southview BSDN G61 .... 65 C1
Southview Ct SPRGB/BLRNK G21 .. 80 B3 🔟
Southview Ter SPRGB/BLRNK G21 .. 80 B3
Southwood Dr LNPK/KPK G44 ..... 129 C1
South Woodside Rd COWCAD G4 .... 19 D2
  MRYH/FIRH G20 .... 19 E1
Soutra Pl STPS/GTHM/RID G33 ...... 98 B2
Spean St LNPK/KPK G44 .... 116 A3
Speirshall Cl SCOT G14 .... 85 D1
Speirshall Ter SCOT G14 .... 71 C4
Speirs Rd BSDN G61 .... 67 C3
Spencer St KNTSWD G13 .... 74 B3
Spence St MRYH/FIRH G20 .... 76 A2
Spey Dr RNFRW PA4 .... 85 C4
Spey Rd BSDN G61 .... 65 C4
Spey St STPS/GTHM/RID G33 .... 97 D2
Spiersbridge Av GIF/THBK G46 ... 124 B3 🔟
Spiersbridge La GIF/THBK G46 ..... 124 A3
Spiersbridge Rd GIF/THBK G46 ..... 124 B4
Spiersbridge Ter GIF/THBK G46 .... 124 A3
Spiers Gv GIF/THBK G46 .... 124 B3
Spittal Rd CSMK G45 .... 130 B2
Spoutmouth CGLE G1 .... 34 B5 🔟
Springbank St MRYH/FIRH G20 .... 7 F4
Springboig Av CAR/SHTL G32 .... 99 C3
Springboig Rd CAR/SHTL G32 .... 99 C3
Springburn Rd COWCAD G4 .... 23 C4
  COWCAD G4 .... 34 C1
  SPRGB/BLRNK G21 .... 11 D5
  SPRGB/BLRNK G21 .... 80 A4
Springburn Wy SPRGB/BLRNK G21 .. 11 E4
Springcroft Av
  BAIL/MDB/MHD G69 .... 101 D4
Springcroft Crs
  BAIL/MDB/MHD G69 .... 101 D4
Springcroft Dr
  BAIL/MDB/MHD G69 .... 101 C4
Springcroft Gv
  BAIL/MDB/MHD G69 .... 101 D4 🔟
Springcroft Rd
  BAIL/MDB/MHD G69 .... 101 D4
Springfield Av BSHPBGS G64 .... 81 C2
Springfield Ct CGLE G1 .... 33 E4 🔟
Springfield Crs BSHPBGS G64 .... 81 C2
Springfield Park Rd RUTH G73 ...... 120 A4
Springfield Quay GOV/IBX G51 ...... 31 E5
Springfield Rd BSHPBGS G64 .... 81 C1
  DEN/PKHD G31 .... 49 F4
  DMNK/BRGTN G40 .... 60 C2
Springfield Sq BSHPBGS G64 .... 81 C2
Springhill Dr South
  BAIL/MDB/MHD G69 .... 101 C4
Springhill Gdns PLKSD/SHW G41 .. 55 D5 🔟
Springhill Pkwy
  BAIL/MDB/MHD G69 .... 101 D3
Springhill Rd BAIL/MDB/MHD G69 ... 108 B1 🔟
Springkell Av PLKSD/SHW G41 ...... 53 D2
Springkell Dr PLKSD/SHW G41 ...... 53 D3
Springkell Gdns PLKSD/SHW G41 .. 53 F4
Springkell Ga PLKSD/SHW G41 ...... 54 A1
Springside Pl DRUM G15 .... 64 A2

Springvale Ter *SPRGB/BLRNK* G21...... **11** D3
Squire St *SCOT* G14................ **14** B2
Staffa Av *RNFRW* PA4 .... **92** A1
Staffa Rd *BLTYR/CAMB* G72 .... **133** D3
Staffa St *DEN/PKHD* G31............ **36** C2
Staffin Dr *SMSTN* G23 .... **76** B1 🔟
Staffin St *SMSTN* G23............ **77** C1
Stafford St *COWCAD* G4 .... **22** A5
Stag St *GOV/IBX* G51 .... **29** D3
Stamford St *DEN/PKHD* G31........ **48** C3
Stanalane St *GIF/THBK* G46 ...... **124** B2 🔟
Standburn Rd *SPRGB/BLRNK* G21 ...... **82** A4
Stanford St *CLYDBK* G81 .... **70** A1
Stanhope Dr *RUTH* G73 .... **132** B1 🔟
Stanley Dr *BSHPBGS* G64 .... **69** D4
Stanley St *PLKSD/SHW* G41.......... **43** D2
Stanley Street La *PLKSD/SHW* G41 ...... **43** D2
Stanmore Rd *GVH/MTFL* G42 .... **116** B2
Startpoint St *STPS/GTHM/RID* G33 .... **98** A2
Station Crs *RNFRW* PA4 .... **85** C2
Station Rd *BSDN* G61 .... **65** D2
GIF/THBK G46 .... **126** A3
MRYH/FIRH G20 .... **76** A2 🔟
RNFRW PA4 .... **84** B2 🔟
STPS/GTHM/RID G33............ **90** A1
Steel St *CGLE* G1 .... **46** A1
Stenton St *CAR/SHTL* G32 .... **97** C3 🔟
Stepford Pl *STPS/GTHM/RID* G33 .. **100** B3 🔟
Stepford Rd *STPS/GTHM/RID* G33...... **100** B3
Stephen Crs *BAIL/MDB/MHD* G69 ...... **58** B1
Stephenson St
CARD/HILL/MSPK G52............ **93** C2
Stepps Rd *STPS/GTHM/RID* G33...... **99** C2
Stevenson St *DMNK/BRGTN* G40 ...... **46** C1
Stewarton Dr *BLTYR/CAMB* G72 ...... **133** C1
Stewart St *COWCAD* G4 .... **21** D4
Stewartville St *PTCK* G11 .... **17** D3
Stirling Av *BSDN* G61 .... **66** A4
Stirling Dr *BSHPBGS* G64 .... **68** A3
RUTH G73 .... **131** D1
Stirlingfauld Pl *GBLS* G5 .... **45** D4
Stirling Gdns *BSHPBGS* G64 .... **68** A3
Stirling Rd *COWCAD* G4 .... **34** B2
Stirrat St *MRYH/FIRH* G20 .... **76** A4
Stobcross Rd *KVGV* G3................ **30** C3
Stobhill Rd *SPRGB/BLRNK* G21 ...... **80** B3
Stockwell Pl *CGLE* G1 .... **33** E5
Stockwell St *CGLE* G1................ **45** F1
Stonedyke Gv *DRUM* G15 .... **64** B4
Stonefield Av *KVD/HLHD* G12 ...... **76** A1 🔟
Stonelaw Dr *RUTH* G73 .... **119** D3
Stonelaw Rd *RUTH* G73 .... **119** D3
Stoneside Dr *PLKSW/MSWD* G43 .... **113** C4
Stoneside Sq *PLKSW/MSWD* G43...... **113** C4
Stonyhurst St *PPK/MIL* G22 .... **78** A4
Stornoway St *PPK/MIL* G22 .... **79** C2
Strachur St *PPK/MIL* G22 .... **78** A3
Straiton St *CAR/SHTL* G32 .... **97** C3 🔟
Stranraer Dr *DRUM* G15 .... **65** C4 🔟
Stratford St *MRYH/FIRH* G20 .... **6** B2
Strathallon Pl *RUTH* G73 .... **132** B2 🔟
Strathbran St *DEN/PKHD* G31 .... **104** B3 🔟
Strathcarron Pl *MRYH/FIRH* G20 .... **76** B4 🔟
Strathclyde Dr *RUTH* G73 .... **119** C3
Strathclyde St *DMNK/BRGTN* G40 .... **60** B3
Strathcona Dr *KNTSWD* G13 .... **74** B3
Strathcona Gdns *MRYH/FIRH* G20.... **75** C3
Strathcona Pl *RUTH* G73 .... **132** B2 🔟
Strathcona St *KNTSWD* G13 .... **74** B3 🔟
Strathdee Rd *LNPK/KPK* G44 .... **127** C4 🔟
Strathdon Av *LNPK/KPK* G44 ...... **127** C4
Strathdon Dr *LNPK/KPK* G44 ...... **127** D4
Strathendrick Dr
PLKSW/MSWD G43 .... **127** C2 🔟
Strathkelvin Av
SPRGB/BLRNK G21 .... **80** B3 🔟
Strathmore Gdns *RUTH* G73 .... **132** B2 🔟
Strathmore Rd *PPK/MIL* G22 ...... **78** B3
Strathord St *CAR/SHTL* G32 ...... **106** A3
Strathtay Av *LNPK/KPK* G44 ...... **127** C4
Strathview Gv *LNPK/KPK* G44 .... **127** C4 🔟
Strathview Pk *LNPK/KPK* G44 .... **127** C4
Strathy Pl *MRYH/FIRH* G20 .... **76** B4 🔟
Strathyre Gdns *BSDN* G61............ **67** D1
Strathyre St *PLKSD/SHW* G41 .... **115** C2 🔟
Stratton Dr *GIF/THBK* G46.......... **125** D4
Strauss Av *CLYDBK* G81 .... **71** C1
Stravanan Ct *CSMK* G45 .... **130** A4 🔟
Stravanan Rd *CSMK* G45 .... **129** D4
Stravanan St *CSMK* G45 .... **129** D4 🔟
Stravanan Ter *CSMK* G45 .... **129** D4 🔟
Strenabey Av *RUTH* G73 .... **132** B2 🔟
Striven Gdns *MRYH/FIRH* G20 .... **7** E5
Stroma St *SPRGB/BLRNK* G21 .... **25** D2
Stromness St *GBLS* G5 .... **44** B4
Stronend St *PPK/MIL* G22 .... **8** C2
Strone Rd *STPS/GTHM/RID* G33 .... **98** B3
Stronsay St *SPRGB/BLRNK* G21 ...... **25** D2
Stronvar Dr *SCOT* G14 .... **86** B2
Strowan Crs *CAR/SHTL* G32 ...... **106** B2
Strowan St *CAR/SHTL* G32 .... **106** B2
Struan Av *GIF/THBK* G46............ **126** A3
Struan Gdns *LNPK/KPK* G44 ...... **128** A1 🔟
Struan Rd *LNPK/KPK* G44 .... **128** A1
Struie St *ESTRH* G34 .... **101** C2 🔟
Stuart Av *RUTH* G73.................. **131** D1
Stuart Dr *BSHPBGS* G64.............. **80** A2
Succoth St *KNTSWD* G13 .... **74** B3
Suffolk St *CGLE* G1.................... **46** B1
Sugworth Av *BAIL/MDB/MHD* G69 .... **109** C3
Sumburgh St *STPS/GTHM/RID* G33 .... **97** D3
Summerfield St *DMNK/BRGTN* G40.... **60** C3
Summerhill Dr *DRUM* G15.......... **64** B2
Summerhill Gdns *DRUM* G15 ...... **64** B2
Summerhill Pl *DRUM* G15 .... **64** B2 🔟
Summerhill Rd *DRUM* G15 .... **64** B2
Summerlea Rd *GIF/THBK* G46...... **124** B2
Summerlee St *STPS/GTHM/RID* G33 .. **99** C3
Summer St *DMNK/BRGTN* G40 ...... **47** F3
Summertown Rd *GOV/IBX* G51 ...... **28** C4
Sunart Gdns *BSHPBGS* G64 .... **82** A1
Sunart Rd *BSHPBGS* G64 .... **82** A1
CARD/HILL/MSPK G52............ **39** C3
Sunningdale Rd *SMSTN* G23 .... **76** B2
Sunnybank Dr *DMNK/BRGTN* G40 .... **60** C3
Sunnylaw St *PPK/MIL* G22 .... **8** C3
Sunnyside Dr *DRUM* G15............ **72** A1
Sunnyside Pl *DRUM* G15 .... **72** A1
Surrey La *GBLS* G5 .... **45** D4
Surrey St *GBLS* G5 .... **45** D4
Sussex St *PLKSD/SHW* G41 .... **42** C2
Sutcliffe Ct *KNTSWD* G13 .... **74** A3 🔟
Sutcliffe Rd *KNTSWD* G13 .... **74** B3 🔟
Sutherland Av *PLKSD/SHW* G41...... **53** D2
Sutherness Dr *STPS/GTHM/RID* G33 .. **98** A3
Swallow Gdns *KNTSWD* G13 .... **71** D3
Swanston St *DMNK/BRGTN* G40 .... **60** B4
Swan St *COWCAD* G4 .... **21** F4
Sween Av *LNPK/KPK* G44 .... **128** A2
Swift Crs *KNTSWD* G13................ **71** D3
Swinton Dr *CARD/HILL/MSPK* G52.... **102** B1
Swinton St *CARD/HILL/MSPK* G52 .. **102** B1
Switchback Rd *BSDN* G61 .... **66** B4
Swordale Pl *ESTRH* G34 .... **101** C2 🔟

Sword St *DEN/PKHD* G31 .... **35** F5
Sydenham La *KVD/HLHD* G12 .... **17** D1
Sydenham Rd *KVD/HLHD* G12 .... **5** E5
Sydney St *DEN/PKHD* G31 .... **35** D5
Syriam Pl *SPRGB/BLRNK* G21 .... **11** F3
Syriam St *SPRGB/BLRNK* G21 .... **11** F2

T

Tabard Pl *KNTSWD* G13 .... **73** C2 🔟
Tabard Rd *KNTSWD* G13 .... **73** C2
Talbot Ct *SCOT* G14 .... **86** B1 🔟
Talbot Dr *KNTSWD* G13 .... **86** B1
Talbot Pl *SCOT* G14 .... **86** B1 🔟
Talbot Ter *SCOT* G14........................... **86** B1
Talisman Rd *KNTSWD* G13 .... **73** C4
Tallant Rd *DRUM* G15 .... **64** B3
Tallant Ter *DRUM* G15 .... **65** C3
Talla Rd *CARD/HILL/MSPK* G52 .... **102** B3
Tambowie St *KNTSWD* G13 .... **74** A3
Tamshill St *MRYH/FIRH* G20 .... **77** D4
Tanar Av *RNFRW* PA4 .... **93** D1
Tanera Av *LNPK/KPK* G44 .... **129** C1
Tanfield Pl *CAR/SHTL* G32 .... **99** C3 🔟
Tanfield St *CAR/SHTL* G32 .... **99** C3
Tankerland Rd *PLKSW/MSWD* G43 .. **116** A4
Tannadice Av
    CARD/HILL/MSPK G52 .... **103** C3
Tanna Dr *CARD/HILL/MSPK* G52 .... **51** F1
Tannahill Rd *PLKSW/MSWD* G43 .. **115** D4 🔟
Tannock St *PPK/MIL* G22........................ **9** D4
Tantallon Rd *BAIL/MDB/MHD* G69.. **109** C1
    PLKSW/SHW G41 .... **115** C3
Taransay St *GOV/IBX* G51 .... **28** A1
Tarbolton Dr *CLYDBK* G81 .... **62** A3 🔟
Tarbolton Rd *PLKSW/MSWD* G43 .... **114** B4 🔟
Tarfside Gdns *CARD/HILL/MSPK* G52.. **38** B5
Tarfside Ov *CARD/HILL/MSPK* G52.... **50** A1
Tarland St *GOV/IBX* G51 .... **27** F5
Tarras Dr *RNFRW* PA4 .... **93** D1
Tassie St *PLKSW/MSWD* G43 .... **114** D2
Tattershall Rd *STPS/GTHM/RID* G33 .. **91** C4
Tavistock Dr *PLKSW/MSWD* G43 ...... **126** B1
Tay Av *RNFRW* PA4 .... **85** C3 🔟
Tay Crs *BSHPBGS* G64........................... **81** D1
    STPS/GTHM/RID G33 .... **97** C1
Taylor Pl *COWCAD* G4........................... **34** B2
Taylor St *CLYDBK* G81 .... **70** A2
    COWCAD G4........................... **34** B3
Taymouth St *CAR/SHTL* G32 .... **106** B3
Taynish Dr *LNPK/KPK* G44 .... **128** B3
Tay Rd *BSDN* G61 .... **65** D4 🔟
    BSHPBGS G64........................... **81** D1
Teal Dr *KNTSWD* G13 .... **72** A3
Tealing Av *CARD/HILL/MSPK* G52 .... **103** C2
Tealing Crs
    CARD/HILL/MSPK G52 .... **103** C2 🔟
Teasel Av *PLK/PH/NH* G53 .... **122** B3
Teith Av *RNFRW* PA4 .... **85** D4
Teith Dr *BSDN* G61 .... **65** C3
Teith St *STPS/GTHM/RID* G33 .... **97** C1 🔟
Templar Av *KNTSWD* G13 .... **73** D3
Temple Gdns *KNTSWD* G13 .... **74** B3 🔟
Templeland Rd *PLK/PH/NH* G53 .... **103** C4
Temple Locks Ct *KNTSWD* G13 .... **74** B3 🔟
Temple Locks Pl *KNTSWD* G13 .... **74** B3 🔟
Temple Rd *MRYH/FIRH* G20 .... **75** C3
Templeton St *DMNK/BRGTN* G40 ...... **47** D3
Tennant St *RNFRW* PA4 .... **84** B2 🔟
Tennyson Dr *DEN/PKHD* G31 .... **105** C2

Terregles Av *PLKSD/SHW* G41.............. **53** D3
Terregles Crs *PLKSD/SHW* G41 .... **53** E3
Terregles Dr *PLKSD/SHW* G41 .... **53** E3
Teviot Av *BSHPBGS* G64....................... **69** C3
Teviot Crs *BSDN* G61 .... **65** C4
Teviot St *KVGV* G3............................... **29** F1
Thane Rd *KNTSWD* G13 .... **73** C4
Tharsis St *SPRGB/BLRNK* G21 .... **23** F5
Third Av *LNPK/KPK* G44 .... **116** B3
    RNFRW PA4 .... **84** A4
    STPS/GTHM/RID G33 .... **90** B1
Third Gdns *PLKSD/SHW* G41 .... **40** B5
Thirdpart Crs *KNTSWD* G13 .... **71** C3 🔟
Thistle St *GBLS* G5 .... **45** E3
Thistle Ter *GBLS* G5 .... **45** D4
Thomas Muir Av *BSHPBGS* G64 .... **81** C2 🔟
Thompson St *DEN/PKHD* G31 .... **36** A5
Thomson St *RNFRW* PA4 .... **84** A4
Thornbridge Av
    BAIL/MDB/MHD G69 .... **109** D1 🔟
    KVD/HLHD G12 .... **5** F1 🔟
Thornbridge Gdns
    BAIL/MDB/MHD G69 .... **109** C1 🔟
Thornbridge Rd
    BAIL/MDB/MHD G69 .... **109** C1
Thorncliffe Gdns *PLKSD/SHW* G41...... **55** D4
Thorncroft Dr *LNPK/KPK* G44............ **129** C1
Thornden La *SCOT* G14 .... **86** A2 🔟
Thorn Dr *BSDN* G61 .... **65** D1
    RUTH G73 .... **132** A2
Thornlea Dr *GIF/THBK* G46 .... **126** B2
Thornley Av *KNTSWD* G13 .... **72** B3
Thornliebank Rd *GIF/THBK* G46 .... **125** C2
    PLKSW/MSWD G43 .... **125** D1
Thorn Rd *BSDN* G61 .... **65** C1
Thornton La *MRYH/FIRH* G20 .... **76** B3
Thornwood Av *PTCK* G11 .... **16** A3
Thornwood Crs *PTCK* G11 .... **15** F1
Thornwood Dr *PTCK* G11 .... **16** A1 🔟
Thornwood Gdns *PTCK* G11 .... **15** F2
Thornwood Pl *PTCK* G11 .... **15** F1 🔟
Thornwood Qd *PTCK* G11 .... **15** F1
Thornwood Rd *PTCK* G11 .... **15** F2
Thornwood Ter *PTCK* G11 .... **15** F2
Threestonehill Av *CAR/SHTL* G32........ **98** B4
Thrums Av *BSHPBGS* G64..................... **82** A1
Thurston Rd *CARD/HILL/MSPK* G52.. **102** A3
Tibbermore Rd *PTCK* G11 .... **16** B1
Tillie St *MRYH/FIRH* G20 .... **19** E1
Tillycairn Dr *STPS/GTHM/RID* G33 ..... **91** D4 🔟
Tillycairn Rd *STPS/GTHM/RID* G33..... **91** D4
Tilt St *STPS/GTHM/RID* G33 .... **89** C4
Tinto Rd *PLKSW/MSWD* G43 .... **126** A1
Tinwald Pth *CARD/HILL/MSPK* G52 .. **102** A1
Tiree Av *RNFRW* PA4 .... **92** A3
Tiree St *SPRGB/BLRNK* G21 .... **25** E2
Tirry Av *RNFRW* PA4 .... **85** D4
Titwood Rd *PLKSD/SHW* G41 .... **53** D3
    PLKSW/SHW G41 .... **54** C5
Tiverton Av *CAR/SHTL* G32 .... **107** D3
Tobago Pl *DMNK/BRGTN* G40 .... **47** E2
Tobago St *DMNK/BRGTN* G40 .... **47** D2
Tobermory Rd *RUTH* G73 .... **132** B3
Todd St *DEN/PKHD* G31 .... **37** F3
Tofthill Av *BSHPBGS* G64..................... **68** B4
Tofthill Gdns *BSHPBGS* G64................. **68** A4
Tollcross Park Gdns *CAR/SHTL* G32 .. **105** D3 🔟
Tollcross Park Gv *CAR/SHTL* G32 .. **105** D3 🔟
Tollcross Park Vw
    CAR/SHTL G32 .... **105** D3 🔟
Tollcross Rd *CAR/SHTL* G32 .... **106** B1
    DEN/PKHD G31 .... **104** B1

Toll La *GOV/IBX* G51 .... **43** D1
Tolsta St *SMSTN* G23 .... **77** C1
Tontine La *CGLE* G1 .... **34** A5
Tontine Pl *RUTH* G73 .... **133** C2
Torbreck St *CARD/HILL/MSPK* G52 ...... **39** E3
Torburn Av *GIF/THBK* G46 .... **125** D3
Torgyle St *SMSTN* G23 .... **76** B1
Tormore St *GOV/IBX* G51 .... **26** A5
Tormusk Dr *CSMK* G45 .... **131** C2
Tormusk Gdns *CSMK* G45 .... **131** C2
Tormusk Gv *PTCK* G45 .... **131** C2 ⬛
Tormusk Rd *CSMK* G45 .... **131** C2
Torness St *PTCK* G11 .... **17** F3
Torogay Pl *PPK/MIL* G22 .... **80** A2 ⬛
Torogay St *PPK/MIL* G22 .... **79** C3
Torogay Ter *PPK/MIL* G22 .... **79** C2 ⬛
Torphin Crs *CAR/SHTL* G32 .... **98** A3
Torphin Wk *CAR/SHTL* G32 .... **98** B3 ⬛
Torrance St *SPRGB/BLRNK* G21 .... **11** E3 ⬛
Torran Rd *STPS/GTHM/RID* G33 .... **100** B3
Torridon Av *PLKSD/SHW* G41 .... **52** C1
Torrington Crs *CAR/SHTL* G32 .... **107** D3
Torrin Rd *SMSTN* G23 .... **76** B1
Torrisdale St *GVH/MTFL* G42 .... **55** F4
Torr Rd *BSHPBGS* G64 .... **82** B1
Torr St *PPK/MIL* G22 .... **10** A3
Torryburn Rd *SPRGB/BLRNK* G21 .... **13** E4
Toryglen Rd *RUTH* G73 .... **118** A2
Toryglen St *GBLS* G5 .... **58** B3
Toward Rd *STPS/GTHM/RID* G33 .... **99** C3
Towerhill Rd *KNTSWD* G13 .... **73** C1
Towerside Crs *PLK/PH/NH* G53 .... **102** A4
Towerside Rd *PLK/PH/NH* G53 .... **102** A4
Tower St *PLKSD/SHW* G41 .... **42** C2
Townmill Rd *DEN/PKHD* G31 .... **36** A1
Townsend St *COWCAD* G4 .... **21** E4
Tradeston St *GBLS* G5 .... **44** B1
Trafalgar St *DMNK/BRGTN* G40 .... **59** E2
Trainard Av *CAR/SHTL* G32 .... **105** D2
Tranent Pl *STPS/GTHM/RID* G33 .... **97** C2 ⬛
Traquair Dr *CARD/HILL/MSPK* G52 ...... **102** B2
Treeburn Av *GIF/THBK* G46 .... **125** D3
Trefoil Av *PLKSD/SHW* G41 .... **114** B2
Tresta St *SMSTN* G23 .... **77** D2
Trinity Av *CARD/HILL/MSPK* G52 .... **103** C2
Trinley Rd *KNTSWD* G13 .... **73** D1
Trondra Pth *ESTRH* G34 .... **100** B2 ⬛
Trondra Pl *ESTRH* G34 .... **100** B2
Trongate *CGLE* G1 .... **34** A5
Troon St *DMNK/BRGTN* G40 .... **60** C1
Trossachs St *MRYH/FIRH* G20 .... **20** A1
Trossachs Rd *RUTH* G73 .... **132** B4
Trossachs St *MRYH/FIRH* G20 .... **20** A1
Truce Rd *KNTSWD* G13 .... **72** B2
Tudor La South *SCOT* G14 .... **3** D5
Tudor Rd *SCOT* G14 .... **3** D5
Tudor St *BAIL/MDB/MHD* G69 .... **108** B3 ⬛
Tullis St *DMNK/BRGTN* G40 .... **47** D5
Tulloch-Ard Pl *RUTH* G73 .... **132** B3 ⬛
Tulloch St *LNPK/KPK* G44 .... **116** A4 ⬛
Tummel St *STPS/GTHM/RID* G33 .... **97** C2
Tunnel St *KVGV* G3 .... **30** C4
Turnberry Av *PTCK* G11 .... **16** C1
Turnberry Dr *RUTH* G73 .... **130** B2
Turnberry Pl *CSMK* G45 .... **130** B2 ⬛
Turnberry Rd *PTCK* G11 .... **16** B1
Turnbull St *CGLE* G1 .... **46** A1
Turnlaw St *GBLS* G5 .... **46** B5
Turret Crs *KNTSWD* G13 .... **73** C2
Turret Rd *KNTSWD* G13 .... **73** C2
Turriff St *GBLS* G5 .... **44** C5
Tweed Crs *RNFRW* PA4 .... **85** C4

STPS/GTHM/RID G33 .... **96** B1
Tweed Dr *BSDN* G61 .... **65** D3
Tweedsmuir Rd
   CARD/HILL/MSPK G52 .... **102** B2
Tweedvale Av *SCOT* G14 .... **71** C4
Tweedvale Pl *SCOT* G14 .... **71** C4 ⬛
Tyndrum Rd *BSDN* G61 .... **67** D1 ⬛
Tyndrum St *COWCAD* G4 .... **21** D4
Tynecastle Crs *CAR/SHTL* G32 .... **98** B3
Tynecastle Pl *CAR/SHTL* G32 .... **98** B3 ⬛
Tynecastle St *CAR/SHTL* G32 .... **98** B3
Tynwald Av *RUTH* G73 .... **132** A2

U

Uig Pl *STPS/GTHM/RID* G33 .... **108** A1 ⬛
Uist St *GOV/IBX* G51 .... **27** E4
Ulva St *CARD/HILL/MSPK* G52 .... **39** E3
Underwood Rd *RUTH* G73 .... **120** A4
Underwood St *PLKSD/SHW* G41 .. **115** C2 ⬛
Union Pl *CGLE* G1 .... **33** D3
Union St *CGLE* G1 .... **33** D3
Unity Pl *COWCAD* G4 .... **20** B3
University Av *KVD/HLHD* G12 .... **18** A2
University Gdns *KVD/HLHD* G12 .... **18** A2
University Pl *KVD/HLHD* G12 .... **18** A2
Uphall Pl *STPS/GTHM/RID* G33 .... **97** C3 ⬛
Upland La *SCOT* G14 .... **87** C2 ⬛
Upland Rd *SCOT* G14 .... **87** C2 ⬛
Upper Bourtree Ct *RUTH* G73 .... **132** A2 ⬛
Upper Bourtree Dr *RUTH* G73 .... **131** D2
Upper Glenburn Rd *BSDN* G61 .... **65** D1
Urquhart Crs *RNFRW* PA4 .... **84** A4
Urrdale Rd *PLKSD/SHW* G41 .... **40** C3
Usmore Pl *STPS/GTHM/RID* G33 .. **108** A1 ⬛

V

Vaila St *SMSTN* G23 .... **77** D3
Valeview Ter *GVH/MTFL* G42 .... **116** A2
Vallay St *PPK/MIL* G22 .... **79** D2
Valleyfield St *SPRGB/BLRNK* G21 .... **11** D5
Vancouver La *SCOT* G14 .... **2** A4
   SCOT G14 .... **87** C2 ⬛
Vancouver Rd *SCOT* G14 .... **87** C3
Vanguard St *CLYDBK* G81 .... **62** B4
Varna La *SCOT* G14 .... **3** D5
Varna Rd *SCOT* G14 .... **3** D4
Vassart Pl *MRYH/FIRH* G20 .... **7** E3
Vennard Gdns *PLKSD/SHW* G41 .... **55** D4
Vermont Av *RUTH* G73 .... **119** C3 ⬛
Vermont St *PLKSD/SHW* G41 .... **42** B3
Verona Av *SCOT* G14 .... **87** C2
Verona Gdns *SCOT* G14 .... **87** C2 ⬛
Verona La *SCOT* G14 .... **87** C2
Vesalius St *CAR/SHTL* G32 .... **106** A1 ⬛
Vicarfield St *GOV/IBX* G51 .... **28** C3
Victoria Circ *KVD/HLHD* G12 .... **5** E5
Victoria Crescent La
   KVD/HLHD G12 .... **17** F1 ⬛
Victoria Crescent Rd *KVD/HLHD* G12 .. **5** E5
Victoria Dr East *RNFRW* PA4 .... **84** A4 ⬛
Victoria Park Cnr *SCOT* G14 .... **2** A4
Victoria Park Dr North *SCOT* G14 .... **2** B4
Victoria Park Dr South *SCOT* G14 ..... **2** A5 ⬛
   SCOT G14 .... **14** B1
Victoria Park Gdns North *PTCK* G11 ... **3** E5
Victoria Park Gdns South *PTCK* G11 ... **3** E5

Victoria Park La North *SCOT* G14 .... 2 A5
Victoria Park La South *SCOT* G14 ..... 14 A1
Victoria Park St *SCOT* G14 .... 14 B1
Victoria Rd *GVH/MTFL* G42 .... 56 B3
   RUTH G73 .... 119 C4 🔲
   STPS/GTHM/RID G33 .... 91 D1
Victoria St *RUTH* G73 .... 119 C2
Viewbank *GIF/THBK* G46 .... 125 C3 🔲
Viewfield Av *BAIL/MDB/MHD* G69 .... 108 B1
   BSHPBGS G64 .... 80 A2 🔲
Viewfield Rd *BAIL/MDB/MHD* G69 .... 108 A1
Viewfield La *KVD/HLHD* G12 .... 18 C3
Viewfield Rd *BSHPBGS* G64 .... 80 A2
Viewmount Dr *MRYH/FIRH* G20 .... 76 B3
Viewpark Av *DEN/PKHD* G31 .... 36 C1
Viewpark Dr *RUTH* G73 .... 119 D4
Viewpoint Rd *SPRGB/BLRNK* G21 ..... 80 B4
Viking Wy *GIF/THBK* G46 .... 124 B1
Villafield Av *BSHPBGS* G64 .... 69 C3
Villafield Dr *BSHPBGS* G64 .... 69 C3
Vine St *PTCK* G11 .... 16 C3
Vinicombe La *KVD/HLHD* G12 .... 6 B5 🔲
Vinicombe St *KVD/HLHD* G12 .... 6 B5
Vintner St *COWCAD* G4 .... 21 E2
Virginia Ct *CGLE* G1 .... 33 E4
Virginia Pl *CGLE* G1 .... 33 F4
Virginia St *CGLE* G1 .... 33 F4
Viscount Av *RNFRW* PA4 .... 92 A1
Voil Dr *LNPK/KPK* G44 .... 128 A2
Vulcan St *SPRGB/BLRNK* G21 .... 11 D4 🔲

W

Waddell St *GBLS* G5 .... 46 A4
Waldemar Rd *KNTSWD* G13 .... 73 C3
Waldo St *KNTSWD* G13 .... 74 B3 🔲
Walkerburn Rd
   CARD/HILL/MSPK G52 .... 102 B2
Walker Ct *PTCK* G11 .... 17 D4
Walker St *PTCK* G11 .... 17 D4
Walkinshaw St *DMNK/BRGTN* G40 ... 48 A4
Wallace St *GBLS* G5 .... 44 C2 🔲
   RUTH G73 .... 119 C4 🔲🔲
Wallacewell Crs *SPRGB/BLRNK* G21 .. 13 D2
Wallacewell Pl *SPRGB/BLRNK* G21..... 13 D2
Wallacewell Qd *SPRGB/BLRNK* G21... 82 A4
Wallacewell Rd *SPRGB/BLRNK* G21.... 12 B2
Walls St *CGLE* G1 .... 34 A4
Walnut Crs *PPK/MIL* G22 .... 10 A1
Walter St *DEN/PKHD* G31 .... 37 D3
Walton St *PLKSD/SHW* G41 .... 115 C2 🔲
Wamba Av *KNTSWD* G13 .... 74 A2
Wandilla Av *CLYDBK* G81 .... 62 B4 🔲
Wanlock St *GOV/IBX* G51 .... 28 B1
Warden Rd *KNTSWD* G13 .... 73 D3
Wardie Pl *STPS/GTHM/RID* G33 ..... 100 B3 🔲
Wardie Rd *BAIL/MDB/MHD* G69 ...... 101 C3
Wardlaw Av *RUTH* G73 .... 119 D3
Wardlaw Dr *RUTH* G73 .... 119 D3 🔲
Wardlaw Rd *BSDN* G61 .... 74 B1
Wardrop St *GOV/IBX* G51 .... 28 A1
Ware Rd *STPS/GTHM/RID* G33 .... 100 B3
Warilda Av *CLYDBK* G81 .... 62 A4 🔲
Warnock St *COWCAD* G4 .... 35 D4
Warren St *GVH/MTFL* G42 .... 57 D5
Warriston Crs *STPS/GTHM/RID* G33 .. 96 B2
Warriston Pl *CAR/SHTL* G32 .... 98 B3 🔲
Warriston St *STPS/GTHM/RID* G33 ... 96 B2
Warroch St *KVGV* G3 .... 31 F4
Washington St *KVGV* G3 .... 32 A5

Waterfoot Av *PLK/PH/NH* G53.......... 111 C2
Waterfoot Ter *PLK/PH/NH* G53........ 111 C2 🔲
Waterford Rd *GIF/THBK* G46 .... 125 D3
Waterloo La *CGLW* G2 .... 32 C3
Waterloo St *CGLW* G2 .... 32 B3
Waterside St *GBLS* G5 .... 46 A5
Watson Av *RUTH* G73 .... 118 B3
Watson St *CGLE* G1 .... 33 F5
Watt Low Av *RUTH* G73 .... 118 B4 🔲
   RUTH G73 .... 119 C4 🔲
Watt Rd *CARD/HILL/MSPK* G52....... 93 D3
Watt St *GBLS* G5 .... 43 E2
Waukglen Av *PLK/PH/NH* G53 .... 122 B3
Waukglen Crs *PLK/PH/NH* G53 .... 123 C3
Waukglen Dr *PLK/PH/NH* G53 .... 122 B3
Waukglen Gdns *PLK/PH/NH* G53.... 122 B3
Waukglen Pth *PLK/PH/NH* G53 ..... 122 B3 🔲
Waukglen Pl *PLK/PH/NH* G53.......... 122 B3
Waukglen Rd *PLK/PH/NH* G53 .... 122 B3
Waulkmill La *GIF/THBK* G46 .... 124 A2
Waverley Dr *RUTH* G73 .... 120 A3 🔲
Waverley Gdns *PLKSD/SHW* G41 ..... 54 C5
Waverley St *PLKSD/SHW* G41 .... 55 D5
Weardale La *STPS/GTHM/RID* G33... 99 C2
Weardale St *STPS/GTHM/RID* G33 ... 99 C2
Weaver St *COWCAD* G4 .... 34 B3
Webster St *DMNK/BRGTN* G40 .... 60 A2
   KNTSWD G13 .... 71 C2 🔲
Wedderlea Dr
   CARD/HILL/MSPK G52............ 102 B1
Weensmoor Rd *PLK/PH/NH* G53...... 122 A2
Weirwood Av *BAIL/MDB/MHD* G69 .. 108 B2
Weirwood Gdns
   BAIL/MDB/MHD G69 .... 108 B2 🔲
Welbeck Rd *PLK/PH/NH* G53 .... 122 B1
Wellcroft Pl *GBLS* G5 .... 44 C4
Wellfield Av *GIF/THBK* G46 .... 125 D3
Wellfield St *SPRGB/BLRNK* G21 ...... 11 F3
Well Gn *PLKSW/MSWD* G43 .... 114 A2 🔲
Wellhouse Crs
   STPS/GTHM/RID G33 .... 100 A3
Wellhouse Rd
   STPS/GTHM/RID G33 .... 100 B2
Wellington La *CGLW* G2 .... 32 B3
Wellington Rd *BSHPBGS* G64 .... 69 C3
Wellington St *CGLW* G2 .... 32 C3
Wellmeadow Rd
   PLKSW/MSWD G43 .... 113 C4
Wellpark St *COWCAD* G4 .... 35 D4
Wellshot Dr *BLTYR/CAMB* G72 ...... 133 D1
Wellshot Rd *CAR/SHTL* G32 .... 105 D2
Wemyss Gdns
   BAIL/MDB/MHD G69 .... 109 C3 🔲
Wentworth Dr *SMSTN* G23 .... 77 C1 🔲🔲
West Av *RNFRW* PA4 .... 84 A3
   STPS/GTHM/RID G33................. 91 D1
Westbank La *KVD/HLHD* G12 .... 18 C3
Westbank Qd *KVD/HLHD* G12........... 18 C3
Westbourne Crs *BSDN* G61 .... 65 C1
Westbourne Dr *BSDN* G61 .... 65 C1
Westbourne Gardens La
   KVD/HLHD G12 .... 5 E4 🔲
Westbourne Gdns North
   KVD/HLHD G12.............................. 5 E4
Westbourne Gdns South
   KVD/HLHD G12.............................. 5 E4
Westbourne Gdns West
   KVD/HLHD G12.............................. 5 E4
Westbourne Rd *KVD/HLHD* G12........ 5 D4
Westbourne Terrace La North
   KVD/HLHD G12............................. 5 D4

Westbourne Terrace La South
  KVD/HLHD G12.. 5 D4
Westbrae Dr KNTSWD G13 .... 2 C3
Westburn Crs RUTH G73 .... 118 B3
West Campbell St CGLW G2 .... 32 B4
Westcastle Crs CSMK G45 .... 129 D3
Westcastle Gdns CSMK G45 .... 129 D3
Westcastle Gv CSMK G45 .... 129 D3 ☑
West Chapelton Av BSDN G61 .... 66 B2
West Chapelton Crs BSDN G61 .... 66 B2
West Chapelton Dr BSDN G61 .... 66 B2
Westclyffe St PLKSD/SHW G41........................ 54 C5
West Coats Rd BLTYR/CAMB G72...... 133 D1 ☑
Westend Park St KVGV G3 .... 19 E4
Westerburn St CAR/SHTL G32 .... 97 D4
Wester Cleddens Rd BSHPBGS G64.... 69 C4
Wester Common Dr PPK/MIL G22 .... 8 B3
Wester Common Rd PPK/MIL G22 .... 8 B3
Westercraigs DEN/PKHD G31........................ 35 F4
Westerhill Rd BSHPBGS G64 .... 69 D2
Westerhouse Rd ESTRH G34 .... 101 D2
Westerkirk Dr SMSTN G23 .... 77 C1
Westerlands KVD/HLHD G12 .... 75 C4 ☑
Western Av RUTH G73 .... 119 C2 ☑
Western Rd BLTYR/CAMB G72 .... 133 D3
Wester Rd CAR/SHTL G32 .... 107 D3
Westerton Av KNTSWD G13 .... 74 B2
Westfield Av RUTH G73 .... 118 B3
Westfield Crs BSDN G61 .... 66 A4 ☑
Westfield Dr BSDN G61 .... 66 A4
  CARD/HILL/MSPK G52.............................. 102 A1
Westfield Rd GIF/THBK G46 .... 125 C4
Westfields BSHPBGS G64 .... 68 A3
West George La CGLW G2 .... 33 D3 ☑
West George St CGLE G1 .... 33 E3
  CGLW G2 .... 32 A2
West Graham St KVGV G3 .... 20 B5
West Greenhill Pl KVGV G3 .... 30 C2
Westhouse Av RUTH G73 .... 118 A3
Westhouse Gdns RUTH G73 .... 118 A3 ☑
Westland Dr SCOT G14 .... 2 A5
Westmoreland St GVH/MTFL G42 .... 56 B4
Westmuir Pl RUTH G73 .... 118 A2
Westmuir St DEN/PKHD G31 .... 104 B1
West Nile St CGLE G1 .... 33 D3
West Prince's La COWCAD G4 .... 19 D2 ☑
West Prince's St COWCAD G4 .... 19 E2
  KVGV G3 .... 19 F4
Westray Circ PPK/MIL G22 .... 79 D4 ☑
Westray Pl PPK/MIL G22 .... 79 D3 ☑
Westray Sq PPK/MIL G22 .... 79 C3
Westray St PPK/MIL G22 .... 79 C3
West Regent La CGLW G2 .... 32 C2
West Regent St CGLW G2 .... 32 A1
Westside Gdns PTCK G11 .... 17 D2 ☑
West St CLYDBK G81 .... 71 C2
  GBLS G5 .... 44 A3
West Whitby St DEN/PKHD G31........ 49 F4
Westwood Av GIF/THBK G46 .... 125 D3
Westwood Qd CLYDBK G81 .... 70 B1
Westwood Rd PLKSW/MSWD G43 .... 113 D4
Weymouth Dr KVD/HLHD G12 .... 75 C4
Wheatfield Rd BSDN G61 .... 65 D4
Wheatley Loan BSHPBGS G64 .... 82 A2
Whinfield Rd PLK/PH/NH G53 .... 122 A2 ☑
Whinhill Rd PLK/PH/NH G53 .... 102 A3
Whins Rd PLKSD/SHW G41 .... 53 F5
Whirlow Gdns
  BAIL/MDB/MHD G69 .... 109 C1
Whirlow Rd BAIL/MDB/MHD G69 .... 109 C1
Whistlefield Ct BSDN G61 .... 66 A3
Whitburn St CAR/SHTL G32.......................... 97 D3

Whitecraigs Pl SMSTN G23 .... 77 C2 ☑
Whitecrook Sreet CLYDBK G81 .... 70 A2
Whitefield Rd GOV/IBX G51 .... 41 E1
Whitehall St KVGV G3..................................... 31 F4
Whitehaugh Crs PLK/PH/NH G53 ... 122 A2
Whitehaugh Rd PLK/PH/NH G53 .... 122 A2
Whitehill Gdns DEN/PKHD G31 .... 36 B4
Whitehill Rd BSDN G61 .... 65 D2
Whitehill St DEN/PKHD G31 .... 36 A2
Whitehill Street La DEN/PKHD G31 ...... 36 A4
Whitekirk Pl DRUM G15 .... 64 A4 ☑
Whitelaw St MRYH/FIRH G20 .... 76 A3
Whitemoss Av LNPK/KPK G44 .... 127 D2 ☑
White St CLYDBK G81 .... 70 B3
  PTCK G11 .... 17 D2
Whitevale St DEN/PKHD G31 .... 48 B1
Whitlawburn Av BLTYR/CAMB G72 .. 133 C2 ☑
Whitlawburn Rd BLTYR/CAMB G72 .. 133 C2 ☑
Whitlawburn Ter
  BLTYR/CAMB G72 .... 133 C2 ☑
Whitslade Pl ESTRH G34 .... 101 C1 ☑
Whitslade St ESTRH G34 .... 101 C1 ☑
Whittingehame Dr KNTSWD G13 .... 3 E2 ☑
  KVD/HLHD G12 .... 3 F2
Whittingehame La KNTSWD G13............ 3 E2
Whittlemuir Av LNPK/KPK G44 .... 127 D2
Whitton Dr GIF/THBK G46 .... 126 B2
Whitton St MRYH/FIRH G20 .... 76 A2
Whitworth St MRYH/FIRH G20 .... 78 A3 ☑
Whyte Av BLTYR/CAMB G72 .... 121 C4
Wilfred Av KNTSWD G13 .... 73 D3
Williamson St DMNK/BRGTN G40........... 49 E5
William St KVGV G3... 31 F2
William Ure Pl BSHPBGS G64 .... 69 D1
Williamwood Dr LNPK/KPK G44........ 127 C4
Williamwood Pk LNPK/KPK G44 ... 127 D4 ☑
Williamwood Pk West
  LNPK/KPK G44 .... 127 D4 ☑
Willock Pl MRYH/FIRH G20 .... 77 C3
Willoughby Dr KNTSWD G13 .... 74 B4 ☑
Willoughby La KNTSWD G13 .... 74 B4 ☑
Willow Av BSHPBGS G64 .... 81 C2 ☑
Willowbank Crs KVGV G3 .... 19 E3 ☑
Willowbank St KVGV G3 .... 19 E4
Willowdale Crs
  BAIL/MDB/MHD G69 .... 109 C2
Willowdale Gdns
  BAIL/MDB/MHD G69 .... 109 C2 ☑
Willow La CAR/SHTL G32 .... 106 B4
Willow St KNTSWD G13 .... 74 B3
Wilmot Rd KNTSWD G13 .... 73 D4 ☑
Wilson St CGLE G1 .... 33 F4
  RNFRW PA4 .... 84 B2
Wiltonburn Rd PLK/PH/NH G53........ 122 A2
Wilton Crescent La MRYH/FIRH G20 .... 7 E5
Wilton Dr MRYH/FIRH G20 .... 7 F5
Wilton St MRYH/FIRH G20..................... 6 C4
Wilverton Rd KNTSWD G13 .... 74 A2
Winchester Dr KVD/HLHD G12 .... 75 D4
Windhill Crs PLKSW/MSWD G43 .... 125 D1
Windhill Rd PLKSW/MSWD G43 .... 125 D1
Windlaw Gdns LNPK/KPK G44 .... 127 D2
Windlaw Park Gdns
  LNPK/KPK G44 .... 127 D2 ☑
Windsor Rd RNFRW PA4 .... 84 A4
Windsor St CAR/SHTL G32 .... 99 C4 ☑
  MRYH/FIRH G20 .... 20 A2
Windsor Ter MRYH/FIRH G20 .... 20 A2
Windyedge Crs KNTSWD G13 .... 87 C1 ☑
Windyedge Pl KNTSWD G13 .... 87 C1 ☑
Winfield Av BLTYR/CAMB G72 .... 121 C3 ☑
Winifred St STPS/GTHM/RID G33......... 88 B2

Winning Rw *DEN/PKHD* G31 .... **104** B1
Winton Av *GIF/THBK* G46 .... **126** A4
Winton Dr *KVD/HLHD* G12 .... **5** E2
Winton La *KVD/HLHD* G12 .... **5** F2
Wirran Pl *KNTSWD* G13 .... **71** C2
Wishart St *DEN/PKHD* G31 .... **35** D2
Wisner Ct *GIF/THBK* G46 .... **124** B3
Woddrop St *DMNK/BRGTN* G40 .... **60** C3
Wolseley St *GBLS* G5 .... **58** A1
Woodburn Rd *PLKSW/MSWD* G43 ...... **126** B1
Woodcroft Av *PTCK* G11 .... **3** F5
Woodend Ct *CAR/SHTL* G32 .... **108** A4
Woodend Dr *KNTSWD* G13 .... **2** C1
Woodend Gdns *CAR/SHTL* G32 .... **107** D4
Woodend La *KNTSWD* G13 .... **3** D2
Woodend Rd *CAR/SHTL* G32 .... **107** D4
.... *RUTH* G73 .... **131** D2
Woodfoot Pl *PLK/PH/NH* G53 .... **122** A2
Woodfoot Qd *PLK/PH/NH* G53 .... **122** B3
Woodfoot Rd *PLK/PH/NH* G53 .... **122** A2
Woodford St *PLKSW/MSWD* G43 ...... **114** B3
Woodgreen Av *LNPK/KPK* G44 .... **116** B4
Woodhall St *DMNK/BRGTN* G40 .... **60** C3
Woodhill Rd *BSHPBGS* G64 .... **82** A1
.... *SPRGB/BLRNK* G21 .... **81** D4
Woodholm Av *LNPK/KPK* G44 .... **117** C4
Woodhouse St *KNTSWD* G13 .... **74** A3
Woodlands Ct *GIF/THBK* G46 .... **124** B4
Woodlands Crs *GIF/THBK* G46 .... **124** B3
Woodlands Dr *COWCAD* G4 .... **19** E3
.... *KVGV* G3 .... **19** E3
Woodlands Ga *GIF/THBK* G46 .... **124** B3
.... *KVGV* G3 .... **19** E4
Woodlands Pk *GIF/THBK* G46 .... **124** B4
Woodlands Rd *GIF/THBK* G46 .... **124** B4
.... *KVGV* G3 .... **19** E4
Woodlands Ter *KVGV* G3 .... **19** D5
Woodlea Dr *GIF/THBK* G46 .... **126** B2
Woodlinn Av *LNPK/KPK* G44 .... **128** B1
Woodneuk Rd *PLK/PH/NH* G53 .... **122** B2
Wood Qd *CLYDBK* G81 .... **71** C2
Woodrow Circ *PLKSD/SHW* G41 .... **42** A4
Woodrow Rd *PLKSD/SHW* G41 .... **42** A5
Woodside Av *GIF/THBK* G46 .... **125** C3
.... *RUTH* G73 .... **120** A3
Woodside Crs *KVGV* G3 .... **19** F5
Woodside Pl *KVGV* G3 .... **19** E5
Woodside Place La *KVGV* G3 .... **19** E5
Woodside Ter *KVGV* G3 .... **19** E5

Woodside Terrace La *KVGV* G3 .... **19** E5
Woodside Gv *RUTH* G73 .... **120** A3
Woodstock Av *PLKSD/SHW* G41 .... **114** B2
Wood St *DEN/PKHD* G31 .... **36** C2
Woodvale Av *BSDN* G61 .... **67** D4
Woodville Pk *GOV/IBX* G51 .... **28** C5
Woodville St *GOV/IBX* G51 .... **29** D5
Wykeham Pl *KNTSWD* G13 .... **73** C4
Wykeham Rd *KNTSWD* G13 .... **73** C4
Wyndford Rd *MRYH/FIRH* G20 .... **6** A1
Wyndham Ct *KVD/HLHD* G12 .... **6** A3
Wyndham St *KVD/HLHD* G12 .... **6** A3
Wyper Pl *DMNK/BRGTN* G40 .... **48** A1
Wyvil Av *KNTSWD* G13 .... **74** A1
Wyvis Av *KNTSWD* G13 .... **71** C2
Wyvis Pl *KNTSWD* G13 .... **71** D2
Wyvis Qd *CLYDBK* G81 .... **71** D2

Y

Yair Dr *CARD/HILL/MSPK* G52 .... **94** A4
Yarrow Gdns *MRYH/FIRH* G20 .... **7** E5
Yarrow Gardens La *MRYH/FIRH* G20... **7** E5
Yarrow Rd *BSHPBGS* G64 .... **69** C2
Yate St *DEN/PKHD* G31 .... **48** C3
Yetholm St *SCOT* G14 .... **71** C4
Yew Dr *SPRGB/BLRNK* G21 .... **12** B5
Yokerburn Pl *KNTSWD* G13 .... **71** C3
Yokerburn Ter *CLYDBK* G81 .... **70** B3
Yoker Ferry Rd *RNFRW* PA4 .... **85** C1
Yoker Mill Gdns *KNTSWD* G13 .... **71** C3
Yoker Mill Rd *KNTSWD* G13 .... **71** C3
York Dr *RUTH* G73 .... **132** B1
Yorkhill Pde *KVGV* G3 .... **17** F5
Yorkhill St *KVGV* G3 .... **30** A1
York St *CLYDBK* G81 .... **62** B4
.... *KVGV* G3 .... **32** B4
Young Ter *SPRGB/BLRNK* G21 .... **12** A4

Z

Zena Pl *STPS/GTHM/RID* G33 .... **88** B2
Zena St *STPS/GTHM/RID* G33 .... **88** B2
Zetland Rd *CARD/HILL/MSPK* G52 ..... **93** D2

Index - featured places

Abercorn Secondary School
.... *COWCAD* G4 .... **20** C3
Acredyke School
.... *SPRGB/BLRNK* G21 .... **82** A3
Albert Primary School
.... *SPRGB/BLRNK* G21 .... **11** E2
**Alexandra Parade
Primary School**
.... *DEN/PKHD* G31 .... **36** B2
All Saints RC Secondary School
.... *SPRGB/BLRNK* G21 .... **13** F3
AMF Bowling
.... *KVGV* G3 .... **31** E3
**The Anderson Doe
Podiatry Clinic**
.... *SCOT* G14 .... **3** E3

Anderston Medical Centre
.... *KVGV* G3 .... **31** D1
Anderston Primary School
.... *KVGV* G3 .... **31** E3
Annfield Medical Centre
.... *DEN/PKHD* G31 .... **35** F4
Anniesland College
.... *CLYDBK* G81 .... **70** A2
**Anniesland College
of Further Education**
.... *KVD/HLHD* G12 .... **4** A1
**Anniesland College
of Further Education**
.... *PTCK* G11 .... **15** E3
Anniesland Industrial Estate
.... *KNTSWD* G13 .... **74** A2

Cathkin High School
BLTYR/CAMB G72 .... **133** C2

Cathkin Primary School
RUTH G73 .... **132** B3

Celtic Football Club
DEN/PKHD G31 .... **49** E3

Central College of Commerce
CGLE G1 .... **33** F2

Central Mosque
GBLS G5 .... **45** E2

Centre Gallery
CGLW G2 .... **32** A1

Charing Cross Clinic
KVGV G3 .... **19** F5

Child Health Clinic
PLKSW/MSWD G43 .... **114** A2

Chinese Medical Centre
KVD/HLHD G12 .... **18** A2

Chirnsyde Primary School
PPK/MIL G22 .... **79** D4

City Chambers
CGLE G1 .... **33** F3

City Council
CGLW G2 .... **32** C2

City Halls & Ticket Office
CGLE G1 .... **33** F4

City of Glasgow Council
CGLE G1 .... **33** E2

City of Glasgow Council
CGLE G1 .... **46** B1

City of Glasgow Council
CSMK G45 .... **130** B3

City of Glasgow Council
GBLS G5 .... **45** F3

Cleveden Secondary School
KVD/HLHD G12 .... **5** E1

Cleveden Secondary School
MRYH/FIRH G20 .... **7** D4

Clydebank Business Centre
CLYDBK G81 .... **70** A2

Clyde Industrial Estate
RUTH G73 .... **120** B2

Clydeway Business Centre
KVGV G3 .... **31** D3

College of Art
CGLW G2 .... **32** B1

College of Building & Printing
CGLE G1 .... **33** F2

College of Food & Technology
CGLE G1 .... **33** F2

**Colquhoun Park
Primary School**
BSDN G61 .... **65** C3

Compass Gallery
CGLW G2 .... **32** B2

Cotton Street Business Park
DMNK/BRGTN G40 .... **59** F3

Cowglen Hospital
PLK/PH/NH G53 .... **111** D1

Craigbank Secondary School
PLK/PH/NH G53 .... **111** D1

Craigholme School
PLKSD/SHW G41 .... **54** A2

Croftcroighn School
STPS/GTHM/RID G33 .... **100** A1

Crookston (NT)
PLK/PH/NH G53 .... **102** B4

Crowngate Business Centre
DMNK/BRGTN G40 .... **47** F3

Cuthbertson Primary School
PLKSD/SHW G41 .... **56** A2

Cyril Gerber Gallery
CGLW G2 .... **32** C2

**Daily Record & Sunday
Mail Offices**
KVGV G3 .... **31** E4

Dalmarnock Industrial Estate
RUTH G73 .... **60** C5

Dalmarnock Primary School
DMNK/BRGTN G40 .... **48** A5

Dalsholm Industrial Estate
MRYH/FIRH G20 .... **75** D3

David Dale College
DMNK/BRGTN G40 .... **47** F2

Dental Hospital & School
CGLW G2 .... **32** B1

Department of General Practice
KVD/HLHD G12 .... **5** E3

Dinmont Doctors Surgery
PLKSD/SHW G41 .... **114** B1

Douglas Inch Clinic
KVGV G3 .... **19** F5

Dowanhill Primary School
PTCK G11 .... **17** F2

Drumchapel Health Centre
DRUM G15 .... **63** D3

Drumchapel High School
DRUM G15 .... **64** A2

Drummore School
DRUM G15 .... **65** C2

Drumoyne Industrial Estate
GOV/IBX G51 .... **26** C5

Drumoyne Primary School
GOV/IBX G51 .... **26** C4

Duchess Industrial Estate
RUTH G73 .... **61** E5

Dunard Primary School
MRYH/FIRH G20 .... **7** E4

**Dunbartonshire
& Lomond Council**
BSHPBGS G64 .... **68** B4

Dundas Business Centre
COWCAD G4 .... **20** C4

East Bank Primary School
CAR/SHTL G32 .... **107** C1

East Dunbartonshire Council
BAIL/MDB/MHD G69 .... **109** D1

East Dunbartonshire Council
BSDN G61 .... **67** C2

East Dunbartonshire Council
BSHPBGS G64 .... **68** A2

East Dunbartonshire Council
BSHPBGS G64 .... **80** B2

Eastmuir Surgery
CAR/SHTL G32 .... **107** C1

Elderpark Clinic
GOV/IBX G51 .... **27** E3

Elder Park Primary School
GOV/IBX G51 .... **26** C2

Elmvale Primary School
PPK/MIL G22 .... **11** D2

Family Planning Clinic
KVGV G3 .... **19** E5

Farm Castle Industrial Estate
RUTH G73 .... **120** A2

Farmeloan Industrial Estate
RUTH G73 .... **119** D2

Fiddle Gallery
MRYH/FIRH G20 .... **7** D4

Film Theatre
CGLW G2 .... **32** C1

Glasgow City Council
PLK/PH/NH G53 .... 110 B4

Glasgow City Council
PLKSD/SHW G41 .... 43 F4

Glasgow City Council
PLKSD/SHW G41 .... 54 B2

Glasgow City Council
PLKSW/MSWD G43 .... 114 A3

Glasgow City Council
PPK/MIL G22 .... 9 E2

Glasgow City Council
PPK/MIL G22 .... 80 A3

Glasgow City Council
PTCK G11 .... 16 C4

Glasgow City Council
PTCK G11 .... 17 E4

Glasgow City Council
SPRGB/BLRNK G21 .... 10 C4

Glasgow City Council
SPRGB/BLRNK G21 .... 22 C1

Glasgow City Council
SPRGB/BLRNK G21 .... 23 E5

Glasgow City Council
SPRGB/BLRNK G21 .... 25 D2

Glasgow City Council
SPRGB/BLRNK G21 .... 80 B4

Glasgow City Council
SPRGB/BLRNK G21 .... 82 A4

Glasgow City Council
STPS/GTHM/RID G33 .... 97 D2

Glasgow City Council
STPS/GTHM/RID G33 .... 99 C2

Glasgow City Council
STPS/GTHM/RID G33 .... 100 B4

Glasgow Nuffield Hospital
KVD/HLHD G12 .... 5 D2

Glasgow Royal Infirmary
DEN/PKHD G31 .... 35 E1

Glasgow School of Art
KVGV G3 .... 20 C5

Glasgow Steiner School
KVGV G3 .... 18 A5

Glasgow Zoo
UD/BTH/TAN G71 .... 109 D4

Glendale Primary School
PLKSD/SHW G41 .... 43 F5

Glenmill Surgery
STPS/GTHM/RID G33 .... 88 B3

Glenpark Industrial Estate
DEN/PKHD G31 .... 36 C5

Glenwood Business Centre
CSMK G45 .... 130 A3

Glenwood Business Park
CSMK G45 .... 130 A3

Golfhill Primary School
DEN/PKHD G31 .... 35 E2

Gorbals Health Centre
GBLS G5 .... 45 F4

Govan Health Centre
GOV/IBX G51 .... 27 D3

Govan High Secondary School
GOV/IBX G51 .... 26 C4

Govanhill Health Centre
CVH/MTFL G42 .... 56 C4

Greater Glasgow Health Board
DEN/PKHD G31 .... 104 B1

Greek Orthodox Cathedral
of St Luke
KVD/HLHD G12 .... 5 F5

Greenfield Street School
GOV/IBX G51 .... 27 E4

Haghill School
DEN/PKHD G31 .... 37 D3

Hamiltonhill Industrial Estate
PPK/MIL G22 .... 9 D5

Hampden School
CVH/MTFL G42 .... 118 A3

The Harvest Clinic
COWCAD G4 .... 20 A4

Heatherbank Museum
of Social Work Trust
KVD/HLHD G12 .... 19 D3

High Court & Court of Justiciary
CGLE G1 .... 45 F1

High School of Glasgow
KNTSWD G13 .... 3 E1

Hillhead High School
KVD/HLHD G12 .... 18 C2

Hillhead Rugby Club
KVD/HLHD G12 .... 5 D3

Hillington Industrial Estate
CARD/HILL/MSPK G52 .... 93 D3

Hillington Primary School
CARD/HILL/MSPK G52 .... 94 A4

Hillpark Secondary School
PLKSW/MSWD G43 .... 126 A1

Hillstrust Primary School
GOV/IBX G51 .... 28 A2

Hindu Temple
KVD/HLHD G12 .... 18 C2

Holmlea Primary School
LNPK/KPK G44 .... 116 A4

Holy Reedemer RC School
CLYDBK G81 .... 70 B3

Holyrood Secondary School
CVH/MTFL G42 .... 117 C1

Homoeopaths Surgery
KVGV G3 .... 31 F1

Househillmuir Road School
PLK/PH/NH G53 .... 122 B1

Howford School
PLK/PH/NH G53 .... 102 A4

The Hui Chun Clinic
KVGV G3 .... 20 B5

Hutchesons Grammar
Junior School
PLKSD/SHW G41 .... 56 A3

Hutchesons St Aloysians
Rugby Club
GIF/THBK G46 .... 125 C1

Hyndland Primary School
PTCK G11 .... 16 C2

Hyndland Senior
Secondary School
KVD/HLHD G12 .... 4 C5

Ibrox Industrial Estate
GOV/IBX G51 .... 41 E1

Ibrox Primary School
GOV/IBX G51 .... 40 C2

Indoor Market
DRUM G15 .... 63 D3

Insomnia Gallery
KVGV G3 .... 19 F5

International Christian College
COWCAD G4 .... 34 B2

Islamic Mosque
KVGV G3 .... 19 F4

John Hillhouse Industrial Estate
BLTYR/CAMB G72 .... 120 B2

John Wheatley College
ESTRH G34 .... 101 D2

Jordanhill College School
KNTSWD G13 .... 2 C1

Junior High School of Glasgow
BSDN G61 .... 65 D2
The Kelly Gallery
CGLW G2 .... 32 B1
Kelvindale Primary School
KVD/HLHD G12 .... 4 B1
Kelvin Gallery
CGLW G2 .... 32 C1
Kennyhill School
DEN/PKHD G31 .... 37 E2
Kerr Practice
DMNK/BRGTN G40 .... 47 F3
Kings Park Secondary School
LNPK/KPK G44 .... 129 C1
Kings Theatre
CGLW G2 .... 32 A1
Kinning Park Medical Centre
GOV/IBX G51 .... 43 D1
Kirklandeuk Primary School
RNFRW PA4 .... 84 A2
Kirkriggs School
CSMK G45 .... 131 C1
Laird Business Park
DMNK/BRGTN G40 .... 60 A3
Lamlash Primary School
STPS/GTHM/RID G33 .... 98 B2
Lanfauld School
DRUM G15 .... 63 D2
Langlands School
GOV/IBX G51 .... 26 C3
Langside College
CSMK G45 .... 130 B3
Langside College
GVH/MTFL G42 .... 116 A2
Langside Galleries
GVH/MTFL G42 .... 115 D2
Lansdowne Clinic
KVD/HLHD G12 .... 4 B1
Leithland Road Primary School
PLK/PH/NH G53 .... 110 B1
Lightburn Hospital
CAR/SHTL G32 .... 98 B3
Lillie Art Gallery
BSDN G61 .... 66 A1
Linburn School
CARD/HILL/MSPK G52 .... 93 D4
Linnvale Primary School
CLYDBK G81 .... 70 B1
Littlehill Primary School
STPS/GTHM/RID G33 .... 88 B3
Lochgoin Primary School
DRUM G15 .... 63 D2
**Lochinch Playing Fields
& Sports Club**
PLKSW/MSWD G43 .... 51 F5
Loch Primary School
RUTH G73 .... 132 B2
London Road Primary School
DMNK/BRGTN G40 .... 49 D4
Lourdes Primary School
CARD/HILL/MSPK G52 .... 103 C2
M8 Trading Estate
PLKSD/SHW G41 .... 43 D3
Madhok Medical Centre
GVH/MTFL G42 .... 116 A3
Markets
SPRGB/BLRNK G21 .... 24 C5
Maryhill Football Club
MRYH/FIRH G20 .... 76 B4
Maryhill Health Centre
MRYH/FIRH G20 .... 77 C4

Mcgill Primary School
PLK/PH/NH G53 .... 103 C4
Mclellan Galleries
CGLW G2 .... 32 C1
Meadowburn Primary School
BSHPBGS G64 .... 69 C3
Meadowside Industrial Estate
RNFRW PA4 .... 70 B4
Megabowl
CLYDBK G81 .... 70 A1
Merrylee Primary School
PLKSW/MSWD G43 .... 127 D1
Middlefield School
PTCK G11 .... 17 D2
Midlock Medical Centre
GOV/IBX G51 .... 41 E2
Miltonbank Primary School
PPK/MIL G22 .... 79 C2
Milton Clinic
PPK/MIL G22 .... 79 C3
Milton School
PPK/MIL G22 .... 80 A3
Mitchell Theatre & Library
KVGV G3 .... 31 F1
**Moore & Dalziel
Doctors Surgery**
PTCK G11 .... 17 D3
Mosque
GVH/MTFL G42 .... 56 B5
Mount Florida Medical Centre
GVH/MTFL G42 .... 116 A2
Mount Florida School
LNPK/KPK G44 .... 116 B3
Mount Manor Business Park
KVGV G3 .... 30 C2
Mount Vernon Primary School
CAR/SHTL G32 .... 107 D3
Munro Business Centre
KNTSWD G13 .... 74 A4
Murano Medical Centre
MRYH/FIRH G20 .... 7 E3
Museum
RNFRW PA4 .... 84 B2
**Museum of Royal
Highland Fusiliers**
CGLW G2 .... 31 F1
Museum of Transport
KVGV G3 .... 18 A4
Napiers Dispensary & Clinic
PTCK G11 .... 17 E3
Natural Therapy Clinic
CGLW G2 .... 32 B1
Nethercraigs Sports Centre
CARD/HILL/MSPK G52 .... 50 B3
Netherlee Primary School
LNPK/KPK G44 .... 127 D4
Netherton School
CSMK G45 .... 129 C4
New Albion Industrial Estate
KNTSWD G13 .... 71 C3
Newmains Primary School
RNFRW PA4 .... 92 A1
Newspaper Offices
CGLE G1 .... 34 A3
Nitshill Primary School
PLK/PH/NH G53 .... 122 A2
Northcote Surgery
KVD/HLHD G12 .... 5 E4
North Glasgow College
SPRGB/BLRNK G21 .... 11 D5

North Glasgow University
Hospital NHS Trust
  SPRGB/BLRNK G21 .... **80** B3
North Woodside Swimming Pool
  COWCAD G4 .... **20** B3
Notre Dame High School
  KVD/HLHD G12 .... **5** E5
Notre Dame Primary School
  KVD/HLHD G12 .... **5** F5
Nuneaton Industrial Estate
  DMNK/BRGTN G40 .... **60** A1
Oakbank Industrial Estate
  MRYH/FIRH G20 .... **20** C2
Oakgrove Primary School
  COWCAD G4 .... **20** B3
Odeon Cinema
  CGLW G2 .... **33** D2
Odeon Cinema
  GOV/IBX G51 .... **43** E1
Open Air Market Stall
  CCGLE G1 .... **45** F1
Optimax Laser Eye Clinic
  CGLW G2 .... **20** A5
Our Lady of Assumption
Primary School
  MRYH/FIRH G20 .... **78** A4
Our Lady of the Annunciation
Primary School
  PLKSW/MSWD G43 .... **127** C1
Our Lady of the Missions
Primary School
  GIF/THBK G46 .... **125** D3
Outdoor Recreation Centre
  BSHPBGS G64 .... **81** C2
Parkhead Hospital
  DEN/PKHD G31 .... **104** B1
Parkhouse School
  PPK/MIL G22 .... **79** D4
Parkview Business Centre
  KVGV G3 .... **19** F5
Partick Market
  PTCK G11 .... **17** E3
Partick Thistle Football Club
  MRYH/FIRH G20 .... **8** A3
The Pavilion Theatre
  CGLW G2 .... **33** D1
Penilee Secondary School
  CARD/HILL/MSPK G52 .... **93** D4
Pentagon Business Centre
  KVGV G3 .... **32** A4
Peoples Palace Museum
  DMNK/BRGTN G40 .... **46** C2
Petershill Football Club
  SPRGB/BLRNK G21 .... **11** F5
Petershill Recreation Centre
  SPRGB/BLRNK G21 .... **25** D1
Pinewood Primary School
  DRUM G15 .... **65** C4
Pollokshields Primary School
  PLKSD/SHW G41 .... **55** E1
Possilpark Health Centre
  PPK/MIL G22 .... **9** E3
Primary School
  RNFRW PA4 .... **84** B4
Provand's Lordship
  COWCAD G4 .... **34** C2
Quarry Brae Primary School
  DEN/PKHD G31 .... **104** B2
Queen's Park FC
  GVH/MTFL G42 .... **116** B3

Ramgarhia Association
Sikh Temple
  KVD/HLHD G12 .... **19** D2
Ramshorn Theatre
  CGLE G1 .... **34** A3
Rangers Football Club
  GOV/IBX G51 .... **29** D5
Rangers Football Club
  CGLE G1 .... **34** A5
Rangers Football Club
  GOV/IBX G51 .... **40** C1
Regency Medical Clinic
  KVGV G3 .... **19** E5
Renfrew Council
  RNFRW PA4 .... **84** B2
Renfrew Health Centre
  RNFRW PA4 .... **84** A4
Renfrew High School
  RNFRW PA4 .... **84** B4
Richmond Doctors Surgery
  PTCK G11 .... **16** A2
Richmond Park School
  GBLS G5 .... **58** B2
Robslee School
  GIF/THBK G46 .... **125** D4
Rosevale School
  PPK/MIL G22 .... **79** D3
Ross Clinic
  KVD/HLHD G12 .... **5** D5
Ross Hall Hospital
  CARD/HILL/MSPK G52 .... **102** A3
Royal College of Nursing
  KVGV G3 .... **19** E5
Royal Concert Hall
  CGLE G1 .... **33** E1
Royal Hospital for Sick Children
  DRUM G15 .... **64** A4
Royal Infirmary
  COWCAD G4 .... **34** A2
Royal Maternity Hospital
  CGLE G1 .... **34** A3
Royston Primary School
  SPRGB/BLRNK G21 .... **23** E5
RSAMD
  CGLW G2 .... **33** D1
Rutherglen Health Centre
  RUTH G73 .... **119** D3
Rutherglen High School
  RUTH G73 .... **119** D2
Rutherglen Swimming Pool
  RUTH G73 .... **119** C3
Sacred Heart Primary School
  DMNK/BRGTN G40 .... **47** F5
SAE Technology College
  PLKSD/SHW G41 .... **43** D2
St Agnes Primary School
  SMSTN G23 .... **77** C2
St Aidans School
  CAR/SHTL G32 .... **96** B4
St Alberts Primary School
  PLKSD/SHW G41 .... **42** C4
St Aloysius College
  KVGV G3 .... **20** B5
St Aloysius College
Junior School
  KVGV G3 .... **20** B5
St Aloysius Preparatory School
  KVGV G3 .... **20** B5
St Andrewes Cathedral
  CGLE G1 .... **33** D5
St Andrews Clinics for Children
  KVD/HLHD G12 .... **18** B1

St Andrews High School
CLYDBK G81 .... 70 A2

St Andrews Secondary
RC School
CAR/SHTL G32 .... 98 A3

St Angelas Primary School
GIF/THBK G46 .... 123 D3

St Annes Primary School
DMNK/BRGTN G40 .... 48 B1

St Anthonys Football Club
GOV/IBX G51 .... 28 A5

St Anthonys RC School
RUTH G73 .... 132 B2

St Anthonys School
GOV/IBX G51 .... 27 F1

St Augustines Primary School
PPK/MIL G22 .... 79 C3

St Batholemews
Primary School
CSMK G45 .... 130 B2

St Benedicts RC School
ESTRH G34 .... 101 C1

St Blanes Primary School
SMSTN G23 .... 76 B1

St Bridgets Primary School
BAIL/MDB/MHD G69 .... 109 D1

St Bridgets School
GVH/MTFL G42 .... 118 A2

St Catherines School
SPRGB/BLRNK G21 .... 13 E2

St Columbas High School
CLYDBK G81 .... 62 A2

St Columbkilles RC School
RUTH G73 .... 119 D3

St Convals Primary School
PLKSW/MSWD G43 .... 114 B2

St Cuthberts Primary School
PPK/MIL G22 .... 8 C3

St Denis's Primary School
DEN/PKHD G31 .... 36 C4

St Dominics Primary School
CSMK G45 .... 130 B4

St Enoch Business Centre
CGLE G1 .... 33 D5

St Enoch Shopping Centre
CGLE G1 .... 33 E5

St Francis of Assisi
Primary School
BAIL/MDB/MHD G69 .... 108 B3

St Francis Primary School
GBLS G5 .... 46 A5

St Georges Medical Centre
KVGV G3 .... 20 A4

St Georges School
CARD/HILL/MSPK G52 .... 102 A1

St Gerards Secondary School
GOV/IBX G51 .... 29 D3

St Gilberts Primary School
SPRGB/BLRNK G21 .... 25 E1

St James Primary School
DMNK/BRGTN G40 .... 46 C2

St James RC Primary School
RNFRW PA4 .... 84 A3

St Joan of Arc School
PPK/MIL G22 .... 78 B3

St Johns Approved
School Springboig
CAR/SHTL G32 .... 99 D3

St Johns RC Primary School
GBLS G5 .... 45 D2

St Josephs RC Primary School
COWCAD G4 .... 20 B3

St Judes Primary School
STPS/GTHM/RID G33 .... 100 A4

St Julies School
CSMK G45 .... 129 D2

St Margaret Marys
Primary School
CSMK G45 .... 129 C4

St Margaret Marys
Secondary School
CSMK G45 .... 129 D3

St Marks Primary School
CAR/SHTL G32 .... 105 C1

St Marks RC Primary School
RUTH G73 .... 131 D1

St Marnocks Primary School
PLK/PH/NH G53 .... 111 C1

St Marthas School
SPRGB/BLRNK G21 .... 12 B1

St Martins Primary School
CSMK G45 .... 130 B4

St Marys Cathedral
COWCAD G4 .... 19 E2

St Marys Primary School
MRYH/FIRH G20 .... 76 A3

St Matthews Primary School
BSHPBGS G64 .... 69 D4

St Michaels Primary School
DEN/PKHD G31 .... 49 F3

St Mirins Primary School
LNPK/KPK G44 .... 129 C1

St Modans School
STPS/GTHM/RID G33 .... 98 A2

St Monicas School
PLK/PH/NH G53 .... 110 B1

The St Mungo Museum
of Religious Life & Art
COWCAD G4 .... 34 C2

St Mungo's Primary School
COWCAD G4 .... 34 B1

St Ninians High School
GIF/THBK G46 .... 124 B4

St Ninians Primary School
KNTSWD G13 .... 73 C1

St Oswalds School
LNPK/KPK G44 .... 127 D1

St Patricks School RC
Primary School
KVGV G3 .... 31 F3

St Pauls Primary School
CAR/SHTL G32 .... 106 A3

St Pauls Primary School
SCOT G14 .... 87 C3

St Peters School
PTCK G11 .... 17 E3

St Philomenas Primary School
STPS/GTHM/RID G33 .... 88 B3

St Pius Primary School
DRUM G15 .... 64 A2

St Raymonds School
LNPK/KPK G44 .... 128 B4

St Rochs Secondary School
SPRGB/BLRNK G21 .... 23 D5

St Rose of Lima Primary School
STPS/GTHM/RID G33 .... 91 C1

St Saviours School
GOV/IBX G51 .... 29 D4

St Stephens Primary School
COWCAD G4 .... 22 C3

St Teresas Primary School
PPK/MIL G22 .... 9 F5

St Thomas Aquinas RC Secondary School
SCOT G14 .... 2 C3

St Timothys Primary School
CAR/SHTL G32 .... 98 A4

Sandaig Primary School
STPS/GTHM/RID G33 .... 100 B4

Sandwood School
CARD/HILL/MSPK G52 .... 102 A1

Saracen Health Centre
PPK/MIL G22 .... 9 D3

Saracen Primary School
PPK/MIL G22 .... 8 C4

Sauchiehall Shopping Centre
CGLW G2 .... 33 D1

School of Art
KVGV G3 .... 20 B5

Scotland Street School Museum
GBLS G5 .... 43 F3

Scottish Exhibition and Conference Centre
KVGV G3 .... 30 B3

Scottish Youth Theatre
CGLE G1 .... 33 D3

Scotus College
BSDN G61 .... 65 C2

Shaftesbury Medical Practice
SCOT G14 .... 14 A1

Sharmanka Gallery & Workshop
CGLE G1 .... 33 F5

Shawbridge Industrial Estate
PLKSW/MSWD G43 .... 113 D3

Shawlands Primary School
PLKSD/SHW G41 .... 114 B1

Shawlands Surgery
PLKSD/SHW G41 .... 114 B2

Sheriff Court
GBLS G5 .... 45 E1

Shettleston Day Hospital
CAR/SHTL G32 .... 105 D2

Shettleston Health Centre
CAR/SHTL G32 .... 106 A1

Sighthill Primary School
SPRGB/BLRNK G21 .... 22 B1

Simshill Primary School
LNPK/KPK G44 .... 128 B2

Sino Herb Clinic
PTCK G11 .... 17 D3

Sir John Maxwell School
PLKSW/MSWD G43 .... 114 A3

Smithycroft Secondary School
STPS/GTHM/RID G33 .... 97 C1

Somerset Eye Clinic
KVGV G3 .... 19 D5

Southern General Hospital NHS Trust
GOV/IBX G51 .... 26 B1

South Lanarkshire Council
RUTH G73 .... 119 D2

Spectrum Business Centre
RUTH G73 .... 119 D2

Spiersbridge Business Park
GIF/THBK G46 .... 124 A3

Spittal School
RUTH G73 .... 130 B1

Springburn Health Centre
SPRGB/BLRNK G21 .... 11 E3

Springburn Museum
SPRGB/BLRNK G21 .... 11 E4

Springburn Sports Centre
SPRGB/BLRNK G21 .... 11 E3

Springfield Primary School
DMNK/BRGTN G40 .... 61 D3

Stathclyde Regional Council
SPRGB/BLRNK G21 .... 13 D4

Steunans Primary School
CLYDBK G81 .... 62 A4

Stirling's Library
CGLE G1 .... 33 E4

Stobhill General Hospital
SPRGB/BLRNK G21 .... 81 C4

Stock Exchange
CGLE G1 .... 33 D3

Stonedyke Primary School
DRUM G15 .... 64 B4

Stonelaw High School
RUTH G73 .... 119 D3

Stow College
KVGV G3 .... 20 B4

Strathclyde Art Centre
KVGV G3 .... 32 A4

Strathclyde Business Centre
GOV/IBX G51 .... 42 A1

Strathclyde Business Centre
PLKSD/SHW G41 .... 42 C2

Street Level Gallery
CGLE G1 .... 33 F5

Summerhill School
DRUM G15 .... 64 B2

Sunnyside School
STPS/GTHM/RID G33 .... 91 C3

Synagogue
GVH/MTFL G42 .... 55 F4

Temple School
KNTSWD G13 .... 74 B3

Templeton Business Centre
DMNK/BRGTN G40 .... 46 C3

Thames Open College
CGLW G2 .... 32 C3

Thornliebank Health Centre
GIF/THBK G46 .... 124 B2

Thornliebank Industrial Estate
GIF/THBK G46 .... 124 A4

Thorntree Primary School
CAR/SHTL G32 .... 98 A4

Thornwood School
PTCK G11 .... 15 F2

Tinto Primary School
PLKSW/MSWD G43 .... 114 A4

Tollcross Industrial Estate
CAR/SHTL G32 .... 106 A3

The Toonspeak Young Peoples Theatre
SPRGB/BLRNK G21 .... 23 F3

Tormusk Primary School
CSMK G45 .... 131 C3

Toryglen School
RUTH G73 .... 118 A2

Townhead Health Centre
COWCAD G4 .... 35 D1

Transmission Gallery
CGLE G1 .... 33 F5

Trinity High School
BLTYR/CAMB G72 .... 121 C3

Trinity High School
RNFRW PA4 .... 84 B2

Tron Theatre
CGLE G1 .... 34 A5

Turnbull High School
BSHPBGS G64 .... 68 A4

Underground Gallery
KVD/HLHD G12 .... 18 A1